War, Culture and Memory

The Open University

War, Culture and Memory

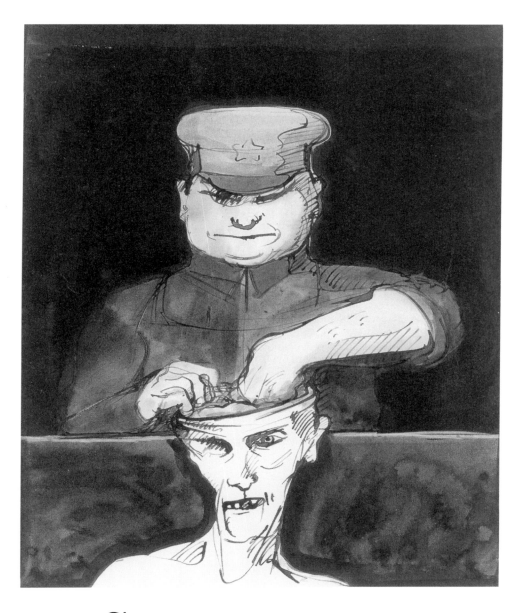

EDITED BY Clive
Emsley

This publication forms part of an Open University course AA300 *Europe: Identities and Culture in a Contested Continent*. Details of this and other Open University courses can be obtained from the Course Information and Advice Centre, PO Box 724, The Open University, Milton Keynes MK7 6ZS, United Kingdom; tel. +44 (0)1908 653231; e-mail general-enquiries@open.ac.uk

Alternatively, you may visit the Open University website at http://www.open.ac.uk where you can learn more about the wide range of courses and packs offered at all levels by The Open University.

To purchase a selection of Open University course materials visit the webshop at www.ouw.co.uk, or contact Open University Worldwide, Michael Young Building, Walton Hall, Milton Keynes MK7 6AA, United Kingdom for a brochure. Tel. +44 (0)1908 858785; fax +44 (0)1908 858787; e-mail ouwenq@open.ac.uk

The Open University
Walton Hall, Milton Keynes
MK7 6AA

First published 2003

Edited, designed and typeset by The Open University

Printed in the United Kingdom by TJ International Ltd, Padstow.

Colour plates origination by Interscan Graphics, Malaysia

Colour plates printed in the United Kingdom by Nicholson & Bass Ltd

ISBN 0 7492 9611 9

1.1

29393B/aa300b3prei1.1

The paper used in this publication contains pulp sourced from forests independently certified to the Forest Stewardship Council (FSC) principles and criteria. Chain of custody certification allows the pulp from these forests to be tracked to the end use (see www.fsc-uk.org).

Mixed Sources
Product group from well-managed forests and other controlled sources
www.fsc.org Cert no. SGS-COC-2482
© 1996 Forest Stewardship Council
FSC

Contents

List of contributors   ix

List of readings   x

Introduction   1
CLIVE EMSLEY

1 War and national and political identities   7
CLIVE EMSLEY

'Two world wars and one World Cup!'   7

Germany: where did it all go wrong?   14

France: another past that will not go away   20

Elsewhere in the west   23

Elsewhere: eastern Europe   30

A European identity – the solution?   31

Some concluding points   36

References   37

2 War in twentieth-century Europe:
cultural images, memories and monuments   39
CLIVE EMSLEY

Die Neue Wache   39

Culture and memory   41

The culture of memorial   56

Some concluding points   65

References   67

3 **Literature, memory and nation**   69
DENNIS WALDER

Introduction   69

Why read *The Reader*?   70

Memory, nation and the novel   80

'The book that we have waited for'   83

What kind of novel is *The Reader*?   85

The inability to mourn   94

Conclusion   100

References   101

4 **Voicing protest:**
three responses to war in art music   103
ROBERT SAMUELS

Introduction   103

Michael Tippett (1905–98): *A Child of Our Time*   105

Benjamin Britten (1913–76): *War Requiem*   121

Dmitri Shostakovich (1906–75): Symphony no. 13, 'Babi Yar'   139

Conclusion: ideology, politics and artistic Modernism   159

References   160

5 **War, cinema and society**   161
JAMES CHAPMAN

Introduction   161

The First World War: from propaganda to anti-war cinema   164

Filming the people's war   172

Nazis and 'good Germans'   181

Resistance and collaboration   187

Conclusions   193

References   194

Select filmography   195

6   Two total wars, the Cold War and postmodernism:
    the arts in Europe, 1910–2000   197
    ARTHUR MARWICK

    Introduction   197

    The First World War   200

    The Second World War and the Cold War   221

    The cultural revolution and postmodernism   223

    Conclusion   228

    References   229

7   Europe and the cultural impact of the Holocaust   230
    TIM COLE

    Introduction   230

    Auschwitz   232

    Budapest   242

    Germany   249

    Conclusion: 27 January – a European Holocaust Memorial
    Day?   256

    References   267

8   Dealing with dictatorship: socialism and the sites of
    memory in contemporary Hungary   269
    MARK PITTAWAY

    Introduction: 'post-socialism' and memory in central and
    eastern Europe   269

    Coming to terms with the past? The politics of
    remembering socialism in post-socialist Hungary   279

    Shaping the politics of memory: Budapest's socialist statues
    and the park of tyranny   287

    A site of different memories? The House of Terror and the
    politics of memory   298

    Conclusion   306

    References   307

9 Identity and managing the memory of war. Yugoslavia: a case study   **309**
CELIA HAWKESWORTH

Introduction: early history and its interpretation   **309**

The Yugoslav lands, 1918–90   **324**

The Yugoslav wars of the 1990s   **330**

Conclusion   **347**

Appendix   **348**

References   **354**

Acknowledgements   **355**

Index   **357**

Contributors

James Chapman, Senior Lecturer in Film and Television History, the Open University

Tim Cole, Lecturer in Social History, University of Bristol

Clive Emsley, Professor of History, the Open University

Celia Hawkesworth, Senior Lecturer in Serbian and Croatian Studies, University College London

Arthur Marwick, founding Professor of History, the Open University

Mark Pittaway, Lecturer in European Studies, History Department, the Open University

Robert Samuels, Lecturer in Music, the Open University

Dennis Walder, Professor of Literature, the Open University

Readings

The readings that appear in this book are extracts from the following works.

Chapter 1

Dominic Lawson, *The Spectator*, Nicholas Ridley interview

Axel Tixhon, 'A bridge too far?'

'Germany has asked pardon', *Le Soir de Bruxelles*

Chapter 2

August Stramm, 'Schlachtfeld'/'Battlefield'

Heinrich Lersch, 'Der Kriegsinvalide'/'The war-invalide'

Ernst Jünger, *Storm of Steel*

Chapter 3

Theodor Adorno, 'Commitment'

Paul Celan, 'Todesfuge'/'Death Fugue'

Bernhard Schlink, *The Reader*

Chapter 4

Michael Tippett, *A Child of Our Time*

Benjamin Britten, *War Requiem*

Dmitri Shostakovich, Symphony no. 13, 'Babi Yar', settings of poems by Yevgeny Yevtushenko

Chapter 5

James Douglas, *Star*, review of *Battle of the Somme*

Jiri Weiss, 'An Allied film unit', *Documentary News Letter*

William Whitebait, 'Bombardment', *New Statesman*

Richard Combs, *Monthly Film Bulletin*, review of *Das Boot*

Chapter 6

Paul Hindemith, letter to Emmy Ronnefeldt

Paul Hindemith, letter to Frieda and Emma Lubbecke

Hugo Ball, *Cabaret Voltaire*

Tristan Tzara, Dada manifesto

Jean (or Hans) Arp, *Dadaland*

Fernand Léger, statement on *The Card Game*

Fernand Léger, statement on the First World War

Fernand Léger, letter to Louis Poughon (12 August 1915)

Fernand Léger, letter to Louis Poughon (25 October 1916)

Fernand Léger, letter to Louis Poughon (23 November 1916)

Fernand Léger, letter to Louis Poughon (7 December 1917)

Roland Barthes, 'The death of the author'

Chapter 7

Auschwitz museum guidebook, 1974, We remember

Auschwitz museum guidebook, 1974, Block 4, Room 4

Auschwitz museum guidebook, 1993, Block 4, Room 1

E. Rubenstein, *For You Who Died I Must Live On ... Reflections on the March of the Living*, accounts by Leigh Salsberg and Jillian Moncarz

Paul Levine, 'To choose to go to Birkenau: reflections on visiting a death camp, August 1996'

Plaque at entrance to the interior room of the *Neue Wache* memorial

Open letter to German newspapers, 30 January 1989

Ceremony programme, Britain's first official national Holocaust Memorial Day, 27 January 2001

Dan Stone, 'Day of remembrance or day of forgetting?'

David Cesarani, 'Seizing the day'

Chapter 8

Dubravka Ugrešić, 'The confiscation of memory'

András Gerő and Iván Pető, *Unfinished Socialism*

Chapter 9

'The downfall of the Serbian empire', traditional song

Petar Petrovic Njegoš, *The Mountain Wreath*

Nena Skopljanac-Brunner, et al., *Media and War*

'The Kosovo girl', traditional song

'The mother of the Jugovichi', traditional song

Introduction

CLIVE EMSLEY

During the twentieth century Europe was a major theatre of conflict. In two world wars Europe's nations fought each other; and during the second of these wars there was a systematic attempt at genocide employing all of the facilities and faculties of a bureaucratic and industrialized modern nation-state. Subsequently, during the Cold War, Europe was divided into two distinct blocs, each of which possessed different economic, political and social ideologies. In many respects 'hot war' and 'cold war' were shared experiences for Europeans and European states during the century, but different parts of Europe, and different communities within those parts, had very different and often quite contrasting experiences.

The nine essays in this book explore the ways in which, in various European countries, these wars have been remembered through history, literature, music, various forms of visual media and other cultural artefacts. They stress throughout that, in addition to drawing on memory, these disciplines and various artefacts also contribute to the formation and reshaping of remembrance, both public and private, and the formation and reshaping of the self-image of combatant nations. Such formation and reshaping might be done, or at least attempted, deliberately and cynically, but they can also be the result of contingency. Moreover, while the bulk of the focus here is on collective memory and remembrance, the authors are also keen to emphasize that collective amnesia can be as significant as collective memory.

The essays are not intended as a comprehensive survey of memory and remembrance of war in twentieth-century Europe. Such a task would be beyond the scope of a single volume, especially given the recent growth of research and publication in the area. Rather, the authors in this book have each contributed a case study on a broad theme, on a particular topic such as the remembrance of the Holocaust, or on a type of cultural artefact such as the war film. There has been an attempt here to pick out what might be considered the most usual and the most significant issues. There has also been an attempt to ensure that the issues are explored across the length and breadth of Europe, hence the inclusion of essays on Hungary and Yugoslavia as well as the more common focus on Britain, France and Germany.

While the events that underpin the content of this collection are historical, the issues tackled are discussed with reference to the ways in which they are reflected through culture. Culture here is conceived broadly as the totality of symbols and artefacts produced by human beings. Thus it includes modes of thinking, feeling and behaving as well as values, customs, traditions and norms. On the basis of this conception of culture, the study of memory and remembrance has a wide perspective. The nine essays are not a collection of separate studies ranging across a variety of disciplines. They seek to connect perspectives that are often artificially separated by the conventional organization of academic disciplines.

The first two chapters provide a broad overview of the main issues addressed. Chapter 1, 'War and national and political identities', ranges widely across Europe, surveying and contrasting how different nations have remembered and re-remembered the experiences of the two world wars. Beginning with the peculiarly 'eurosceptic' attitudes of some members of British society, the chapter moves on to survey German attempts to come to terms with defeat after the First World War, and defeat, division and guilt after the Second World War. It discusses French difficulties in facing up to the trauma of the second war, and then looks at a variety of other experiences, notably in Belgium and Poland. It concludes by indicating how the shock and agony of these wars, which might be said finally to have buried the European Enlightenment project of progress, led some individuals to seek some system of unification for Europe to prevent similar conflicts in the future. The first chapter is concerned principally with public memory, and there is particular reference to the role of politicians and historians in the construction and use of memory. Private memory is given greater emphasis in Chapter 2, 'War in twentieth-century Europe: cultural images, memories and monuments'. Again the range of this chapter is wide both in the countries and regions covered and in its subject matter – cemeteries, memorials, paintings and different forms of literature. The main focus of these two chapters is the two world wars, but they also draw attention to the issues of how the Cold War is remembered and of how the collapse of the Soviet Union has both complicated and forced the rethinking of the remembrance of 1914–18 and 1939–45.

The point is made in Chapter 2 that much of our understanding and 'remembrance' of war comes from the written word, in the form of either history or creative literature. In the following chapter, 'Literature, memory and nation', Dennis Walder narrows the previously wide focus, providing a close analysis of Bernhard Schlink's novel *The Reader*. Schlink's novel is not about the Second World War as such, but deals with the experience of a German, born at the end of the war, who seeks to come to terms with that war and with the appalling atrocities inflicted on the so-called enemies of the *Volksgemeinschaft*. There are important questions raised here explicitly about the extent to which a work of fiction can engage with difficulties in the perception of national identity, and implicitly about how far a literary text can address such issues as acutely as a sociological or historical work.

Chapter 4 continues the narrow focus. In 'Voicing protest: three responses to war in art music' Robert Samuels looks at three pieces of music by three different composers, each of which was intended as a statement about war: Michael Tippett's *A Child of Our Time*, Benjamin Britten's *War Requiem* and Dimitri Shostakovitch's Thirteenth Symphony, 'Babi Yar'. It is relatively easy to see how a novelist or poet can seek to influence society through his or her use of words and the way in which a theme is addressed. In this chapter Samuels stresses how the three composers who come under his spotlight saw their role in such terms. Their political attitudes and commitment were different, and they employed different musical forms – oratorio, requiem and symphony – to express themselves with respect to war, but they each shared a commitment to communicate and to influence society at large.

The high art form of classical music appears inaccessible to many; the popular medium of cinema seems just the opposite. If much contemporary understanding and awareness of war originates in literature, how much more can be said to come from film, both actuality films and narrative features? In Chapter 5, 'War, cinema and society', James Chapman looks at the diverse genre of the war film, comparing the various forms and drawing attention to the importance of different contexts. If the individuals responsible for high culture seek to communicate and influence society, what is the potential for such influence among those appealing directly to a broad, popular audience? Chapman stresses that most war films have been made within the context of a particular national cinema and tell a story in a version that is comfortable to that country. He notes too the ways in which film deals with the specific rather than the general, and that its story is invariably invested with allegorical meaning that has as much relevance for the present in which it was made as for the past that it purports to portray. This brings us back to the questions of the formation and reshaping of remembrance and of identity.

If we are to understand how the arts arguably mediate war and shape and reshape many of our perspectives on war and national identity, then we need some recognition of how war – 'hot' and 'cold' – affected the arts. In Chapter 6, 'Two total wars, the Cold War and postmodernism: the arts in Europe, 1910–2000', Arthur Marwick revisits controversies in which he has actively participated over many years: how far did the total wars of the twentieth century affect artists and their work? He challenges the view that the First World War fostered a return to traditional forms among artists, and suggests that the impact of both wars on the arts was similar, even though the predominant movements in the two periods were different. He concludes with some suggestions regarding the impact of the Cold War on the cultural movements of the 1960s and beyond.

The memory of the Holocaust, the Nazi attempt to annihilate European Jewry as well as Gypsies, large numbers of Slavs and various groups and individuals labelled 'asocial' or enemies of the German national community, is a theme picked up in many of the chapters. In Chapter 7, 'Europe and the cultural impact of the Holocaust', Tim Cole focuses on the topic directly. Beginning with the manner in which the Holocaust, especially with reference to the Jews, was Americanized during the 1980s and 1990s as the antithesis of all that the United States holds dear, he proceeds to an exploration of how far it has been, or indeed can be 'Europeanized'. Cole discusses the shifting representations of Auschwitz within Poland, the various Holocaust memorials in Budapest and, finally, the contrasting memory and memorials within a divided and then a reunited Germany.

Memorials and their various meanings are the subject of Mark Pittaway's 'Dealing with dictatorship: socialism and the sites of memory in contemporary Hungary' (Chapter 8). This chapter looks at two particular sites in Budapest, the House of Terror and the Statue Park. The former was a clear attempt by a political grouping to shape the memory of the communist regime; there are echoes here of the attempt in West Germany during the 1950s and 1960s to link Nazi and Soviet regimes under the woolly category 'totalitarian'. The content of the House, however, was geared particularly towards emphasizing the unbridled might and brutality deployed under Soviet domination. The Statue Park, by contrast, is no less critical but it is a far more subtle site of memory. Moreover, Pittaway implies, it is probably a far better reflection of contemporary Hungarian ambivalence towards, even nostalgia for, the good economic years under the communist regime of János Kádár.

In the wake of the disintegration of Yugoslavia during the 1990s there were those who were nostalgic for the regime of Marshal Tito. At least he had held the state together and prevented civil war, massacre and ethnic cleansing. In the final chapter of this volume, 'Identity and managing the memory of war. Yugoslavia: a case study', Celia Hawkesworth examines the power of national myths, and how they have been deployed and reshaped over time, particularly during the 1990s. The ethnic tensions within the Yugoslav state were not, she argues, the cause of the wars of the 1990s; rather, the memory of previous conflicts, together with various cultural assumptions drawn from that memory, were mobilized and glossed in the service of the new wars. This is a convenient point at which to conclude since, while the disintegration of Yugoslavia was commonly described in the west as another example of the failure of communism and the violence of the wars was commonly portrayed as peculiarly Balkan, this mobilization of memory and of cultural assumptions based on that memory are matters that the previous essays have noted across those European states that experienced the total wars of the twentieth century.

This is the third of four books in the series *Europe: Culture and Identities in a Contested Continent*. They form the main texts of an Open University level 3 course of the same name.

1

War and national and political identities

CLIVE EMSLEY

'Two world wars and one World Cup!'

On 14 July 1990 *The Spectator* published an interview that its editor, Dominic Lawson, had conducted with Nicholas Ridley, then secretary of state for trade and industry in Margaret Thatcher's government. The interview caused a furore, and Ridley was forced to resign his cabinet post. The first reading is an extract from this interview.

Saying the unsayable about the Germans

Nicholas Ridley's passion for illusion is most definitely only a pastime. In modern political life there is no more brutal practitioner of the home truth. Not even Mrs Thatcher – whose own views owe much to his – is more averse to hiding the hard facts behind a patina of sympathy or politician's charm ...

Even knowing this, I was still taken aback by the vehemence of Mr Ridley's views on the matter of Europe, and in particular the role of Germany. It had seemed a topical way to engage his thoughts, since the day after we met, Herr Klaus-Otto Pöhl, the president of the Bundesbank[,] was visiting England to preach the joys of a joint European monetary policy.

'This is all a German racket designed to take over the whole of Europe. It has to be thwarted. This rushed take-over by the Germans on the worst possible basis, with the French behaving like poodles to the Germans, is absolutely intolerable.'

'Excuse me, but in what way are moves toward monetary union, "The Germans trying to take over the whole of Europe"?'

'The deutschmark is always going to be the strongest currency, *because of their habits.*'

'But Mr Ridley, it's surely not axiomatic that the German currency will always be the strongest ...?'

'It's because of the *Germans*.'

'But the European Community is not just the Germans.'

Mr Ridley turned his fire – he was, as usual[,] smoking heavily – onto the organisation as a whole.

'When I look at the institutions to which it is proposed that sovereignty is to be handed over, I'm aghast. Seventeen unelected reject politicians ... with no accountability to anybody, who are not responsible for raising taxes, just spending money, who are pandered to by a supine parliament which also is not responsible for raising taxes, already behaving with an arrogance I find breathtaking – the idea that one says, "OK, we'll give this lot our sovereignty," is unacceptable to me. I'm not against giving up sovereignty in principle, but not to this lot. You might just as well give it to Adolf Hitler, frankly.'

We were back to Germany again, and I was still the devil's – if not Hitler's – advocate:

'But Hitler was elected.'

'Well he was, at least *he* was ... but I didn't agree with him – but that's another matter.'

'But surely **Herr Kohl** is preferable to Herr Hitler. He's not going to bomb us, after all.'

Helmut Kohl was German chancellor from 1982 to 1998. It was during his chancellorship that the two Germanies were reunited in 1990.

'I'm not sure I wouldn't rather have ...' – I thought for one giddy moment, as Mr Ridley paused to stub out his *n*th cigarette, that he would mention the name of the last Chancellor of a united Germany – 'er ... the shelters and the chance to fight back, than simply being taken over by ... *economics*. He'll soon be coming *here* and trying to say that this is what we should do on the banking front and this is what our taxes should be. I mean, he'll soon be trying to take over *everything*.' ...

Mr Ridley's confidence in expressing his views on the German threat must owe a little something to the knowledge that they are not significantly different from those of the Prime Minister, who originally opposed German reunification, even though in public she is required not to be so indelicate as to draw comparisons between Herren Kohl and Hitler.

What the Prime Minister and Mr Ridley have in common, which they do not share with many of their Cabinet colleagues, is that they are over 60. Next question, therefore, to Mr Ridley: 'Aren't your views coloured by the fact that you can remember the second world war?' I could have sworn I saw a spasm of emotion cross Mr Ridley's face. At any rate he answered the question while twisting his head to stare out of the window:

'Jolly good thing too. About time somebody said that. It was pretty nasty. Only two months ago I was in Auschwitz, Poland. Next week I'm in Czechoslovakia. You ask them what they think about the second world war. It's useful to remember.' It is also useful to know that Mr Ridley's trips to Poland and Czechoslovakia are efforts, in the company of some of Britain's leading businessmen, to persuade the East Europeans of the virtues of doing business with Britain. How very annoying to see the large towels of Mr Kohl and his businessmen already covering those Eastern beaches.

But, hold on a minute, how relevant to us, now, is what Germany did to Eastern Europe in the war? Mr Ridley reverted to the sort of arguments he must have inhaled with his smokes when he was a Minister of State at the Foreign Office:

'We've always played the balance of power in Europe. It has always been Britain's role to keep these various powers balanced, and never has it been more necessary than now, with Germany so uppity.'

'But suppose we don't have the balance of power; would the German economy run Europe?'

'I don't know about the German economy. It's the German *people*. They're already running most of the Community.' ...

The rumbustious tone of Mr Ridley's remarks and the fact that our conversation was post-prandial may give the misleading impression that the politician was relaxing, and not choosing his words too carefully. Far from it. Mr Ridley had the smallest glass of wine with his lunch, and then answered all my questions with a fierce frown of concentration, one hand clutched to his forehead, the other helping to provide frequent supplies of nicotine.

(*The Spectator*, 14 July 1990, pp. 8–9)

EXERCISE

Having read the extract, consider the following questions.

1   What, do you suppose, was the reason for the furore over Ridley's words?

2   What does Ridley consider to be the traditional role of Britain in European politics?

3   What does Lawson present by way of an excuse for Ridley's strong sentiments? And who does he suggest shares those sentiments for similar reasons?

DISCUSSION

1   Ridley expresses a hostile attitude towards the German people, whom he accuses of seeking to take over Europe through the European Community in line with their 'habits', as previously demonstrated by their military behaviour. Not only do such comments break all of the diplomatic niceties of relations between friendly states, it was, at the very least, injudicious for a government minister to draw a parallel between the German chancellor, Helmut Kohl, and Adolf Hitler.

2   Ridley regards Britain's traditional role as ensuring a balance between the various European powers. It might be argued that what Ridley does in this interview is to ascribe a kind of persona to nations and/or nation-states. Thus Germany is a state that always acts in a particular way; as does England/Britain, although its role is different. I shall return to this perception of nation-states and their behaviour.

3   Lawson explains that Ridley and Margaret Thatcher (who, Lawson maintained, had similar ideas) are both aged over 60, and that their views are coloured by remembrance of the Second World War. It is probably worth noting also that Lawson is at pains to stress Ridley's abstemiousness over lunch – this is not the drink talking. Nicholas Ridley's sentiments may seem surprising when expressed publicly by a leading member of a government, yet would probably seem less so when heard in private conversations. Similar ideas could be found underpinning the euroscepticism of many members of the Tory party, and others in the United Kingdom, from the 1980s onwards. They are also significant in the popular memory of British history.

It is arguable that England was the first country where 'a genuine national memory developed at the popular level' (Fentress and Wickham, 1992, pp. 129–30), with local celebrations during the seventeenth century commemorating moments when the small Protestant state affirmed its triumph over its Roman Catholic enemies. Subsequent conflicts added new layers to such memory, as the Protestant island and the 'freeborn Englishman' (with the assistance of Irish, Scots and Welsh) stood steadfast and 'saved Europe' from (in turn) Louis XIV, the French Revolution, Napoleon, 'Kaiser Bill' and Hitler. A series of moments from wars, especially the world wars of the twentieth century, continue to be used by politicians, the media and ordinary individuals to renew and reconstitute the self-identification of a heroic island race. In 1914 Britain went to the aid of 'gallant little Belgium'; in 1940 the British showed 'the Dunkirk spirit', were saved by 'the Few', stood alone against Nazi-occupied Europe and could boast of 'their finest hour'. Two years later the popular historian Sir Arthur Bryant (1899–1985) published the first volume of his trilogy on Britain during the Revolutionary and Napoleonic wars. 'In that struggle there were only two constant factors', he declares in the preface to this work.

> One was the French resolve to create a New Order; the other was the British refusal to admit any Order not based on law. Other nations were tossed in and out of the storm like leaves. Only Britain, though she bent, never broke. For a generation, sometimes with powerful allies but as often alone, she fought on against a nation with twice her population and animated by a strange revolutionary fanaticism which gave its devotees the strength of a man in a delirium. Such was its power that at times Britain found herself fighting almost the whole of Europe, including her former allies, without, apparently, the slightest chance of victory and with very little of survival.
>
> Yet her patient, rock-like people never compromised, never gave in, never despaired.
>
> (Bryant, 1942, p. ix)

Bryant goes on to stress the parallels between the Younger Pitt, prime minister for much of the period of the French wars, and Winston Churchill; between the defence of the Channel ports in 1914 and 1918; between Jacobinism and Nazism; between Napoleon and Hitler.

But there is another side to the British popular memory of war. As well as reaffirming and reconstructing self-identification, it enables the construction of the opponent. Almost a decade after Bryant wrote the preface quoted above another British historian (but this time one with an academic post) expressed an attitude towards 'the German problem' akin to that which was later to get Nicholas Ridley into trouble. 'How can the peoples of Europe be secured against repeated bouts of German aggression? And how can the Germans discover a settled, peaceful form of political existence?' asked A. J. P. Taylor (1906–90) in the preface to the new edition of *The Course of German History* (Taylor, 1951, p. 9). The first problem was resolvable if Germany's neighbours were united and friendly. The second problem required keeping Germany disarmed and with 'rigorously defined' frontiers. 'The disappearance of Germany from the ranks of the Great Powers will be a blow to the pride of German army officers and of German university professors; it will not inflict hardship on the German people.' Moreover, it would give a chance to the 'democratic Germans of who we hear so much' (Taylor, 1951, p. 9). Some years later Taylor returned to the problem in *The Origins of the Second World War* where, in rather more measured tones, he argued that the war was brought about by Germany's ability to act as a great power. 'In international affairs there was nothing wrong with Hitler except that he was a German' (Taylor, 1964, p. 27). There is an unspoken assumption here that Germany's size and geographical position predestined the country, once united, to be a threat to its neighbours.

While, at the close of the twentieth century, England's football fans might lament that their team had won the World Cup only once (as opposed to the German team's three victories, not to mention its three European Nations Cups since 1945), the unpleasant extremists among them could respond with a chant which principally celebrated military victories: 'Two world wars and one World Cup!' Similarly, during the Euro 2000 soccer competition bewildered Belgians were treated to the chant 'If it wasn't for the English you'd be Krauts!' There is an alternative vision, exemplified by Edward Heath, the Tory prime minister who took the United Kingdom into the European Economic Community in 1973. Like others in Britain and in continental Europe, Heath, who had served as an artillery officer during the Second World War, saw the community, at least in part, as a way of preventing future conflicts. Participating in (and being on the winning side in) these two wars has had a significant impact on British/English identity, though, as these examples demonstrate, the effects have not been the same for everyone and have not always been for the better. It has reaffirmed some old self-beliefs and has also contributed to the construction and reconstruction of beliefs, not always flattering, about some of the peoples and some of the states of continental Europe.

Not everything is, or indeed can be, remembered. This raises important questions about why some things may be forgotten, or at least marginalized, while others are remembered and given considerable significance. There are also questions centring on *how* things are remembered, as reflected in the behaviour of certain English soccer fans, the demonization of Germany as the dangerous 'other' by Ridley and Taylor, and the contrasting perspective of Heath. To some extent all of this may simply demonstrate that we need a way of making sense of the past and the present, a way of putting some kind of pattern and/or meaning on events to provide a measure of security in the present or hope for the future. Arthur Marwick has argued that

> It is only through a sense of history that communities establish their identity, orientate themselves, understand their relationship to the past and to other communities and societies. Without history (*knowledge* of the past) we, and our communities, would be utterly adrift on an endless and featureless sea of time.
>
> (Marwick, 2001, p. 32)

But then how can similar people make such different sense of the same history, even of similar memories? When approaching the problem of how historians treat memory in the shape of memoirs, eyewitness testimony and the recent fascination with oral history, James Fentress, an anthropologist, and Chris Wickham, a medieval historian, comment,

> When we remember, we represent ourselves to ourselves and to those around us. To the extent that our 'nature' – that which we truly are – can be revealed in articulation, we are what we remember. If this is the case, then a study of the way we remember – the way we present ourselves in our memories, the way we define our personal and collective identities through our memories, the way we order and structure our ideas in our memories, and the way we transmit these memories to others – is a study of the way we are.
>
> (Fentress and Wickham, 1992, p. 7)

So are personal and, by extension, national memories of war essentially a way of defining identities at a particular moment? During the 1990s there were heated debates between British historians and cultural theorists about whether or not, or the extent to which, British identity had been successively reconfigured in the half century following the Second World War. Geoff Eley has argued, for example, for three distinct British memories of the war over this period, all of them contributing to the shaping of identity. First, in the decade or so following the war, he identifies 'a narrative of popular democratic accomplishment'. This was overturned by the cultural radicalisms of the 1960s and 1970s which 'thoroughly destabilised the post-war settlement, angrily and exuberantly exposing its deficiencies and denouncing its congealing of values'. Finally, during the 1990s, there was 'an aggressive reimagining of British identity' under Margaret Thatcher which evoked the Winston Churchill 'of late imperial militarism and racialized cultural superiority, exchanging ideas of social justice for a patriotism straight and pure' (Eley, 2001, pp. 821–3). But is Eley right? And are such variations in the memory of war and the shaping of identity as a result of war unique to the English/British experience?

Germany: where did it all go wrong?

German memory of the experience of the two wars of the twentieth century is, for obvious reasons, very different from that of the English/British. There is no tradition similar to the English self-image of the 'patient, rock-like' island race. Germany was only united into a modern political entity in 1871, in the aftermath of the Franco-Prussian war. Up until 1945, unification under Prussia was seen as a great climax in German history and one worthy of celebration. After 1945, following defeat in two wars and the division of the country into the Federal Republic (the FDR, or West Germany) and the Democratic Republic (the GDR, or East Germany), that earlier unification was not something to celebrate. It appeared to many, both inside and outside Germany, that the events of 1871 had led inexorably to the emergence in 1933 of a singularly brutal and repellent regime. The Germans themselves had to come to terms with their recent past and, as a corollary of this, with their identity as Germans. Historians of Germany sought explanations for why events had taken the direction that they had. Why did the unification of 1871 culminate in two military defeats and in Nazism? For many the answer lay in the notion of Germany's *Sonderweg*, literally its 'special path'.

The idea of a distinct German path to the present was not a new one. During the nineteenth century and during the short-lived Weimar Republic that followed the First World War, many German intellectuals regarded their culture and society as less 'materialistic' and more 'spiritual' than those of their contemporaries. A popular example of this is to be found in the oft-quoted quip of the historian Heinrich von Treitschke (1834–96), a staunch partisan of Prussian power and unification, who denigrated the English for believing that 'soap is civilization'. But after 1945, in the Federal Republic, a new slant was put on the German *Sonderweg*. The belief now was that German economic, political and social development had diverged from the 'normal' path detectable in other European powers (notably Britain and France), where industrialization had produced a movement towards democratization. According to this interpretation the nineteenth-century German bourgeoisie, rather than striking out in its own interest, opted for socialization within the ranks of the old, pre-industrial elite of landowners, military officers and bureaucrats. Moreover, when crisis hit the Weimar Republic in the early 1930s the old elite and its new supporters sought to solve the problems by backing Hitler in the mistaken belief that they could control him.

Defeat in 1945 toppled the old elite and finally enabled West Germany to follow the route of western liberal democracies.

EXERCISE

That was a necessarily over-simplified account of the *Sonderweg*. Other analysts of the concept have been criticized even though their accounts are much more extended and penetrating (Blackbourn and Eley, 1984, especially the introduction). However, recognizing the limitations of what has been said up to now, can you identify a theoretical problem with the presupposition upon which the concept is based?

DISCUSSION

The presupposition here is that if there was a special, or abnormal, path for Germany, then there was a 'normal' path for the liberal democracies whereby the processes of industrialization led, ultimately, to a democratic system principally because of the pressure exerted on the old order by those responsible for the changes. The problem with this presupposition is that the histories of England and France are so different, and the debate about whether each country underwent a 'bourgeois' revolution (and what these may have entailed) is so complex, that to say Germany was different begs many questions. Weren't England and France also very different from each other?

The problem is complicated further by the fact that much recent historical research and argument have tended to suggest that other European 'bourgeoisies' were as keen on joining the old elite as those in Germany. Martin J. Wiener has argued that the English 'industrial spirit' declined from the mid nineteenth century onwards because a '"gentrified" bourgeois culture, particularly the rooting of pseudoaristocratic attitudes and values in upper middle class educated opinion, shaped an unfavourable context for economic endeavour' (Weiner, 1985, p. 10). Arno J. Mayer has insisted that it was 'the persistence of the old regime' across Europe, a regime both 'preindustrial and prebourgeois', that was the underlying cause of the First World War, and that this old system revived in the aftermath of the conflict to contribute to the resumption of war in 1939 (Mayer, 1981).

Might it also be argued that the idea of the *Sonderweg* is a way of avoiding responsibility, by implying there was some sort of inevitability in the way events unfolded after unification was achieved? Or else might it be argued that the concept is a way of pinning the blame on to social groups who were to disappear? Thus Germany's problems and its murderous Nazi regime were really the fault of an old order that no longer existed after 1945. We might find echoes of this in the way that elements of the German army and sections of society sought to pass the buck after the First World War. The theory of 'the stab in the back' (*der Dolchstoß*) absolved the army from blame for losing that war; the fault could then be laid at the door of feeble left-wing politicians, of Marxists, Jews and other groups allegedly keen to undermine Germany. The fact that many German regiments marched back from France and Belgium in 1918 in good order added weight to the idea that the army was never defeated; although in truth many of these soldiers probably realized that they would get home quicker by acting in a disciplined, organized way rather than just packing up and leaving on their own. In the aftermath of the Second World War there were many who insisted that any blame was the sole responsibility of the Nazis. There was a collective amnesia about the extent to which the Gestapo had relied upon denunciations by ordinary Germans and the extent to which soldiers of the *Wehrmacht* (the ordinary army, as opposed to SS units) had participated in atrocities in the east. This amnesia can be said to have begun at the Nuremberg trials when a succession of senior German officers insisted that they and their men had simply fought a war in the conventional way and had nothing to do with the mass killings of Jews, Poles, Russians and others. There were moments when the official story was challenged by a younger generation, notably during the students' disorders of 1968 and at the beginning of 1979 when, over four successive evenings, West German television broadcast the US-made mini-series *Holocaust* about the destruction of a German-Jewish family. The official perspective, however, remained relatively intact for at least a quarter of a century among the commanders of the new *Bundeswehr* (West Germany's army) and German politicians, many of whom had served their apprenticeships during the Third Reich. Then, during the mid 1980s, there was a heated debate (*der Historikerstreit*) involving historians and philosophers, and dragging in politicians and others, over the extent to which the Nazi period could be normalized within the historical record.

The *Historikerstreit* was sparked by Chancellor Kohl's invitation to the US president, Ronald Reagan, to visit the Second World War cemetery in Bitburg in May 1985, the fortieth anniversary of VE Day. Kohl planned a meeting that would demonstrate that the Federal Republic of Germany was now just a normal nation-state. The previous September he had held a similar meeting at Fort Douamont on the First World War battlefield of Verdun with the French president, François Mitterand. There, during a moment's silence, chancellor and president had clasped hands to demonstrate the new Franco-German unity that had succeeded the two world wars. But the plans for Bitburg went badly awry. It was revealed that the cemetery did not just contain the remains of ordinary German soldiers, but also those of members of the SS. A well-known academic, Jürgen Habermas, wrote a furious letter to the press accusing Kohl of seeking to obscure Germany's Nazi past behind a veil of rapprochement, of presenting the two former enemies on equal terms – as if both had been honest combatants during the war. Habermas insisted that any modern German identity had to be based on a continual public debate over the nation's history, together with a recognition of the Nazi role. The subsequent debate was fought publicly and acrimoniously in the national press as well as in academic publications.

The *Historikerstreit*, the rise of a new generation in the army and in politics, the end of the Cold War, and the growing awareness of new research and publications by historians combined to provoke a reappraisal of the recent past. Significant in the 1990s was the publication of Christopher Browning's *Ordinary Men* (1992) and Daniel J. Goldhagen's *Hitler's Willing Executioners* (1996). These two books were by American scholars, and they differed significantly in their interpretation of the same events, but they both demonstrated that it was not just Nazi party members and SS troops who had been involved in mass killings. Other historians, many of them from the

Figure 1.1 Germans of all ages studying some of the non-harrowing images from the exhibition that opened in Karlsruhe in January 1997 called *Vernichtungskrieg: Verbrechen der Wehrmacht 1941 bis 1944* (War of Extermination: Crimes of the Army 1941 to 1944). Photo: Noel Tovia Matoff

younger generation of German scholars, revealed, for example, the Gestapo's reliance on denunciations by members of the public, while the role of the military was examined in an exhibition organized by the Hamburg Institute for Social Research, *Vernichtungskrieg: Verbrechen der Wehrmacht 1941 bis 1944* (War of Extermination: Crimes of the Army 1941 to 1944). The exhibition opened in Karlsruhe in January 1997 before going on to tour other German cities. It attracted large crowds who were generally shocked and disquieted by the images presented of ordinary German soldiers involved in mass murder.

The concept of 'totalitarianism' was widely used in West Germany during the 1950s, to denote the difference between the new society and political system in the Federal Republic, as opposed to both the old Nazi system and the neighbouring system in the Democratic Republic of East Germany. Being critical of 'totalitarianism', a term which could encompass both Nazism and Stalinism, was a means of demonstrating sympathy for and identification with liberal democracy. Moreover, the general nature of the concept could further help to exonerate the German people from any responsibility for Nazism if it were accepted that totalitarian regimes were common and could be explained as a malaise of modern, mass society. Christian Democrat governments in the Federal Republic refused to have anything to do with the GDR and right-wing politicians were furious when Willy Brandt, a socialist politician sworn in as federal chancellor in October 1969, began his policy of *Ostpolitik* which sought to normalize relations between the two Germanies. The political right in the Federal Republic, however, could hardly accuse Brandt of being a 'fellow traveller' for he had shown himself to be courageously anti-communist while mayor of Berlin between 1957 and 1963. The East Germans and the Soviets also had difficulty with him since he could not be slotted into their usual category of West German politicians. Brandt was a lifelong socialist who had fought against the Nazis and had spent the war in Norway.

In East Germany people were encouraged to see their new state as the product of the struggle against fascism that had begun in the interwar period; indeed the leaders of the GDR had cut their political teeth during these years as young communists in political conflict with the Nazis. The two world wars were, for the GDR, the product of different stages of doomed capitalism; the Cold War was another manifestation of the struggle of the progressive forces (which had defeated fascism) against capitalism. Questions about national responsibility for the development of Nazism, for causing the wars and for committing crimes against humanity did not need to be asked by East Germans since the answers were self-evident; these problems were nothing to do with either their country or their people. In the reunified Germany of the 1990s, however, people brought up in the GDR were forced to confront these issues as well as their own involvement with a state whose secret police was considerably more numerous and intrusive than the Gestapo.

Reunification, and the end of the Cold War, led to new debates about German identity across the political spectrum. All political groupings saw a need to redefine the nation and establish some sort of German identity and national normalcy. But the problem of responsibility for Nazism and how to cope with its crimes remained. Some members of the new right took a radical line, arguing that the Nazi regime should be understood, at least in part, as a progressive modernizing force that destroyed the old social divisions of class and religion. Individuals on the left, in contrast, saw this as presenting far too positive an image of the Nazis and marginalizing their crimes. In his textbook *Klein deutsche Geschichte* (a short history of Germany), published in 1996, the mainstream liberal Hagen Schulze hoped for a return to a normal national identity in the reunited country. The problem, of course, is whether the notion of 'normal national identity' has any more meaning than the 'normal political development' assumed within the concept of the *Sonderweg*.

EXERCISE

The discussion above has focused very much on politics and historical interpretations of the German experience of the world wars. It has concentrated largely on how German people sought to come to terms with Nazism and their 'responsibility' for it. But is there another way, scarcely touched upon above, that Germans might have thought (and think) collectively about the wars and their national experience?

DISCUSSION

Much of the British myth-memory of the Second World War centres around the Blitz and mucking in together through hardship and shortage. The Germans also suffered terror bombing and food shortages. At the end of the war many of their finest cities were in ruins; their economy and infrastructure were destroyed; millions of their people were dead or missing; while invasion, particularly from the east, brought the appalling experience of mass looting and mass rape. German memory of the war could also mean memory of hardship, comradeship and, above all, of being the victims of the victors. This was not so much official memory as personal, or centred on the local community. It fed into and interreacted with the public debates, but in ways that are rather more difficult to untangle.

France: another past that will not go away

For much of the interwar period the French could look back on the First World War with sorrow – for the dead and maimed – but also with a degree of satisfaction; they had won the war, emasculated their opponent and reunited Alsace into their republic. Remembrance of the Second World War was, and arguably remains, more painful and, because of the conflicting loyalties of wartime, much more difficult. The Third Republic was defeated in the summer of 1940. It sued for an armistice and then the National Assembly, reconvened in the spa town of Vichy, voted by an overwhelming majority to grant full executive powers to Marshal Philippe Pétain, a hero of the 1914–18 war. The neo-fascist Vichy regime ruled for the next four years in alliance with Nazi Germany. Large numbers of German troops were stationed first in northern and western France, and subsequently (from 1942) across the whole country. From February 1943 young Frenchmen were required to contribute to the German war effort under the system of *Service du Travail Obligatoire* (STO – obligatory labour service), either in Germany proper or in German industries established in France.

Most of the population within France between 1940 and 1944 were not resisters. The Resistance, such as it was, received a boost from Communist party members when the Soviet Union was invaded in June 1941 and resisting then became the duty of French party members. The Resistance was subsequently strengthened too by young men seeking to avoid STO; they hid in the countryside and, in the south particularly, became involved in the armed groups of the *Forces Françaises de l'Intérieure* (**FFI** – French interior forces). Outside of France French servicemen continued to fight in alliance with Britain in distinct French units under the command of General Charles de Gaulle; these units returned to mainland France with Allied forces in the summer of 1944.

The FFI comprised both communists and Gaullists, who were organized into military units to fight within France for liberation. They were principally active in the aftermath of D-Day.

EXERCISE

From the brief description given in the preceding paragraph consider the following questions.

1 How many different kinds of wartime memory can you associate with the French people?

2 Does there appear to you to be a dominant French memory of the Second World War?

DISCUSSION

1   You could list here: the supporters of Vichy; the internal
     Resistance (and remember that this was divided between
     communists and non-communists); the servicemen who fought
     alongside British and American troops; and those who positively
     supported neither Vichy nor the Resistance, but simply tried to
     get on with their lives.

2   I think that it would be difficult to detect a dominant memory
     from that paragraph. It might be tempting to suggest that most
     people opted to get on with their lives without committing
     themselves to either Vichy or the Resistance, except when it was
     prudent or when they were compelled to make a commitment.
     But then if that was how most people behaved in reality, is that
     likely to constitute a satisfactory national or political memory?

The Popular Front was an anti-fascist coalition of left and centre parties during the 1930s. It formed the government in France from June 1936 to October 1938.

The historian Henry Rousso has argued that the 'crucial feature' of the Vichy regime was the fact that a large number of internal conflicts erupted into a form of civil war. One of these conflicts was the hostility between the political left and right, both of whom had perceived the existence of 'an enemy within' during the 1930s – for the left this was fascism, while for the right it was communism and the **Popular Front**. There were also old, unresolved divisions that went back to the great revolution that had broken out in 1789 and which Vichy brought back to the top of the political agenda with its moves against republican institutions and a revival of state support for the Catholic church. Finally, there is every justification for believing that Vichy's anti-semitism owed as much to an anti-semitic tradition within France as to Nazism. Rousso argues that these internal divisions linked with the trauma of occupation to form what he has labelled 'the Vichy syndrome', a set of 'symptoms' which have continued since the war and which periodically flare into crises within political, social and cultural life (Rousso, 1991).

Rousso's 'syndrome' broadly manifested itself in four distinct stages. The first was a brief purge (*l'Épuration*). The second, occupying the decade after the war, was a period of mourning punctuated by calls for forgiveness and reconciliation, even while the old wounds and hostilities still simmered, occasionally bubbling over in court cases. In the third stage, however, from the mid 1950s until the end of the 1960s, the Vichy period became less controversial, and during the presidency of Charles de Gaulle the whole nation tended to become identified with the Resistance. The students of 1968 who clashed with the CRS (*Compagnies Républicains de Sécurité*) riot police sometimes chanted 'CRS – SS' and 'Nous sommes tous des juifs allemands' (We

Maurice Papon, the prefect of police in Paris in 1968 and therefore responsible for coordinating police deployment against student demonstrators, had been a Vichy functionary in Bordeaux from 1942 to 1944. It was alleged that he had been instrumental in organizing the deportation of Jews during this period. In 1998, at the age of 88, Papon was found guilty of this offence and sentenced to ten years in prison. He was released on compassionate grounds, owing to ill health, in September 2002.

are all German Jews), but the lasting significance of their protest with reference to the war was a re-investigation of the period and a challenge to the Gaullist image of Resistance. Particularly notable in this reassessment was the documentary film made in 1969 by Marcel Olphus, *Le Chagrin et la Pitié* (*The Sorrow and the Pity*), which chronicles the daily life of the people of Clermont-Ferrand (in central France) under the occupation. The film had a long run, but in a limited number of cinemas; it was shown overseas to considerable acclaim, yet it took ten years for French television to show it. The former *résistant* Jean-Jacques de Bresson, who was head of French radio and television in 1971, explained to the cultural committee of the French senate that the film 'destroys myths that the people of France still need' (quoted in Rousso, 1991, p. 110). Finally Rousso's fourth stage, a period of obsession, began in the mid 1970s, ignited by a heightened Jewish consciousness within France and, more broadly, by an international awareness of the scale of the Holocaust.

Throughout the 1990s the law and attempted political pragmatism continued to throw up problems and paradoxes over the memory of the Second World War in France. In April 1992 there was a judicial ruling that Paul Touvier, formerly chief of the vicious Vichy militia in Lyon, had no case to answer on a charge of crimes against humanity since the definition of such a crime required that it be committed at the behest of a state practising a policy of ideological hegemony. The Axis powers had pursued such policies, but Vichy had not; therefore it was necessary to prove that Touvier had acted at the behest of the Germans, which did not seem possible. At roughly the same time 200 prominent public figures petitioned the socialist president, François Mitterand, to admit publicly that the French state was responsible for crimes against the Jews of France. Mitterand refused on the grounds that there was no analogy between what the German 'nation' had done, for which Chancellor Willy Brandt had made a public apology, and what the French 'nation' had done. Besides, taking a line similar to De Gaulle's assertion that the Vichy state was always illegitimate, Mitterand insisted that the Fifth Republic could not take responsibility for things done by Vichy. These responses were made at the same time that Mitterand authorized the publication of details about his own ambiguous past and his personal involvement with the Vichy regime. Three years after Mitterand's refusal a Gaullist president, Jacques Chirac, conceded the responsibility of the French state. But by admitting that Vichy was a legitimate regime, Chirac was also implying that De Gaulle's call to arms and refusal to accept the French government's armistice in June 1940 constituted, in some degree at least, an act of rebellion.

Elsewhere in the west

Elsewhere in Europe the memory and the legacy of the war have created similar kinds of pain and paradox. In Italy the second half of the Second World War was essentially a civil war; many old wounds left from the *Risorgimento* (the nationalist movement that led to the unification of Italy in 1870) were reopened and individuals had to make decisions about where to focus their loyalty. Meanwhile, for a long time in Austria there appeared to be a consensus to portray the country as the first victim of Nazism, occupied following the *Anschluss* of 1938. As one Austrian teacher expressed it in 1946, urging that Austrian cultural achievements be stressed over those of Prussia and Saxony,

> Little Austria is a great power in the area of culture and spirit: the university, Burgtheatre, [and] opera are living proof of this ... And this Austria fell victim to National Socialist aggression after heroic resistance.
>
> And this Austria, with all of its wonderful achievements, had to keep quiet in recent years. Instead the Greater German Reich had to be praised, which, as everyone knows today, only brought Austria unspeakable unhappiness and a sea of blood and tears, until it collapsed of its own doing into the greatest catastrophe of all time, pulling our innocent *Heimat* [homeland] along with it into the rottenness.
>
> (Quoted in Utgaard, 1999, p. 143)

But the involvement of Austrians in Nazi crimes against humanity was brought to the fore in the mid 1980s when Kurt Waldheim, former secretary-general of the United Nations, stood for the post of president of Austria. Waldheim's unsavoury wartime activities were uncovered and questions began to be pressed, again by a younger generation that had grown up since 1945.

Finally in this brief survey, Switzerland was neutral in both world wars, yet various revelations, particularly during the 1990s first about the behaviour of Swiss banks regarding the money and possessions of Jewish families caught up in the Holocaust, and secondly about those banks' financial relations with the Nazis, have caused embarrassment, heart-searching and pain.

So far we have concentrated on national experiences and memories, but I want you now to read extracts from two documents relating to a Belgian municipal experience and memory. The first is the appendix to a master's thesis originally written in 1995 by a young historian at the Université catholique de Louvain whose father had been the mayor of Dinant, a town in southeast Belgium. The second is extracted from a newspaper report published in 2001.

A bridge too far?

A history of the difficult relations between Dinant and the German flag

On 6 May next [2001] in ten days' time, a solemn ceremony will take place in Dinant. During the ceremony the German flag will be officially raised on the town's bridge where, for several decades, the flags of the other European countries have flown. For the uninitiated this might seem curious. Why, in a region very dependent on tourism and normally welcoming strangers, more than fifty years after the end of the Second World War and more than eighty years after the Great War, has the German tricolour not been tolerated until the beginning of the twenty-first century? The reason for this curiosity originates in the tragic days of August 1914 when nearly 700 civilians were shot and three-quarters of the town was razed to the ground. The German High Command, accusing the civilian population of openly siding with the French army and of participating in the fighting of 15 August which checked the first Prussian offensive, planned the sack of Dinant in the days preceding 23 August [when the massacre took place].

During the occupation that followed the invasion, the [German] authorities forbade all commemoration of the days of August and continued to justify the massacres of 1914 by insisting that those executed were *francs-tireurs* ...

After the armistice, the *Dinantais* hastened not only to rebuild their town but also to develop a cult of martyrs. Permanently sullied by the *francs-tireurs* accusation, the memory of the dead could not be properly honoured as long as this German calumny remained as official justification for the events of 1914. The inscriptions on the monuments to the dead, raised in the shadow of Bayard's Rock and the citadel, spoke of Saxon barbarism, Teutonic fury and German cowardice. Several times in the 1920s tourists coming from across the Rhine were violently abused and forced to leave the town in haste. In 1925 the war council of Namur symbolically condemned to death the executioners of 23 August. Two years later a committee was established to transmit to the Weimar Republic tens of thousands of pamphlets, written in German, refuting the German argument of *francs-tireurs*. Responses poured in to the town hall. A tiny minority, coming mainly from pacifist associations, supported the *Dinantais* ...

Francs-tireurs are irregular fighters. The Germans had encountered them during their invasion of France in the Franco-Prussian war of 1870–1. When they launched their invasion in 1914 they were extremely concerned about sniping activities hitting their supply lines and the rear of their army.

The determination of the *Dinantais* to denounce the executioners of 1914 did not diminish in the 1930s. Quite the contrary. In August 1936, while Belgian diplomacy was seeking to follow a path of neutrality, the Liberal mayor (*bourgmestre*), Sasserath, inaugurated a monument known as *Furore teutonico*. Again, like other monuments erected in the town, this forcefully declared the innocence of those massacred in 1914 and the barbarism of Germany which continued to defend the label of *francs-tireurs*.

In June 1940, when German troops entered the town, this memorial was totally destroyed. The inscriptions on all the town's monuments were chiselled away. In addition, the bas-reliefs that explicitly showed scenes of the shooting of civilians were destroyed. During the occupation the Gestapo set up offices in the town so as to deal more effectively with the acts of resistance in the countryside and the large forests in the south of the province. On 6 September 1944 a group of young *Dinantais*, encouraged by the rapid advance of the Allied army, tore down the German flag flying from the local church. Discovered, they were imprisoned and executed.

After the war there were important trials of collaborators, even in the town martyred in 1914. These ended in several death sentences, which were carried out in the heart of the town, within

Figures 1.2 and 1.3 *Furore teutonico*, the memorial to the civilian victims of the 1914 massacres in Dinant, Belgium. The memorial, with a central section showing a priest's hand raised in blessing and a dead child, was razed to the ground by the German army in 1940. Postcards courtesy of Dr Axel Tixhon

prison walls a few metres from the wall where more than 100 *Dinantais* had been executed in August 1914.

Restoration of the various monuments mutilated in 1940 had to wait until the beginning of the 1950s. The inscriptions were restored to what they had been on the eve of the conflict. They kept their overtly anti-German character. *Furore teutonico*, however, was not restored. After the war, the spot where it had stood was earmarked for sports and swimming facilities designed to attract tourists who seemed, more than ever, to be the principal means of filling the community's coffers ...

The 1950s saw the inauguration of a new bridge at Dinant, replacing the one destroyed at the beginning of the town's liberation. Flags were displayed upon it from the moment it opened, at the end of 1954. We cannot be certain if the German flag flew from the bridge then, but it seems unlikely since in 1953 the town authorities refused to offer a welcome to the participants in a Volkswagen rally when they reached the town. In 1955 and 1956 protests were voiced in the town's tourist office regarding tourist publicity circulated in Germany, and the problem always came back to the German thesis of the Dinant *francs-tireurs*.

The 1950s were also marked by the Treaty of Rome which established Belgium, Luxembourg, the Netherlands, France, Italy and the German Federal Republic as the European Economic Community, and by the organization of the Universal Exhibition of 1958. Increasingly the *Dinantais*, more and more dependent upon tourism, recognized that they must offer the most attractive image possible to foreigners who were coming to spend their money in local shops and businesses.

In July 1967 the mayor, himself one of the main owners of tourist attractions in the town, invited representatives of different local patriotic associations to give their opinion on raising the German flag in Dinant 'at a moment when the hour of Europe is with us, when customs barriers are being lowered, bringing better commerce, and promising better and better to follow, in cultural and tourist exchange as well as in trade'. These societies accepted, in writing, the presence of the flag of the Federal Republic of Germany providing that they did not see it raised during the commemoration of the events of 23 August.

Following this process of consultation the tourist office received authorization to display the German flag in several parts of the town alongside the flags of the other European nations. However, in May 1968 this flag was torn down and ripped into pieces at the tourist office. The person responsible, an individual well known in the town who had been responsible for investigating the tragedies of the two wars, sent a letter to the mayor explaining his actions:

> It is important to do everything possible for peace between peoples. But no one will think that it contributes to anything allowing the flag of those responsible for the massacres of Dinant, **Oradour-sur-Glane**. ... etc. to fly over the places where they have dishonoured themselves. Moreover, we are still waiting for the criminals of August 1914 and others to retract the accusations that they have levelled against their victims. We are still waiting for them to make amends.

A few days later the town council discussed the affair and decided it would no longer permit the German flag in Dinant except during sports events organized in the town in which German athletes were to participate. But the tourist office, arguing that the council had no right to impose such a decision, continued to fly the German flag. The flag was ripped down and replaced on several occasions. In the press several important *Dinantais*, notably from the legal profession, expressed their support for these acts of 'civic vandalism'. The decision of whether or not to permit the German flag was finally left to the mayor and his power to establish

On 10 June 1944, 642 inhabitants of the French village of Oradour-sur-Glane in the Limousin region of west central France were massacred by German troops from the *Waffen SS* tank division *Das Reich*.

Figure 1.4 The ruins of Oradour-sur-Glane, preserved, as it was left, as a monument to the massacre of June 1944. Photo: Imperial War Museum, London

by-laws (*règlements de police*). Following a new meeting at the town hall, the mayor reserved his right officially to ban the flag but, on his part, the head of the tourist office agreed no longer to fly it.

The authorities maintained this situation throughout the years that followed. They would not fly the German flag from the town's bridge. Occasionally some German tourists complained. A few, more aware of the situation, expressed their regrets for the tragedy of 23 August, notably, at the beginning of the 1980s, a group who came from Bochum. At the end of this decade the town council discussed the German flag again. It was decided that unanimity was necessary to permit the flag to be flown. Three councillors, one from each of the parties represented, refused. Thus the situation remained until the dawn of the twenty-first century.

(From annexe to Tixhon, 1995, transl. Clive Emsley)

Germany has asked pardon

The German minister of defence has come to ask pardon for the events of August 1914. A page is turned, even if the arguments between *Dinantais* are not over.

The first symbolic image of this historic day for many *Dinantais* families: the German minister of defence, Walter Kolbow, bowed before the monument to the dead erected in the courtyard of the town hall. He placed a wreath at the foot of the stone which bore the inscription: 'To the 674 *Dinantais* martyrs, innocent victims of German barbarism'. The tone of the ceremony was set.

The ceremonies unfolded in the noted absence of the *Dinantais* opposition, led by the socialist group ...

'It must be done for the young and for the future'
Interview
Name. Van Espen.
Christian name. Lucien.
Age. 75 years.
Role. President of the *Interfédérale des associations patriotiques de Dinant*.

Has it been easy to convince the patriotic associations to associate themselves with the ceremonies of rapprochement with Germany?
The patriotic associations have been looking into this problem for three or four years. We reached a common decision at the beginning of the last local elections and we sent a letter to all the candidates. We outlined in it the conditions under which we would agree to participate in these ceremonies. We required that the Germans ask pardon and not just express regrets. That said, the more the organization of the ceremonies advanced, the more you heard reservations being expressed. On the part of political prisoners particularly. I understand those who would prefer not to be present.

But you have decided to be present personally ...
I think that it must be done for the young and for the future. Dinant can't remain an isolated island in Europe. But that is not to say that we must not remain vigilant. Peace is fragile.

A page is turned?

The page must be turned. But the memory, the sufferings are not eliminated by that. Those who have lost family members cannot forget like that.

'It would be better to let these events die'

Interview

Name. Metzeler.

Christian name. Lucienne.

Age. 74 years.

Role. Local and regional secretary of the *Confédération des prisonniers politiques*, formerly detained in Ravensbrück.

You decided not to take part in the ceremony on 6 May; why?

I was unable to accept the idea. There has been too much suffering to go to see things like that. We don't forgive and we don't want to forgive. I had thought of leaving town during the ceremony. Then I said to myself:

I don't see why I should leave my home because a German is coming to Dinant.

What do you say to those who say that it is time to think of the future, of the young?

I visit concentration camps every year with the young. They are not all in favour of reconciliation.

Is it difficult to turn the page?

It would be better to let these events die of their own accord. Why rake over all these ashes? And can I doubt the sincerity of their asking forgiveness? That said, this won't impede Belgium from commercial relations with Germany. There's nothing to see.

Do you think that the German flag will stay on the bridge for long?

In my opinion, no!

But it won't be you who climbs the pole to bring it down?

Certainly not! I don't wish to put my hands on it.

(*Le Soir de Bruxelles*, 7 May 2001, transl. Clive Emsley)

EXERCISE

How do these two extracts amplify the issues already discussed in this chapter?

DISCUSSION

These extracts illustrate the long municipal memory of the people of Dinant and their refusal to forget, let alone to forgive, the events of 1914 and what they see as a calumny against their 'martyred' fellow townsfolk. They suggest that, whatever the national memory – and certainly the national experience of Belgium in two world wars was not a happy one – local, personalized memory can still be the more significant and potent. It might be argued (and probably would be argued by the *Dinantais*) that theirs was a stand on principle; they were prepared to see their tourist industry suffer because officially the Germans continued to insist on the story of the *francs-tireurs*. Looking back to the ideas of Fentress and Wickham quoted at the end of the first section of this chapter ('Two world wars and one World Cup!'), the memory of August 1914 and of the subsequent events that developed as a result of that memory can be seen as an essential part of being a citizen of Dinant.

Elsewhere: eastern Europe

In the second section above ('Germany: where did it all go wrong?'), I briefly noted a contrast between the way that the west and the east of Europe viewed the war against Nazism. In the west during the 1950s and 1960s the resistance to Hitler and the Nazis was portrayed as a struggle against totalitarianism, against a brutal anti-democratic regime that trampled on human rights and civil liberties – in other words a regime that paralleled the Soviet bloc, and especially the Soviet bloc under Stalin. By contrast, in eastern Europe the emphasis was put on the struggle for social liberation and the linked oppression of capitalism and fascism. Interestingly, the interpretations in both east and west during the 1950s and 1960s tended to marginalize the genocide committed against the Jews.

In Chapter 7 (p. 234) Tim Coles notes the lack of reference in the Soviet bloc to Jewish victims of the Nazis.

In April 1967 the Auschwitz Memorial was inaugurated. It was declared a monument to the international victims of the struggle against fascism, but above all to the Poles who had died. Given that Auschwitz stood on Polish territory, this is in part understandable. It was not until the collapse of Soviet power that the Poles, like citizens of the DDR and other former communist countries, were compelled to confront some of the memories that had been hidden by the old interpretation of the war in eastern Europe. The fact that the Red Army had rested outside Warsaw while the occupying Germans destroyed the anti-communist Polish Home Army during its uprising of 1 August to 3 October 1944 had been one such taboo subject. But this memory portrayed the Poles heroically as victims; the existence of Polish anti-semitism was a much more difficult issue.

The appearance of Jan Gross's book *Neighbors* in 2001 was a watershed in confronting this aspect of the past. The book chronicles the massacre perpetrated by the Polish townsfolk of Jedwabne on 1,600 of their Jewish neighbours in July 1941. A small group of Germans in the town stood by and took propaganda photographs. The prosecution of some twenty of the ringleaders between 1949 and 1953 was low-key, and those convicted were released before serving the full term of their sentences. Gross, a Pole from a mixed marriage (Jewish father, Catholic mother), had left Poland in 1969 for the United States, where he became a professor of political science in New York. He was vilified by many Poles over his book, accused of washing dirty linen in public. Some even condemned him and his book as part of a Jewish conspiracy. But the book also led to the Polish president appearing on television and urging his fellow citizens to seek forgiveness for the massacre.

A European identity – the solution?

War was a European experience during the twentieth century, yet so far we have focused largely on national identity, or at least on some form of identity related to a geographical area.

1 Why, do you suppose, have national identities been so central, given the subject matter here?

2 Can you think of any alternative identities that transcend those discussed up to this point?

DISCUSSION

1 The title of this chapter is 'War and national and political identities', and it might be argued that the identities given greatest prominence during the experience of war are invariably the national and political. The world wars of the twentieth century were fought between nation-states. War is among the most acute tests for such states. National war efforts require internal stability and solidarity; legislation and propaganda seek to maintain these. With peace will come either a national celebration of such commitment, if the outcome has been successful; or, if the result has been failure, there may be national heart-searching and attempts to redefine and renew the national image.

2 Political identities might transcend the national identities discussed so far. For example, some individuals in the period under discussion were internationalist – particularly those who were card-carrying members of Communist parties and who saw themselves engaged in an international struggle against fascism and capitalism during the 1930s. Then there were those who believed that the best way to ensure peace in the future was to break down national barriers and create some sort of united Europe. Communist party members, at least from the 1930s onwards, were invariably required to follow a line dictated by Moscow and the genuinely international, liberal and progressive aspirations of many such members were corroded by Stalinism. The collapse of the Soviet Union and its empire in east and central Europe largely brought an end to this kind of international identity, but the other idea of some sort of unified Europe continues. The immense costs and the destruction wrought by wars in twentieth-century Europe fostered ideas of union, a union that was not to be established at bayonet point and enforced by the secret police. Such ideas were not new. At

the end of the seventeenth century, for example, the Quaker William Penn had advocated a European parliament to preserve peace and maintain international harmony. But the two twentieth-century wars appeared to many to create both a new urgency and a new opportunity for the idea. If the existing nation-states and national identities had brought about the wars (and this is one major argument as to why the wars occurred), then peace might best be secured by establishing a broader European identity.

In 1923 Richard Coudenhove-Kalergi (1894–1972) published *Pan-Europe*. In this he writes,

> Europe as a political concept does not exist. The part of the world with that name covers peoples and States in chaos, a powder keg of international conflicts, the breeding ground of future conflicts. This is the European Question: the mutual hatred of Europeans for each other poisons the international atmosphere and is a perpetual worry to even the most peace-loving countries of the world ... The European Question will be resolved only by the union of the peoples of Europe. This will come about either voluntarily, by the construction of a pan-European federation[,] or coercively by Russian conquest.

(Quoted in Salmon and Nicoll, 1997, p. 7)

Coudenhove-Kalergi had mixed ancestry – Cretan, Flemish and Japanese – and had been born a subject of the Austro-Hungarian empire. After the First World War he took Czech citizenship. His ideas for a European federation found some sympathizers, even among politicians. The French minister of foreign affairs, Aristide Briand, developed similar ideas and in September 1929 addressed the League of Nations, hinting at such a union. Briand, together with his German opposite number Gustav Stresemann, sought Franco-German reconciliation and considered that some sort of a European umbrella was the best way forward. At the beginning of May 1930, now promoted to prime minister of France, Briand presented a memorandum to the League that outlined new European political structures as a precursor to economic union. But the project foundered, not least because of the economic uncertainties generated by the Wall Street crash of October 1929, the death of Stresemann in the same month and Briand's own death in 1932.

Coudenhove-Kalergi remained active throughout the 1930s. In 1938 he fled Vienna as the Nazis arrived, settling in Switzerland. When war broke out the following year he published *Europe Must Unite*, urging a

Swiss-style federation for the continent and suggesting that English, as a *lingua franca*, might be considered its official language while other national languages and cultures could still be preserved within the system. As France crumbled and British troops were taken from the beaches at Dunkirk, Jean Monnet (1888–1979), a French businessman who had organized war supplies during the First World War and who had subsequently served as deputy secretary of the League of Nations, sponsored a plan for a Franco-British union in which the peoples would have joint citizenship and there would be joint institutions for defence, foreign affairs and economic management. The government in France, believing the war to be already lost, rejected the notion. Monnet began to contemplate a rather broader European union, while elsewhere other anti-fascists developed similar ideas. Two Italian political prisoners, Ernesto Rossi (1897–1967) and, rather more important, Altiero Spinelli (1907–86), published the Ventotene manifesto in June 1941. This was an attack on fascism and the Catholic church, which the authors saw as a supporter of the right. It urged a socialist solution to Europe's problems, arguing that social reform and freedom could be achieved through some sort of European union. In May 1944 representatives of the national resistance movements in Czechoslovakia, Denmark, France, the Netherlands, Italy, Norway, Yugoslavia and Germany itself met in Geneva and adopted a draft declaration on European federation. This declaration was also written by Rossi and Spinelli.

While they aspired to similar ends, Monnet and Spinelli adopted rather different approaches as to how some form of European unity might be achieved. Monnet was a pragmatist who considered that, from small practical beginnings, integration would develop its own momentum, increasingly restricting national governments and creating a general awareness of the greater benefits achievable through union. Spinelli hoped that federal idealists could create some sort of mass popular movement within Europe that would sweep away the old order of nationalists, soldiers and bureaucrats. While Spinelli went on to become a member of the European parliament and to prepare the draft treaty on European union adopted by the parliament in 1984, but never submitted to the member states for ratification, it is fair to say that Monnet's pragmatism and gradualism produced greater achievements.

The years immediately following the Second World War witnessed considerable debate about why and how Europe might be brought together. In September 1946, for example, Winston Churchill spoke of 'the tragedy of Europe'.

> This noble continent, comprising on the whole the fairest and the most cultivated regions on earth, enjoying a temperate and equitable climate, is the home of the greatest

parent races of the western world. It is the fountain of Christian faith and Christian ethics. It is the origin of most of the culture, arts, philosophy, and science both of ancient and modern times. If Europe were once united in the sharing of its common inheritance, there would be no limit to the happiness, to the prosperity and glory which its three or four hundred million people would enjoy.

(Quoted in Nelson and Stubb, 1998, p. 8)

Unfortunately, since the beginning of the twentieth century Europe had been wracked by war. Churchill's remedy for this was a 'United States of Europe'. He urged that France and Germany should come together to lead the new entity. He did not see Britain as having a role in this union, however. Rather, Britain and its Commonwealth, together with the USA and the USSR, would be friends, sponsors and champions of the continent. Churchill's exclusion of Britain from his proposal for European unity prefigures the ambivalence of subsequent British politicians towards the idea.

In April 1951 France and West Germany, together with Belgium, Italy, Luxembourg and the Netherlands, took the first positive steps towards economic unity by signing the treaty establishing the European Coal and Steel Community (ECSC). The idea had been developed by Monnet and was taken up and pressed by the French foreign minister, Robert Schuman (1886–1963). Schuman, who had a French father, was born in Luxembourg, educated at German universities and continued to be an exponent of Franco-German cooperation while on the run from the Gestapo. He openly stated that the intention of the ECSC was to render war impossible. The treaty bound together those industries central to the production of munitions. Two subsequent treaties were signed in Rome in March 1957, creating the European Atomic Energy Community (Euratom) and, more significantly, the European Economic Community (EEC). Arguably, a subtle shift was detectable in the attitude of the signatories to these later treaties. While peace remained the central goal, the preamble to the EEC treaty expressed a determination 'to lay the foundations for an ever closer union among the peoples of Europe' and the overall stress appears to point rather more towards material improvements.

EXERCISE _____

1   A simple and obvious question: the signatories of these treaties labelled their new institutions 'European', but how far was the label justified?

2   Given the political situation of Europe in the aftermath of the
     Second World War, can you see any political accusations that
     might be levelled at these new institutions?

DISCUSSION

1   Of course these institutions were European in the sense that they
     were situated in Europe and involved European states, but these
     states were, initially, only six in number and were located in the
     most industrially advanced areas of the western part of the
     continent.

2   Postwar Europe was divided by the Iron Curtain, and since the
     countries involved in the new institutions lay in the west it was
     possible to accuse them of perpetuating that division by adding
     an economic dimension to the political and ideological one. In
     1957 the Moscow Institute of World Economics and International
     Relations published seventeen theses criticizing the EEC and
     related developments precisely in these terms. In this view the
     community was part of an aggressive bloc directed against the
     USSR and the 'People's Democracies', backed by the USA and
     linked to Nato. Rather than being a force for peace and stability,
     the EEC would accentuate the struggle for raw materials across
     the world, exploit the underprivileged of the Third World and
     impede movements for national liberation. It was designed by
     capitalists, for capitalists, and the peoples of Europe had not been
     consulted on its creation. In some respects the Moscow Institute
     had a point. The USA had indeed been keen to see these
     developments, and the peoples of the countries involved had
     never been formally consulted about them.

One motive for the construction of the EU lay in the destruction and
division the Second World War created, yet, paradoxically, the
memory of the same war (and of its predecessor) has fed the hostility
of those who have vehemently opposed further development of the
EU, especially any development which has implied some sort of
federal system. Historians have played a significant role in
constructing national identities by constructing national pasts; might
they now do they same for Europe and European identity? Norman
Davies has suggested that '[s]ooner or later, a convincing new picture
of Europe's past will have to be composed to accompany the new
aspirations for Europe's future' (Davies, 1996, p. 45). But any
attempts so far in this direction, as Davies himself points out, have
not been encouraging. For example, the European Commission
financed (though it did not originate) an attempt to present the

history of Europe through a 500-page book, a ten-part television series and a school textbook, all of which were to be published simultaneously in the eight languages of the community. The school textbook (Delouche, et al., 1992), written by twelve historians from twelve different countries, could not find an English publisher and moreover illustrated some of the problems inherent in efforts to reach agreement about issues interpreted differently in different countries. The 500-page survey (Duroselle, 1991), which argued that nation-states were only recent inventions that were not set in stone and that people could rise above 'national instincts' – especially following the triumph of liberal democracy over totalitarianism in the west (by which the author meant the end of the neo-fascist regimes in Spain and Portugal) – received a bad press and the European Commission was obliged to disassociate itself from the work.

Some concluding points

At the turn of the century there continued to be debate about the direction to be adopted by the European Union, as the EEC had become. There were those, especially in continental Europe, who called for ever closer union between member states, while British eurosceptics in particular insisted that in 1973 the UK had joined an economic union, not an organization intended to become the United States of Europe. Moreover, for the majority of the people living within the EU national identity appeared to remain more significant than any European one and concerns were expressed in many quarters about the loss of national identity, though not always because of the development of Europe.

In the year 2000 the Press and Information Office of the German government published a small pamphlet on the developing EU. It argued that the union was evolving into a completely new form of political organization that was much better suited to the conditions and difficulties of the world. It urged that war within Europe was no longer possible, and it set out to alleviate concerns about the replacement of the deutschmark by the euro. It posed many of these anxieties as questions, and provided brief answers.

> *But won't Europe lose its diversity and won't individual states lose their national identity?*

> Has Munich lost since the foundation of the German Reich in 1871, is it indistinguishable from Hamburg? Is there no longer a distinction between Swabia and Frisia, or a loss if you can travel from Kempten to Husum without border controls? Don't worry: the diversity of ethnicities, mentalities, traditions and cultural behaviour remains supported by the EU.

> (*Europa*, 2000, p. 21)

It is instructive that even in a country where, as a result of two world wars, there is concern about the past effects of nationalism and where people have discussed the need to create a new national identity, the government still felt it necessary to stress that national identity would not be lost through a broader, inter-state union.

References

Blackbourn, David and Eley, Geoff (1984) *The Peculiarities of German History: Bourgeois Society and Politics in Nineteenth-Century Germany*, Oxford, Oxford University Press.

Browning, Christopher R. (1992) *Ordinary Men: Reserve Police Battalion 101 and the Final Solution in Poland*, New York, HarperCollins.

Bryant, Arthur (1942) *The Years of Endurance 1793–1802*, London, Collins.

Davies, Norman (1996) *Europe: a History*, Oxford, Oxford University Press.

Delouche, Frédéric, et al. (1992) *Histoire de l'Europe*, Paris, Hachette.

Duroselle, Jean-Baptiste (1991) *Europe: a History of its Peoples*, London, Viking.

Eley, Geoff (2001) 'Finding the people's war: film, British collective memory, and World War II', *American Historical Review*, 106, pp. 818–38.

Europa 2000: Die Europäische Union wird größer (2000), Berlin, Presse- und Informationsamt der Bundesregierung.

Fentress, James and Wickham, Chris (1992) *Social Memory*, Oxford, Blackwell.

Goldhagen, Daniel J. (1996) *Hitler's Willing Executioners: Ordinary Germans and the Holocaust*, London, Little, Brown.

Gross, Jan T. (2001) *Neighbors: the Destruction of the Jewish Community in Jedwabne*, Princeton, NJ, Princeton University Press.

Marwick, Arthur (2001) *The New Nature of History*, London, Palgrave.

Mayer, Arno J. (1981) *The Persistence of the Old Regime: Europe to the Great War*, London, Croom Helm.

Nelson, Brent F. and Stubb, Alexander C-G. (eds) (1998) *The European Union: Readings on the Theory and Practice of European Integration*, 2nd edn., London, Macmillan.

Rousso, Henry (1991) *The Vichy Syndrome: History and Memory in France since 1944*, Cambridge, MA, Harvard University Press (originally published as *Le Syndrome de Vichy: de 1944 à nos jours*, Paris, Editions du Seuil, 1987).

Salmon, Trevor and Nicoll, Sir William (eds) (1997) *Building European Union: a Documentary History and Analysis*, Manchester, Manchester University Press.

Schulze, Hagen (1996) *Klein deutsche Geschichte*, Munich, C. H. Beck.

Taylor, A. J. P. (1951) *The Course of German History*, new edn., London, Hamish Hamilton.

Taylor, A. J. P. (1964) *The Origins of the Second World War*, Harmondsworth, Penguin.

Tixhon, Axel (1995) 'Le souvenir des massacres du 23 août 1914. Étude des commemorations organisées à Dinant durant l'entre-deux-guerres', master's dissertation in history, Université catholique de Louvain.

Utgaard, Peter (1999) 'From *Blümchenkaffee to Wiener Melange*: schools, identity, and the birth of the "Austria-as-Victim" myth, 1945–55', *Austrian History Yearbook*, 30, pp. 127–58.

Wiener, Martin J. (1985) *English Culture and the Decline of the Industrial Spirit*, Harmondsworth, Penguin.

2

War in twentieth-century Europe:
cultural images, memories and monuments

CLIVE EMSLEY

Die Neue Wache

At the eastern end of Unter den Linden, the avenue that was once the heart of imperial Berlin, stands *Die Neue Wache* (the new guardhouse). Situated between the Humboldt University and the massive *Zeughaus* (the arsenal, now the Museum of German History), *Die Neue Wache* is a relatively small structure, little more than a classical portico with a large room behind. Built between 1816 and 1818 it was designed by Karl Friedrich Schinkel, the architect responsible for much of the building in early nineteenth-century Berlin. It served as the headquarters for the royal palace guard from 1818 until the fall of the Prussian monarchy in 1918. In 1931 *Die Neue Wache*, redesigned on the orders of the Prussian government, was inaugurated as a memorial to those who had fallen in the 'Great War'. In the centre was situated a block of granite surrounded with a wreath of silver oak leaves. During the Second World War the building, like much else in the city, was damaged by Allied bombing. In the aftermath of this war Unter den Linden fell within the Soviet sector of Berlin but *Die Neue Wache* was restored in 1960 by the German Democratic Republic as a memorial to the victims of fascism and militarism. In 1969 the remains of an unknown soldier and an unknown concentration camp victim were interred within the building, surrounded by earth from the battlefields and the concentration camps, and an eternal flame was lit in the centre of the room. In 1993, with Germany reunited, *Die Neue Wache* became the central memorial of the country. The interior design of the old Weimar memorial was restored but, in the place of the block of granite, there was placed a reproduction of a *pietà*, a mother cradling the body of her dead son, by Käthe Kollwitz (Kollwitz's own son had been killed in action in 1914). In front of the statue are the words *Den Opfen von Krieg und Gewaltherrschaft* (to the victims of war and tyranny).

The implications of placing the *pietà* in this memorial are discussed by Tim Cole in Chapter 7 (p. 251).

Figure 2.1 *Die Neue Wache.* The photograph shows soldiers of the GDR changing guard in front of the building in 1955. Photo: BPK

Several aspects and images of the remembrance of war can be found in the story of *Die Neue Wache*. The building was first established for the military in a kingdom whose name has often been regarded as synonymous with militarism. Since the fall of the kingdom of Prussia it has become the focus for remembering the dead of both war and oppressive regimes. The rituals of remembrance deployed there at different times and by different regimes are well known throughout Europe: wreaths, earth from the scenes of war or oppression, an eternal flame, unknown warriors/victims, dedications, statues of dead sons and weeping mothers – all the more poignant in the case of Kollwitz, given her personal tragedy. But *Die Neue Wache* has also raised fierce controversy. The GDR could be criticized for remembering the victims of fascism and militarism, yet at the same time ignoring those of Stalinism or those who fell to the guns of border guards while trying to cross the Berlin Wall less than 2 kilometres from the memorial. More recently several intellectuals of the new united Germany have protested that Kollwitz's *pietà* is essentially a Christian image. Can it therefore be seen as easily and readily including Jewish victims of the Holocaust? Does the image, and do the words of the dedication, not also blur the important distinction between the victims and the perpetrators of the Nazi regime and its crimes against humanity? Does such a blurring tend to absolve Germany from an unprecedented degree of responsibility for both the world wars and these crimes? Is this simply a German problem?

The world wars of the twentieth century began in Europe; the Cold War was initiated in the division of Europe. But how far do Europeans have a common memory of these events and how far is there a common way of commemorating them? How far might these images be said to have contributed to common identities – national, or even supranational? The experience of war leaves individuals with memories that are often painful and harrowing. While not wishing to marginalize or trivialize such memories, what follows will explore very broadly the public memory of war by focusing on what might be termed cultural artefacts of memory and remembrance.

Culture and memory

On the night of 9–10 November 1989, following a flustered response at a press conference by a member of the East German Politburo, crowds danced atop the Berlin Wall and set about it with sledgehammers. This was the most dramatic moment in the dismantling of the Iron Curtain and the end of the Cold War; it led, in turn, to the reunification of Germany. Within a matter of months the 106-kilometre wall, with its electric fences, bunkers and watchtowers, was all but destroyed. Some pieces were used as hardcore for new construction work; some of the more brightly coloured parts (decorated on the western side of the wall by Berlin's graffiti artists) were given away to foreign governments or sold off to entrepreneurs who profited by selling them on to tourists. Ten years later it was still possible to buy a piece of the wall in Berlin tourist shops, sometimes in a gift box with a toy model of the East German car, the Trabant, crashing into it. Attempts to preserve parts of the wall as a monument were rejected by local Berliners who protested that they had had to look daily at the physical division of their city for twenty-eight years, and had no wish to be reminded of this. In 1996 a Berlin newspaper carried out a poll of 12-year-olds to see what they remembered of the momentous events of 1989, and discovered that few had any recollection. The year 1989 had also seen the fiftieth anniversary of the beginning of the Second World War, by which time most surviving veterans of that war would have been in retirement. Moreover, by 1989 most of those who had survived the First World War were dead. Yet the world wars and (probably to a much lesser extent) the Cold War still reverberate in popular memory. They are also, in varying degrees, commemorated and remembered publicly by nation-states, thus contributing to national memories and identities.

EXERCISE

1   What is the abiding image of the First World War?

2   Where does that image come from?

3   Would you consider this image to be international?

4   Would you consider this image to be gendered?

DISCUSSION

1   Perhaps everyone has their own image of the First World War, but I suspect that your response here was to mention muddy trenches and a pointless waste of life, with men being mown down by machine-gun fire in a no man's land of barbed wire, shattered trees and shell-holes. You might also have mentioned shallow, even wicked politicians, bungling generals and corrupt capitalists profiteering at the expense of the brave victims in the trenches.

2   In his history of the First World War, *The Pity of War*, Niall Ferguson writes:

> It is not from historians that the majority of modern readers gain their impression of the First World War, but from [modern novels like Pat Barker's 1990s trilogy, *Regeneration*, *The Eye in the Door* and *The Ghost Road*, and Sebastian Faulks's *Birdsong*] – and, of course, from newspapers, television, theatre and cinema.
>
> (Ferguson, 1998, p. xxxii)

3   Trench warfare was to be found on all fronts during the First World War, but in the east and the Balkans there was also considerable movement, very different from the stalemate of the Western Front that dominates British and French perceptions. In short, the war may have been experienced across Europe, but national and regional experiences of the conflict may have been very different.

4   War for most of the twentieth century, and in most societies in earlier centuries too, was generally considered to be the public business/duty of men. Female roles, especially as defined in

Europe (though not just in Europe), tended to be confined to the private sphere or, where they were 'public', to managing and delivering forms of welfare. War re-emphasized these male/female, public/private roles and identities. The best-known personal narrative by a British woman to come out of the Great War was that of Vera Britten, who served as a nurse – a welfare, caring and, arguably, maternal role. Wartime novels written by women in France commonly stressed similar roles and duties for women (O'Brien, 1996). The First World War occurred as feminist movements were becoming increasingly influential across Europe and convincing many men that women should be enfranchised. During the war, however, many of the feminists in the combatant countries, like many of the socialists there, subordinated their politics to the national cause.

Historians still argue about the causes of the First World War, and many have challenged the blame that has been heaped upon the politicians and generals associated with it. Yet the images of corruption and incompetence, many of which go back to the war itself, persist and they cross national boundaries. The French historian Jean-Louis Robert, having explored the press of Berlin, London and Paris during the war with particular reference to the image of the profiteer, has suggested that during the conflict a new moral code began to be expressed on the different home fronts.

> This normative code ruled out of bounds in wartime a whole panoply of sins: dissoluteness, frivolousness, the display of conspicuous wealth, egotism, cynicism, vulgarity, an uncompromising search for personal advantage, sloth, incompetence.

(Robert, 1997, p. 131)

It has become a cliché to contrast the pre-war poetry of early twentieth-century Britain with, for example, the pain, suffering and complete antithesis of military glory expressed by Wilfred Owen or the angry cynicism, often assumed to reflect that of the ordinary soldiers, presented at times by Siegfried Sassoon (1886–1967) in war poems such as 'Blighters'.

> The House is crammed: tier beyond tier they grin
> And cackle at the Show, while prancing ranks
> Of harlots shrill the chorus, drunk with din;
> 'We're sure the Kaiser loves our dear old Tanks!'

> I'd like to see a Tank come down the stalls,
> Lurching to rag-time tunes, or 'Home, sweet Home',
> And there'd be no more jokes in Music-halls
> To mock the riddled corpses round Bapaume.

Henri Barbusse's *Le Feu* (commonly translated as 'under fire', though *feu* (fire) has much broader connotations and meanings, especially given the inundation that concludes the novel), the story of a squad of French soldiers, was a best-seller from its first publication in 1916.

Arnold Zweig's *Der Streit um den Sergeanten Grischa* (*The Case of Sergeant Grischa*), initially drafted as a play in 1921 but published as a novel seven years later, contains a scene in which a Prussian general, who dreams of annexing vast tracts of central Europe, meets with a powerful industrialist and member of the *Reichstag* (German parliament), who is speculating on the currency markets, to discuss

> all for the good of the Fatherland – the transference of twenty or thirty thousand civilian workmen from the occupied territory, since General Headquarters had kindly consented to relieve [the industrialist] of the care of his turbulent and embittered malcontents, and the fellows had been called up.
>
> (Zweig [1928] 2000, p. 211)

Erich Maria Remarque's *Im Westen nichts Neues* (*All Quiet on the Western Front*) encapsulates the image of a lost generation. In the final chapter Paul, the central character who has described the gradual destruction of his squad of German infantrymen, speculates on the future.

> Had we returned home in 1916, out of the suffering and the strength of our experiences we might have unleashed a storm. Now if we go back we will be weary, broken, burnt out, rootless, and without hope. We will not be able to find our way any more.
>
> And men will not understand us – for the generation that grew up before us, though it has passed these years with us already had a home and a calling; now it will return to its old occupations, and the war will be forgotten – and the generation that has grown up after us will be strange to us and push us aside.
>
> (Remarque [1929] 1963, p. 190)

I used the word 'encapsulates' above; might I rather have used the word 'creates'? To what extent is our memory of the First World War a literary or, more generally – thinking of paintings such as Paul Nash's *We Are Making a New World* (Plate 2), Georges Leroux's *L'Enfer* (Plate 3) and Otto Dix's triptych *Krieg* (Plate 4), and films such as G. W. Pabst's *Westfront 1918*, Abel Gance's *J'Accuse*, Lewis Milestone's *All*

Figure 2.2   The war dead rise up to protest; from Abel Gance's film *J'Accuse*, made in 1919 in the immediate aftermath of the First World War. Photo: Ronald Grant Archive

All Quiet on the Western Front and Jean Renoir's *La Grande Illusion* – an artistic creation, rather than one established by people who lived through it or, subsequently, by historians? The stark, often brutal portrayal of war by artists during and immediately after 1914–18 has led several cultural critics to argue that the conflict contributed significantly to a new Modernist language in poetry, prose and the visual arts. There was simply no other way to portray the event, and no other way to remember it. The literary critic Paul Fussell, for example, has suggested that much of the modern literary vision of war in general emanates from the images of the First World War, with many modern writers eschewing the Second World War as a source of image, phrase and myth (Fussell, 1975). The term 'no man's land' provides a good example. During and immediately after the First World War it was used to describe the space between the front-line trenches. Such lines rarely existed in a similar way during the Second World War, and indeed 'no man's land' primarily describes a characteristic of the Western Front rather than other fronts of 1914–18. Yet the term continued, and continues, to be used both for its evocation of a particular kind of space and also as a part of the literary language employed when describing aspects of war or some

Figure 2.3 Paul's platoon at rest; from Lewis Milestone's *All Quiet on the Western Front*, made in 1930. Photo: Ronald Grant Archive

other form of conflict. The term, moreover, is the same in both English and French, while the German *das Niemandsland* is a literal equivalent.

The 'Modernist' notion that the First World War is a key moment in the shift to a new kind of literary and visual language has not gone unchallenged. The historian Jay Winter, for example, has insisted that in some respects the poetry of the Great War, rather than ushering in Modernism, 'reinforced romantic tendencies about war ... [with] a refashioned set of ideas and images drawn from a range of older traditions' (Winter, 1995, p. 221). According to Winter, the soldier poet, especially significant in the British memory of the war,

> was in the end a romantic figure ... Many sought to reach the sacred through the metaphor of resurrection. What better means of evoking feeling for the brotherhood of the living and the dead by hearing them speak again?

> (Winter, 1995, p. 221)

Figure 2.4 At a later stage of the war (note the changed German helmets) Paul comforts a comrade in a makeshift trench. Photo: Ronald Grant Archive

Yet, despite these caveats, the war poets are commonly credited with bringing readers face to face with the horrors of industrialized war and challenging, in the words of Wilfred Owen in his wartime poem 'Dulce et Decorum est',

> The old Lie: *Dulce et decorum est*
> *Pro patria mori*

The cultural critic George Steiner has suggested, however, that 'nearer than any writer, nearer even than the poets to forcing language into the mould of total war' was the German writer Ernst Jünger.

> This is in part a matter of technique: the lapidary sentences, so different from the sinuous hesitance of normal German literary and philosophic prose, the violent similes, the play of graphic, uncontrolled turbulence against abstraction. In part it stems from Jünger's resolve to make the job of writing a counterpart to that of combat.

> (Steiner, 1970, p. 7)

Yet Jünger's vision of war is rather different from that of the poets.

The first reading begins with two poems from the First World War, one by August Stramm (1874–1915) and the other by Heinrich Lersch (1889–1936). In each case the original German is printed beside the English version to give an idea of the use of language in the original. The poems are followed by a prose extract, from Ernst Jünger's *Storm of Steel*.

Schlachtfeld

Schollenmürbe schläfert ein das Eisen

Blute filzen Sickerflecke

Roste krumen

Fleische schleimen

Saugen brünstet um Zerfallen.

Mordesmorde

Blinzen

Kinderblicke.

August Stramm

Battlefield

Clod softness lulls iron off
to sleep

Bloods clot ooze patches

Rusts crumble

Fleshes slime

Sucking ruts around decay

Child eyes

Blink

Murder upon murder

(Bridgewater, 1985,
pp. 43–4, 171)

Der Kriegsinvalide

Ihr könnt mein Lächeln, Leute, nicht verstehn?

Ich lächle, wo ich immer geh und bin.

Ich darf noch einmal in das Leben gehn.

Für mich hat alles andern Sinn.

Ob auch mein linker Arm sich nach dem rechten sehnt

The War-Invalid

You cannot understand my smile, comrades?

I smile wherever I go and wherever I am.

I am returning to life.

For me everything has a different meaning.

Even if my left arm longs for the right one (which is rotting somewhere), the feeling of loss

(der irgendwo verfault), das brennt wie Gift;

und doch, der linke, der sich mächtig dehnt,

der packt das Leben, wo er es nur trifft.

Ich weiss ein Land, das voll von Toten liegt.

Einst lag ich mitten unter ihnen – wund.

So oft mein Auge rückwärts schauend fliegt,

Schmeckt mir die Zung wie Blut im Mund.

Noch gräbt man täglich tausend Tote ein –

ich sah sie fallen, Stück um Stück.

Ich aber lebe und die Welt ist mein.

Es gibt auf Erden ja kein grössres Glück,

als nicht Soldat, als nicht im Krieg zu sein!

Heinrich Lersch

burning like poison;

yet the left one, which has quite a stretch,

grabs life wherever it meets it.

I know a land full of dead men.

I once lay among them, wounded.

Whenever my mind's eye recalls the scene,

I taste blood in my mouth.

A thousand dead are still being buried daily,

I saw them fall, one by one.

But I am alive and the world is mine.

There is no greater happiness on earth

than that of not being a soldier, not being in the war!

(Bridgewater, 1985, pp. 131–2, 194)

In the midst of this tumult I was struck to the earth by a terrific blow. Sobered, I tore off my helmet, and saw with horror two large holes in it. The N.C.O. Mohrmann, who sprang to my help, comforted me by the assurance that nothing was to be seen on the back of my head but a scratch. The shot of a far-distant rifle had pierced my helmet and grazed the skull. I was half-dazed and was forced to give way. With my head bound up I made my way out of the thick of the fight. I had scarcely passed the next traverse when a man ran up behind me and gasped out that Tebbe had been killed by a shot in the head at the very same spot.

This news finished me. I could scarcely realize that a friend with whom for years I had shared joy and sorrow and danger, and who had sung out a jest to me a few minutes before, had met his end from a senseless piece of lead. Unhappily it was too true.

All the leading N.C.Os. and a third of the company had fallen too in this murderous piece of trench; Lieutenant Hopf, also, an elderly man and a teacher by profession, a German 'Ideal-Schulmeister' in the best sense of the word. My two Fähnrichs and many more were wounded. In spite of this the 7th Company held the trench they had gloriously won, and remained there under the command of Lieutenant Hoppenrath, the only officer left, until the relief of the battalion.

Even modern battle has its great moments. One hears it said very often and very mistakenly that the infantry battle has degenerated to an uninteresting butchery. On the contrary, to-day more than ever it is the individual that counts. Every one knows that who has seen them in their own realm, these princes of the trenches, with their hard, set faces, brave to madness, tough and agile to leap forward or back, with keen bloodthirsty nerves, whom no despatch ever mentions. Trench warfare is the bloodiest, wildest, and most brutal of all warfare, yet it too has had its men, men whom the call of the hour has raised up, unknown foolhardy fighters. Of all the nerve-racking moments of war none is so formidable as the meeting of two storm-troop leaders between the narrow walls of the trench. There is no retreat and no mercy then. Blood sounds in the shrill cry that is wrung like a nightmare from the breast.

(Jünger [1929] 1975, pp. 234–5)

Figure 2.5 Wilfred Owen (1893–1918)   **Figure 2.6** Ernst Jünger (1895–1998)
War poet, war hero, but can we accept 'princes of the trenches'?

EXERCISE _____

After you have read the two poems and the prose extract, consider the following questions.

1 What image of war do these extracts contain? Are they similar?

2 Do you find that you can empathize in equal measure with each of the authors?

DISCUSSION _____

1 This is a very subjective question. My own feeling is that all three pieces touch on the appalling nature of death and destruction in industrialized war (and perhaps not just 'industrialized' war). Stramm's poem is suggestive of artillery fire thumping into the earth, producing destruction and then decay. Lersch's speaker is a man who has survived the horrors of war and is overjoyed at being alive, though disabled. Jünger describes the violence of war, the loss of friends, but he also puts considerable emphasis on the exhilaration of battle.

2 This too is a highly subjective question. You may have found it easier to empathize with the poems of Lersch and Stramm which, I would suggest, fit with the way that we tend to think about and remember war, especially the First World War. Jünger too describes horror and violence, but you may have found his portrayal of tough, masculine, chivalric warriors ('princes of the trenches') rather hard to take. It is arguable that the personal clout of poetry is stronger than the more abstract power of prose. And yet the prose is autobiography, written in the first person, which makes a difference (translation might also make a difference). Furthermore, there is a significant difference between the poems. Stramm's poem is imagist, while that of Lersch is much more personal (note how the 'I' is repeated). For that reason you may have found Lersch and Jünger rather more human and hence easier to sympathize with.

_____

Jünger is a difficult individual to come to terms with. There is no doubt about his courage; he was wounded several times and won the highest military decoration of the Wilhelmine army, the *Pour le Mérite*. *The Storm of Steel* (*In Stahlgewittern*) was first published in Germany in 1920, and went through numerous editions and translations. In the immediate aftermath of the First World War Jünger dabbled in right-wing politics, before turning to the study of botany and zoology and the writing of novels. He served in the German army again during the Second World War and was on the fringe of the bomb plot against Hitler in 1944. When he died in 1998 at the age of 102 he was, literally, the grand old man of German literature and was eulogized as such. It has been suggested that his life and longevity were both a witness to and a testimony of the shift away from military violence and a kind of conservative masculinity within twentieth-century German society (Weisbrod, 2000). And if Jünger's adrenalin-charged accounts of battle and heroic masculinity may seem hard to take, it is perhaps worth remembering that before his protest against war in 1917 Siegfried Sassoon was known as 'Mad Jack' for his courageous behaviour; doubtless Jünger would have considered him a fellow 'prince'.

There is no single great work of literature, no painting, no film that can be said to encapsulate the memory of the First World War for a single national group, let alone for Europe as a whole. The cultural historian Daniel Pick reviewed an exhibition of art from the Great War held at London's Barbican in 1994 and, commenting specifically on the paintings of Otto Dix, suggested that there was a

> problem of ethics, of what should guide us as we look upon and admire this body of work. What are we to do with [Dix's] curious 'aestheticising' of the disgusting, his intricate – or

Figure 2.7   Men of the Border Regiment resting in a front-line trench, the battle of the Somme, Thiepval wood, August 1916. A typical image of the Western Front. Photo: Imperial War Museum, London, Crown Copyright

morbid – attempt to attribute form to the most visceral aspects of violence? How are we, the viewers of the work, thereby implicated? ... What is at stake when the artist and the viewer take pleasure in experimental forms, in the creativity evident amidst (or out of?) the slaughter? What does 'admiring' Dix's work consist in? Are we to relish or recoil from his images, even of the putrescence of bodies? Is our satisfaction in the art linked with the way he produces that recoil? Dix is exemplary because he so starkly raises the problem ... of how to represent war ... of how to find 'an adequate language'.

(Pick, 1995, pp. 196–7)

Not all works of art or literature concerned with war, or wartime, have to focus on its violence and brutality. These are not the only elements which make up the memory of war. Jaroslav Hašek succeeded in producing only about three-quarters of the one book by which he is now best remembered. *The Good Soldier Švejk* is often described as the funniest book to emerge from the First World War. Josef Švejk, a dog-trader and fancier from Prague, serves as the orderly to a drunken chaplain and subsequently as the batman for an infantry lieutenant. While the officers regard Švejk as stupid, at times it is difficult to discern how far this is really the case and how far he is acting out of a shrewd sense of self-preservation. Many of Švejk's adventures would find echoes in every army that participated in the war: sick and injured men classified as 'malingerers'; meaningless orders regarding food and equipment sent from a headquarters that is totally out of touch with what is going on in units bound for, or at, the front. Others are rooted in the Austro-Hungarian experience: the police

Figure 2.8 Švejk in trouble with superior officers again. 'His eyes asked: "Have I done something wrong, please?" His eyes spoke: "Don't you see that I'm as innocent as a lamb?"' The drawings of Švejk by Josef Lada are now permanently linked with the character, even though only one of what turned out to be over 500 was completed and approved by Hašek before his death in 1923. Lada perfectly captures the image portrayed in the novel of Švejk's innocence, shrewdness or perhaps even dumb insolence. Cartoon: Josef Lada

cell containing six men, five of whom are there for political comment on the war and one who 'did not want to have anything to do with them, in case any suspicion should fall on him. He was only detained here for attempted robbery with murder' (Hašek, 2000, p. 16).

Švejk is the only celebrated literary figure to have been resurrected as a Second World War character, although Bertolt Brecht's *Schweyk im Zweiten Weltkrieg* (*Švejk in the Second World War*) is not regarded as one of his finest plays. Perhaps the biggest problem with the play is the way the central character has been uprooted from the Austro-Hungarian empire and its war effort, and replanted into Nazi-occupied Prague and, subsequently, the Eastern Front a few kilometres from Stalingrad. The old empire was, and continues to be, perceived as ramshackle and inefficient; the Nazi regime is generally regarded as brutal and effective (even if recent historical research has pointed to massive inefficiency and a hierarchy divided by petty hostility and rivalries). Brecht's aim is to puncture the pretensions of the powerful and to show how the little man can be a survivor, even without being a hero of the Resistance. One of the key songs in the play concludes:

Am Grunde der Moldau wandern die Steine.	At the bottom of the [River] Moldau the stones are shifting.
Es liegen drei Kaiser begraben in Prag.	Three emperors lay buried in Prague.
Das Grosse bleibt gross nicht, und klein nicht das Kleine.	The powerful won't stay powerful, and the small not small.
Die Nacht hat zwölf Stunden, dann kommt schon den Tag.	Night has twelve hours, and then comes day.

Arguably one of the problems here is that Brecht is letting his romantic view of 'the people' – derived from his Marxism – cloud any critical assessment of the peoples of Nazi Germany and Nazi-occupied Europe. Just how many opportunistic 'little men' like Brecht's Schweyk were there? And is it realistic to believe that their ability to survive, largely by going along with brutal and oppressive systems, ultimately brings such systems down? The play may be extremely funny but it remains literature with a message; moreover it is a message that we can see through, and which we probably have difficulty in accepting. This brings me to a more general issue about the 'messages' of war literature. How important is what we bring to our reading and understanding? And what might this do for our acceptance of and empathy with an author? Brecht's message is Marxist, and some would dismiss him simply because of that. Jünger's message, however it is interpreted, is uncomfortable. But how should we handle it? It is very different from that of Brecht and not the usual anti-war message, but we cannot simply dismiss it as misleading, proto-fascist and therefore 'bad'. Did people simply not wish to see through the messages of Lersch, Owen, Remarque, Sassoon, Stramm and Zweig? Or was it rather that those messages struck a chord in the popular memory of the conflict, helped the healing process following the war, and have, perhaps as a consequence, come to dominate (as Fussell argues) the subsequent view of war?

EXERCISE

Švejk's transportation from Austro-Hungary to Nazi Prague brings us to a necessary consideration of the remembrance of the 1939–45 war.

1   Is the Second World War remembered in a similar way to its predecessor?

2   What is the abiding image of the Second World War?

3   Where does that memory come from?

DISCUSSION

I don't know what you may have come up with in response to these questions. The answers are not, I think, quite as clear-cut as they are with reference to the First World War. I would suggest that the two wars are not remembered in quite the same way. It could be argued, for example, that the way people have subsequently interpreted the reasons for fighting makes the First World War appear all the more futile. In 1914 men went to war 'For King and Country', '*Pour la Patrie*', '*Für Gott und Vaterland*'. For many in the aftermath it became the Great War and the 'war to end wars'; notions of fighting for the kinds of idea trumpeted in 1914 seemed hollow, while the slaughter as men were pitted against barbed wire, machine-guns and artillery emphasized futility. Europeans entered the Second World War with a much greater awareness of what industrialized warfare actually meant, due at least in some measure to the artistic productions of the interwar years. After 1945 many found themselves able to look back on the second war as a just conflict in a rather different way from that in which people had looked back on the first war. The 1939–45 conflict was regarded as a struggle with an evil system that had harnessed modern bureaucracy and modern industry in the service of genocide. In the Federal Republic of Germany some historians felt the need to stress the heroism of German soldiers fighting in the east against the Soviet armies, the vanguard of another oppressive and repressive regime. The enormous scale of rape and plunder inflicted by those armies as they fought their way into Germany in 1944–5 gave strength to their case; so too did the use of the concept of totalitarianism to embrace both Nazi and Stalinist regimes. Individual German soldiers on the Eastern Front were thus regarded as defenders of women, of property, even of basic freedoms.

As for the abiding images of the Second World War, quite probably you mentioned the extermination camps such as Auschwitz and crimes against humanity; you might have mentioned the Blitz, strategic bombing (another 'crime'?) and the fact that this was a war of movement, of *Blitzkrieg* (lightning war), as opposed to the deadlock of the Western Front. Equally important, the memory of the Second World War is not so rooted in one battlefront; there is a much greater recognition of the different theatres of the conflict – war in Italy, in the deserts of North Africa, in the Far East; war on the home fronts, the clandestine war of resisters and secret agents; and that titanic struggle between Nazi Germany and the Soviet Union. Without the single, searing image of the Western Front, memories, and the cultural constructions of the Second World War, are rather more disparate. Nevertheless, it is probably the case that most impressions of the war derived from reading come not from historians but from novels, and most other impressions come from representations in feature films, television series and documentaries.

The culture of memorial

Even before the armistice of 1918 a determination was apparent at government level and among the wider population to commemorate and remember those who had died during the First World War. The French law of 29 December 1915 was the first to mandate a perpetual resting place for each of the war dead; other nations quickly followed suit. And continuing with French examples, in Lyon on All Souls' Day 1916 a popular service of remembrance was organized in the cemetery of the *quartier* of La Guillotière by men wounded in the war or invalided out of the service. Such determination led to the building of war memorials in cities, towns and villages across Europe, to the consecration of cemeteries on the battlefields, and to elaborate public ceremonies of remembrance. War memorials were not a new phenomenon to emerge from the Great War, but the scale on which they now appeared and the mixture of state and private participation in their construction and in their use as sites of public mourning were new. Remembrance of the war became a European phenomenon, but it developed differently in different national contexts. Arguably, it also developed differently according to individual experiences and identities.

'Armistice Day', according to Adrian Gregory, 'was part of a sustained and creative effort to give meaning and purpose to the terrifying and unexpected experience of mass death' (Gregory, 1994, p. 19). Early on in his book Gregory quotes the following two newspaper leaders referring to the first Armistice Day remembrance services in Britain in 1919.

> In quiet graves beyond the seas sleep a million British men who paid the price of victory ... It is our duty to see that they did not die in vain, and for the accomplishment of that duty all classes must combine as they did to win the war, unselfishly and harmoniously. There must be a truce in domestic quarrels, an end to industrial strife. We must all pull together lest the rewards of victory be thrown away.
>
> (*Daily Express*, 11 November 1919; quoted in Gregory, 1994, p. 11)

> You are asked to be silent for two minutes to-day, to be silent and pause in your labours, to remember this day and this hour last year ...
>
> What will you remember and what will you forget? You will remember, mothers, the gay sons you have lost; wives, you will think of the husbands who went out into the mist of the winter morning – the mist that sent cold chills round the heart – never to come back. And brothers will think of brothers and friends of friends, all lying dead today under an alien soil.
>
> But what will you forget? The crime that called these men to battle ... The war that was to end war and in reality did not? ...
>
> Make the most of this day of official remembrance. By the sacred memory of those lost to you, swear to yourself this day at 11 o'clock, that never again, God helping you, shall the peace and happiness of the world fall into the hands of a few cynical old men.
>
> (*Daily Herald*, 11 November 1919; quoted in Gregory, 1994, p. 12)

EXERCISE

What similarities and what different emphases do these two extracts present?

DISCUSSION

Both editorials make a plea for an act of genuine remembrance and a commitment to ensure that the dead servicemen did not die in vain. But there is a different understanding of what the latter means. The

Daily Express urges an end to any internal strife within the country, and it singles out industrial conflict as an example of such strife. The *Daily Herald*, however, stresses the need to ensure that an event such as the Great War cannot happen again through the actions of poor leaders. It is interesting too how the two pieces stress different things regarding the act of remembrance itself: on the one hand the social unity of the war years, and on the other the personal remembrance of family and friends.

Divisions of this sort can be seen elsewhere across Europe. In Britain in the immediate aftermath of war there was conflict over who best spoke for the veterans: the British Legion, a non-political body headed by the last commander of the British armies in France, Earl Haig; or the politically radical National Union of Ex-Servicemen (NUX). Membership of the former never reached 20 per cent of the eligible ex-servicemen, and was commonly less than 10 per cent. The latter, with around 100,000 members at the end of 1919 and double that a year later (ten times the number in the British Legion in its first year), rapidly settled for reorganizing into a loose federation of local branches, many of which were absorbed by the Labour party or the Independent Labour party. In France during the interwar years socialists were known to organize counter-demonstrations to remembrance parades on Armistice Day, singing the *Internationale* and chanting *À bas la guerre* (down with war); while socialist mayors were known to seek to prohibit the carrying of flags and 'militarist emblems' on such occasions. Some groups shared (and still share) an assumption that the remembrance of war was, in itself, militarist. This was reflected in the 'anti-capitalism' demonstration held in London on 1 May 2000 when, among other targets, the Cenotaph in Whitehall was daubed with graffiti. Yet Gregory argues that in interwar Britain, while the official ceremonies of remembrance can be seen to reflect traditional values such as order, fairness, social harmony, they also put stress on the sacrifice of family, and especially women. They were also, he contends, rooted in the Christian concept of redemption and renewal through blood sacrifice. Antoine Prost, in a three-volume study of the war veterans' associations in interwar France, rejects the notion that either the associations or their ceremonies were in any way militaristic. Rather the *mouvement combattant*, which mobilized almost three and a half million French people, was both patriotic and pacifist. It was rooted in the civic and egalitarian education of the French Third Republic; it stood for renewal but it also built upon a traditional view of French rural life. There were pilgrimages, most notably to Verdun (the site of a crucial, prolonged and bloody battle in 1916); but there were also local dinners and fêtes, collections and distributions on behalf of the needy (Prost, 1977).

In Germany the remembrance of the First World War was painful in similar but also in rather different ways – for Germany, after all, this was a war lost, with some land gained (from Russia), but other territory lost. Britain and France buried their unknown warriors in 1920; the monument in *Die Neue Wache* was not established for another eleven years. But as in Britain and France the authorities in Weimar Germany intended remembrance to be dignified and solemn. For example, Tannenberg was the scene of a decisive German victory over the Russians in the early months of the war; yet its memorial, completed in 1927, was not triumphal but focused rather on a tomb containing twenty unknown soldiers. As mentioned above, the memorial in *Die Neue Wache* was designed by Käthe Kollwitz, whose son Peter was killed in Belgium in October 1914. Before the war she was an internationalist, hostile to the militarism that she saw in imperial Germany, yet at the same time she believed that the fatherland underpinned the life of an individual. Inspired by patriotic ideals, Peter had volunteered for the army at the age of 18. Two years after his death she confided to her diary, 'Is it a break of faith with you, Peter, if I can now see only madness in the war?' (quoted in Winter, 1995, p. 110). She completed a memorial to her son early in 1931; it was exhibited in Berlin later that year and finally moved to the German cemetery at Vladslo, Belgium, where it remains close to the entrance and close to her son's grave. The memorial, *Die Eltern* (the parents) (Plate 5), shows Kollwitz and her husband on their knees. Simple and timeless, it also draws on Christian images of prayer and lamentation; perhaps too it is a female, and above all a mother's, comment. The German cemetery at Langemarck (Plate 6), a few kilometres south of Vladso, has rather different Christian imagery. Scattered throughout, and between the black slabs with the names of the dead, are black stone crosses; they resemble the German medal the Iron Cross, but, clustered as they are in threes, they also look like so many Calvarys.

Crucifixion was a recurrent image in art and literature, used to represent what had happened to individual soldiers – and in some instances to hapless civilians as well. It was also a theme played upon by the German right wing in the aftermath of the war. British and French war veterans' associations had been resolutely non-political – with the brief exception of the NUX. In Germany, and to some extent in Italy too, the opposite was more commonly the case. This has led the historian George Mosse to see the memory of the First World War in Germany as constructed for the celebration of nationalist impulses that led to the Second World War and the monstrosity of the Holocaust (Mosse, 1990). From the end of the

Photographs of First World War memorials and cemeteries form a key component of the colour plates section of this book.

1920s onwards nationalist students and right-wing political organizations held an annual celebration in November – the link and challenge to Armistice Day was deliberate – to mark Langemarck Day. The battle of Langemarck had been an unsuccessful assault on British positions near Ieper (Ypres) in November 1914, but a legend grew up of the German soldiers, many fresh from university, heroically linking arms and advancing on the British positions singing patriotic songs. The young men of the legend were held up as models of patriotic heroism for the youth of Weimar. All of this was a far cry from Kollwitz's *Die Eltern*.

Christian imagery was significant in many memorials irrespective of the nation involved, at least in the west and in central Europe. British war cemeteries, for example, all have a 'cross of sacrifice' – a stone cross with a bronze sword affixed to it (see Plate 7). Classical images were also incorporated. Laurel wreaths abound on the monuments. Sir Edwin Lutyens's Cenotaph in Whitehall took its inspiration from Greek commemorative architecture. The Trench of Bayonets at Verdun has elements of a Roman memorial, while the French unknown warrior and eternal flame were placed under the Arc de Triomphe, a Napoleonic monument which is itself based on classical models. But the France of the Third Republic was officially a secular state and overtly religious images are consequently far less common than in, for example, the staunchly Catholic and francophone Belgian province of Wallonia. And there were also significant national elements to many of the memorials. The British cemetery at Tyne Cot near Ieper (Ypres) has an entrance resembling that of an English country churchyard; some French monuments are surmounted by Gallic cocks, or by a mourning woman who could be a soldier's mother or wife, or Marianne, the female spirit of France. The national element is also implicit in terms such as 'Our Glorious Dead', or 'We [the people of the nation who survived, or who came after] will remember them'. But local monuments were also built emphasizing the immediate identity of those killed, and those who remembered them. The principal term of dedication on the monuments in Wallonia is *enfants* as, for example, in 'La commune de ... à ses enfants morts pour la Patrie' (Tixhon and Van Yersele, 2000, p. 99). Moreover, national and local experience also influenced the monuments. Most of Belgium was occupied during the First World War, and consequently, alongside the soldiers who died in the fighting, its monuments also remember people deported and those 'martyred' in German atrocities, particularly during the summer of 1914. (See *Furore teutonico*, Figures 1.2 and 1.3, p. 25.)

Towns and villages built their own memorials in the aftermath of the Great War; in France they were part-funded by the state, in Britain they were generally built by public subscription. All carried the names of local men who were killed and became the focus for local Armistice Day ceremonies during the interwar years. Indeed it might be argued that the relationship emerging here between memorialization and national identity was a developing form of civic religion, drawing on both Christian and classical traditions in the search for legitimacy in an increasingly secular age.

After 1945 new names were added to the monuments and new war cemeteries were built. However, public remembrance after 1945 was different. Gregory suggests that the Armistice Day emphasis on family and sacrifice and the use of high-flown rhetoric were already being viewed with scepticism by many people towards the end of the 1930s; this became more pronounced after 1945 (Gregory, 1994, Chapter 7). In both France and West Germany there was some collective amnesia about national remembrance with reference to the Second World War, which it turn contributed to a certain scepticism among some of the younger generation. In France a comparison has been drawn between the enormous effort at central government level in the aftermath of the First World War to prepare accurate lists of the dead for local mayors to inscribe on their memorials and the inferior effort after the Second World War. Deportees and resistance fighters commonly appeared on the memorials only when the mayor acted on local information, while Jews were generally ignored, as were Gypsies. Indeed the head of the historical branch of the Department of War Veterans and War Victims could write, 'Ces monuments aux morts de 1939–1945 ne sont pas justes, alors que ceux de 1914–1918 sont globalement justes' (These monuments to the dead of 1939–1945 are incomplete [though note that the original French word 'justes' carries additional overtones] compared with those to the dead of 1914–1918) (Barcellini, 1991, p. 71). Alf Lüdtke, a sceptic from the generation that grew up after the war, commented critically on the annual *Volkstrauerntag* (national mourning day) in Göttingen, where he worked. A monument erected to 'fallen comrades' by the survivors of an infantry regiment based in the town was the focus for the ceremony. The mayor, local political leaders and representatives of the German army were present to lay wreaths.

> The line has not changed over the years: the poor fellows who had nonvoluntarily fulfilled their duties in the army had paid 'their price.' Weren't they similarly true victims of 'the brown terror regime'? For the past three years, some dozen people have tried to disrupt each gathering, but of course, police pushed them aside. Some of the critics are now demanding a memorial to the deserters.
>
> (Lüdtke, 1993, p. 560)

Lüdtke's concerns were similar to those voiced by critics of *Die Neue Wache*, but there is also no doubt that right-wing, often neo-Nazi, groups have sought to appropriate part of these ceremonies and/or to remember publicly, and with sympathy, individuals responsible for war crimes. In the early summer of 2000, for example, a group of concerned Italians urged the German government to remove the remains of three SS officers from a military cemetery on the slopes of Monte Baldo close to the shore of Lake Garda because the spot was becoming a shrine for German visitors of the extreme right.

The discussion so far has focused on the remembrance of the First World War and the continuation of remembrance in the aftermath of the second war, but primarily in Britain, France and Germany. These countries may have had different experiences of war (victory, defeat, occupation or not), but their broad perceptions of war (of a lost generation expiring in the mud and blood of trench warfare during the first war; more complex and often more difficult memories of the second) and their patterns and symbols of remembrance (ceremonies for 'the fallen', Christian and classical as well as national and local memorials) were largely similar. Above all there was public, national mourning for dead servicemen in all of these countries. However, moving the focus to the extreme east of Europe presents a very different picture.

The Russian empire entered the First World War at the very beginning, but withdrew following the 1917 revolution and was wracked by a civil war that lasted into the early 1920s. The series of conflicts helped bring about famine, and between them war, famine, the excesses of the regime and the purges of the 1930s left millions dead. The triumphant Bolshevik regime, governing not the Russian empire but the Union of Soviet Socialist Republics (USSR), had no interest in remembering the hundreds of thousands who had been killed fighting for the capitalist regime of the tsar. According to the *Great Soviet Encyclopaedia*, 'Only the capitalists gained any advantages from the war'. However, on the positive side in the Soviet view, the war aggravated

> the class struggle and accelerated the ripening of the objective prerequisites for the Great October Socialist Revolution, which opened a new epoch in world history – the epoch of the transition from capitalism to socialism.
>
> (*Great Soviet Encyclopaedia*, 1974, p. 737)

There were no Soviet monuments to the dead of the 1914–18 war and no public ceremonies of remembrance. But there were Soviet demonstrations. The annual parade to celebrate the October Revolution of 1917 closely coincided with the public mourning of Armistice Day elsewhere in Europe, though it manifestly celebrated

Soviet might and promise for the future rather than remembering the 'sacrifice' of servicemen. There were public ceremonies to honour heroes of the revolution, but there were occasionally difficulties in designing rites appropriate to an avowedly atheist regime. Initially the organizers of Lenin's funeral in 1924 contemplated requiem masses by Mozart and Verdi, but these were rejected on the grounds of their Christian connotations; Wagner was rejected for aesthetic reasons, and the decision was eventually made to opt for a mix of Beethoven and Chopin with regular bursts of the *Internationale*. The ordinary people of the USSR had no opportunity to mourn their dead as elsewhere, while their traditional religious burial practices came under ferocious assault along with the rest of Orthodox Christian ritual.

It should be stressed that it was not only the Soviet authorities that agonized over music for ceremonies of remembrance. In 1927 the BBC consciously decided against including any music by a German composer in its Armistice Day concert (Gregory, 1994, p. 138).

Although avowedly internationalist, during the Second World War the Soviet authorities had to resort to nationalist rallying calls for the defence of Mother Russia and the conflict became known as 'the Great Patriotic War'. In its aftermath the regime built a cluster of massive war memorials. Just outside Kiev was erected an enormous aluminium statue of a woman brandishing a sword and shield. In Berlin a monument to the Soviet soldiers killed in the assault on the city was fashioned out of stone from the ruined *Reichstag*; tanks and field guns were positioned on either side, and a towering figure of a Soviet soldier was placed on top (see also Plate 11). But how far were these two memorials in particular primarily for remembrance of the dead? Kiev is now the capital of Ukraine, and throughout the time that it was part of first the Russian empire and then the USSR there were Ukrainians who resented Russian encroachments on their identity. Indeed in 1941 many Ukrainians welcomed the Nazis in preference to the Soviets. Thousands of Soviet soldiers were killed in the assault on Berlin in 1945, but situating a memorial in the Tiergarten in the centre of the city close to both the Brandenberg Gate and the remains of the *Reichstag* appears to have been designed to give other messages. Moreover, the memorial fell in what had been the British sector of the city and on occasions, while the city was divided, the Soviet honour guard, which was changed daily, had to be put under the protection of British soldiers.

Unlike the countries of western Europe the Soviet Union had never held Armistice Day remembrance ceremonies following the First World War. But widespread public commemoration was introduced for the Great Patriotic War; it was held in May on the anniversary of the end of the Second World War. Catherine Merridale has argued that Soviet commemoration was 'oppressively masculine', with its demonstrations of modern weaponry, its young soldiers on parade and its medalled male veterans in the stands. The majority of those who mourned, however, were women; there were 20 million more women than men in the USSR at the end of the war. Possibly also

> commemoration and the re-enactment of national solidarity enabled individuals to transcend earlier griefs which had few other outlets. The woman whose husband had disappeared in 1937 ... could bring her grief, if not her story about it, to the solemn meetings in May every year as easily as her neighbour the war widow.
>
> (Merridale, 1999, pp. 76–7)

With the fall of the Soviet Union the Russians continued to commemorate the defeat of Nazi Germany. It was easier to view the conflict in the simpler terms of the Great Patriotic War now that the Russian people could jettison the political overlay of the international workers' struggle for liberty and the notion of fascism as a particular stage or manifestation of capitalism. But there were also problems in reorganizing the commemorative parades. Dominic Lieven, a historian of modern Russia, watched the fiftieth anniversary parade in 1995 and commented upon it for Canadian television.

> Russia's veterans marched in their old Soviet uniforms, but they did so under the command of serving officers in a new uniform, more tsarist than Soviet and bearing the double-headed eagle of the Romanovs on their caps. By contrast the naval units which participated in the ceremony looked more Soviet than tsarist, but marched under the flag of Saint Andrew, the standard of the pre-Revolutionary fleet. Given Russia's immense sacrifices during the Second World War, the parade was a highly emotional event. On such occasions, music best captures, symbolises and heightens the feelings of participants and observers alike. At the parade's climax it would have been most appropriate to play the Soviet anthem but in the political circumstances ... this was impossible. To play the current national anthem would have been meaningless, since few could even recognise it. Instead it was decided to play that great showpiece of Russian patriotism, Chaikovsky's 1812 symphony. In Chaikovsky's original composition, to which after 1917 the rest of the world adhered but the USSR did not, the climax of the symphony is the Russian Imperial hymn, God Save the Tsar. Whether because it was deemed inappropriate or because they simply possessed a Soviet score the massed bands that day followed the Soviet tradition. At the centre of this supremely national day and event there was therefore, very symbolically, a void within a void.
>
> (Lieven, 1998, pp. 268–9)

EXERCISE

1 Do you find Lieven's critical account of the parade satisfactory?

2 How might the participants have responded to such an account?

DISCUSSION

1 This is another question to which any response is bound to be subjective. I find Lieven's account satisfactory on the intellectual level. He clearly indicates the contradictions in the event on its public, ceremonial level.

2 However, I suspect that the individual participants would have rejected Lieven's criticisms. It seems logical that the individual veterans knew what they were marching for (though they may have resented the new uniforms and new flags). Similarly, both the young servicemen in the parade and the Russian spectators were remembering the sacrifice and victory of a previous generation, whatever the contradictions that lay in the trappings of the ceremony.

In the aftermath of the collapse of the Soviet Union perhaps the myth of the Great Patriotic War (and I use the word 'myth' advisedly, since the traditional, and probably the current memory of the war shared the sort of collective amnesia found elsewhere in Europe in this instance with reference to, among other things, the Nazi–Soviet Pact of 1939; the enforcement of loyalty to Stalin and the Communist party by political commissars and NKVD (political police) detachments; Soviet massacres of Poles; the rape of German women) constitutes one of the last elements of the previous regime to remain unproblematic and untarnished. As such, it can continue to be a proud memory and a significant element within contemporary Russian identity.

Some concluding points

There is a series of general issues which, I believe, we have seriously to ponder. In what ways, if at all, can art or literature contribute to our memory of war and to our understanding of the twentieth-century European experience of war? What do we look for in a painting, statue, photograph or film? What do we expect from a poem or piece of prose? Do we empathize primarily with those that reflect sentiments that we already have, or feel we ought to have? Do we, wittingly or unwittingly, discard or marginalize elements in a cultural artefact that do not suit our perspective? If so, how can these cultural artefacts contribute to our knowledge and understanding of the memory of a shared national or of a shared European experience? War may have been a shared experience, but does the national experience of war come through more strongly than any concept of 'front' or war generations? Can we speak of a 'front generation' (or, given the fact that there were two world wars, of 'front generations') in any meaningful way? Did the men who made up these front generations share an identity with their opponents? Did they continue to have such an identity once they returned to civilian or peacetime life? Do combatants have a wartime identity which is rather different from that of peacetime?

Similar questions might be posed with reference to the sites and ceremonies of mourning. Do these essentially remain national sites and ceremonies? And if we agree with this perception, are we implicitly accepting the criticisms levelled at German officialdom (by other Germans) that the attempts to include all victims of war in a specific memorial simply muddies the issue of who holds responsibility? Do these sites and ceremonies contribute above all to a careful collective structuring of the national past, with a collective amnesia about the difficult bits? And if this is the case should there be more open discussion about the subject of remembrance and its attendant ceremonies?

The bulk of this chapter has focused on the two world wars though, through the early comments on the end of the Berlin Wall, there was some reference to the Cold War. The Cold War was a shared European experience; it lasted more than forty years, longer than the two 'hot' world wars, and, given the nuclear capabilities of the two superpowers that faced each other in Europe, it was potentially far more destructive. It was enormously expensive, especially for European states such as Britain and France which insisted on clinging to great power status with their own nuclear weaponry. It gave a forced unity to European states in as much as it compelled virtually everyone to take a side. It fostered a sub-genre of literature and film – the spy thriller – but few other cultural artefacts. It has few sites of remembrance, and these are more commonly tourist attractions and oddities, like the 'Portakabin' in Friedrichstraße that used to be Checkpoint Charlie. Nor is it something that countries – even the supposed 'victors' – have significantly absorbed into their national memories with annual, public ceremonies. The question might be posed: what would the victors be commemorating or remembering? The cost was in money rather than blood. But even though the victors would readily admit to the identity of being liberal capitalist states, they have never considered publicly remembering the liberal expenditure of their financial capital in international conflict.

References

Barcellini, Serge (1991) 'Il n'y a pas des lenteurs propres à la Seconde Guerre mondiale', in Georges Kantin and Gilles Manceron (eds), *Les Échos de la mémoire: tabous et enseignement de la seconde guerre mondiale*, Paris, Le Monde Editions.

Bridgewater, Patrick (1985) *The German Poets of the First World War*, London, Croom Helm.

Ferguson, Niall (1998) *The Pity of War*, London, Allen Lane.

Fussell, Paul (1975) *The Great War and Modern Memory*, Oxford, Oxford University Press.

The Great Soviet Encyclopaedia (1974), 3rd edn., New York/London, Macmillan/Collier Macmillan.

Gregory, Adrian (1994) *The Silence of Memory: Armistice Day 1919–1946*, Oxford/Providence, RI, Berg.

Hašek, Jaroslav (2000) *The Good Soldier Švejk*, transl. Cecil Parrott, Harmondsworth, Penguin.

Jünger, Ernst [1929] (1975) *The Storm of Steel: from the Diary of a German Storm-Troop Officer on the Western Front*, transl. Basil Creighton, New York, Howard Fertig.

Lieven, Dominic (1998) 'Russian, imperial and Soviet identities', *Transactions of the Royal Historical Society*, 6th series, VIII, pp. 253–69.

Lüdtke, Alf (1993) ' "Coming to terms with the past": illusions of remembering, ways of forgetting Nazism in West Germany', *Journal of Modern History*, 65, pp. 542–72.

Merridale, Catherine (1999) 'War, death, and remembrance in Soviet Russia', in Jay Winter and Emmanuel Sivan (eds), *War and Remembrance in the Twentieth Century*, Cambridge, Cambridge University Press.

Mosse, George L. (1990) *Fallen Soldiers: Reshaping the Memory of the World Wars*, Oxford, Oxford University Press.

O'Brien, Catherine (1996) 'Beyond the can[n]on: French women's responses to the First World War', *French Cultural Studies*, 7, pp. 201–13.

Pick, Daniel (1995) 'A bitter truth: avant garde art and the Great War', *History Workshop Journal*, 39, pp. 196–200.

Prost, Antoine (1977) *Les Anciens combattants et la société française 1914–1939*, 3 volumes, Paris, Presses de la Fondation Nationale des Sciences Politiques (abbreviated English-language version, *In the Wake of War: 'Les Anciens Combattants' and French Society*, Oxford/Providence, RI, Berg, 1992).

Prost, Antoine (1997) 'Les monuments aux morts. Culte républicaine? Culte civique? Culte patriotique?', in vol. I of Pierre Nora (ed.), *Les Lieux de mémoire: la république, la nation, les France*, 3 volumes, Paris, Quarto Gallimard.

Remarque, Erich Maria [1929] (1963) *All Quiet on the Western Front*, transl. A. H. Wheen, London, Mayflower.

Robert, Jean-Louis (1997) 'The image of the profiteer', in Jay Winter and Jean-Louis Robert (eds), *Capital Cities at War: Paris, London, Berlin 1914–1919*, Cambridge, Cambridge University Press.

Steiner, George (1970) 'Introduction', to Ernst Jünger, *On the Marble Cliffs*, Harmondsworth, Penguin.

Tixhon, Axel and van Yersele, Laurence (2000) 'Du sang et des pierres: les monuments de la guerre 1914–1918 en Wallonie', *Cahiers d'Histoire du Temps Present*, 7, pp. 83–126.

Weisbrod, Bernd (2000) 'Military violence and male fundamentalism: Ernst Jünger's contribution to the conservative revolution', *History Workshop Journal*, 49, pp. 69–94.

Winter, J. M. (1995) *Sites of Memory, Sites of Mourning: the Great War in European Cultural History*, Cambridge, Cambridge University Press.

Zweig, Arnold [1928] (2000) *The Case of Sergeant Grischa*, London, Prion.

3

Literature, memory and nation

DENNIS WALDER

Introduction

When I began writing this chapter I came across an intriguing item in the news, about a man who had lost his memory two years before as a result of being mugged in a Toronto street. Without a wallet or other form of identification, wearing clothes from widely available brands, speaking English 'with a public school accent', the man was young, and white, and claimed to have no memory of events prior to waking up in hospital. He had been unable to open a bank account, or receive state benefits, and the Canadian authorities had offered him temporary citizenship only, while a lawyer had appealed worldwide for someone to say who he was (Borger, 2001). So while his gender, race, language and class were known, he lacked an identity.

As philosophers since at least the eighteenth century have pointed out, without our individual memories we do not know who we are, nor can we say to what larger community we belong – family, clan or nation. And without some kind of formal record of these memories, the state refuses to recognize us. One of the things that may destroy memory, in an individual as well as on a collective basis, is trauma: physical, emotional and/or psychological – such as the assault which, apparently, turned the Toronto man into a baffling amnesiac. It is a commonplace that people forget what has happened to them during an accident; equally familiar is the idea that, nonetheless, the details of the event may sometimes be retrieved, for example through therapy. At the same time there is no guarantee that what is 'remembered', through therapy or other means, actually happened. Or what is 'remembered' may be just a version of what happened. This is at the heart of the debate about what has been called 'false memory syndrome'.

Similarly, events are remembered by groups or communities in quite different ways, especially where much is invested in the difference. The most notable example of large-scale trauma, remembering and forgetfulness in late twentieth-century Europe is the matter of the Holocaust (a word of Latin origin meaning human sacrifice, bringing purification through fire). This has become more of an issue than the memory of the Second World War itself. Although the peoples of Europe continue to memorialize the conflict in various ways, it is striking how interest in remembering the Holocaust – or guarding against forgetting it – has grown: the first marking of Holocaust Remembrance Day in the United Kingdom took place on 27 January 2001, and immediately generated argument about its continuing relevance (see Holocaust Memorial Day website). Michael Burleigh, whose history of *The Third Reich* (first published 2000) won the Samuel Johnson prize, the leading UK prize for non-fiction, in 2001, worried publicly that schoolchildren know too much about the Holocaust and not enough about other aspects of modern history; while in the USA Peter Novick caused a storm of controversy in 1999 by arguing, in *The Holocaust and Collective Memory* (UK edition 2000), that the remarkable rise of postwar Jewish and American Holocaust consciousness devalues, or even trivializes, memory of the event.

If there is bound to be an argument about whether or not, and how far, the Holocaust should be part of the collective memory of the former Allies, presumably there is no argument about its central importance in the lives of its victim-survivors, and of its perpetrators too? We might add (since our main focus here is on European identities) that there is no argument about its central importance for Germany, and the Germans, either. As Mary Fulbrook has suggested, the idea of German national identity 'in the shadow of the Holocaust' has been 'uniquely problematic, uniquely tortured' (Fulbrook, 1999, p. 19). In this chapter I want to suggest some ways of reflecting on the complexities and ambiguities of memory, identity and nation as these issues are foregrounded in a recent German literary text. Since the Second World War there has been a considerable amount of writing that attempts to deal with Germany's past, and its relation to the present. I can do no more than touch on that here. Instead I shall take as my main example a single literary text, Bernhard Schlink's recent novel *The Reader* – or, to give its original title, *Der Vorleser* (the German title implies a reader who reads aloud, *to* someone), first published in 1995 (an English translation first appeared in the UK in 1997). I shall also refer to other literary texts, but very selectively, and by way of contextualizing discussion of *The Reader*.

Why read *The Reader*?

My reasons for selecting *The Reader* are as follows.

1   It is one of the few literary works from Germany in several decades to find very large numbers of readers not only in that country but around the world – by January 2002 sales in Germany had surpassed the half-million mark, while 100,000 had been sold

Figure 3.1   Street scene near the Marienkirche, Danzig, 1937. This is from the front cover of *Frauen: German Women Recall the Third Reich*, by Alison Owings (2001), which contains a remarkable series of interviews with 'ordinary' German women, including Resistance workers, Nazi party members, a survivor of the death camps and a former concentration camp guard. It reflects the memories of a whole generation of women whose voices have barely been heard up to now. How would you describe the class and background of the women in the foreground? Does Schlink's novel also offer a voice for German women, on some level? Photo: Hans Hubman/BPK/Berlin

in France, 200,000 in the UK and 750,000 in the USA; it is a set text on school and university syllabuses internationally, and it has been translated into twenty-five languages.

2   It is an accessible, compellingly written, well-translated and relatively short book.

3   It is controversial.

4   It prompts us to examine how a literary text may engage with the problems faced by a European people still questioning their national identity as a result of a traumatic past.

5   In particular, it suggests how 'the second generation' in Germany is still struggling in the post-reunification era to come to terms with their past – that is, the generation of those now in middle age whose parents were adults during the Nazi era.

The 'first generation' of postwar Germans included writers such as the Nobel prize-winner Günter Grass (born 1927), author of *Die Blechtrommel* (*The Tin Drum*), which since its publication in 1959 has sold over a million copies worldwide and has been turned into a play and a film. This generation of writers have asked questions of themselves and of the German people as a whole in the light of the Second World War, eventually (in Grass's case) going so far as to question the right of the German nation-state to continue in existence at all. This was on the occasion of the reunification of Germany in 1990 – an event that was otherwise almost universally welcomed. Writers in both East and West Germany have long felt an obligation to bring questions of responsibility for the Nazi past into public view. For many, it has seemed as if such issues were not being addressed by politicians or the media, much less by the public at large. But Schlink's novel represents something new in this national self-questioning, and he seems to have taken the public and the media along with him. The novel has been credited with providing a richer, more nuanced account than before of the perpetrators and bystanders of this past, going beyond the usual outright condemnation (for example, by the students of 1968) of the older generation.

To begin with, it is important to point out that there has been a lengthy debate about whether or not literature is an appropriate discourse for recalling the Holocaust at all.

The first reading comes from the eminent social philosopher and returned German-Jewish exile, Theodor Adorno (1903–60). It is an extract from a work first published in Germany in 1965.

I have no wish to soften the saying that to write lyric poetry after Auschwitz is barbaric; it expresses in negative form the impulse which inspires committed literature. The question asked by a character in Sartre's play *Mort Sans Sépulture* [*Men without Shadows*, 1946], 'Is there any meaning in life when men exist who beat people until the bones break in their bodies?', is also the question whether any art now has a right to exist; whether intellectual regression is not inherent in the concept of committed literature because of the regression of society ... Yet ... suffering ... also demands the continued existence of art while it prohibits it; it is now virtually in art alone that suffering can still find its own voice, consolation, without immediately being betrayed by it. The most important artists of the age have realized this ... [But] the so-called artistic representation of the sheer physical pain of people beaten to the ground by rifle-butts contains, however remotely, the power to elicit enjoyment out of it. The moral of this art, not to forget for a single instant, slithers into the abyss of its opposite.

(Adorno [1965] (1977), pp. 188–9)

EXERCISE _____

1   What do you think about Adorno's remarks? Do you share his views?

2   What is the case against depicting extreme suffering, and what is the argument (if there is one) to justify literary representations of it?

DISCUSSION _____

1   Adorno's views are complex, and appear both to condemn and to justify representations of the Holocaust – or at least one manifestation of it, the experience of Auschwitz.

2   The unique barbarity of Auschwitz is such, the suffering of the victims so extreme, that any art at all now seems pointless. Yet, paradoxically, art can provide a unique voice for the suffering, as '[t]he most important artists of the age have realized'. However, even if we allow such 'committed literature' a place, it brings with it the potential for enjoying the suffering of the victims.

Adorno's conclusion here is that the moral justification for representations of the Holocaust may slither into its opposite: not forgetting becomes a wrong kind of remembering. His position was shared by many, yet the phrase (which he first used in 1949) that lyric poetry after Auschwitz was barbaric, he later withdrew, possibly because of the extraordinary lyric poetry of Paul Celan (1920–70), whose writings drew on his experiences of the war years and the loss of his parents in the death camps. Yet even if poetry is more than merely the expression of pleasure or beauty – as the English war poetry of Wilfred Owen or Keith Douglas (1920–44) long ago demonstrated – it would indeed seem as if the terrible, industrialized form of mass killing that was central to the Holocaust goes beyond what may be legitimately captured in verse.

There is a further argument, most powerfully advanced by the cultural critic George Steiner, that the German language itself was contaminated by the horrors of Nazism, infected by the grammar of lies, the rhetoric of extermination, and so it would be better for German writers to remain silent. Steiner made these remarks in an essay, 'The hollow miracle', first published in 1959 but reprinted many times since (despite, and while acknowledging, the furore it aroused in Germany and beyond). For Steiner, 'Nazism found in the language precisely what it needed to give voice to its savagery ... the latent hysteria, the confusion, the quality of hypnotic trance ... [Hitler] sensed in German another music than that of Goethe, Heine and Mann', injecting it with falsehood to such an extent that even after his death the 'post-war history of the German language has been one of dissimulation and deliberate forgetting' (Steiner [1959] 1969, pp. 140, 151).

I should like you now to turn to the second reading on pages 76–7. This poem, 'Todesfuge', written by Celan in 1948, is perhaps the most famous that has been written on the subject of the death camps. It has been widely anthologized and numerous composers have set it to music, while the artist Anselm Kiefer has inscribed phrases from it into some of his unsettling paintings. Read it now and then complete the exercise below.

EXERCISE

How far does your experience of the poem support Adorno's and Steiner's arguments? Does it minimize the horrors of the camps with its lilting, sing-song rhythms and stark transitions – juxtaposing the golden-haired, stereotypically Aryan Margarete with the ashen-haired, stereotypically Jewish Shulamith? Do you think Celan was right to ask editors to exclude it from anthologies, after it had become a standard text in German schools?

DISCUSSION

I do not think my questions are easy to answer. But I would say the following at least. First, my own response was one of shock at the strange, almost surreal directness of the imagery of life and death in the camps, which reminded me of the horrors I have read about in a way that did not seem to me to cheapen or undermine them.

Secondly, I can nevertheless understand the author wanting to exclude this poem after a time, when it became so well known that its effect could have been blunted, its message hollowed, by over-familiarity and its 'classic' status in Germany – if not abroad.

Perhaps the key point concerning Celan's poem is how you respond to the combination of a playful, lilting rhythm and ballad-like refrain, the use of stereotypes (the blue-eyed murderer of Jews), with images of terror – a question which also arises in relation to certain poets writing in English (such as Sylvia Plath), but not for a specifically German-speaking audience. The phrase 'der Tod ist ein Meister aus Deutschland' (death is a master from Germany) became widely known in Germany, where it was used as the title of various books and of a major television documentary, although responses to this were ambivalent. Interestingly, Steiner himself argued in favour of Celan's work, contending that readers should take the risk of allowing this poetry to enter their lives and alter their 'inner existence' (cover blurb, Celan, 1996). Perhaps the German language had not, after all, been irrevocably tainted by Nazism. It all came down to the question of who used a word or a phrase, and how they did so. Adorno might well have rethought his position as a result of reading Celan. Yet Celan was speaking as a victim and an exile, whose parents had died in the camps – not as somebody like Schlink, whose parents might have been classed among the perpetrators of or among those complicit in Nazism. (In fact Schlink's father was a professor of theology who was sacked in 1937 for being a follower of Martin Niemöller, the Protestant clergyman who called for a break from the church in protest at Hitler's policies, but remained a pastor.) As mentioned above, later Celan himself felt his poem should not continue to be read.

Celan's name and personal history reflect a radical uncertainty about his identity as a German-speaker directly affected by the rise of Nazism and the Second World War. Paul Antschel – who changed his name to Ancel and then to Celan (an anagram adopted in 1947, when his first poems appeared in a Romanian periodical) – was born in Czernowitz (now Chernovtsy) in Bukovina (now in Romania) on 23 November 1920. His parents were – like many others in this

Todesfuge

Schwarze Milch der Frühe wir trinken sie abends
wir trinken sie mittags und morgens wir trinken sie nachts
wir trinken und trinken
wir schaufeln ein Grab in den Lüften da liegt man nicht eng
Ein Mann wohnt im Haus der spielt mit den Schlangen der schreibt
der schreibt wenn es dunkelt nach Deutschland dein goldenes Haar
Margarete
er schreibt es und tritt vor das Haus und es blitzen die Sterne er
pfeift seine Rüden herbei
er pfeift seine Juden hervor läßt schaufeln ein Grab in der Erde
er befiehlt uns spielt auf nun zum Tanz

Schwarze Milch der Frühe wir trinken dich nachts
wir trinken dich morgens und mittags wir trinken dich abends
wir trinken und trinken
Ein Mann wohnt im Haus der spielt mit den Schlangen der schreibt
der schreibt wenn es dunkelt nach Deutschland dein goldenes Haar
Margarete
Dein aschenes Haar Sulamith wir schaufeln ein Grab in den Lüften da
liegt man nicht eng

Er ruft stecht tiefer ins Erdreich ihr einen ihr andern singet und spielt
er greift nach dem Eisen im Gurt er schwingts seine Augen sind blau
stecht tiefer die Spaten ihr einen ihr andern spielt weiter zum Tanz auf
Schwarze Milch der Frühe wir trinken dich nachts
wir trinken dich mittags und morgens wir trinken dich abends
wir trinken und trinken
ein Mann wohnt im Haus dein goldenes Haar Margarete
dein aschenes Haar Sulamith er spielt mit den Schlangen
Er ruft spielt süßer den Tod der Tod ist ein Meister aus Deutschland
er ruft streicht dunkler die Geigen dann steigt ihr als Rauch in die Luft
dann habt ihr ein Grab in den Wolken da liegt man nicht eng

Schwarze Milch der Frühe wir trinken dich nachts
wir trinken dich mittags der Tod ist ein Meister aus Deutschland
wir trinken dich abends und morgens wir trinken und trinken
der Tod ist ein Meister aus Deutschland sein Auge ist blau
er trifft dich mit bleierner Kugel er trifft dich genau
ein Mann wohnt im Haus dein goldenes Haar Margarete
er hetzt seine Rüden auf uns er schenkt uns ein Grab in der Luft
er spielt mit den Schlangen und träumet der Tod ist ein Meister aus
Deutschland

dein goldenes Haar Margarete
dein aschenes Haar Sulamith

Death Fugue

Black milk of daybreak we drink it at sundown
we drink it at noon in the morning we drink it at night
we drink and we drink it
we dig a grave in the breezes there one lies unconfined
A man lives in the house he plays with the serpents he writes
he writes when dusk falls to Germany your golden hair Margarete
he writes it and steps out of doors and the stars are flashing he whistles
his pack out
he whistles his Jews out in earth has them dig for a grave
he commands us strike up for the dance

Black milk of daybreak we drink you at night
we drink in the morning at noon we drink you at sundown
we drink and we drink you
A man lives in the house he plays with the serpents he writes
he writes when dusk falls to Germany your golden hair Margarete
your ashen hair Shulamith we dig a grave in the breezes there one lies
unconfined

He calls out jab deeper into the earth you lot you others sing now and
play
he grabs at the iron in his belt he waves it his eyes are blue
jab deeper you lot with your spades you others play on for the dance
Black milk of daybreak we drink you at night
we drink you at noon in the morning we drink you at sundown
we drink and we drink you
a man lives in the house your golden hair Margarete
your ashen hair Shulamith he plays with the serpents
He calls out more sweetly play death death is a master from Germany
he calls out more darkly now stroke your strings then as smoke you will
rise into air
then a grave you will have in the clouds there one lies unconfined

Black milk of daybreak we drink you at night
we drink you at noon death is a master from Germany
we drink you at sundown and in the morning we drink and we drink you
death is a master from Germany his eyes are blue
he strikes you with leaden bullets his aim is true
a man lives in the house your golden hair Margarete
he sets his pack on to us he grants us a grave in the air
he plays with the serpents and daydreams death is a master from Germany

your golden hair Margarete
your ashen hair Shulamith

(Celan, 1996, pp. 62–5)

eastern region of the former Austrian empire – German-speaking Jews, steeped in German popular and classical culture. He was a student when Soviet troops occupied Czernowitz in June 1940. A year later German and Romanian forces occupied the region, forcing the Jews into a ghetto. Two years later Celan's parents were deported to an internment camp, where his father died of typhus and his mother was shot. After working in a Romanian labour camp he returned to Bukovina, which had by then been annexed to Ukraine by the Soviets. In December 1947 he left Romania illegally for Vienna, where he published his first book of poems, *Der Sand aus den Urnen* (*Sand from the Urns*), before settling in Paris, where he married and taught German literature. This remained his home until his suicide by drowning in 1970.

By the time of his death Celan had become an acclaimed poet, receiving many prizes and invitations to read his poetry in West Germany. Personal crises and breakdowns did not interfere with the flow of his creative work – which, however, became increasingly private and inward, unlike the public and political trend of German writing during the 1950s and 1960s.

Most other West German writers, including playwrights and novelists as well as poets, hesitated to try to deal directly with the Holocaust, despite the immediate postwar flood of documentaries, history books, exhibitions and witness accounts – most of which, however, focused upon the labour camps rather than the extermination camps. This may appear to bear out Steiner's claim of 'deliberate forgetting'. While it is a commonplace to refer to West Germany's recovery from the Second World War in terms of the *Wirtschaftswunder* (economic miracle) it experienced, less familiar has been the simultaneous recovery of literary achievement. But what did that recovery involve? The answer to this question helps us to see how extraordinary Celan's poetry is.

In West Germany the term *Stunde Null* (zero hour) was used to designate 1945, suggesting that a totally new beginning was possible in the aftermath of the war, but although the Nuremberg trials were accompanied by a process of denazification this process petered out as a result of the Cold War, and many former Nazis became members of the new civil service. Hence what began as a 'literature of the ruins' (*Trümmerliteratur*), describing the sufferings of the population during and immediately after the war, turned to questions about how and why the Nazis had come to power. Yet details about the roles of German citizens, about the camps and about the millions who had disappeared were notably absent. Exiled German writers such as

Thomas Mann (whose *Doktor Faustus*, published in 1947, mythologized Nazism as a pact with the devil) exhorted Germans to acknowledge their guilt.

But if many (West and East) German writers were prominent in participating in the politics of their respective communities, this was a politics of the present. It was as if the sought-for *Schlußstrich* (concluding line) had succeeded in separating the problematic past from the present. Thus Günter Grass made speeches on behalf of the Social Democrats, while Heinrich Böll (another Nobel laureate) spoke up as president of the PEN club, on behalf of persecuted intellectuals in the Soviet Union, eastern Europe and Latin America. Böll, an ex-*Wehrmacht* soldier, focused in his semi-documentary fiction upon the experiences of 'ordinary' German people (for example in *Der Zug war pünktlich* or *The Train Was on Time*). Grass, who served only briefly in the war before being taken prisoner by the Americans, also used his personal experience to create more complex, semi-allegoric, satirical works. Other members of the postwar writers' group known as *Gruppe 47* (group of 47), such as the playwright Wolfgang Borchert (author of *Draussen vor der Tür*, or *The Man Outside*, 1946), agonized over the powerlessness of language to express the Nazi past. In East Germany, despite the fact that literature was regarded almost exclusively in terms of its social function and that the approved mode was Soviet-inspired, anti-fascist social realism, novelists such as Christa Wolf and Stefan Heym sowed the seeds of a more critical, self-aware spirit during the 1960s. Wolf's *Kindheitsmuster* (*Pattern Childhood*, 1976) confronted the subject of Nazi collaboration; while Heym's speech in 1988 on the fiftieth anniversary of the Kristallnacht pogrom, or 'Schreiben nach Auschwitz' (writing after Auschwitz), challenged the view that the past was over and could be forgotten.

But by then attitudes in the west were changing too. Perceptions were challenged in particular by the American television series *Holocaust*, which was viewed by 20 million people in West Germany early in 1979. The GDR claimed that it did not need to remind its citizens of the past and refused to broadcast the series (although millions there were able to pick up the West German broadcast anyway). For all its Hollywood-style sentimentality, *Holocaust* led to a new generation of Germans knowing about that past, and wanting to recall and discuss it. A few years later the trauma of the war and of the Nazi period gained new prominence – again in West Germany – through the *Historikerstreit* (1986–7), or historians' controversy, as mentioned in Chapter 1: a controversy that had been simmering for some time. The main figures in the debate were Karl Jaspers, who argued (as he had done earlier in *Die Schuldfrage*, or *The Question of Guilt*, 1946) for the liability of all Germans as regards the war, and the importance of remembering what had happened; and Ernst Nolte, who 'contextualized' the Holocaust so as to remove its stigma of unique barbarity from the Germans by referring to other atrocities of the twentieth century, such as Stalin's.

When unification came, both East and West German writers continued to consider the Holocaust a moral touchstone, while finding it difficult to face in their writings. One of the most extreme expressions of the writers' view was given by Grass in a lecture at the University of Frankfurt on 13 February 1990. He concluded that

> [T]he horror summarized in the name 'Auschwitz' has remained inconceivable; precisely because it is not comparable, cannot be historically contextualized, is not open to any confession of guilt, it is not far-fetched to date the history of mankind and our concept of human existence as occurring before and after Auschwitz.
>
> (Quoted in Schlant, 1999, p. 204)

Hence, he argued, unification was not a good idea: the breach between the two Germanys should be kept, as a reminder of this breach in history brought about by the German nation itself. Clearly, changes in the political status of what was identified as Germany left national identity a deeply troubling issue for writers because of the impossibility of ignoring the shadow of the Holocaust which, nonetheless, they could not write about directly.

Memory, nation and the novel

If we agree that literature may play a role even in conceiving 'the inconceivable', what makes it worth reading something as apparently innocuous and subjective as a novel to gauge a nation's sense of itself? One answer is that novels and nations have for some time been thought of as linked in a crucial, yet often obscure way. For Benedict Anderson, the 'imagined communities' of nationality were conceived in the eighteenth century, when two cultural forms first flowered that provided the 'technical means' for '"re-presenting" the *kind* of imagined community that is the nation': the novel and the newspaper (Anderson, 1991, p. 25). As an increasingly popular form of imagining that constructed secular, historically informed and chronologically organized narratives about figures whose lives represented the desires and beliefs of a given linguistic community, the novel can be thought of as playing a key role in the growing self-awareness of communities in late eighteenth- and early nineteenth-century Europe.

In particular, novels may be said to contribute to the formation of memory as a collective, rather than a merely individual phenomenon. But was memory thought of as so important in the first place, in the construction of the idea of the nation in Europe?

Consider the following excerpt from the historian Ernest Renan's famous lecture on 'Qu'est-ce qu'une nation?' (what is a nation?), delivered at the Sorbonne in 1882.

> Or, l'essence d'une nation est que tous les individus aient beaucoup de choses en commun et aussis que tous aient oublié bien de choses ... Tout citoyen français *doit avoir oublié* la Saint-Barthélemy, les massacres du Midi au XIIIe siècle.
>
> (Yet the essence of a nation is that all individuals have many things in common, and also that they have forgotten many things ... Every French citizen *has to have forgotten* Saint Bartholomew, the massacres in the Midi [south of France] in the thirteenth century.)
>
> (Quoted in Anderson, 1991, p. 199, transl. Dennis Walder)

EXERCISE

1 What does Renan say the citizens of a nation need to have in common, in order to constitute a nation?

2 What implications might we draw from what Renan urges his French audience to think about?

DISCUSSION

1 Among much else, in order to constitute a nation the citizens need to 'have forgotten many things'. These include certain historical memories, such as Saint Bartholomew's Day (the date of the anti-Huguenot pogrom of 24 August 1572) and the mass killings of an even earlier period, about which presumably Renan's audience was aware (the massacres of the heretical Albigensians throughout the thirteenth century, instigated by Pope Innocent III).

2 One implication is that the paradoxical, complex involvement of long-term memories of atrocity in nation-construction (and deconstruction) – such as Renan refers to – continues to this day. Across the new nations of former Yugoslavia, for instance, there are still calls to remember (as well as to forget) not just the persecution of ethnic minority Serbs by Ustashe (extreme nationalist) Croatians during the Second World War, but also 28 June 1389: the date when the Serbian army was destroyed by the Ottomans at the battle of Kosovo. An example from further afield is South Africa's Truth and Reconciliation Commission

(TRC), set up in 1996 in response to calls to build a new nation by providing through testimony, witnessing and remembering the means for reconciling without violence the deeply divided people of the former apartheid state. The aim of the TRC has been to tell the truths of the past in a spirit of reparation rather than vengeance, although questions remain. What about justice? Attempts to bring alleged war criminals from former Yugoslavia to face the International Court at the Hague demonstrate that this is a continuing concern, while reminding us too of the Nuremberg trials that followed the Second World War.

Novels that engage with recent attempts to deal with mass atrocities have yet to be written, although the issue has already found a place in the more immediate field of drama. There is always a time-lag before events are incorporated, one way or another, within novels, which is a more reflective genre than lyric poetry or drama – even if the events are already incorporated within the narratives of individual and collective memory by the media of the day. This was true of the Holocaust too: narratives of that experience emerged in diaries (such as Anne Frank's), memoirs (Elie Wiesel's, for example) and various other kinds of testimony, before poems, plays and eventually novels followed, while attempts were made by historians and others to synthesize all of these into some larger narrative.

These narratives, both fictional and non-fictional, raise in acute form the question of memory and forgetting: they make a claim that 'we must never forget', while having to recognize that inevitably, as time passes, we do indeed forget – and perhaps we have to, in order to live on. But is this good enough, as far as Germany is concerned? What does it mean to be a German today?

There are no simple answers to these questions. But German identity is bound to be a troubled one. Following the postwar division into East and West Germany, with each country trying to define itself (and being defined) in a different way in relation to the past and the present, reunification after 1990 meant that Germany became yet another state, part of an unprecedented combination of former communist dictatorship and successful capitalist democracy. This caused new strains and tensions, some of which were evident in an upsurge of right-wing extremism, aimed once again at ethnic 'others'. The American reporter Martha Gellhorn, who had witnessed the liberation of the Dachau concentration camp, decided in 1990 to tour German universities where, she observed, there were 'good Europeans' now, who thought and spoke for themselves. But an outbreak of widespread violence against refugees in former East

Germany prompted her to ask why the German government, which had set up liberal immigration policies as a penance for the past, was doing nothing about this. And why weren't the students protesting? She asked a Turkish taxi driver who had lived in the country for thirteen years why he didn't apply for German citizenship. He replied, 'I do not wish to be German' (Gellhorn, 1992, pp. 199–208). In fact, despite the amendment of citizenship laws after the Second World War, so as to repudiate utterly the racist elements of Nazi rulings on citizenship and to allow in political refugees of any kind, the definition of 'Germans' as a community of ethnic descent remained, to the extent that it would have been extremely difficult, if not impossible, for this Turkish taxi driver to have become a German citizen – in contrast to ethnic Germans (*Volksdeutsche*) from Russia, Poland and elsewhere in eastern Europe who had never set foot on postwar German soil (see Fulbrook, 1999, pp. 183–4). This consideration is also part of the context of *The Reader*.

'The book that we have waited for'

Bernhard Schlink is a German who has had no choice about his identity. Like the narrator of his novel *The Reader*, he was born in 1944. Hence his relationship to the past of his parents' generation is inevitably part of who he is. Yet, unlike many other German writers of his generation, he did not represent that relationship in his earlier fictions. An academic and practising lawyer, Schlink had already published three successful crime novels when he wrote *The Reader*. The last of these, *Selbs Betrug* (*Selb's Deception* or, punningly, 'Self-deception'), whose hero Gerhard Selb is an ageing private detective with a Nazi past, appeared in 1992, when Schlink became professor of law at Humboldt University in Berlin. Happy to have these earlier works published first in German and in Germany (although by a Swiss publisher), Schlink hoped that *Der Vorleser* would appear first in the USA and, unusually, commissioned and paid for an English translation (by Carol Brown Janeway) at the outset. According to the German newspaper *Der Spiegel* this was because he was concerned that 'in Deutschland falsch verstanden zu werden', or in other words that he would be misunderstood in his own country. He felt that the book might be thought (in the English phrase) 'politically incorrect' (Hage, 1999).

Why? Perhaps Schlink was conscious of going against the grain of recent writing about Germany's past. But if it was 'politically incorrect' in German terms to write a love story that brought in the Holocaust, he need not have worried about the book's reception. As Christoph Stölzl, chief feature editor of *Die Welt* newspaper remarked at a prize-winning ceremony for the novelist in 1999, the German reviews had demonstrated that 'Das ist das Buch, auf das wir so lange gewartet haben, ohne es zu wissen' (This is the book that we have waited for for so long, without realizing it). Over the previous four years and without any publicity campaign, the novel had quietly overwhelmed its German readers, said Stölzl, by involving them with their own inner dialogue about *Schuld* (guilt) and *Sühne* (atonement) (Stölzl, 1999). The book has now been included in the German school curriculum.

Yet Schlink was, apparently, right to assume that an American audience would be especially receptive: not only did the novel earn high praise from all the usual highbrow newspapers and journals in the USA (such as the *New York Times* and the *New York Review of Books*) when it was published in English in 1997, but the author was also invited to tour the country. Thereafter *The Reader*'s success was ensured: chosen by the television talk-show host Oprah Winfrey for her book club in 1999, it was a best-seller as well as a critical success. D. J. Enright praised it for taking on 'a grievously formidable subject' and making us 'think too much about things we would rather not think about, issues which the book leaves open and we might wish to have closed one way or another' (*New York Review of Books*, 26 March 1998). And this success was not confined to the USA. In the UK the *New Statesman* described the book as a 'magnificent chiaroscuro novel' grappling with 'the legacy of those who carried out the Final Solution', while laying bare 'the agony of Germany's post-war generation without diminishing the profanities perpetrated by many of their parents' (Toby Mundy, *New Statesman*, 9 January 1998). Perhaps most magisterial of all, George Steiner gave Schlink's novel nothing less than a rave review in the London *Observer* of 2 November 1997, describing it as a 'touchstone of moral literacy'.

Despite all this enthusiasm from within and outside Germany, Schlink himself continued to express doubts. On the Oprah Winfrey show he returned to his reservations about publishing his book in Germany, 'because I thought maybe people might misunderstand it as apologetic, sort of whitewashing book [*sic*]' (quoted in Donahue, 2001, p. 63). And there has been a growing resistance towards the novel, most persuasively argued by Ernestine Schlant in *The Language of Silence* (Schlant, 1999, pp. 209–16) and by William Donahue in 'Illusions of subtlety' (Donahue, 2001, pp. 60–81).

Before considering these reactions and thinking about how to develop a position in relation to them, I should like now to consider the novel in some detail.

What kind of novel is *The Reader*?

Novels are of course narratives of particular kinds. This has to be taken into account when considering how any specific novel engages with its society and history. To get to grips with the kind of narrative provided by *The Reader*, I should like to look at its opening chapter and consider the way that it conveys its subject from the start. If you already know the novel, you might like to ask yourself as you read the following extract if there is a particular moment, indeed a particular sentence, when the later development of the plot is anticipated here.

All the references to and quotes from the English-language version of *The Reader* in this chapter are based on the 1998 paperback edition.

When I was fifteen, I got hepatitis. It started in the autumn and lasted until spring. As the old year darkened and turned colder, I got weaker and weaker. Things didn't start to improve until the new year. January was warm, and my mother moved my bed out onto the balcony. I saw sky, sun, clouds, and heard the voices of children playing in the courtyard. As dusk came one evening in February, there was the sound of a blackbird singing.

The first time I ventured outside, it was to go from Blumenstrasse, where we lived on the second floor of a massive turn-of-the-century building, to Bahnhofstrasse. That's where I'd thrown up on the way home from school one day the previous October. I'd been feeling weak for days, in a way that was completely new to me. Every step was an effort. When I was faced with stairs either at home or at school, my legs would hardly carry me. I had no appetite. Even if I sat down at the table hungry, I soon felt queasy. I woke up every morning with a dry mouth and the sensation that my insides were in the wrong place and pressing too hard against my bones. I was ashamed of being so weak. I was even more ashamed when I threw up. That was another thing that had never happened to me before. My mouth was suddenly full, I tried to swallow everything down again, and clenched my teeth with my hand in front of my mouth, but it all burst out of my mouth anyway straight through my fingers. I leaned against the wall of the building, looked down at the vomit around my feet, and retched something clear and sticky.

When rescue came, it was almost an assault. The woman seized my arm and pulled me through the dark entrance into the courtyard. Up above there were lines strung from window to window, loaded with laundry. Wood was stacked in the courtyard; in an open workshop a saw screamed and shavings flew. The woman turned on the tap, washed my hand first, and then cupped both of hers and threw water in my face. I dried myself with a handkerchief.

'Get that one!' There were two pails standing by the tap: she grabbed one and filled it. I took the other one, filled it, and followed her through the entrance. She swung her arm, the water sluiced down across the walk and washed the vomit into the gutter. Then she took my pail and sent a second wave of water across the walk.

When she straightened up, she saw I was crying. 'Hey, kid,' she said, startled, 'hey, kid' – and took me in her arms. I wasn't much taller than she was, I could feel her breasts against my chest. I smelled the sourness of my own breath and felt a sudden sweat as she held me, and didn't know where to look. I stopped crying.

(pp. 1–3)

EXERCISE

How would you define what kind of fiction this is, based on these lines?

DISCUSSION

It is a first-person, realist novel in the style of an autobiography.

The Reader is in fact about a German schoolboy whose sexual relationship with an older woman draws him into a relationship with his country's troubled past. It is told in the first person. The narrator later goes on to question himself and his motives, ultimately as a result of being drawn into witnessing the woman's trial and imprisonment for her involvement in the Holocaust. Here, however, at the opening of the novel, we are presented with the first, accidental encounter between the woman and the narrator as a 15-year-old schoolboy. We are given a very precise, realistically detailed idea of his feelings from the start, when he first falls ill in the street and is helped by the woman, who cleans him up so that he can go home. All this is conveyed as the memories of the older man who tells us the story.

'When rescue came, it was almost an assault.' This sentence, at the beginning of the third paragraph, is striking and, if you think about it, anticipates later developments: in particular, the shock of the older woman's sexual advance upon the (not unwilling) youth. If you have read the novel, you may also have recalled, from later in the story, that as an SS guard the woman used to select young people in the camps to join her in her quarters; which is when the question arises as to just how far her behaviour was then and is now blameworthy.

You may not have noticed the sentence to which I have drawn attention here, especially not on a first reading. But even if you have not yet read the novel, you will be aware from the blurb that it is about the relationship between a young boy and an older woman, relayed through his memories. So from the very beginning there is an interaction between past and present, or different time-zones, in the narrative. The second chapter (pp. 4–7) brings this out more strongly, by informing us that the building on Bahnhofstrasse is no longer there (as with other old buildings, it has evidently been replaced in the process of Germany's 'economic miracle') and that the narrator has a recurrent dream about it, a dream that presses in on him wherever he may be, either living in his current home in Germany or travelling abroad.

But as you re-read the opening chapter, you may well notice that the moment when the woman helps the boy as he collapses in the street will become the start of a relationship; and that when she seizes his arm and takes him off to clean him up, she is unconsciously setting in motion a train of events – which we see from the narrator's selective point of view, although there are some clues as to her motives from time to time. Notice, too, the momentary, involuntary sensuality of the encounter: 'I could feel her breasts against my chest. I smelled the sourness of my own breath and felt a sudden sweat as she held me, and didn't know where to look.' If you have already read the novel, you might further realize that the relationship initiated here will draw both the boy and us as readers into Hanna's predicament, and into the moral issues that predicament raises for the older narrator; although, like him, we do not know how far this is going to take us until later on – or to what extent, if at all, we should think of him as one more of her victims.

Interestingly, the sentence I have highlighted, which hints at the moral ambivalence of the 'rescue' of the boy by the woman (whose assistance is in retrospect less straightforward than it seems at first) is absent from the original. In the German text the third paragraph begins *Die Frau, die sich meiner annahm, tat es fast grob* (Schlink [1995] 1997, p. 6). Yet if you know German you will know that the literal translation, 'The woman, who took hold of me, did so quite roughly', may well justify the additional sentence in English comparing this rescue to an 'assault', since that helps to bring out the anticipatory weight of *grob* in the original, a word which also means 'rudely' or 'coarsely' (although the English translation does not manage the associative nuance of *annahm*, which can also mean 'adopted', as in adopting a child). 'Assault' carries more serious overtones than 'coarsely', yet it can be argued that these are appropriate overtones nevertheless, since they hint at what is to come. This is not only because *meiner annahm* means 'took care of me', anticipating the emotional hold the woman will develop over the boy, but also because, even before the revelation of her wartime past, we discover an element of violence in the woman's behaviour towards him: once, when she believes he has deserted her on a bicycle outing, she hits him so hard across the mouth with her belt that he bleeds (Schlink [1995] 1997, p. 53).

Translating a literary text always involves difficulties: even if the general meaning is accurately conveyed, and the conceptions and responses generated by the text are well enough understood, the immediate quality of the language is likely to resist the process of translation. But since this is a realist text, apparently offering an authentic account of 'real life' in relatively 'transparent' language, it is more amenable to translation than a denser, more allusive kind of fiction, or a poem, might have been. Moreover, like some of the postwar generation of German writers such as Böll (and unlike, say, Thomas Mann), Schlink writes in short, clear sentences, organized within short paragraphs and brief chapters. This may be the result of his having written crime fiction (*Kriminalromane*), but in any case it suggests a clear break from the traditional manner of German writing – once somewhat unfairly characterized by Mark Twain as a cumbersome conglomeration of parentheses within parentheses, which keep the reader in dark suspense, awaiting the accumulating bank of verbs at the end (Twain [1880] 1997, p. 391).

Yet Schlink is writing within an identifiable European literary tradition. Do you recognize it? The following exercise may help you in this.

EXERCISE

There is a more general term for the kind of fictional narrative we appear to be dealing with here, which may broadly be described as having to do with the growth in moral understanding of a young man, structured around a series of lessons, initiations or awakenings through which the hero must pass in order to reach maturity. The characteristic tone of such novels is generated by meditating upon the past, through memory. Can you guess what kind of novel this might be? Many such novels were written within this tradition during the nineteenth and twentieth centuries.

DISCUSSION

The Reader is, I would suggest, a twentieth-century version of the *Bildungsroman*, or novel of education, a realist narrative form to be found, for example, in Charles Dickens's *David Copperfield* (1849–50) or Gustave Flaubert's *L'Éducation sentimentale* (*Sentimental Education*, 1869). (Charlotte Bronte's *Jane Eyre*, 1848, is a female version.)

What you may not be aware of is that the *Bildungsroman* form, as its name implies, was established in Europe by a German writer. Specifically, it dates from Johann Wolfgang von Goethe's widely popular *Wilhelm Meister*, which appeared in two volumes separated by thirty-odd years: *Wilhelm Meisters Lehrjahre* (*Wilhelm Meister's Apprenticeship Years*, published in 1796), and *Wilhelm Meisters Wanderjahre* (*Wilhelm Meister's Travel Years*, first published in 1821 and revised in 1829). Goethe's influence upon German literature can hardly be overestimated: he was the virtual creator (with the sixteenth-century theologian Martin Luther) of modern German cultural expression, and a key figure in the creation of German 'national consciousness' – a rather nebulous description of the sense of collective identity which developed during the late eighteenth and early nineteenth centuries, well before the unified state of Germany came into being under the so-called Iron Chancellor, Otto von Bismarck, in 1871.

The key to the influence of the *Bildungsroman* is its emphasis (especially in the German context) upon the individual struggle towards self-awareness, in terms implying a deeper moral and even political struggle, ultimately a struggle for national self-understanding. The form arose in the Romantic period, when Germany existed less as a nation-state than as an idea – an idea of the nation as a unique cultural expression, rather than a state designed to ensure the equality of its citizens, as elsewhere in western Europe. The gap between German nationalist feeling, and the territory or state which might contain it, has been the central problem of modern German history.

The key figures of the *Bildungsroman*, whose inner lives we are invited to follow so closely and with whom we are encouraged to identify, have a representative quality, in their inwardness and insecurity. What seems on the surface of the traditional *Bildungsroman* to be primarily a domestic romance story has a wider resonance within the society to which it is addressed. This is one reason why these works and their European successors were so popular and lasting. Typically, such novels deal with relations across the classes, often involving a frustrated love between the humble and the mighty which ends in marriage or death. Their impact upon the course of European fiction has been profound, although nowadays the relationship between the individual and his or her community is more commonly presented as an experience of fracture or total alienation.

How might knowing all this about the generic literary context of *The Reader* help our understanding of the novel? In particular, does it help our understanding of how the book uses the idea of memory? To explore this issue further, I shall take as an example the following extract, from Chapter 9 of the novel, after the love affair between the boy and the woman has begun.

Why does it make me so sad when I think back to that time? Is it yearning for past happiness – for I was happy in the weeks that followed, in which I really did work like a lunatic and passed the class, and we made love as if nothing else in the world mattered. Is it the knowledge of what came later, and that what came out afterwards had been there all along?

Why? Why does what was beautiful suddenly shatter in hindsight because it concealed dark truths? Why does the memory of years of happy marriage turn to gall when our partner is revealed to have had a lover all those years? Because such a situation makes it impossible to be happy? But we were happy! Sometimes the memory of happiness cannot stay true because it ended unhappily. Because happiness is only real if it lasts forever? Because things always end painfully if they contained pain, conscious or unconscious, all along? But what is unconscious, unrecognized pain?

I think back to that time and I see my former self ... I didn't like the way I looked, the way I dressed and moved, what I achieved and what I felt I was worth. But there was so much energy in me, such belief that one day I'd be handsome and clever and superior and admired ... Sometimes I see the same eagerness and belief in the faces of children and teenagers and the sight brings back the same sadness I feel in remembering myself. Is this what sadness is all about? Is it what comes over us when beautiful memories shatter in hindsight because the remembered happiness fed not just on actual circumstances but on a promise that was not kept?

She – I should start calling her Hanna, just as I started calling her Hanna back then – she certainly didn't nourish herself on promises, but was rooted in the here and now.

I asked her about her life, and it was as if she rummaged around in a dusty chest to get me the answers. She had grown up in a German community in Rumania, then came to Berlin at the age of sixteen, taken a job at the Siemens factory, and ended up in the army at twenty-one. Since the end of the war, she had done all manner of jobs to get by ... Things I wanted to know more about had vanished completely from her mind, and she didn't understand why I was interested in what had happened to her parents, whether she had had brothers and sisters, how she had lived in Berlin, and what she'd done in the army. 'The things you ask, kid!'

It was the same with the future – of course I wasn't hammering out plans for marriage and future. But I identified more with Julien Sorel's relationship with Madame de Renal than with his one with Mathilde de la Mole. I was glad to see Felix Krull end up in the arms of the mother rather than the daughter. My sister, who was studying German literature, delivered a report at the dinner table about the controversy as to whether Mr von Goethe and Madame von Stein had had a relationship, and I vigorously defended the idea, to the bafflement of my family ...

It all happened because of reading aloud. The day after our conversation, Hanna wanted to know what I was learning in school. I told her about Homer, Cicero, and Hemingway's story about the old man and his battle with the fish and the sea. She wanted to hear what Greek and Latin sounded like, and I read to her from the *Odyssey* and the speeches against Cataline.

(pp. 35–40)

EXERCISE _____

1   What is the tone of this chapter? (Tone is a matter of the feelings suggested by specific sentences, words, of which we may be hardly aware as we read.)

2   What do you make of the literary references in this extract, and how do they contribute to that tone?

DISCUSSION _____

1   The tone is nostalgic, yearning. The chapter begins with the words 'Why does it make me so sad when I think back to that time?' It is also questioning: 'Is [sadness] what comes over us when beautiful memories shatter in hindsight because the remembered happiness fed not just on actual circumstances but on a promise that was not kept?' This also anticipates the theme of betrayal that is to become increasingly important in the book.

2   References in the extract to the classics of European literature, from Homer and Cicero to Goethe, Stendhal (Julien Sorel) and Thomas Mann (Felix Krull), and also to Ernest Hemingway, provide a sense of the cultural distance between the young boy reader and his listener Hanna Schmitz, while asserting the long history of the theme of doomed love that entangles the ill-assorted pair in this novel. It is also notable that the first work the boy reads to his lover is Homer's epic poem about a wanderer

who, in stark contrast to the boy, is finally able to find wife, home, peace and reconciliation after war.

The German word for the feeling of nostalgia overtaking Michael, the narrator, is *Sehnsucht*: a word familiar to German readers as an inherited, Romantic commonplace that reflects a yearning for the ideal, the barely remembered, the lost – a yearning that typically overcomes the Romantic hero. Knowing this helps us to understand that *The Reader* is a highly self-conscious novel, calling on the reader's awareness of other literary texts as it explores the common theme of memory. But to what purpose? It does appear as if the novel is justifying itself, and its theme, by implicitly placing itself within the mainstream of western classical literature, traceable back to Homer. In that sense it is claiming to deal with a common, rather than a unique phenomenon. Perhaps this explains why the book translates so well into other European languages and cultures.

Yet we also have to consider this reference (in the same chapter): 'I had already done the reading about the Weimar Republic and the Third Reich while I was in my sickbed' (p. 39). German history is, apparently, a safe distance away at this stage. It may seem quite natural that when Hanna tells the schoolboy about her life there is a gap in her account. If on a first reading of the book we are hardly conscious of this, any more than the boy is, in the proleptic manner of this narrative it is a gap that draws attention to itself, as it does to his innocence and her knowledge:

> Things I wanted to know more about had vanished completely from her mind, and she didn't understand why I was interested in what had happened to her parents, whether she had had brothers or sisters, how she had lived in Berlin, and what she'd done in the army. 'The things you ask, kid!'
>
> (p. 37)

The overall tone of the first part of the three-part narrative is personal and intimate, the tone of a mind speaking to itself, both engaging and sympathetic, taking the reader through the affair between the boy and his mistress. Yet all the time there is both a sense of how distant this teenage affair is to the consciousness revealing it to us – 'today I can recognize that events back then were part of a lifelong pattern' (p. 18) – as well as a sense of impending disaster, most notably at that moment just before Michael Berg realizes he has 'betrayed' Hanna by keeping their relationship secret.

That moment of realization, of betrayal and guilt, occurs at a significant point in the narrative, in Chapter 14. It is the beginning of the end of their relationship; it is also near the end of Part One of the novel. As the boy takes his place among young people his own age, he begins to resent Hanna and their secret affair. I was particularly struck by the extended metaphor at the beginning of the chapter, which is quoted below.

> When an aeroplane's engines fail, it is not the end of the flight. Aeroplanes don't fall out of the sky like stones. They glide on, the enormous multi-engined passenger jets, for thirty, forty-five minutes, only to smash themselves up when they attempt a landing. The passengers don't notice a thing. Flying feels the same whether the engines are working or not. It's quieter, but only slightly: the wind drowns out the engines as it buffets the tail and wings. At some point, the earth or sea look dangerously close through the window. But perhaps the film is on, and the stewards and air hostesses have closed the blinds. Maybe the very quietness of the flight strikes the passengers as an improvement.
>
> That summer was the glide path of our love. Or rather, of my love for Hanna. I don't know about her love for me.

(pp. 67–8)

EXERCISE _____

What do you make of the contribution of this passage to the novel and to our responses to the affair between the boy and the woman?

DISCUSSION _____

The extremity of this image prepares us for the discoveries to follow. At the same time, it suggests how penetrating the layers of memory can have serious, even disastrous results. Over the following few pages of the book, the narrator reveals how as a youth he experienced shame, denial, guilt – words he uses of himself, which we may feel at first are excessive, yet which fairly represent the way a teenage boy might exaggerate his sense of what he has done, while also anticipating the more serious kinds of social and historical betrayals we will encounter in Parts Two and Three of the novel. The comparison of his affair with a plane gliding down to catastrophe, of which its passengers are blissfully unaware, is doubly appropriate.

_____

The issue is: how can such a small-scale emotional involvement as young Michael's affair with Hanna be mapped on to large-scale events involving whole communities and peoples? Is this a way of internalizing German guilt, and making it accessible to outsiders as well? Or a way of excusing a lack of such guilt? When the narrator accuses himself as a boy in such harsh terms for denying his lover, do we understand this as comparable in any way to the German denial of their country's secret past, their inextricable involvement with those who carried out the dreadful crimes of the Nazi era?

The inability to mourn

In 1967, the year before student rebellions erupted across western Europe, two social psychologists, Alexander and Margarete Mitscherlich, published an influential study entitled *Die Unfähigkeit zu Trauern* (*The Inability to Mourn*; Mitscherlich and Mitscherlich, 1975), which tried to explain what they called the German people's inability to mourn the loss of the Führer. The Mitscherlich argument (based on a Freudian approach) was that by failing to address their past, in particular their past idealization of the leader, and by their consequent silence about the Holocaust, the German people showed that they were unable to 'work through' (*durcharbeiten*) the crimes of the Nazis. The result was that they had become apathetic and indifferent to these crimes. According to Ernestine Schlant, if this is true of the older generation it may also be part of the inheritance of their children. As she puts it,

> They, too, may be unable to recoup the affective dimension required for genuine mourning – not remorse for deeds they did not commit or mourning for a Hitler who to them is at most a historical figure, but a mourning for the parents' generation, the deeds committed by them, and for the victims.

(Schlant, 1999, pp. 13–14)

I find this a persuasive perspective within which to try to understand Schlink's novel, particularly the latter sections of the narrative, which reveal a 'numb' and detached Michael Berg failing in all his relationships and learning the 'truth' about Hanna: her illiteracy (which we have already guessed ahead of him) and her involvement in two Holocaust crimes – as a camp guard selecting inmates to be sent to Auschwitz, and later failing to rescue women prisoners trapped inside a burning church.

In an attempt to fashion an identity for its (both German and non-German) readers which involves coming to terms with the legacy of the past, *The Reader* takes us into the courtroom where Nazi crimes are tried, and then into the prison where the guilty are punished. But we see all this through the eyes of its narrator, the older Michael Berg, who describes his failure to mention his secret love affair with

Figure 3.2 Photo of former women prisoners in the wooden bunks that served as beds in Auschwitz concentration camp. Still photo from a Soviet film. After 27 January 1945. What is running through these women's minds as they return to the scene of their imprisonment and degradation? Photo: USHMM Photographic Archive

Figure 3.3 Inge Viermetz testifies in her own defence at the RuSHA trial, 28 January 1945. Nuremberg. Compare the courtroom scene in *The Reader*, Part Two, and especially the narrator's memory of Hanna's appearance in the dock. Photo: USHMM Photographic Archive

Figure 3.4 The deportation of women and children to an unidentified concentration camp in 1942. Yugoslavia. The poet Paul Celan's parents were deported from further east, in what is now Romania. What, if any, clues are we given as to the origins of the women who feature in *The Reader*? Photo: USHMM Photographic Archive

one of the accused as an act of betrayal. He goes on to reveal to us that he failed to mention Hanna's illiteracy at her trial, although he was aware that her sentence would have been commuted if the judge had known of it – not merely because it was at least an explanation for her decision to join the army, but also because it meant that she could not have written the report which the other female guards claimed had been written by her; a claim designed to shift the blame for the church atrocity to Hanna (pp. 124–5, 128).

But the question now becomes: how do we as readers respond to what is depicted in the courtroom and afterwards? As Hanna says to the judge, 'What would you have done?' (p. 127). The question may seem to be primarily addressed to German readers, whose recent history it brings back, but given the wider availability of the text to all of us (and the evidence of its widespread warm reception) the question also applies to all of us, however we might identify ourselves – as victims, perpetrators, witnesses, bystanders, or as even more distant from the events portrayed. How we answer the question, though, depends, I would suggest, in the first place upon how we respond to the novel, although that in turn depends to some extent upon our individual circumstances and histories. With whom do we identify and sympathize, and why? And what then do we make of the narrator's attitude towards the Jewish victim–survivor he goes on to find in New York? And her response to him? How far are we invited to criticize the narrator? Is he, in the end, a bad reader, in the sense that he is unwilling or unable to read or interpret the past, despite having been able to 'read' Hanna in the end? (The relevant sections of the novel are to be found in Chapters 7 and 9 of Part Two, and Chapters 10 and 11 of Part Three.)

These are difficult questions to answer, but they take us to the heart of the novel and its claim to represent the views of those many readers who have responded positively to the book as a morally sensitive and profound attempt by a German writer to plumb the legacy of the Holocaust – a legacy which, while regarded as uniquely German in some respects, is also increasingly understood as a legacy belonging to all. I can only give my own personal responses for you to test yourself against.

Briefly, then, in the first place I was surprised at what I learned about Hanna's involvement in the Nazi past, while intrigued by the courtroom procedure (an aspect of the novel which resembles the crime-fiction narratives Schlink used to write). Further, prompted by such cues from the narrator as his wish that the judge would ask why Hanna chose certain women as 'favourites' before they were deported to Auschwitz – so that the court would learn 'she wanted to make that final month bearable' for them (p. 116) – I found myself wanting to moderate her guilt.

Secondly, since the narrator is the centre of the narrative we not only identify and sympathize with him, we are also led to accept his judgements upon others. When Hanna confronts the judge with 'What would you have done?' and the narrator tells us that nobody was willing to understand her position, we sympathize with the 'confusion and helplessness' that he claims she experienced when, faced with 'two equally compelling duties' after the church fire broke out and her superiors had disappeared, she nonetheless felt her prime duty was not to let the women escape (p. 127).

Thirdly, we are encouraged even more to sympathize with Hanna when we read that she spent her last years in prison, where she learned to read and write at last, before finally hanging herself. The narrator's reaction to this news, which is to 'stammer and weep' (p. 205), suggests that he feels his inadequacy in the face of her act, which in turn prompts him to carry out her request that her savings be given to the sole survivor of the church fire. His appearance before the survivor once again suggests inadequacy on his part – and on Hanna's. The 'absolution' that both of them wish for will not be granted, although 'recognition' will be (pp. 210–13). Is that sufficient?

I have focused on this area of the novel in some detail, because I think it is the key to how we may sum up our evaluation of the work. Some readers have found the ending ultimately hopeful and as a way of helping to lay the past to rest; others find it a cop-out on the novelist's part, since important issues about complicity with the Nazi past have been raised without satisfactorily concluding them. A crucial point to consider is how we view the role of the narrator: is he to be identified with the author, or not? If not, then we can view his behaviour critically, at least. His perspective is evidently limited by his viewpoint, which Schlink has chosen as one effective and moving way of providing access to the dilemmas of Germans of his generation who wish to deal with the Nazi past of their parents' generation. Implicitly, however, the novel is also about the past which remains present for all of us, a presence recalled when events like those of former Yugoslavia or Rwanda remind us of how ordinary people can turn into the slayers of those of their compatriots who become identified as different.

For Ernestine Schlant, 'It is not surprising that Michael wants to salvage the image of the woman he has loved, but his lack of abhorrence at Hanna's acts and the way she speaks – or does not speak – about them is amazing'. Moreover, by having Hanna learn to read in her cell, where Michael goes after her suicide to find books by victims of the Holocaust and the autobiography of Rudolf Hess, the author suggests that overcoming her illiteracy was enough to make Hanna 'morally alert'. But 'Illiteracy cannot serve as an explanation for co-operating in and committing criminal acts'; nor is it an excuse; and if not, what purpose does it serve in the novel? 'At the very point where Schlink needs to make a strong case with respect to the Nazi crimes and those who perpetrated them, the novel is weakest' (Schlant, 1999, p. 213).

A more subtle version of this argument is made by William Collins Donahue, in his essay 'Illusions of subtlety', where he argues that the narrator is the first to accuse himself for inadequately realizing the moral problem of Hanna's role in Nazi crimes, 'thereby [blunting] any impulse we may feel to judge him' (Donahue, 2001, p. 66). Moreover, the way in which Michael's 'numbness' emerges whenever the details of the trial are brought out (particularly those of the Jewish witnesses) is generalized to become part of our own assumed exhaustion at the apparently endless retelling of Holocaust horrors, thus allowing us to join him in not facing up to 'the patent absurdities' involved in associating perpetrators, victims, the dead, the living as if they were indistinguishable – as Michael does, for example, during the trial (Donahue, 2001, pp. 68–9).

As Donahue puts it, we as readers are finally placed in the invidious position of seeing not only Hanna as a kind of victim, but Michael too – to the extent that in the penultimate chapter (Part Three, Chapter 11) the Jewish survivor that he goes to visit is made to confirm Hanna's 'brutality' towards him as a boy, as if that were more important than her earlier crimes as a Nazi. Nevertheless, Donahue admits that if the aim of the novel is to involve us in its author's moral uncertainty, it succeeds, and it may be beyond any novel to show the kind of moral understanding 'in the light of real historical constraints' that is required of Holocaust narratives. At least this one, Donahue concludes, shows the authentic, deep anguish of 'the second generation's understandable difficulty in coming to terms with the Holocaust' (Donahue, 2001, pp. 80–1).

In my own view, the very last chapter of the novel – which most commentators appear to forget or ignore – suggests something different. This is where the narrator reveals that he wrote the story to be free of it, but that he has failed in this because the past always extends into the present, building the inevitable 'geological layers of our lives' (p. 215). In other words he admits his personal agenda, which may be taken as an admission of the questionable nature of some aspects of his story, such as the eroticization of Hanna, which leads to his desire to excuse her from guilt, and his inability to mourn her, except in the very last line of the book, when we are told he stands at her grave. Earlier he has said that 'my love for Hanna was, in a way, the fate of my generation, a German fate' (p. 169). But when Michael stands by Hanna's grave he does so while he has in his pocket a computer-generated letter from a Jewish charity thanking her for the donation he has made in her name. Does this mean that the novel's attempt to redeem the past for a whole generation of Germans is upset – usefully upset – at the end? I believe it does, leaving us with a literary text which, while exhibiting the features of a realist, *Bildungsroman*-type of novel, resists the moral closure usually

Figure 3.5 Bernhard Schlink, author of *The Reader*, as he is today (2001). Photo: Sara Krulwich/The New York Times

associated with that kind of fiction. When Michael goes over the list of titles he recorded reading for Hanna, he notices that 'they testify to a great and fundamental confidence in bourgeois culture' (p. 183), and remarks that he does not remember ever asking himself

> whether I should go beyond Kafka, Frisch, Johnson, Bachmann, and Lenz, and read experimental literature, literature in which I did not recognize the story or like any of the characters. To me it was obvious that experimental literature was experimenting with the reader, and Hanna didn't need that and neither did I.

(p. 183)

Yet these remarks, while justifying the predominantly realist and traditional shape of the narrative, themselves promote the possibility of uncertainty, of writing and reading things in a way that suggests what more 'experimental' literature does, that is to emphasize the subjectivity of experience and hence the uncertainty of judgement. Schlink's project reminds us of the importance of the status of the text – a factor given particular prominence by a publication that appeared in the same year as *Der Vorleser*, Binjamin Wilkomirski's *Bruchstücke: aus einer Kindheit 1939–1948* (translated as *Fragments: Memories of a Childhood 1939–1948* in 1996), which earned instant fame as a gruelling memoir of growing up in the concentration camps but subsequently became notorious when it transpired that the work was a fabrication by a disturbed Swiss Gentile named Bruno Grosjean. How do we separate 'cashing in' on the eminently commodifiable subject of the Holocaust from genuine engagement with it? It is a matter of how we read, the assumptions we bring to reading, and our ability to develop a critical awareness of what we read.

Conclusion

In this chapter I have tried to suggest various contexts in which it may be helpful to read *The Reader*, and to take you as readers through some aspects of it that seem to me to bear most upon questions of German self-awareness, although this is not ultimately separable from questions of our self-awareness as readers, wherever we are coming from. The novel acknowledges the continuing need to break the silence, as it were, to remember – although it offers an unusual kind of remembering, involving deep problems of moral accountability, and the role of literature and art. Like the novelist W. G. Sebald (see his *Austerlitz*, 2001) – who was also born in Germany in 1944, although he chose to live in exile in the UK – Schlink belongs to a generation of Germans who have looked at their past but who, instead of avoidance or silence, have chosen to recall it, if indirectly and through the medium of literature, raising questions about their sense of who they are in both the present and the future. What does the Nazi past still mean for Germans as a relatively new national community? Can the country simply take its place as one nation like any other in the European Union? Or should its citizens continue to face up to its unique identity? Does one have to choose between these alternatives? Schlink has brought us into what Celan called in the title-poem of *Der Sand aus den Urnen* 'das Haus des Vergessens' (the house of forgetting), but it is not a comfortable place for anyone, even for those of us who may be fortunate enough in some sense to enter this house through translation, and at a distance.

References

Adorno, Theodor (1977) 'Commitment', transl. Francis MacDonagh, in R. Livingstone, P. Anderson, F. Mulhern (eds), *Aesthetics and Politics*, London, New Left Books, pp. 177–95 (first published as *Noten zur Literatur III*, 1965, Frankfurt, Suhrkamp).

Anderson, Benedict (1991) *Imagined Communities*, rev. and extended edn., London, Verso.

Borger, Julian (2001) 'Does anybody know who this man is?', *Guardian: G2*, 13 June.

Burleigh, Michael [2000] (2001) *The Third Reich: a New History*, London, Pan.

Celan, Paul (1996) *Selected Poems*, transl. and intro. Michael Hamburger, Harmondsworth, Penguin.

Donahue, William Collins (2001) 'Illusions of subtlety: Bernhard Schlink's *Der Vorleser* and the moral limits of Holocaust fiction', *German Life and Letters*, vol. 54, 1 January.

Fulbrook, Mary (1999) *German National Identity after the Holocaust*, Cambridge, Polity.

Gellhorn, Martha (1992) '*Ohne mich*: Why I shall never return to Germany', *Krauts!, Granta* 42 (winter).

Hage, Volker (1999) 'Gewicht der Wahrheit', *Der Spiegel*, 29 March.

Holocaust Memorial Day website: http://www.holocaustmemorialday. gov.uk

Mitscherlich, Alexander and Mitschelich, Margarete (1975) *The Inability to Mourn*, New York, Grove (first published as *Die Unfähigkeit zu Trauern*, 1967).

Novick, Peter (2000) *The Holocaust and Collective Memory*, London, Bloomsbury.

Owings, Alison (2001) *Frauen: German Women Recall the Third Reich*, Harmondsworth, Penguin.

Schlant, Ernestine (1999) *The Language of Silence: West German Literature and the Holocaust*, London/New York, Routledge.

Schlink, Bernhard [1995] (1997) *Der Vorleser*, Zurich, Diogenes.

Schlink, Bernhard [1997] (1998) *The Reader*, transl. Carol Brown Janeway, London, Phoenix.

Sebald, W. G. (2001) *Austerlitz*, transl. Anthea Bell, London, Hamish Hamilton.

Steiner, George [1959] (1969) 'The hollow miracle', reprinted in *Language and Silence: Essays 1958–1966*, Harmondsworth, Penguin.

Stölzl, Christoph (1999) 'Ich hab's in einer Nacht ausgelesen', *Die Welt* website: http://www.welt.de/daten/1999/11/13/11131w13/6/1.htx

Twain, Mark [1880] (1997) 'The awful German language', appendix D in *A Tramp Abroad*, New York, Penguin.

Wilkomirski, Binjamin (1996) *Fragments: Memories of a Childhood 1939–1948*, transl. Carol Brown Janeway, London, Picador (first published as *Bruchstücke: Aus einer Kindheit 1939–1948*, 1995).

4

Voicing protest:

three responses to war in art music

ROBERT SAMUELS

Introduction

It is something of a platitude that war is an extreme experience for both combatants and non-combatants. The harsh conditions of the Second World War gave rise to some remarkable anecdotes concerning the forms of human activity commonly considered perhaps those most distanced from warfare: artistic production and performance. Among musicians and scholars of music, several of these tales have become oft-repeated, for example that of the BBC's continued broadcasts of chamber music from London during the Blitz; or the composition and first performance of Olivier Messiaen's *Quatuor pour la fin du temps* (Quartet for the End of Time), written while he was interned in Silesia (the slightly unusual combination of instruments, piano, clarinet, violin and cello, was forced upon the composer by the resources available). And in recent years there has been considerable renewed interest in the musical activities pursued in concentration camps. For instance, the transit camp at Terezin in Bohemia had a rich musical life, due in part to the presence of several active composers, three of whom (Viktor Ullmann, Pavel Haas and Hans Krása) eventually died on the same day, 18 October 1944, in the Auschwitz gas chambers. Auschwitz itself had no fewer than six orchestras of Jewish musicians at one time, whose personnel included the distinguished soloist Alma Rosé, daughter of Arnold Rosé, leader of the Vienna Philharmonic Orchestra, and niece of the composer Gustav Mahler.

While all these are undoubtedly stories of great pathos, they are also indicators of the value that artistic consumption and production continue to have within western culture, even (or perhaps especially) when the political and social existence of that culture is under threat. This chapter looks at three works of 'art music', all of which, in different ways, owe their genesis to the experience of war. Through them the reaction to war not just of individual composers but of western culture generally can be gauged.

One of these works dates from wartime itself: Michael Tippett's oratorio *A Child of Our Time*, written in 1939–41 and first performed at the Adelphi Theatre, London, in 1944. The other two were both written in 1961–2, at the height of the Cold War. One is the quasi-official musical war memorial, *War Requiem* by Benjamin Britten; the other is Dmitri Shostakovich's Thirteenth Symphony, which the composer subtitled 'Babi Yar' and which sets poetry by Yevgeny Yevtushenko (written for this symphony) in each of its five movements.

These three works furnish rich sources of comparison: between wartime and postwar works, between works of cultural protest and works of establishment sanction, between western European and eastern European responses. They are also works which bear within their structures a problematized but self-aware relationship to the history of musical form. All three are examples of musical forms with long histories in western culture: the oratorio, the requiem, the symphony. The survival of these forms of art music into the twentieth century was dependent on the conscious will of composers to continue to utilize them beyond the historical periods in which they were intrinsically bound up with social activities: the theatre, liturgy or the public concert. This continued survival was, obviously, even more radically threatened by the Second World War, which was perceived by the three composers, from their different perspectives, as a threat to the entirety of European culture. For Britten and Shostakovich, this sense of cultural disaster (although with hindsight we know it was avoided) was placed against the background – one might say, placed in counterpoint with – the even greater perceived threat of global destruction in the Cold War. For Britten, indeed, the use of poetry from the First World War as part of his text intentionally creates resonances between these cataclysmic threats.

In these works two contexts are clearly evident: on the one hand the Modernist artist's characteristic anxiety over his or her relationship to tradition and the continued viability of his or her craft; and on the other, the political crisis of the mid twentieth century, in which the Enlightenment ideals of nation-statehood appeared to many people to be reaching a catastrophic yet logical conclusion. This confluence is acted out within the musical works as an immanent critique of form. These two situations of crisis – the aesthetic and the political – were in any case parallel results of European history, rather than accidentally coincidental. The study of musical responses to the war is a far from marginal activity within the aim of understanding the marks which that conflict left upon European society, marks that are still visible today.

Michael Tippett (1905–98): *A Child of Our Time*

Tippett began to write his oratorio on the day that war was declared between Britain and Germany. He was a relatively little-known composer who had already become sincerely attached to what were to remain lifelong commitments, to left-wing politics and to pacifism. The text of the oratorio coalesced after a period in which Tippett had first considered writing an opera based on the Irish **Easter Rising** of 1916. In the event, the text is a combination of three main elements.

First, some sections embody narrative. Here, Tippett bases his work on two stories. The principal one is that of Herschel Grynspan, a Polish-German émigré Jew who, on hearing of the expulsion of his mother and sister from Germany to Poland (where they were refused entry) in late 1938, shot a third secretary in the German embassy in Paris. The assassination, for which Grynspan did not attempt to resist arrest, provoked the anti-semitic pogrom that included the Kristallnacht atrocities. The other story used by Tippett is the novel that provided his eventual title, *Ein Kind unserer Zeit* by Ödön von

The Easter Rising (24 April–1 May 1916) was an armed insurrection against British rule in Ireland. About 2,000 members of the Irish Volunteers and the Irish Citizen Army, led by Pádraic Pearse and James Connolly, seized the main post office in Dublin, along with other strategic buildings. A provisional Irish republic was proclaimed on 24 April, but the British swiftly counterattacked, securing a military victory by 29 April. Sixteen of the leaders of the rising were executed the following month. However, in the 1918 general elections the Sinn Fein (Republican) party won the majority vote, and British rule of Ireland became untenable by 1921.

Figure 4.1 Michael Tippett in 1944, at rehearsals for the first performance of *A Child of Our Time*. Photo: *Picture Post*, Hulton Archive

Horváth, translated into English in 1938. The novel tells the story of a young Nazi soldier, whose gradual disillusionment results in his committing murder, becoming deranged and eventually dying an anonymous death frozen in the snow on a park bench.

The second element in Tippett's material is provided by more general, reflective passages, in which the themes or 'message' of the Grynspan and von Horváth stories are seen as representative both of society and of individual psychology. Tippett focuses in particular on the image of the scapegoat, which was his characterization of both Grynspan and von Horváth's protagonist; it is the literary device through which he implicates both sides of the European conflict and, at a deeper level, humankind itself in the evils described. In writing these more reflective passages Tippett draws heavily on religious imagery (reflecting the heritage of religious oratorios which form the context of his composition), and also relies on ideas drawn from the **Jungian** concepts of archetype and the collective subconscious.

The third, and at first hearing the most striking, feature of the text is the incorporation of arrangements of five Negro spirituals. Here Tippett made use of texts and melodies from a 1926 collection, *The Book of American Negro Spirituals*, whose publication was itself indicative of the growing interest in this music, as in other folk traditions and non-western music, in the early decades of the twentieth century.

At this point you should read through the text of *A Child of Our Time*, given below.

Carl Jung (1885–1961) is one of the founding fathers of modern psychology. His idea of the 'collective unconscious' refers to a level of the psyche deeper than the individual's 'personal unconscious', and which is shared by all humans. The collective unconscious is composed of a number of archetypes (such as the 'wise old man' or the 'great mother'), which are therefore universal to all human cultures.

A Child of Our Time

PART I

1. CHORUS
The world turns on its dark side.
It is winter.

2. THE ARGUMENT (Alto Solo)
Man has measured the heavens with a telescope,
driven the gods from their thrones.
But the soul, watching the chaotic mirror, knows that the gods return.
Truly, the living god consumes within and turns the flesh to cancer.

Interludium (instrumental)

3. SCENA (Chorus & Alto Solo)

Chorus
Is evil then good?
Is reason untrue?

Alto
Reason is true to itself;
But pity breaks open the heart.

Interludium (instrumental)

Chorus
We are lost.
We are as seed before the wind.
We are carried to a great slaughter.

4. THE NARRATOR (Bass Solo)

Now in each nation there were some cast out by authority and
tormented, made to suffer for the general wrong.
Pogroms in the east, lynching in the west;
Europe brooding on a war of starvation,
And a great cry went up from the people.

5. CHORUS OF THE OPPRESSED

When shall the usurers' city cease,
And famine depart from the fruitful land?

6. TENOR SOLO

I have no money for my bread; I have no gift for my love.
I am caught between my desires and their frustration as between
the hammer and the anvil.
How can I grow to a man's stature?

7. SOPRANO SOLO

How can I cherish my man in such days,
Or become a mother in a world of destruction?
How shall I feed my children on so small a wage?
How can I comfort them when I am dead?

8. A SPIRITUAL (Chorus & Soli)

Steal away, steal away, steal away to Jesus;
Steal away, steal away home – I han't got long to stay here.
My Lord, He calls me, He calls me by the thunder,
The trumpet sounds within-a my soul,

I han't got long to stay here.
Green trees a-bending, poor sinner stand a-trembling,
The trumpet sounds within-a my soul,
I han't got long to stay here.
Steal away, steal away, steal away to Jesus;
Steal away, steal away home – I han't got long to stay here.

PART II

9. CHORUS

A star rises in mid-winter.
Behold the man! The scape-goat!
The child of our time.

10. THE NARRATOR (Bass Solo)

And a time came when in the continual persecution
One race stood for all.

11. DOUBLE CHORUS OF PERSECUTORS AND PERSECUTED

Away with them!
Curse them! Kill them!
They infect the state.
Where? How? Why?
We have no refuge.

12. THE NARRATOR (Bass Solo)

Where they could, they fled from the terror,
And among them a boy escaped secretly, and was kept in hiding in
a great city.

13. CHORUS OF THE SELF-RIGHTEOUS

We cannot have them in our Empire.
They shall not work, nor beg a dole.
Let them starve in No-Mans-Land!

14. THE NARRATOR (Bass Solo)

And the boy's mother wrote a letter, saying:

15. SCENA (Solo Quartet)

Mother (Soprano)
O my son! In the dread terror they have brought me near to
death.

Boy (Tenor)
Mother! Mother!
Though men hunt me like an animal, I will defy the world to reach you.

Aunt (Alto)
Have patience.
Throw not your life away in futile sacrifice.

Uncle (Bass)
You are as one against all.
Accept the impotence of your humanity.

Boy
No! I must save her.

16. A SPIRITUAL (Chorus & Soli)

Nobody knows the trouble I see, Lord,
Nobody knows like Jesus.
O brothers, pray for me,
O brothers, pray for me,
And help me to drive Old Satan away.
O mothers, pray for me,
O mothers, pray for me,
And help me to drive Old Satan away.
Nobody knows the trouble I see, Lord,
Nobody knows like Jesus.

17. SCENA (Duet – Bass & Alto Soli)

Narrator (Bass)
The boy becomes desperate in his agony.

Alto
A curse is born.
The dark forces threaten him.

Narrator
He goes to authority.
He is met with hostility.

Alto
His other self rises in him, demonic and destructive.

Narrator
He shoots the official –

Alto
But he shoots only his dark brother –
And see – he is dead.

18. THE NARRATOR (Bass Solo)

They took a terrible vengeance.

19. THE TERROR (Chorus)

Burn down their homes! Beat in their heads!
Break them in pieces on the wheel!

20. THE NARRATOR (Bass Solo)

Men were ashamed of what was done.
There was bitterness and horror.

21. A SPIRITUAL OF ANGER (Chorus & Bass Solo)

Go down, Moses, way down in Egypt land;
Tell old Pharaoh, to let my people go.
When Israel was in Egypt's land,
Let my people go.
Oppressed so hard they could not stand,
Let my people go.
Thus spake the Lord, bold Moses said,
Let my people go.
If not, I'll smite your first-born dead,
Let my people go.
Go down, Moses, way down in Egypt land;
Tell old Pharaoh, to let my people go.

22. THE BOY SINGS IN HIS PRISON (Tenor Solo)

My dreams are all shattered in a ghastly reality.
The wild beating of my heart is stilled: day by day.
Earth and sky are not for those in prison.
Mother! Mother!

23. THE MOTHER (Soprano Solo)

What have I done to you, my son?
What will become of us now?
The springs of hope are dried up.
My heart aches in unending pain.

24. ALTO SOLO

The dark forces rise like a flood.
Men's hearts are heavy: they cry for peace.

25. A SPIRITUAL (Chorus & Soprano Solo)

O, by and by, by and by,
I'm going to lay down my heavy load.
I know my robe's going to fit me well,
I tried it on at the gates of hell.
O, hell is deep and a dark despair,
O, stop, poor sinner, and don t go there!
O, by and by, by and by,
I'm going to lay down my heavy load.

PART III

26. CHORUS

The cold deepens.
The world descends into the icy waters where lies the jewel of great price.

27. ALTO SOLO

The soul of man is impassioned like a woman.
She is old as the earth, beyond good and evil,
The sensual garments.
Her face will be illumined like the sun.
Then is the time of his deliverance.

28. SCENA

Bass
The words of wisdom are these:
Winter cold means inner warmth, the secret nursery of the seed.

Chorus
How shalt we have patience for the consummation of the mystery?
Who will comfort us in the going through?

Bass
Patience is born in the tension of loneliness.
The garden lies beyond the desert.

Chorus
Is the man of destiny master of us all?
Shall those cast out be unavenged?

Bass
The man of destiny is cut off from fellowship.
Healing springs from the womb of time.
The simple-hearted shall exult in the end.

Chorus
What of the boy, then? What of him?
He, too, is outcast, his manhood broken in the clash of powers.
God overpowered him – the child of our time.

29. GENERAL ENSEMBLE (Chorus & Soli)

Preludium (instrumental)

Tenor
I would know my shadow and my light,
so shall I at last be whole.

Bass
Then courage, brother, dare the grave passage.

Soprano
Here is no final grieving, but an abiding hope.

Alto
The moving waters renew the earth.
It is spring.

Chorus
repeats the words of the soloists

30. A SPIRITUAL (Chorus & Soli)

Deep river, my home is over Jordan,
Deep river, Lord, I want to cross over into camp-ground.
O chillun! O don't you want to go,
To that gospel feast,
That promised land,
That land where all is peace?
Walk into heaven, and take my seat,
And cast down my crown at Jesus' feet.
Deep river, my home is over Jordan,
I want to cross over into camp-ground, Lord!

(Adapted from Tippett, 1944)

EXERCISE _____

Can you identify the ways in which Tippett interleaves the three
different varieties of text identified above into the libretto of *A Child
of Our Time*?

DISCUSSION

The bulk of the libretto is made up of the sections of narrative, although these contain more in the way of expressions of anguish or despair than depictions of events. Numbers 4–7, 10–15, 17–20 and 22–4 fall into this category. The more general, reflective sections open each part of the work (numbers 1–3, 9 and 26–9). There are five spirituals, including the closing number of each part (numbers 8, 16, 21, 25 and 30). Therefore, Part I is split fairly evenly between these varieties of text, while Part II is made up almost entirely of narrative, and Part III of general reflection.

When Tippett began to consider writing an oratorio, he approached the poet T. S. Eliot, with whom he had already discussed music, text-setting and dramatic poetry, and asked him if he would write the libretto. Eliot's response was to ask for an outline of what Tippett required. As Tippett relates,

> I put down on paper for Eliot a 'scenario' under the title 'Sketch for a Modern Oratorio' (the final title for the piece had not then appeared). Eliot considered this sketch for some weeks, and then gave me the surprising advice to write all the words myself. He felt that the sketch was already a text in embryo (as, in fact, it was), and whatever words he, Eliot, wrote would be of such greater *poetic* quality they would 'stick out a mile'. While remaining true to his belief in the primacy of the *musical* imagination in opera and oratorio, he considered the *poetically* imaginative words of a real poet to be often unnecessary.

(Tippett, 1995, p. 111)

While this response was somewhat equivocal, Eliot's point, that in musical text-setting the poetic qualities of the text should not be in competition with the music, is borne out by many examples of highly successful musical settings of minor poets or unimaginative librettists – one thinks for instance of Franz Schubert's settings of **Wilhelm Müller** and **Ludwig Rellstab** in the early nineteenth century.

In any case, Tippett took Eliot's advice and completed the text himself. His style may occasionally suffer from mixed metaphors or pedestrian metre, but it has a directness of expression which is to the advantage of the political message of the work as protest. The text does not have a straightforward narrative structure (as an opera does), nor is it familiar to an audience (as the liturgy is). Clarity of expression is therefore highly important. Tippett scored the work for fairly conventional forces (as far as oratorios are concerned),

Müller's poetry is set in *Die Schöne Müllerin* and *Winterreise*, and Rellstab's in seven of the songs of *Schwanengesang*. Rellstab, a Berlin music critic, also tried to interest Beethoven in writing an opera.

consisting of four soloists (soprano, alto, tenor and bass), chorus and large orchestra. The constant concern for clarity of expression informs Tippett's style in the musical text-setting, particularly in the choral sections, where the melody avoids extremes of virtuosity. An added consideration must also have been the potential performance of the work by amateur choral societies, who formed a highly influential constituency (and indeed market) in British musical life from the mid nineteenth century onwards.

This necessity, of adapting the musical style and structure to accommodate the political force of the text, is something Tippett shared with Shostakovich and Britten. Shostakovich's symphony also has poetry set for chorus and soloist, and here too the vocal lines carrying the text are considerably less florid and virtuosic than in the operatic tradition. Britten utilizes the contrast between liturgical texts and additional, interleaved poetry to tread the line between familiarity and confrontation for his audience. This self-conscious avoidance of any trace of bombast or 'high style', evident in all three of the works considered in this chapter, is essentially bound up with the twentieth-century memorialization of war. Musical celebrations of military victory written in the nineteenth century have no sense of irony in their style – whether one is thinking of the relatively conformist Beethoven's *Wellingtons Sieg*, or the much more socially alienated Tchaikovsky's *1812 Overture*. The contrast between the artistic treatment of war in the two centuries is something that fascinates Paul Fussell in his literary history of the First World War (Fussell, 2000). He describes the watershed between the nineteenth-century and twentieth-century attitudes in his chapter 'A Satire of Circumstance', subtitling a whole section 'Never such innocence again'. Fussell tabulates this '"raised", essentially feudal' language typical of descriptions of war before 1914, contrasting them with the much more prosaic phrasings typical of the war poets and later writers, commenting that 'this system of "high" diction was not the least of the ultimate casualties of the war' (Fussell, 2000, p. 22).

While directness of expression and an aversion to portentous musical rhetoric were perhaps even more evidently prized by Tippett than by Britten and Shostakovich, it must nevertheless be acknowledged that the music of the past was essential to him. There are two musical works which above all provided Tippett with the model for the structure of *A Child of Our Time*, a debt he freely acknowledged in both cases. The first is the *St Matthew Passion* by J. S. Bach (1685–1750). From 1723 to his death in 1750 Bach was employed as *Kantor* – effectively, the civic music director – in Leipzig. Part of his duties was to provide music each week for the city's four main churches, including a setting of the complete Passion narrative from one of the gospels for the Good Friday services. Bach wrote three Passions, but the *St Matthew* (1727) is probably the most celebrated. Tippett wished to find some equivalent to Bach's practice in these works of incorporating Lutheran chorales as points of reflection and repose within the narrative. He admired this incorporation of 'everyday', almost folk-inspired music into the much more cerebral sequence of solo arias and recitatives; the possibility for congregational participation in the chorales also appealed to his socialist outlook. His solution was the five Negro spiritual arrangements. There are also other resemblances between *A Child of Our Time* and the Passions, notably the designation of the bass soloist as the 'narrator' (like Bach's evangelist) in Parts I and II. And there are moments where Tippett's music seems directly to recall the *St Matthew Passion*. In particular, the rhythmic character of the general ensemble which closes Part III (before the final spiritual) resembles that of the opening chorus of Bach's work.

The influence of the other work which Tippett used as a model goes much deeper than the technical procedures that he drew from Bach's Passions. It is difficult for any oratorio with an English text to avoid the legacy of Handel's *Messiah*, undoubtedly the most famous example of the genre ever written. Handel (1685–1759) wrote the work in 1741, originally for performance in Dublin; however, it is part of a sequence of oratorios which he wrote on religious themes for the London public from the mid 1730s onwards. Handel developed this genre because of the church's disapproval of stage drama, and his *Messiah* is untypical in having much less dramatic action in its storyline than works such as *Saul* (1738) or *Samson* (1742). This unusually contemplative character – the work constitutes a musical meditation on the person of Christ, with texts compiled from the Bible – led to initial failure in London, followed by acclaimed performances in the 1750s and continuous success ever after.

Tippett took from Handel's work an aspect which he felt had not previously been explicitly recognized: the overall structuring of the subject matter in the text. Handel's oratorio is divided into three parts, a plan that Tippett followed. In the Handel, the first part sets forth the prophetic background to the appearance of the Messiah; the second part gives the narrative of Christ's incarnation, passion and redemption of the world; and the final part is again more reflective, interpreting the mystery of the drama of salvation. This movement from general to particular, and back again to general, is used in the Tippett so that Part I sets out the sense of foreboding and menace which Tippett felt to be increasingly characteristic of the 1930s; Part II dramatizes the narrative of the 'child of our time', the composite figure based both on Grynspan and on von Horváth's protagonist; and Part III seeks to universalize the message of the oratorio. The opening lines of each part indicate this progression: 'The world turns on its dark side'; 'A star rises in mid-winter'; and 'The cold deepens'. This movement, from an initial statement to a specific narrative and then to reflection, is also a feature of the internal structure of each part. The lines just quoted are each sung by the chorus as an initial evocation of the subject matter of each part. The following solo for alto in Part I is even titled 'The Argument'. There is a repeated sequence of chorus, dramatic exchanges and then Negro spiritual as a point of repose and reflection. The personae of the dramatic exchanges are sometimes indicated in the titles ('Chorus of the Oppressed', 'Double Chorus of Persecutors and Persecuted' and so forth). This sequence is repeated three times in Part II, so that there are five Negro spirituals in the work as a whole.

Although abstract, this echo in the work of what Tippett analysed as the dramatic structure of Handel's *Messiah* is indicative of several issues which recur in all the works discussed here (and frequently elsewhere in music of the twentieth century). One is the straightforward desire to control material, through the use of a formal archetype or a kind of structural ground-plan, justified by reference to either traditional practice or internal logic; both such references are in evidence here. Perhaps more significant, in a piece inescapably bound up with political and social crisis leading to war, is the parody of the Christian drama of salvation which this choice of structure and of model implies. Tippett was quite explicit in linking his work to the experience of conducting a complete performance of *Messiah* in 1931, and Meirion Bowen (Tippett's life partner, biographer and editor) considered that the opening chorus of Part II, which sets the words 'Behold the man! The scape-goat! The child of our time', is modelled on the opening chorus of Part II of *Messiah*, which sets the text 'Behold the lamb of God' (Bowen, 1997, pp. 86–7). (This analysis is followed by Kenneth Gloag – see Gloag, 1999, pp. 47–9.) The similarity of rhythm, texture and melodic shape is indeed telling. This is a typical moment where Tippett simultaneously engages with and distances himself from the past. Handel's text is a prophecy of the birth of Christ, whereas Tippett's 'Behold the man!' is an equally celebrated biblical text ('*ecce homo*'), but recalls Christ's suffering, rejection and crucifixion. The image of the scapegoat is an Old Testament one in biblical terms, and the phrase 'child of our time' perhaps suggests the incarnation (or Christ's own self-identification as 'Son of Man' and his statement 'my time has not yet come'), but the sequence of images does not present a clear, focused narrative, nor does it straightforwardly attempt to subvert the Christian texts it parodies. Rather, the text situates itself (as does the music) within a particular tradition, readily identifiable and known to the anticipated audience; but it both refuses the consummation and fulfilment of the original texts, and places its contemporary concerns (marginalization, suffering and violence) on an equivalent level of significance to the redemption of the whole of humankind. There is an implicit distrust of Christian theology and cosmology, but not an outright rejection. The imagery which has become central to artistic expression in the west is employed, but its signifying value altered. The word 'God' in the line that precedes the final general ensemble in Part III, 'God overpowered him – the child of our time', must be interpreted as naming a social and psychological truth, rather than a metaphysical reality. Such was Tippett's own opinion, at least:

> When the chorus ask: 'What of the boy then, what of him?', they are answered by 'He too is outcast, his manhood broken in the clash of powers. God overpowered him, the child of our time.' This answer is terrible; but the use of the word 'God' is in no way inappropriate. We grope our way towards compassion and understanding, because the shock of the collective tragedy is so great each time any part of the archetypal drama of violence and division is re-enacted.

(Tippett, 1995, p. 184)

Tippett has a complex and self-aware relationship with the history, both of religious belief and of music, that created the oratorio as a form. In particular, he knows himself to be in dialogue with *Messiah*, which more than any other work represents that history. Tippett is not content simply to present his work as one more example of the genre, extending its history into the mid twentieth century. In this respect he is at variance with other artists, such as the Modernist composer Arnold Schoenberg (1874–1951), whose innovations in musical language are directed entirely towards maintaining the viability of the forms he uses (including oratorio in the abandoned *Jakobsleiter*), without compromising artistic integrity or aesthetic truth. Tippett's complex and self-conscious interaction with the text and ideology of *Messiah* is mirrored in the relationship of his musical language with earlier styles. This relationship constitutes an example of what Harold Bloom, writing about literature, terms the 'anxiety of influence' (Bloom, 1973). Handel, whose work is a fundamental point of reference for Tippett, is a father-figure who must be resisted as much as acknowledged. While Tippett does at times come close to direct quotation of *Messiah*, his style is never capable of being mistaken for parody. The complexity of reference, which characterizes both the subject matter of the libretto and the musical language, is foregrounded through the work's self-questioning.

In some respects Tippett's music is notably conservative, by comparison for instance with Schoenberg's: it does not eschew tonality (writing in a key); it relies on a balance of melody and accompaniment not greatly different from eighteenth-century or nineteenth-century choral works; it is presented in a recognizable form. And yet it uses this apparent conservatism in a way which underlines the difference (to use a musical term, the dissonance) between its language and that of the eighteenth century. This dissonance is not simply a mark of the work's sounding 'modern'; it stems from a lack of the certainty and confidence which so recognizably characterize Handel's style. Music of the high baroque (especially that of Handel and J. S. Bach) is always orientated towards clear harmonic goals; it is in this sense deeply teleological. It displays a combination of complexity of surface and lucidity of goal-directedness. It is more than tempting, when talking of religious works such as *Messiah* or Bach's Passions, to equate this with certainty of religious faith; one might equally equate it with an age much more trusting of the transcendence of the human spirit over the natural world. In any case it is this certainty, of musical procedure as much as of religious or Enlightenment idealism, which Tippett's work patently lacks, although his technique of composition makes constant reference to it. Like Stravinsky, Tippett uses an eclectic array of musical reference within his melodic and harmonic material, sometimes approaching collage in his technique. But at every moment the gap is apparent between the Modernist's collection of material and the ideology of the age which furnished that material. One is reminded of a line from *The Waste Land* which T. S. Eliot would certainly have regarded as poetry that would 'stick out a mile' if included in Tippett's text: 'These fragments I have shored against my ruins'.

It is a strangely appropriate fact that the two musical works which are most evident in the background to *A Child of Our Time* are respectively in German and English. While this seems to be no more than coincidence (they are, after all, arguably the most celebrated choral compositions of their age in any case), they are emblematic of the divided Europe which formed the background to Tippett's work. The memory of an integrated society which they bring into the musical language functions perhaps as an indicator of what stands to be lost in the violence and inhumanity chronicled by the soloists and chorus. This in turn raises the question of what forms of identity are presented by the oratorio.

EXERCISE _____

Read again the libretto of *A Child of Our Time*. In what ways does it depict different forms of individual, national and transnational identity?

DISCUSSION _____

I would identify the following three levels.

1   First, the 'child', the protagonist of the narrative sections, especially in Part II, displays an identity which is on the one hand intensely individual, and on the other hand generalized. Some exchanges contain details from the Grynspan story in particular, such as:

> And the boy's mother wrote a letter, saying:
>
> O my son! In the dread terror they have brought me near to death.

At crucial moments, however, Tippett deliberately undercuts the identity of the 'child' as simply victim. He makes use of a Jungian concept, the 'shadow' of the individual personality, a term which names an unconscious identity and which forbids the dissociation of the individual from society. Tippett insists that both persecutor and persecuted are caught in the collective violence, and both share responsibility:

> He goes to authority.
> He is met with hostility.
>
> His other self rises in him, demonic and destructive.
>
> He shoots the official –
>
> But he shoots only his dark brother –
> And see – he is dead.

2   Secondly, it is notable that no particular nation or ethnic grouping is identifiable within the text. The only references to nationhood are negative. The persecuted 'infect the state', and the persecutors 'cannot have them in our Empire'. The oratorio announces itself as rooted in a specific time and place in Part I:

> Europe brooding on a war of starvation ...
>
> When shall the usurers' city cease,
> And famine depart from the fruitful land?

But it is 'Europe' which is afflicted here, not an individual nation. Tippett even carefully avoids specifying the Jews as the persecuted race of the narrative: 'And a time came when in the continual persecution one race stood for all.'

3   Thirdly, Part III presents an ultimately hopeful vision. But this is one which is couched in terms of individual identity, not nationhood. Once again using Jung's symbolism, Tippett suggests that the rediscovery of 'the soul of man', which is personified as female, is the locus of hope:

> Her [the soul's] face will be illumined like the sun.
> Then is the time of his ['man's'] deliverance.

Perhaps surprisingly, Tippett does not conceive the answer to victimization and terror to be located either in resistance or in social action. Rather, the transformation of society through the transformation of the individual is what is needed:

> I would know my shadow and my light,
> so shall I at last be whole.

This utopian impulse is implicitly internationalist. National identities lead only to the 'clash of powers'. As was noted above, the totality of the transformation required is indicated by Tippett's use of the word 'God' to personify the forces that oppose the 'child of our time'.

Tippett's oratorio had to wait three years from its completion until its first performance, in 1944. In the intervening period Tippett served a short term of imprisonment for refusing to serve as a wartime air raid precautions warden. *A Child of Our Time* owed its eventual presentation to the public in great part to Benjamin Britten, who had moved to America before the outbreak of war but returned in 1942 and (with some difficulty) secured exemption from military service as a conscientious objector. Tippett showed him the score of the oratorio in response to being asked what unperformed works he had composed, and Britten effectively arranged both venue and performers for the première; his life partner, Peter Pears, took part as tenor soloist. Both composers felt a personal identification with the figure of the social outcast; in addition to this being a common sentiment for a creative artist in modern European society, their shared anti-war beliefs and their homosexuality contributed to this self-perception. The relative fortunes of the two pacifists, and the role played by the younger man in arranging the première of Tippett's oratorio, are indicative of Britten's easier relationship with the

Figure 4.2 The only known photograph of Tippett and Britten together, at Tippett's 60th birthday party in 1965. Photo: Hulton Archive

Establishment (political and musical), as well as demonstrating the many shared agendas which united the two.

While the inhumanity of war certainly left its mark both directly and indirectly on the music Britten composed at the time (above all the opera *Peter Grimes*), his major work addressing the issues surrounding modern warfare was to wait nearly twenty years after Tippett's composition for its realization.

Benjamin Britten (1913–76): *War Requiem*

In complete contrast to *A Child of Our Time*, Britten's great response to the horrors of total war was from the outset a quasi-Establishment work. In 1958 he was asked to write a piece for the arts festival planned to celebrate the consecration of the new Coventry cathedral. That Britten should have been approached in this way (the festival was organized under the auspices of the Arts Council) indicates his standing at this time as the most prominent figure in British musical life. Coventry cathedral had been almost totally destroyed by bombing in 1940–1, and the entire project of its rebuilding assumed colossal importance as a statement of cultural achievement – a literal and metaphorical rebuilding – following the war. The new building was to stand alongside the ruins of the bombed cathedral, left as a poignant legacy of war; artists perceived as the most significant of the

Figure 4.3 The St Michael's Porch, Coventry cathedral, featuring a bronze sculpture by Jacob Epstein. The porch links the modern building and the ruins of the medieval cathedral. Photo: CV One

time, Graham Sutherland, John Piper and Jacob Epstein among others, were commissioned to contribute to the fabric. Britten's work was to be the centrepiece of the festival marking the cathedral's opening: in effect, it was to be the nation's musical war memorial.

The piece that resulted, *War Requiem*, cannot be dissociated from the event for which it was commissioned. Its première on 30 May 1962 was broadcast and Britten recorded it a few months later, using many of the same performers. For many years this recording was unchallenged in the catalogue, apparently unsurpassable as the authentic interpretation of the work; much more than Tippett's oratorio, *War Requiem* has come to have a permanent cultural value. Even before a note of it had been heard, the critic Alec Robertson wrote in the *Musical Times* that the combination of poetry and liturgy was 'carried through ... with triumphant success; it is Britten's finest work so far' (Robertson, 1962, p. 301). This is in marked contrast to the disquiet about the effectiveness of the Negro spirituals which marked much of the early response to *A Child of Our Time*.

Britten conceived the fundamental outline of the work almost immediately on receiving the commission. Like Tippett, he wanted to utilize the rich store (and long history) of religious imagery in western music and literature, but without accepting its ideology unquestioningly. Indeed in his submission to the local tribunal that

Despite his name, Owen was a genuine 'Shropshire lad', from the English side of the Welsh border region, born in Oswestry and educated in Shrewsbury. (See Johnstone, 1964, p. 167.)

initially refused to exempt him from non-combatant military duties in 1942, Britten stated, 'I do not believe in the divinity of Christ, but I think that his teaching is sound and his example should be followed.' A straightforward setting of the requiem mass would therefore not be sufficient for his purpose, and Britten began very early in the compositional process to seek copyright permission to set poetry by **Wilfred Owen**, the most celebrated English poet of the First World War, interleaved with the Latin liturgical texts.

Owen's poetry has something of the status of a war memorial itself, particularly for someone of pacifist leanings like Britten or Tippett. Its use by Britten in this work marks a significant stage in its gradual incorporation into the canon of English literature. By the end of the 1960s Owen's poems were widely set for examination in school literature syllabuses, and had in their way become as much a part of the paraphernalia of war remembrance in Britain as the overtly militaristic rituals of Remembrance Day. It is hardly surprising that both Tippett's oratorio and Britten's *Requiem* draw on Owen's poetry as part of their protest against mechanized, total war. As Ian Kemp writes (see Kemp, 1987, p. 153), Tippett told T. S. Eliot that the lines which open *A Child of Our Time*,

> The world turns on its dark side.
> It is winter

are an echo of Owen's poem, *The Seed*:

> War broke. And now the winter of the world
> With perishing great darkness closes in.

The importance of the experience of the First World War to the memorialization of the second war is another subject explored by Fussell. Discussing Thomas Pynchon's novel *Gravity's Rainbow*, he comments, 'The presence of Brigadier Pudding in the novel proposes the Great War as the ultimate origin of the insane contemporary scene. It is where the irony and the absurdity began' (Fussell, 2000, p. 329).

I should like you now to read through the texts that make up *War Requiem*, reproduced below.

War Requiem

I Requiem aeternam

CHORUS

Requiem aeternam dona eis Domine,
et lux perpetua luceat eis.

Rest eternal grant them, Lord;
and may everlasting light shine upon them.

BOYS' CHOIR

Te decet hymnus, Deus in Sion;
et tibi reddetur votum in Jerusalem;
exaudi orationem meam,
ad te omnis caro veniet.

Songs of praise are due to Thee, God, in Zion;
and prayers offered up to Thee in Jerusalem;
hear my prayer,
all flesh shall come to Thee.

TENOR SOLO

What passing-bells for these who die as cattle?
Only the monstrous anger of the guns.
Only the stuttering rifles' rapid rattle
Can patter out their hasty orisons.
No mockeries for them from prayers or bells,
Nor any voice of mourning save the choirs, –
The shrill, demented choirs of wailing shells;
And bugles calling for them from sad shires.

What candles may be held to speed them all?
Not in the hands of boys, but in their eyes
Shall shine the holy glimmers of good-byes.
The pallor of girls' brows shall be their pall;
Their flowers the tenderness of silent minds,
And each slow dusk a drawing-down of blinds.

['Anthem for Doomed Youth']

CHORUS

Kyrie eleison,
Christe eleison,
Kyrie eleison.

Lord have mercy,
Christ have mercy,
Lord have mercy.

II Dies irae

CHORUS

Dies irae, dies illa,	Day of anger, that day,
Solvet saeclum in favilla,	Shall dissolve this generation into ashes,
Teste David cum Sibylla.	With David and the Sibyl as witness.
Quantus tremor est futurus,	How much quaking there will be,
Quando Judex est venturus,	When the Judge will come,
Cuncta stricte discussurus!	To weigh all things strictly.
Tuba mirum spargens sonum	The trumpet pouring forth its awful sound
Per sepulchra regionum	Through the tombs of the lands
Coget omnes ante thronum.	Drives everyone before the throne.
Mors stupebit et natura,	Death shall be stunned, and nature,
Cum resurget creatura,	When life shall rise again,
Judicanti responsura.	To answer for itself before the Judge.

BARITONE SOLO

Bugles sang, saddening the evening air,
And bugles answered, sorrowful to hear.

Voices of boys were by the river-side.
Sleep mothered them; and left the twilight sad.
The shadow of the morrow weighed on men.

Voices of old despondency resigned,
Bowed by the shadow of the morrow, slept.

[untitled]

SOPRANO SOLO AND CHORUS

Liber scriptus proferetur,	A book inscribed shall be brought forth,
In quo totum continetur,	In which all is contained,
Unde mundus judicetur.	From which the world shall be judged.
Judex ergo cum sedebit,	When the Judge, therefore, shall sit,
Quidquid latet, apparebit:	Whatever is concealed shall appear:
Nil inultum remanebit.	Nothing unavenged shall remain.
Quid sum miser tunc dicturus?	What am I, a wretch, to say then?
Quem patronum rogaturus,	To whom as defender shall I entreat,
Cum vix justus sit securus?	Since the just man is scarcely safe?
Rex tremendae majestatis,	King of fearful majesty,
Qui salvandos salvas gratis,	Who freely savest those who are to be saved,
Salva me, fans pietatis.	Save me, fountain of compassion.

TENOR AND BARITONE SOLOS

Out there, we've walked quite friendly up to Death;
Sat down and eaten with him, cool and bland, –
Pardoned his spilling mess-tins in our hand.
We've sniffed the green thick odour of his breath, –
Our eyes wept, but our courage didn't writhe.
He's spat at us with bullets and he's coughed
Shrapnel. We chorused when he sang aloft;
We whistled while he shaved us with his scythe.

Oh, Death was never enemy of ours!
We laughed at him, we leagued with him, old chum.
No soldier's paid to kick against his powers.
We laughed, knowing that better men would come,
And greater wars; when each proud fighter brags
He wars on Death – for life; not men – for flags.

['The Next War']

CHORUS

Recordare Jesu pie,	Recall, kind Jesus,
Quod sum causa tuae viae:	That I am the reason for your being:
Ne me perdas illa die.	Lest Thou do away with me on that day.
Quaerens me, sedisti lassus:	Searching for me, Thou didst sit exhausted:
Redemisti crucem passus:	Thou hast redeemed me by suffering the cross:
Tantus labor non sit cassus.	So much toil should not be in vain.
Ingemisco, tamquam reus:	I sigh, so great a sinner:
Culpa rubet vultus meus:	Guilt reddens my face:
Supplicanti parce Deus.	Spare the supplicant, God.
Qui Mariam absolvisti,	Thou who hast forgiven Mary,
Et latronem exaudisti,	And hast listened to the robber,
Mihi quoque spem dedisti.	And hast also given hope to me.
Inter oves locum praesta,	Set me down amongst the sheep,
Et ab haedis me sequestra,	And remove me from the goats,
Statuens in parte dextra.	Standing at Thy right hand.
Confutatis maledictis,	With the damned confounded,
Flammis acribus addictis,	To the crackling flames consigned,
Voca me cum benedictis.	Call me with your saints.
Oro supplex et acclinis,	I pray, kneeling and suppliant,
Cor contritum quasi cinis:	My heart worn away like ashes:
Gere curam mei finis.	Protect me at my ending.

BARITONE SOLO

Be slowly lifted up, thou long black arm,
Great gun towering toward Heaven, about to curse;

Reach at that arrogance which needs thy harm,
And beat it down before its sins grow worse;

But when thy spell be cast complete and whole,
May God curse thee, and cut thee from our soul!

[from 'Sonnet: On Seeing a Piece of Our Artillery Brought into Action']

CHORUS AND SOPRANO SOLO

Dies irae, dies illa,
Solvet saeclum in favilla,
Teste David cum Sibylla.

Day of anger, that day,
Shall dissolve this generation into ashes,
With David and the Sibyl as witness.

Quantus tremor est futurus,
Quando judex est venturus,
Cuncta stricte discussurus!

How much quaking there will be,
When the Judge will come,
To weigh all things strictly.

Lacrimosa dies illa,
Qua resurget ex favilla,
Judicandus homo reus,
Huic ergo parce Deus.

That tearful day,
On which shall arise again from the ashes,
The sinner to be judged,
Spare him accordingly, God.

TENOR SOLO

Move him into the sun –
Gently its touch awoke him once,
At home, whispering of fields unsown.
Always it woke him, even in France,
Until this morning and this snow.
If anything might rouse him now
The kind old sun will know.

Think how it wakes the seeds, –
Woke, once, the clays of a cold star.
Are limbs, so dear-achieved, are sides,
Full-nerved – still warm – too hard to stir?
Was it for this the clay grew tall?
– O what made fatuous sunbeams toil
To break earth's sleep at all?

['Futility']

CHORUS

Pie Jesu Domine,
dona eis requiem.
Amen.

Kind Jesus, Lord,
grant them rest.
Amen.

III Offertorium

BOYS' CHOIR

Domine Jesu Christe,
Rex gloriae,
libera animas omnium fidelium
defunctorum de poenis inferni,
et de profondo lacu:
libera eas de ore leonis,
ne absorbeat eas tartarus,
ne cadant in obscurum.

Lord Jesus Christ,
King of glory,
free the souls of all the faithful
dead from the tortures of hell,
and from the bottomless pit:
free them from the mouth of the lion,
that hell may not swallow them up,
nor may they fall into darkness.

CHORUS

Sed signifer sanctus Michael
repraesentet eas in lucem sanctam:
quam olim Abrahae promisisti,
et semini ejus.

But the holy standard-bearer Michael
shall bring them back into the holy light:
as Thou once didst promise to Abraham,
and his offspring.

BARITONE AND TENOR SOLOS

So Abram rose, and clave the wood, and went,
And took the fire with him, and a knife.
And as they sojourned both of them together,
Isaac the first-born spake and said, My Father,
Behold the preparations, fire and iron,
But where the lamb for this burnt-offering?
Then Abram bound the youth with belts and straps,
And builded parapets and trenches there,

And stretchèd forth the knife to slay his son.
When lo! an angel called him out of heaven,
Saying, Lay not thy hand upon the lad,
Neither do anything to him. Behold,
A ram, caught in a thicket by its horns;
Offer the Ram of Pride instead of him.
But the old man would not so, but slew his son, –
And half the seed of Europe, one by one.

['The Parable of the Old Man and the Young']

BOYS' CHOIR

Hostias et preces	Sacrifices and prayers
tibi Domine laudis offerimus:	we offer to Thee, Lord, with praise:
tu suscipe pro animabus illis,	receive them for the souls of those
quarum hodie memoriam facimus:	whose memory we recall today:
fac eas, Domine,	make them, Lord,
de morte transire ad vitam.	to pass from death to life.

IV Sanctus

SOPRANO SOLO AND CHORUS

Sanctus, sanctus, sanctus	Holy, holy, holy
Dominus Deus Sabaoth.	Lord God of Hosts.
Pleni sunt coeli et terra gloria tua,	Full are heaven and earth with Thy glory.
Hosanna in excelsis.	Hosanna in the highest.
Benedictus qui venit in nomine Domini.	Blessed is he who comes in the name of the Lord.
Hosanna in excelsis.	Hosanna in the highest.

BARITONE SOLO

After the blast of lightning from the East,
The flourish of loud clouds, the Chariot Throne;
After the drums of Time have rolled and ceased,
And by the bronze west long retreat is blown,

Shall life renew these bodies? Of a truth
All death will He annul, all tears assuage? –
Fill the void veins of Life again with youth,
And wash, with an immortal water, Age?

When I do ask white Age he saith not so:
'My head hangs weighed with snow.'
And when I hearken to the Earth, she saith:
'My fiery heart shrinks, aching. It is death.
Mine ancient scars shall not be glorified,
Nor my titanic tears, the sea, be dried.'

['The End']

V Agnus Dei

TENOR SOLO

One ever hangs where shelled roads part.
In this war He too lost a limb,
But His disciples hide apart;
And now the Soldiers bear with Him.

CHORUS

Agnus Dei,   Lamb of God,
qui tollis peccata mundi,   who takest away the sins of the world,
dona eis requiem.   grant them rest.

TENOR SOLO

Near Golgotha strolls many a priest,
And in their faces there is pride
That they were flesh-marked by the Beast
By whom the gentle Christ's denied.

CHORUS

Agnus Dei,   Lamb of God,
qui tollis peccata mundi,   who takest away the sins of the world,
dona eis requiem.   grant them rest.

TENOR SOLO

The scribes on all the people shove
And bawl allegiance to the state,
But they who love the greater love
Lay down their life; they do not hate.

['At a Calvary near the Ancre']

CHORUS

Agnus Dei,   Lamb of God,
qui tollis peccata mundi,   who takest away the sins of the world,
dona eis requiem sempiternam. grant them rest everlasting.

TENOR SOLO

Dona nobis pacem.   Grant us peace.

VI Libera me

CHORUS AND SOPRANO SOLO

Libera me, Domine, de morte aeterna,
in die illa tremenda:
Quando coeli movendi sunt et terra:
Dum veneris judicare
saeculum per ignem.
Tremens factus sum ego, et timeo,
dum discussio venerit,
atque ventura ira.
Libera me, Domine, de morte aeterna,
Quando coeli movendi sunt et terra.
Dies illa, dies irae,
calamitatis et miseriae,
dies magna et amara valde.
Libera me, Domine …

Free me, Lord, from eternal death,
on that dreadful day.
When the skies and ground shall quake:
When Thou comest to judge
our generation through fire.
I am made to tremble, and am afraid,
until the trial shall come,
and the anger arrive.
Free me, Lord, from eternal death,
When the skies and ground shall quake.
That day, day of anger,
of disaster and misery,
a great day and intensely bitter.
Free me, Lord …

TENOR SOLO

It seemed that out of battle I escaped
Down some profound dull tunnel, long since scooped
Through granites which titanic wars had groined.
Yet also there encumbered sleepers groaned,
Too fast in thought or death to be bestirred.
Then, as I probed them, one sprang up, and stared
With piteous recognition in fixed eyes,
Lifting distressful hands as if to bless.
And no guns thumped, or down the flues made moan.
'Strange friend,' I said, 'here is no cause to mourn.'

BARITONE SOLO

'None,' said the other, 'save the undone years,
The hopelessness. Whatever hope is yours,
Was my life also; I went hunting wild
After the wildest beauty in the world.

For by my glee might many men have laughed,
And of my weeping something had been left,
Which must die now. I mean the truth untold,

The pity of war, the pity war distilled.
Now men will go content with what we spoiled.
Or, discontent, boil bloody, and be spilled.
They will be swift with swiftness of the tigress,
None will break ranks, though nations trek from progress.
Miss we the march of this retreating world
Into vain citadels that are not walled.
Then, when much blood had clogged their chariot-wheels,
I would go up and wash them from sweet wells,
Even from wells we sunk too deep for war,
Even the sweetest wells that ever were.

I am the enemy you killed, my friend.
I knew you in this dark; for so you frowned
Yesterday through me as you jabbed and killed.
I parried; but my hands were loath and cold.'

TENOR AND BARITONE SOLOS

'Let us sleep now ...'

['Strange Meeting']

BOYS' CHOIR, CHORUS AND SOPRANO SOLO

In paradisum deducant te Angeli:	To heaven may the Angels escort you:
in tuo adventu suscipiant te Martyres,	on your arrival may the Martyrs accept you,
et perducant te	and lead you
in civitatem sanctam Jerusalem.	to the sacred city Jerusalem.
Chorus Angelorum te suscipiat,	May the Choir of Angels receive you,
et cum Lazaro quondam paupere	and with Lazarus, once a pauper,
aeternam habeas requiem.	may you have rest eternal.
Requiem aeternam dona eis, Domine;	Rest eternal grant them, Lord,
et lux perpetua luceat eis.	and may everlasting light shine upon them.
Requiescant in pace.	May they rest in peace.
Amen.	Amen.

(Reproduced in Cooke, 1996, pp. 92–100)

EXERCISE _____

Can you identify the 'counterpoint' created by Britten between Owen's poetry and the words of the *Requiem* liturgy?

DISCUSSION _____

While Britten has not altered either the texts of the poems or the text of the liturgy in any way, there are continual points of contact between them which are brought out by placing them together. For instance, the opening prayer, 'Rest eternal grant them, Lord' immediately finds a specific resonance in the first line of poetry set, 'What passing-bells for these who die as cattle?'. Or again, the anger contained in the final line of another poem, 'May God curse thee, and cut thee from our soul!', leads into the setting of the *Dies irae*. There are, additionally, sections where Britten interleaves a poem with a liturgical text, as where the religious references and imagery of Owen's 'At a Calvary near the Ancre' are combined with the *Agnus Dei*.

_____

Given Britten's role in arranging the première of *A Child of Our Time*, it seems likely that Tippett's work was a direct model for him in designing *War Requiem*. The differences are extremely significant, however. Britten's task in assembling the text was one of selection and juxtaposition, and the familiarity of all the words he set precluded the accusations of excessive didacticism which characterized some of the early responses to the Tippett. While Britten clearly has just as deeply felt and politically charged a message to communicate, he relies upon the positioning of the different elements within his text, and the interaction of his musical setting with the meaning of the words, to make his points. His forces are even larger than those of *A Child of Our Time*, comprising two choruses (one of boys), three soloists (soprano, tenor and bass) and a chamber orchestra in addition to the main symphony orchestra. The chamber ensemble is used to accompany the Owen poems, which are sung by the male soloists. The two sorts of text-setting combined in the libretto are therefore set against each other musically, dramatizing this large-scale dialogue. This distribution of forces took into account the physical layout of the new building for which the work was written, as letters from Britten to John Lowe, a member of the festival committee, make clear:

> I am all in favour of as big a chorus as possible, without passengers ... The orchestra will be big, however, as I am planning for certainly triple woodwind and a nice assortment of brass for the 'Tuba Mirum' (possibly as many as fourteen).

> Then there is the chamber orchestra to make room for, and I think the best position would be immediately in front of the conductor with the two male soloists. The boys, however, I would like to have placed at a distance; they perform throughout only with the organ, so it would be good if they were near the organ console.
>
> (Letter of 12 May 1961, quoted in Cooke, 1996, p. 24)

The various ways in which these forces can be made to interact are explored throughout the work with constant inventiveness. One of the most striking moments, and indeed one which carries astonishing emotional charge, is the very first entry of Owen's poetry. The opening setting of 'Requiem aeternam' is hesitant, predominantly staccato, intoning statements of the words on single notes to the accompaniment of bells. The ethereal texture of the boys' choir interrupts this with the 'Te decet hymnus', but the opening pleas for eternal rest are far from restful, with the musical accompaniment constantly suggesting the sounds of battle through musical devices familiar from military music, and indeed film. The slowly pulsating, dissonant orchestral accompaniment leads without a break into the chamber orchestra's accompaniment for 'Anthem for Doomed Youth', sung by the tenor soloist. The two notes played by the bells throughout the first section, which also dominate the lines sung by the chorus, are taken up as a tremolando on the harp, giving tremendously powerful, bitter irony to the line 'What passing bells for these who die as cattle?' Owen's poem goes on to list a sequence of religious images: orisons, prayers and candles in addition to bells. The (implicitly political) message is created through the combination of elements: the musical language of the opening, which sounds most non-devotional for liturgical text-setting; the provocative choice of words for the tenor's first entry; and the sudden switch to much faster-paced accompaniment when the chamber orchestra enters, full of musical word-painting (including, for instance, memorable imitation of 'The shrill, demented choirs of wailing shells' by the flute and clarinet). As Mervyn Cooke comments, the effect is 'quite out of proportion to the simplicity of the means employed' (my comments here draw on the detailed discussion in Cooke, 1996, pp. 61–2).

While Britten's work is just as firmly placed within a continuing genre of composition as Tippett's, Britten was much more reticent than Tippett about the specific works which he looked to as models for aspects of *War Requiem*. There may have been no individual work providing inspiration for method in the way that the *St Matthew Passion* did for *A Child of Our Time*, nor an equivalent father-figure to Handel, with whose ghost Tippett struggles; but there are many echoes in *War Requiem* of celebrated requiem settings of the past. The most obvious example is the 1874 *Missa di Requiem* by Guiseppe Verdi (1813–1901). Comparisons with Verdi featured in early reviews, and Britten's somewhat grudging recognition of his indebtedness in a 1969 interview may betray a certain irritation with the often-made comparison:

> I think that I would be a fool if I didn't take notice of how Mozart, Verdi, Dvorak – whoever you like to name – had written their Masses. I mean, many people have pointed out the similarities between the Verdi *Requiem* and bits of my own *War Requiem*, and they may be there.

> (Mitchell, 1984, p. 90)

Although all three requiem settings mentioned by Britten are audible as influences in the work, Verdi casts by far the longest shadow. Similarities in various places include the rhythms of certain melodic lines and the keys of the harmony. Perhaps the most important debt to Verdi, though, is more general, and that is Britten's unashamed use of techniques associated with operatic text-setting to create extremes of expression in the setting of the liturgical text as well as the Owen poems. The curious, halting, monotonal statements by the chorus at the very opening are highly reminiscent of Verdi's treatment of the words 'requiem aeternam', and Verdi himself was criticized for his apparent lack of devotional intent. The description of Verdi's *Requiem* as his 'greatest opera' has become something of a cliché; but his example in extracting every dramatic possibility from the words so easily rendered impotent through their familiarity is turned to spectacular benefit by Britten. There are recurrent images in the poems chosen by Britten which he exploits throughout the work for their poignancy and drama: bells and bugles in particular, and the description of soldiers as 'boys'. The 'Tuba mirum' to which Britten alludes in the letter quoted above has certainly been influenced by Verdi's mastery of spectacular sound effects; but it also shades without any discontinuity into the contrast to the trumpets summoning the dead to judgement, the bugles summoning 'boys' to their deaths:

> Bugles sang, saddening the evening air
> And bugles answered, sorrowful to hear.

Britten's reference to Verdi in *War Requiem* is unlike Tippett's encounter with Handel and Bach in some crucial respects. It does not legitimate the use of the liturgical form by recalling a language of unquestioning acceptance, indeed celebration, of Christian ideology. Quite the reverse, in fact: Verdi was most adept at dramatizing the references to terror, wrath and so forth in the text. But one observation remains valid for both Britten and Tippett's works: *War Requiem* is self-conscious of its place in the tradition of western art

135

music, and it bears the signs of its ancestry in its use of musical language.

It is not possible here to talk in any detail about Britten's musical style, which is complex and subtle in any case. However, some general points about the way in which he handles harmony have implications for the nature of the work as cultural protest against and memorialization of war. Throughout, Britten uses a pair of individual notes as a constantly recurring point of harmonic reference. This interval, always appearing at the same pitch though in the context of many different keys, is used to disrupt and complicate the nature of the tonal writing around it. The notes in question are C natural and F sharp, which together form a 'tritone'. This is the most dissonant interval in traditional western harmony, the use of which was regarded in the medieval period as always incorrect: it was termed *diabolus in musica*. These notes are the ones on which the chorus first enters (the sopranos and tenors sing 'Requiem aeternam' on F sharps, and the basses and altos repeat the words on C naturals), and they are heard on the bells throughout the opening section. They recur in countless different contexts through the whole of the rest of the work, often subverting the sense of a key, in places where either C natural or F sharp is a note not contained in the key signature. At the very end, the tritone is still being sounded repeatedly on the bells, and F sharp is the focus of the melody for 'Requiescant in pace', until the final 'Amen' eventually resolves this tension in the harmony by cadencing on to an ineffably serene F major chord.

The role of these two repeated notes in Britten's harmony has been much discussed by music analysts ever since the work's première. The 'tritone' is the most unstable of all intervals, and yet it is used constantly by Britten, without being developed or incorporated into harmonic progressions, as if it were paradoxically a stable point of reference. One of the most perceptive comments encapsulating Britten's approach to harmony is also one of the very earliest, made by the musicologist Arnold Whittall:

> It has long been obvious that Britten's use of tonality is closely connected with his involvement in the state of society today. The *War Requiem* represents in many ways his most 'involved' statement, and it is therefore to be expected that the style of the work will reflect the composer's sense of acute instability as well as his hatred of suffering and his hopes for peace. In the work tonalities are perpetually collapsing, harmonic resolutions are continually postponed, and the rare moments of unambiguous diatonicism tend to represent fear or grief rather than repose.
>
> (Whittall, 1963, p. 201)

There is a subtle difference in the social critique that implicitly informs *War Requiem* compared with *A Child of Our Time*. Where Tippett's eventual consolation and utopian vision remain rather nebulous, located in the possible transformation of the individual, Britten offers a hope of eventual peace that involves a vision of society. He chooses, for the final Owen setting, the poem 'Strange Meeting', in which two soldiers meet after death and are, in a sense, reconciled. They recognize that 'the march of this retreating world' will continue despite their deaths, and the poem ends with the phrase 'Let us sleep now', which Britten then alternates after 'Requiescant in pace' at the close of the work.

Reconciliation, rather than transformation, is therefore at the centre of Britten's message. This is one way in which this is a postwar, rather than a wartime work. Tippett withdraws in horror from the 'terror' that was still rampant in Europe when *A Child of Our Time* was first performed; Britten is addressing a point in time when society was still in existence after the closure of the conflict, but when the Cold War rendered reconciliation a goal of continuing urgency. Once again, this aspect of the piece cannot be separated from the occasion of its first performance. Britten had two of the soloists in mind while writing the work: the tenor Peter Pears (whose voice is, thanks to recordings, forever identified with Britten's music), and the baritone Dietrich Fischer-Dieskau. For the soprano soloist he wished to engage the Russian singer Galina Vishnevskaya, in order to have soloists representing the three major European parties in the Second World War conflict. It is one of the most famous ironies of cultural politics in the Cold War that the Soviet authorities recalled Vishnevskaya to Moscow, preventing her from travelling to Coventry for the première (her part was taken at very short notice by an English singer, Heather Harper). The sticking point was initially assumed to be the religious character of the occasion; but it seems in fact to have been the multinational cast of soloists itself which her authorities found unacceptable (Cooke, 1996, pp. 26–7). Vishnevskaya was, however, allowed to participate in the recording of the work in January 1963, ensuring the permanency of the symbolism sought by Britten (although Harper's interpretation of the part was widely preferred by critics).

While Tippett's own recording of *A Child of Our Time* is an affectionate retrospective performance, dating from 1992, thanks to Britten's apparently definitive cast of performers *War Requiem* is arguably an event rather than a work, despite its many performances over the years. This is perhaps the most striking example of a recording participating in creating the identity of a musical art object. It was this original recording, inevitably, that was used by the film director Derek Jarman when he created his 1988 film *War Requiem*, in

Figures 4.4 and 4.5 Two scenes from Derek Jarman's film *War Requiem* (1988). These show the range of imagery distinctive of the film: on the one hand, historical documentary rooted in the First World War which produced Owen's poetry; and on the other, a more symbolic interpretation of Britten's music. Figure 4.4 shows the scene that accompanies the setting of the untitled poem 'Bugles sang, saddening the evening air', in the *Dies irae* section of *War Requiem*. Owen is seen writing the poem, with the Unknown Soldier looking over his shoulder and the men under his command washing in the evening light in the trench behind him, before falling asleep exhausted. Figure 4.5 shows the scene that accompanies 'The Parable of the Old Man and the Young', from the *Offertorium*. This poem is interpreted in the film as a melodrama, with Abraham played by a Victorian bishop, and Isaac by Wilfred Owen. The bishop is seen elevating the sacrament in front of an altar built in the rubble of a trench, before adminstering it to Wilfred, binding him and killing him with a cut-throat razor, in a symbolic re-enactment of Owen's death in 1918. Photos: Ronald Grant Archive

which a loose narrative set in the First World War is complemented by footage from more recent conflicts – the Second World War, Vietnam, Angola and others. The textured history of the work, in which both world wars and the Cold War are inscribed, is thus used to suggest a general, universalizing potential for the protest nature of the work.

It is worth building on Fussell's observation, quoted earlier, of resonances between periods of conflict in the twentieth century (Fussell, 2000, pp. 310–35). Just as the poetry written in the First World War becomes essential to the articulation of the remembrance of the second war, so Britten's music cannot be considered autonomously of the changes wrought in Europe by the Cold War. This is perhaps even more true, however, of our third example of war-inspired music, written by a composer who did not have the comforting experience of physical or temporal distance from the events which led to its creation.

Dmitri Shostakovich (1906–75): Symphony no. 13, 'Babi Yar'

The history of Shostakovich's relations with the Soviet authorities is, to say the least, chequered. He was given public and civic honours and described as 'composer laureate of the Soviet State', but at other times he was publicly condemned and performances of his works were banned. By 1962, however, he had achieved such a profile internationally as a composer that official disapprobation of his works no longer extended to sanctions against him as an individual. It was at this date, however, that he wrote his most explicit piece of anti-war music, which also amounts to a protest against the Soviet system itself, as a betrayal of the Russian people: his Thirteenth Symphony, subtitled 'Babi Yar' after the poem set in its first movement.

Shostakovich's Seventh Symphony, the 'Leningrad', was the work written in wartime which responded most explicitly to the war itself. It was, however, described by the composer as a depiction of events, rather than a document of protest. Indeed it understandably focuses on the heroism of the Russian people of the city of Shostakovich's birth in resisting the siege by Hitler's forces in 1941. The Eleventh and Twelfth Symphonies are both concerned with the twentieth-century history of Russia. The Eleventh is subtitled 'The Year 1905', and is a portrait of pre-Soviet Russia at the time of the unsuccessful revolts in St Petersburg and Sevastopol. The Twelfth, subtitled '1917', depicts the October Revolution itself. The Twelfth Symphony, in particular, comes close to being a work of straightforward political propaganda, described by one critic as 'for me (and, I believe, many

Figure 4.6 Jews leaving Kiev. Local Jews were ordered by the German military to assemble at 6 p.m. on 29 September 1941 for 'relocation'. An official report states that 33,771 Jews were then executed at the Babi Yar ravine. Photo: Hessisches, Hauptstaatsarchiv, Wiesbaden

others) the most disappointing of Shostakovich's symphonies' (MacDonald, 1982, p. 126). The Thirteenth Symphony, which carries the next opus number to the Twelfth, appears to complete a triptych of works portraying different phases of Russia's twentieth-century society, dealing as it does with post-Stalinist conditions. But it is a very different kind of work in many ways. Principally, its message is both much less officially acceptable and much more explicitly stated, since the entire work consists of poems by Yevgeny Yevtushenko set for bass soloist and chorus in addition to the symphony orchestra.

Yevtushenko, a younger man than Shostakovich (he was born in 1933), was another artist whose international reputation afforded him some protection from official sanction. His poem 'Babi Yar' was even published in the official newspaper *Pravda*. Its publication gave Shostakovich the impulse to begin the composition of his symphony, which eventually included four other Yevtushenko poems. You should now read through the five of his poems set by Shostakovich, which are reprinted below.

Symphony no. 13 ('Babi Yar')

I. BABI YAR (Adagio)

CHORUS

Nad Babim Yarom pamyatnikov nyet.
Krutol obriv, kak gruboye nadgrobye.
Mne strashno.
Mne sevodnya stol'ko let,
kak samomu yevreiskomu narodu.

SOLO

Mne kazhetsya seichas – ya iudei.
Vot ya bredu po drevnemu Yegiptu.
I vot ya, na kreste raspyati, gibnu,
i do sikh por na mne – sledi gvozdei.
Mne kazhetsya, chto Dreyfus – eto ya.
Meshchanstvo – moi donoschik i sud'ya.

Ya za reshotkoi. Ya popal v kol'tzo,
zatravlenni, opliovanni, obolganni;
i damochki s bryussel's kimi oborkami,
vizzha, zontami tychut mne v litzo.

Mne kazhetsya – ya mal'chik v Belostoke.

Above Babi Yar there are no monuments.
The steep cliff is like a crude tombstone.
I'm frightened.
Today I am as old
as the Jewish people.

It seems to me now that I am a Jew.
Now I am wandering through ancient Egypt.
And now I am on a cross, crucified, dying,
and to this moment I show traces of the nails.
It seems to me that Dreyfus – I am he.
The Philistines are my informers and my judges.
I am behind bars. I have fallen into a circle,
poisoned, spat upon, lied about;
and fancy ladies, dressed in Brussels lace,
squealing, jab me in the face with their parasols.
It seems to me I am a youth in Belostok.

CHORUS

Krov liotsya, rastekayas' po polam.
Beschinstvuyut vozhdi traktirnoi stoiki.
i pakhnut vodkoi s lukom popolam.

Blood is pouring, spilling over the floors.
The saloon barkeeps commit their outrages
and smell of vodka and onions, half and half.

SOLO

Ya, sapogom otbroshenni, bessilen.
Naprasno ya pogromshchikov molyu.

Kicked aside by a boot, I am helpless.
In vain I beg the pogromists.

CHORUS

Pod gogot, 'Bei zhidov, spasai Rossiu!'
labaznik izbivayet mat'moyu.

To the cackle, 'Beat the kikes, save Russia!'
a grain marketeer beats up my mother.

SOLO

O russki moi narod! Ya znayu ti
po sushchnosti internatzionalen.
No chasto te, ch'i ruki nechisty,
tvoim chisteishim imenem bryatzali.
Ya znayu dobrotu moei zemli.
Kak podlo, chto i zhilochkoi ne drognuv,
antisemity narekli sebya

O my Russian people! I know that
in essence you are international.
But often those whose hands were unclean
tarnished your clean name.
I know the kindness of my land.
How vile that, without a flicker of a vein,
the anti-Semites proclaimed themselves

(with Chorus)

'Soyuzom russkovo naroda!'

'The Union of the Russian People!'

SOLO

Mne kazhetsya – ya – eto Anna Frank,
prozrachnaya, kak vetochka v aprele.
I ya lyublyu. I mne ne nado fraz.
Mne nado, chtob drug v druga my smotreli.
Kak malo mozhno videt', obonyat'!
Nel'zya nam list'ev
i nel'zya nam neba,
no mozhno ochen' mnogo – eto nezhno
drug druga v tiomnoi komnate obnyat'.

It seems to me I am Anne Frank,
transparent as a branch in April.
And I love. And I have no need for phrases.
But I need for us to gaze into each other.
There is so little one can see or smell!
We cannot have the leaves,
and we cannot have the sky,
but much is allowed – to embrace
one another in a dark room.

CHORUS

Syuda idut?

Are they coming here?

SOLO

Ne boisya, eto guly samoi vesny –
ona syuda idiot.
Idi ko mne. Dai mne skoreye guby.

Don't fear, those are the roars of spring –
it is coming here.
Come to me. Quickly, give me your lips.

CHORUS

Lomayut dver'?

Are they battering down the door?

SOLO

Nyet – eto ledokhod ...

No – it is the breaking up of the ice ...

CHORUS

Nad Babim Yarom shelest dikikh trav.
Derevya smotryat grozno, po-sudeiski.

Vsio molcha zdes' kritchit,
i, shapku snayav,
ya chuvstvuyu, kak medlenno sedeyu.

SOLO

I sam ya, kak sploshnoi bezzvuchni krik,
nad tysyachami tysyach pogrebionnikh.
Ya – kazhdi zdes' rasstrelyanni starik.

Ya – kazhdi zdes' rasstrelyanni rebionok.

Nichto vo mne pro eto ne zabudet!

CHORUS

'Internatzional!' pust' progremit,
kogda naveki pokhoronen budet
poslendi na zemle antisemit.

SOLO

Yevreiskoi krovi net v krovi moei.
No nenavisten zloboi zaskoruzloi
ya vsem antisemitam, kak yevrei.

(with Chorus)

I potomu, ya nastoyashchi russki!

Above Babi Yar the rustle of wild grass.
The trees gaze sternly, as though they are judges.
Everything here cries out silently,
and, having removed my cap,
I feel how bit by bit I am turning gray.

And I am like a gigantic silent scream,
above the thousands upon thousands buried.
I am each old man who has been shot dead here.
I am each small child who has been shot dead here.
Nothing in me will forget about this!

Let the 'Internationale' thunder forth,
when for the ages is buried
the last anti-Semite on earth.

There is no Jewish blood in my blood.
But I am hated with a bitterness
by all anti-Semites, as if I were a Jew.

For this reason, I am a true Russian!

II. HUMOR (Allegretto)

SOLO

Tzari, koroli, imperatory –
vlastiteli vsei zemli –
komandovali paradami.
No yumorom, no yumorom ne mogli,
ne mogli.
V dvortsy imenitykh osob,
vse dni vozlezhashchikh vykholenno,
yavlyalsa brodyaga Ezop,
i nishchimi oni vyglyadeli.

CHORUS

Yavlyalsa brodyaga Ezop,
i nishchimi oni vyglyadeli.

Czars, kings, emperors –
rulers of all the earth –
commanded parades.
But humor, humor they could not.

In the palaces of the wealthy people,
where daily they reclined at ease,
appeared the beggar Aesop,
and impoverished they appeared.

Appeared the beggar Aesop,
and impoverished they appeared.

SOLO

V domakh gde khanzha nasledil	In homes soiled by hypocrites
svoimi nogami shchuplymi,	with their puny feet,
vsyu poshlost' Khadzha Nasr-ed-Din	Hadji Nasr-ed-Din swept away this vulgarity
sshibal kak shakhmaty shutkami!	like clearing a chessboard – with jokes!

CHORUS

Vsyu poshlost' Khadzha Nasr-ed-Din	Hadji Nasr-ed Din swept away this vulgarity
sshibal kak shakhmaty shutkami!	like clearing a chessboard – with jokes!

SOLO

Khoteli yumor kupit',	They wanted to buy humor,

CHORUS

da tol'ko evo ne kupish!	but one cannot buy it!

SOLO

Khoteli yumor ubit',	They wanted to kill humor,

CHORUS

a yumor pokazyval kukish!	but humor thumbed his nose!

SOLO

Borotsa s nim delo trudnoe.	To battle with him is a difficult task.
Kaznili evo bez kontza.	They executed him time and again.

CHORUS

Evo golova otrublennaya	His severed head
torchala na pike strel'tza.	was hoisted upon a pike.

SOLO

No lish' skomorosh i dudochki	But hardly had the ceremonial pipes
svoi nachinali skaz,	started their knell
on zvonko krichal,	when in a ringing voice he cried,

(with Chorus)

'Ya tutochki! Ya tutochki!'	'I am here! I am here!'
i likho puskalsa plyas.	and began to dance dashingly.

SOLO

Potriopannom kutzem pal'tishke,	In a shabby, scanty overcoat,
ponuryas' i slovno kayas',	downcast and as if repenting,
prestupnikom politicheskim on, poimanni	caught as a political prisoner,
shol na kazn'.	he was going to his execution.
Vsem vidom pokornost' vkyazyval,	To all appearances he showed his obedience,
gotov k nezemnomu zhit'yu,	he was ready for his afterlife,
kak vdrug iz pal'tishka vyskal'zyval,	when suddenly he slipped from his overcoat,
rukoi makhal,	waved his hand,

(with Chorus)

i tyu-tyu!	and ta-ta!

SOLO

Yumor pryatali v kamery,
no chorta sdva udalos'.

SOLO and CHORUS

Reshotki i steny kamennye
on prokhodil na skvoz'.
Otkashlivayas' prostuzhenno kak ryadovoi
boetz,
shagal on chastushkoi prostushkoi
s vintovkoi na Zimni Dvoretz.

SOLO

Privyk on ko vzglyadam sumrachnym
no eto emu ne vredit.
I sam na sebya s yumorom
yumor poroi glyadit.
On vechen.

CHORUS

Vechen.

SOLO

On lovok.

CHORUS

Lovok.

SOLO, then CHORUS

I yurok.

SOLO

Proidiot cherez vsio, cherez vsekh.

SOLO and CHORUS

I tak, da slavitza yumor.
On muzhestvenni chelovek.

They hid humor in cells,
but the devil may care.

The iron bars and walls of stone
he walked straight through.
Coughing from a cold like the rank and file,

with a popular song and a rifle
he marched upon the Winter Palace.

He is used to stern glances,
but this does not bother him.
And sometimes humor
even looks at himself with humor.
He is immortal.

Immortal.

He is sly.

Sly.

And nimble.

He will walk through everything, through
everyone.

And so, all glory to humor.
He is a manly person.

III. AT THE STORE (Adagio)

SOLO

Kto v platke, a kto v platochke.
kak na podvig, kak na trud,

v magazin po odinochke, molcha,
zhenshchiny idut.

Some in shawls, some in scarves,
as though preparing for some heroic deed or
exploit,
into the store, one by one, silently,
the women come.

CHORUS

O, bidonov ikh bryatzan'e,
zvon butylok i kastryul',
pakhnet lukom, ogurtzami,
pakhnet sousom 'Kabul´.'

Oh, the clatter of cans,
the clanking of bottles and saucepans,
the smell of onions, cucumbers,
the smell of the sauce 'Kabul´.'

SOLO

Zyabnu, dolgo v kassu stoya,

no pokuda dvizhus' k nei,
ot dykhanya zhenshchin stol'kikh
v magazine vsio teplei.
Oni tikho podzhidayut,
bogi dobrye sem'i,
i v rukakh oni szhimayut
den'gi trudnye svoi.

I'm freezing, standing so long in line for the
cashier,
but as I move closer,
from the breathing of so many women
it grows warmer in the store.
They wait quietly,
kind family-goddesses,
and in their hands
they clutch their hard-earned money.

CHORUS

Oni tikho podzhidayut,
bogi dobrye sem'i,
i v rukakh oni szhimayut
den'gi trudnye svoi.

They wait quietly,
kind family-goddesses,
and in their hands
they clutch their hard-earned money.

SOLO

Eto zhenshchiny Rossii,
eto nasha chest' i sud.
I beton oni mesili,
i pakhali, i kosili.
Vsio oni perenosili,
vsio oni perenesut.

These are the women of Russia,
they are our honor and judgment.
They have mixed concrete,
and plowed and reaped.
They endured everything,
they will endure everything.

CHORUS

Vsio oni perenosili,
vsio oni perenesut.

They endured everything,
they will endure everything.

SOLO

Vsio na svete im posil'no,
stol'ko sily im dano.

Everything on earth is within their power,
so much strength has been given to them.

SOLO and CHORUS

Ikh obshchityvat' postydno,
ikh obveshivat' greshno.

It is shameful to cheat them,
it is sinful to overweigh their goods.

SOLO

I, v karman pel'meni sunuv,

ya somtryu surov i tikh,
na ustalye ot sumok
ruki pravednye ikh.

And having tucked the dumplings into my pocket,
I gaze, stern and subdued,
on their righteous hands,
tired from shopping bags.

IV. FEARS (Largo)

CHORUS

Umirayut v Rossii strakhi,
slovno prizraki prezhnikh let.
Lish na paperti, kak starukhi,
koe gde eshchno prosyat na khleb.

Fears are dying in Russia,
like phantoms of former years,
lingering only on church steps, like old women,
in a few places, who beg for bread.

SOLO

Ya ikh pomnyu vo vlasti i sile,
pri dvore torzhestvuyushchei lzhi.
Strakhi vsyudu, kak teni, skol'zili,
pronikali vo vse etazhi.
Potikhon'ku lyudei priruchali
i na vsio nalagali pechat'.
Gde molchat' by krichat' priuchali,

i molchat gde by nado krichat'.
Eto stalo sevodnya daliokim,
dazhe stranno i vspomnit' teper'.
Taini strakh pered ch'im to donosom,
taini strakh pered stukhom v dver'.
Nu, a strakh govorit' s inostrantzem?
S inostrantzem to chto, a s zhenoi?
Nu, a strakh bez otchotni ostatsa

posle marshei vdvoiom s tishinoi?

I remember them in power and strength,
at the court of triumphant falsehood.
Fears, like shadows, slithered about everywhere,
they penetrated every floor.
Bit by bit they tamed the people
and placed their seal upon everything.
Where there should be silence, they taught shouting,
and silence where it was necessary to shout.
This, today, has become distant,
it is strange even to remember now.
The secret fear of someone informing,
the secret fear of a knock on the door.
Well, wasn't it fearsome to talk to a foreigner?
With a foreigner, or even your wife?
And, what of the unaccountable fear of remaining
after some march, two together in silence?

CHORUS

Ne boyalis' my stroit' v meteli,
ukhodit' pod snaryadami v boi,
No boyalis' poroyu smertel'no
razgovarivat' sami s soboi.
Nas ne sbili i ne rastlili,
i ne darom seichas vo vragakh,
pobedivshaya strakhi Rossiya,
eshcho bol'shii rozhdaet strakh!

We were not afraid to build in snowstorms,
to go into battle under fire,
but we were deathly afraid
to talk to ourselves.
We were not thrown down or corrupted,
and no wonder that now in our enemies
Russia, having overpowered her fears,
spreads even greater fear!

SOLO

Strakhi novye vizhu svetleya,
strakh neiskrennoi byt' so strannoi,
strakh nepravdoi unizit' idei
chto yavlyayutsa pravdoi samoi.
Strakh fanfarit' do oduren'ya,
strakh chuzhie slova povtoryat',
strakh unizit' drugikh nedover'em,
i chrezmerno sebe doveryat'.

New fears I see appearing,
the fear of being insincere with one's country,
the fear of debasing with lies ideas
that are truths themselves.
The fear of self-elevation to excess,
the fear of repeating someone else's words,
the fear of debasing others with distrust,
and of trusting one's own self excessively.

CHORUS

Umirayut v Rossii strakhi.

Fears are dying in Russia.

SOLO

I kogda ya pishu eti stroki,
i poroyu nevol'no speshu,
to pishuikh v edinstvennom strakhe,
chto ne v polnuyu silu pishu.

And as I write these lines,
and at times unconsciously rush,
I write them with the sole fear
that I am not writing in full force.

V. A CAREER (Allegretto)

SOLO

Tverdili pastyri, chto vreden
i nerazumen Galilei.

The priests insisted that evil
and unwise was Galileo.

CHORUS

Chto nerazumen Galilei,
chto nerazumen Galilei.

That unwise was Galileo,
that unwise was Galileo.

SOLO

No, kak pokazyvaet vremya,
kto nerazumnei tot umnei.

But, as time shows,
he who is unwise is more wise.

CHORUS

Kto nerazumnei tot umnei,
kto nerazumnei tot umnei.

He who is unwise is more wise,
he who is unwise is more wise.

SOLO

Uchoni – sverstnik Galileya –
byl Galileya ne glupee.

A scholar – a contemporary of Galileo –
was no more stupid than Galileo.

CHORUS

Byl Galileya ne glupee,
byl Galileya ne glupee.

Was no more stupid than Galileo,
was no more stupid than Galileo.

SOLO

On znal, chto vertitsa zemlya,
no u nevo byla sem'ya.

He knew that the earth revolves –
but he had a family.

CHORUS

No u nevo byla sem'ya,
no u nevo byla sem'ya.

SOLO

I on, sadyas' s zhenoi v karetu,
svershiv predatel'stvo svoio,
schital, chto delaet kar'eru,
a mezhdu tem gubil eio.

CHORUS

A mezhdu tem gubil eio,
a mezhdu tem gubil eio.

SOLO

Za osoznanie planety
shol Galilei odin na risk,
i stal velikim on.

CHORUS

I stal velikim on.

SOLO

Vot eto –

(with Chorus)

Ya ponimayu kar'erist!

CHORUS

Itak, da zdravstvuet kar'era,
kogda kar'era takova,
kak u Shekspira i Pastera,
Nyutona i Tolstovo – i Tolstovo.

SOLO, then CHORUS

L'va? ... L'va!

CHORUS

Zachem ikh gryazyu pokryvali?
Talant – talant, kak ne kleimi.

SOLO

Zabyty te, kto proklinali.

CHORUS

No pomnyat tekh, kovo klyali,
no pomnyat tekh, kovo klyali.

But he had a family,
but he had a family.

And he, sitting with his wife in a carriage,
having committed his betrayal,
thought he was establishing a career,
but actually he was destroying it.

But actually he was destroying it,
but actually he was destroying it.

To comprehend our planet
Galileo risked alone,
and he became great.

And he became great.

Now this –

I understand as a careerist!

And so, hail to a career,
when a career is like that of
a Shakespeare and Pasteur,
Newton and Tolstoy – and Tolstoy.

Leo? ... Leo!

Why did they slander them?
Talent is talent, no matter what.

They are forgotten, those who cursed.

But those are remembered who were cursed,
but those are remembered who were cursed.

SOLO

Vse te, kto rvalis' v stratosferu,	All those who reached for the stratosphere,
vrachi, chto gibli ot kholer –	the doctors, who perished from cholera –
vot eti delali kar'eru!	they were the ones who made careers!
(with Chorus)	
Ya s ikh kar'er beru primer.	From their careers I take my example.
SOLO	
Ya veryu v ikh svyatuyu veru.	I believe in their sacred belief.
Ikh vera muzhestvo moio.	Their belief is my manhood.
Ya delayu sebe kar'eru	I make my own career
tem, chto ne delayu eio!	by not working at it!

(Buketoff (transl.), 1970–2, after Shostakovich, 1970)

EXERCISE _____

Before continuing to read the discussion of the work which follows, make your own notes on the variety of subject matter and individual portrayals within the poems.

DISCUSSION _____

There is a huge spectrum of tone within these poems, which is in turn a reflection of the variety needed by the different movements of a symphony. The poems range from quite prosaic description in 'At the Store' to intense melancholy in 'Babi Yar' and grim humour in 'Humor' and 'A Career'. The narrating voice is personalized throughout, demonstrating that the poems are the outcome of an individual's observations, and it is made clear that these observations are specific to Russia, so that together the poems make up a portrait of contemporary Russian society.

_____

Babi Yar is a ravine near Kiev, in Ukraine. In 1941 nearly 34,000 Jews were murdered by being machine-gunned on the brink of the cliff, in reprisal by the occupying Nazi forces for terrorist acts in Kiev. Some estimates put the eventual death-toll (of Jews and non-Jews) at the ravine between 1941 and 1943 at 150,000. The appearance of Yevtushenko's poem 'Babi Yar' brought the significance of the site and its history ineradicably into the public domain: its first line, 'Above Babi Yar there are no monuments' is a protest against the attempts by first the German occupying forces, and later the Ukrainian government, to ignore the atrocities committed there. This

Figure 4.7 The ravine at Babi Yar near Kiev. German soldiers can be seen at the top of the cliff, while auxiliaries sift through the clothing of the victims of the mass murder. Photo: Hessisches, Hauptstaatsarchiv, Wiesbaden

Figure 4.8 The dedication of the modern memorial at Babi Yar. It was erected in the 1970s, perhaps partly in response to the feeling summed up in the bitter accusation of the first lines of Yevtushenko's poem. Photo: United States Holocaust Memorial Museum

reflected an official discomfort with criticism of anti-semitism; Stalin's regime had sympathized with much of the ideology of the Third Reich. The last line of the poem, in which the poet, having identified himself with the Jews, declares, 'For this reason I am a true Russian!', was a direct criticism of the attitudes of the Soviet regime. The poem is a rare example of a literary work which has contributed to the course of historical events, since today there is indeed an officially commissioned monument at Babi Yar, although the inscription refers only to 'citizens of Kiev' rather than specifically to Jewish victims.

Shostakovich had not set any text to music in a large-scale work (although he had written songs for chamber performance) for twenty-eight years before writing the Thirteenth Symphony. His previous foray in this direction was his opera *Lady Macbeth of Mtsensk* of 1934, a work that had caused him enormous problems and even real danger after it attracted a storm of official protest, which was compounded greatly when Stalin himself attended a performance in 1936. The opera was suppressed, and Shostakovich's famous epigraph to his Fifth Symphony (1937), 'A Soviet artist's reply to just criticism', was his attempt at professional rehabilitation (which was successful, if only temporarily).

It was Yevtushenko's poetry, though, rather than Shostakovich's music which aroused official displeasure with the Thirteenth Symphony. Khrushchev himself was angered by the prospect of having the poem 'Babi Yar' publicly performed, and after two performances the symphony was banned. It remained so for several years under the Brezhnev regime. The work was first heard in the west only in 1970. This in itself locates the piece as much more a product of the Cold War than a protest against the atrocities of the Second World War. Yevtushenko's trenchant criticism of the Soviet regime found a response in some of Shostakovich's most committed and powerful music. Throughout his life the composer was prepared to compromise with the authorities in order to protect himself and his family, most famously in accepting the instruction to attend the Cultural and Scientific Conference for World Peace in New York in 1949. (Tippett writes of this as one of two 'non-meetings' with Shostakovich, since he refused the invitation to attend – see Tippett, 1995, pp. 79–82.) In writing this symphony, he was clearly trying to exploit what he hoped was a resulting position of strength.

Nevertheless, Yevtushenko's poem takes as its starting point an atrocity of war, and Shostakovich's symphony deserves to be considered alongside *A Child of Our Time* as a depiction of similar horrors, and alongside *War Requiem* as an exactly contemporary Cold War statement.

Just as with the other two works we have studied, Shostakovich's Thirteenth Symphony is very conscious of its place in the European tradition of art music. The very title 'symphony' immediately creates all sorts of expectations, and this is the more significant because there are ways in which Shostakovich's work is not structured according to the most common pattern of the genre. Indeed Shostakovich might just as well have described the work as a 'song-cycle', or even an 'oratorio'. Not that the idea of a symphony incorporating voices was new – far from it. Moreover, the best-known precedents are as important to the statement Shostakovich is making in the work as Handel and Verdi are to Tippett and Britten respectively.

The first symphony to be scored for chorus and soloists in addition to orchestra was the work which became during the nineteenth century possibly the most celebrated in the entire history of music: Beethoven's Ninth. Composers as different as Brahms and Wagner (indeed, especially Brahms and Wagner) considered it the most significant work of all time. Beethoven (1770–1827) was the composer more than any other who raised the profile of the symphony as a genre from that of a relatively lightweight piece (which was true for Haydn and Mozart even in their late symphonies), to the level of the most serious and weighty artistic statement. Beethoven's Ninth Symphony sets, as its final movement, Friedrich Schiller's 'Ode to Joy', and Wagner regarded the resort to words as the culmination of the work; the point at which the implicit programme, already apprehensible to an educated listener in the earlier movements, becomes fully articulate. Not only did any subsequent attempt to compose a symphony incorporating voices inevitably invite comparison with Beethoven, it also usually indicated a desire to buy into the ideology of metaphysical significance and lofty sentiment with which that earlier work was credited.

Perhaps the clearest example of this is a work by a composer deeply revered by Shostakovich and extremely influential on his style, Gustav Mahler (1860–1911). Mahler's Second Symphony is another work which uses soloist and chorus; it is often known as the Resurrection Symphony, after the ode by Friedrich Klopstock which provides the text of the finale. As with Beethoven's Ninth, voices are used only at the end of the work, and in order to make explicit affirmative and aspirational ideals. Mahler used text-setting in his Third, Fourth and Eighth Symphonies as well as the Second, and one of the most likely direct models for Shostakovich's symphony is Mahler's symphonic song-cycle, *Das Lied von der Erde* (the song of the earth), for soprano, baritone and orchestra. This work, which Mahler could have titled his Ninth Symphony, combines the structural plan of a symphony with the linked narratives of a series of poems, something associated with song-cycle form. Its texts are translations by Hans Bethge of Chinese poetry, which portray different aspects of earthly life in the early movements and constitute a farewell to the world itself in the tremendously powerful last movement, 'Der Abschied' (the farewell). Mahler's compositional technique in this last movement in particular was extremely influential on those composers of the next generation who looked to his music as a model, including Shostakovich perhaps above all others (Britten too was a great devotee of Mahler). The combination of absolute seriousness of intent, eclectic musical source material (from 'intellectual' counterpoint to folk-idioms) and a taste for mordant, ironic humour are all characteristics of Shostakovich's music that are also found throughout Mahler's oeuvre.

This, then, is part of the background which provides the context for Shostakovich's work. Rather than reserving text-setting for the final part of the symphony, Shostakovich matches five poems by Yevtushenko in a sequence of movements which constitute a recognizable symphonic framework. The usual pattern for a symphony is to locate the greatest rhetorical weight in the opening and final movements, and this is followed by Shostakovich with the poems 'Babi Yar' and 'A Career'. The central movements of a symphony often include a fast scherzo, which here is the second movement, setting the poem 'Humor'. The other two are both slow movements, with the poems 'At the Store' and 'Fears'.

Earlier great symphonies which also set poetic texts create expectations of significant, public subject matter: for Beethoven this is the common ties uniting humanity; for Mahler it is faith in redemption and renewal. Such topics make the bleakness of Yevtushenko's description of Soviet society, treated in the way Shostakovich presents it, all the more shocking. The implication is that, despite a war waged against the inhumanity and terror of events such as those at Babi Yar, the society forged in its wake is scarcely tolerable. For Shostakovich, the truth-content of the music is the source of its aesthetic worth. His musical language, which uses recognizable points of reference in order to retain the power to subvert the expectations thus generated, is integral to this process. His own justification of the symphony contrasts this attitude bitterly with the 'crowd-pleasing' style officially encouraged by the Communist party leader Andrei Zhdanov, instigator of the cultural purge which condemned Shostakovich along with Prokofiev and Khachaturian, among others, in 1948–9.

The authenticity of Shostakovich's memoirs was fiercely contested both within and outside the USSR on their appearance in the late 1970s, shortly after Shostakovich's death. Their portrayal of Soviet society as characterized by intimidation and fear was challenged, both on grounds of accuracy (particularly within the regime) and as a true representation of Shostakovich's attitudes. Scholarly opinion now generally regards the memoirs as largely correct and authentic; see for example Ho and Feofanov, 1998.

People knew about Babi Yar before Yevtushenko's poem, but they were silent. And when they read the poem, the silence was broken. Art destroys silence.

I know that many will not agree with me and will point out other, more noble aims of art. They'll talk about beauty, grace, and other high qualities. But you won't catch me with that bait ... Zhdanov, a great specialist in the musical arts, also stood fast for beautiful and graceful music. Let anything at all go on around you, but serve high art, and nothing but, at the table ...

I've always protested harshly against this point of view and I strove for the reverse. I always wanted music to be an active force. That is the Russian tradition.

(Shostakovich, 1979, pp. 120–1)

It is notable that Shostakovich links his ideology of music as an 'active force', or as having cultural value beyond the merely entertaining or decorative, with his identity as a Russian. Elsewhere in his memoirs he acknowledges admiration for Beethoven's Ninth Symphony (mingled with distrust of its use by the Communist party), and declares Mahler, along with Schoenberg's pupil Alban Berg (a devoted follower of Mahler), to be his favourite composers. However, it is Mussorgsky (1839–81), the quintessential Russian nationalist, whom he credits time and again as a model, especially for his symphonies. Clearly, national identity is of central importance to Shostakovich. The question of identity is indeed central to the contrasts between the three composers we have encountered in this chapter.

EXERCISE

1   In what ways does the poetic persona of Yevtushenko's poems contrast with those of Tippett's oratorio and Britten's *Requiem*?

2   What is the contribution that memory of the Second World War makes to each piece?

DISCUSSION

1   The fundamental contrast in terms of national identity has already been suggested. Tippett is avowedly internationalist in his stance, resistant to the idea of a Europe of competing identities. Britten is also seeking to avoid, or transcend, such questions in his ideology of reconciliation. This is evident both in the texts and ordering of the Owen poems he selects, and in the careful arrangements he made concerning the première and recording of the work. Shostakovich, though, sets the reclamation of a 'true' Russian identity as a goal.

Figure 4.9 Shostakovich in 1960, about the time that he began work on the Thirteenth Symphony. Photo: Hulton Archive

2   The Second World War features in different ways in the three works. Paradoxically, although on the one hand *War Requiem* is unavoidably a reaction to the conflict, because of the circumstance of its commission, on the other hand its use of poetry from the First World War avoids any direct commentary on the later war as history. For Tippett and Shostakovich, the experience focused on is inhumanity and atrocity. In *A Child of Our Time* the violence of Kristallnacht is inextricable from other forms of violence and is constantly generalized as a feature of human social organization; it seems that nationalism will always lead to ethnic hatred. In 'Babi Yar', however, the Nazi atrocity is important not as part of war, but as a stage in the continuing persecution of the Jewish people. Yevtushenko adds other examples of anti-semitism to the catalogue: biblical accounts,

Anne Frank, Dreyfus, a Stalinist pogrom in Belostok. This last example, as a Russian atrocity, links into the theme throughout the poems set by Shostakovich: that (to use a cliché) while the Russian people may have won the war, their leaders have comprehensively lost the peace.

The nature of the 'true Russian' evidently needs some exploration. On the one hand, Yevtushenko is explicitly anti-nationalist:

> O my Russian people! I know that
> in essence you are international.

and

> Let the 'Internationale' thunder forth,
> when for the ages is buried
> the last anti-Semite on earth.

Yet, on the other hand, there is no suggestion at all that international socialism should efface national identities. Yevtushenko is determined that Russian identity should be preserved, despite the political betrayal of such identity in the name of preserving ethnic purity. This is made explicit in the depiction of national identity throughout the poetry: courageous individualism is described in 'Babi Yar', 'Fears' and 'Career'; the ultimate triumph of the ludic quest for truth is depicted in 'Humor'; and the deprivations of life for the women of Russia is made a subject for outrage in 'At the Store'. Shostakovich underlines this characterization of Russian identity through the music in several ways. The choice of a bass as soloist is typically Russian in itself; the most relevant examples are two of Mussorgsky's operatic characters, Boris in *Boris Godunov* and Prince Ivan in *Khovanshchina* (which Shostakovich named as an influence on the Thirteenth Symphony). The musical language is full of distinctively Russian characteristics, from its implicit appeal to Mussorgsky as a legitimating figure, to its occasional semi-quotation of Russian folk melody. Shostakovich and Yevtushenko are united by a belief that the only hope of salvation within the world of the Thirteenth Symphony lies not in the discovery of personal transformation (as for Tippett), nor in reconciliation and transnational unity (as for Britten), but in the restoration of Russian identity to the Russian people.

Conclusion: ideology, politics and artistic Modernism

Although they are full of fascinating contrasts, and utterly different in originating contexts, the three musical works considered in this chapter have some fundamental points of similarity.

All three composers display striking similarities in their ideology of the function of the artist. They are all committed to the idea that the artist has a role at the centre of society, able to effect social change. This carries responsibility with it, so that it becomes a duty to respond to the most pressing issues of the time, including political issues. The aim is to preserve both the possibility of individuality within society, and the most valuable elements of the culture. The musical styles of Tippett, Britten and Shostakovich are very different from each other, and also strikingly individual and distinctive in each case. But they share a concern for comprehensibility, a kind of aural legibility which stems from a belief that art only functions if it successfully communicates with its audience. While the institution of art music is in itself elitist, any retreat to the position of a cultural mandarin, addressing only the cognoscenti, is anathema to the three composers.

The desire for comprehensibility of language informs the attitude to the tradition of composing music which is of crucial importance in each of these works. They require an understanding of their historical precedents and contexts in order to articulate their different critiques of the social moments at which they were created. In all three, there is a confluence of tendencies that typify musical Modernism in the twentieth century, given the perceived pressing needs of the moment. The three works are not just remarkable responses to the conflict which divides the mid point of twentieth-century history; they are also permanent reminders of the inadequacy of considering music (or any other art) as an autonomous domain divorced from the historical forces which shape it.

References

Bloom, Harold (1973) *The Anxiety of Influence: a Theory of Poetry*, Oxford, Oxford University Press.

Bowen, Meirion (1997) *Michael Tippett*, London, Robson.

Buketoff, Igor (transl.) (1970–2) sleeve notes to Shostakovich, Symphony no. 13, recording RL 01284 (3), RCA Red Seal.

Cooke, Mervyn (1996) *Britten:* War Requiem, Cambridge, Cambridge University Press.

Fussell, Paul (2000) *The Great War and Modern Memory*, 2nd edn., Oxford, Oxford University Press.

Gloag, Kenneth (1999) *Tippett:* A Child of Our Time, Cambridge, Cambridge University Press.

Ho, Allan and Feofanov, Dmitry (eds) (1998) *Shostakovich Reconsidered*, London, Toccata Press.

Horváth, Ödön Josef von [1938] (1985) *A Child of Our Time*, transl. R. Wills Thomas, London, Methuen (originally published 1938 as *Ein Kind unserer Zeit*, Frankfurt am Main, Suhrkamp).

Johnstone, John H. (1964) *English Poetry of the First World War*, Princeton, NJ, Princeton University Press.

Kemp, Ian (1987) *Tippett: the Composer and his Music*, Oxford, Oxford University Press.

MacDonald, Malcolm (1982) 'Words and music in late Shostakovich', in Christopher Norris (ed.), *Shostakovich: the Man and his Music*, London, Lawrence & Wishart.

Mitchell, Donald (1984) 'Mapreading: Benjamin Britten in conversation with Donald Mitchell', in Christopher Palmer (ed.), *The Britten Companion*, London, Faber & Faber.

Robertson, Alec (1962) 'Britten's *War Requiem*', *Musical Times*, vol. 103, pp. 308–10.

Shostakovich, Dmitri (1970) *Symphony no. 13 for Bass Solo, Male Chorus and Orchestra*, opus 113, words by Yevgeny Yevtushenko, Willowdale, Leeds Music.

Shostakovich, Dmitri (1979) *Testimony: the Memoirs of Shostakovich*, ed. Solomon Volkov, transl. Antonina W. Bouis, London, Hamish Hamilton.

Tippett, Michael (1944) *A Child of Our Time*, London, Schott edn. 10065.

Tippett, Michael (1995) *Tippett on Music*, Oxford, Clarendon.

Whittall, Arnold (1963) 'Tonal instability in Britten's *War Requiem*', *Music Review*, vol. 24, pp. 201–4.

5

War, cinema and society

JAMES CHAPMAN

Introduction

Let me start as I mean to go on – with reference to a film. You may have seen *A Bridge Too Far* (1977), based on the ill-fated attempt by British, American and Polish airborne troops to capture the Rhine bridges at Arnhem and Nijmegen in September 1944. It was the last in a cycle of big-budget, all-star war films that reconstructed particular campaigns of the Second World War – a cycle that began with *The Longest Day* (1962) and also included the likes of *Battle of the Bulge* (1965), *Anzio* (1968) and *Battle of Britain* (1969). There's a scene early in the film where General Horrocks (Edward Fox) is explaining the strategy of the operation to his men. This is how he summarizes the plan:

> I like to think of this as one of those American western films. The paratroops, lacking substantial equipment, always short of food – these are the besieged homesteaders. The Germans, well naturally they're the bad guys. And 30 Corps – we, my friends, are the cavalry on the way to the rescue.

Why do I single out this small moment in the film? Well, it strikes me as interesting for the way in which military strategy is explained through a filmic analogy, specifically in this case the Hollywood western. The western is such a familiar genre that the reference would have been readily understood both by the troops Horrocks is addressing in the film itself and by cinema audiences watching the film in 1977. It exemplifies the way in which war is represented in film – turning complicated historical events into intelligible narrative, complete with 'bad guys' and the promise that the 'cavalry' will arrive in the nick of time.

'War is cinema and cinema is war', declares French film theorist Paul Virilio (Virilio, 1989, p. 26). Meaningless in itself, Virilio's statement nevertheless suggests a relationship of some sort between war and cinema. Pierre Sorlin suggests, more precisely, that 'where war is concerned ... something changed dramatically with the invention of the cinema' (Sorlin, 1994, p. 358). If, on the one hand, cinema was an extension of photography, on the other hand it added the immediacy and drama of narrative. Many of our impressions of war have been shaped and moulded by the cinema. This is especially true for those of us who are too young to have experienced the devastation wrought upon Europe by the two total wars of the twentieth century. We have no knowledge of what war was 'really like'; our images of it are mediated – through stories, books, comics, computer games, television and film.

Of all the media, film is the one that has done most to create myths about war. This is especially so in Britain where, as Clive Emsley has already noted in Chapter 2, there is an abiding popular memory of war, especially the Second World War. Much of this popular memory, I would argue, has its origins in the cinema. Consider this statement by historian Philip Taylor:

> For a particular generation that was too young to remember the Second World War, or for those who were born in the decade or so after it, film has remained a vital source of 'evidence' for providing substance to the oral history on which they were weaned. For such people, in their formative years, moving pictures provided direct access to the past, the nearest they could get to the experience which had done so much to shape the world into which they were born. Churchill was the hero; Hitler the villain. The Italians were cowards; the Japanese were inexplicable. Dunkirk was a victory; Dresden was necessary. The Germans may have been formidable opponents, but their defeat made the Allied victory seem all the greater. Douglas Bader looked like Kenneth More, Rommel looked like James Mason and every RAF pilot should have looked like David Niven.
>
> (Taylor, 1988, p. 1)

Film is thus a powerful medium in the creation of a popular memory of war, all the more so because, as Taylor indicates, the postwar generation in Britain were exposed to these myths in their 'formative years'. And while war films are no longer a staple of British cinema, the popular memory of war lives on through their almost continuous presence on television, not to mention the continued replaying of television series such as *Dad's Army*, which similarly contribute to the mythologizing of the war experience (Richards, 1997, pp. 351–66). While the British have been especially adept at mythologizing war through cinema, however, other nations have also expressed some of their dominant cultural myths through films. In France, for example, films about the Resistance have proliferated, while in the former Soviet Union film was the dominant medium for telling the epic story of the Great Patriotic War of 1941–5. In Germany, as one would expect, the legacy of war has been examined critically and with much discomfort, but even there film has been a prominent means of expression for a nation coming to terms with its own past.

This chapter examines the representation of war – specifically the two total wars – in European cinema. It discusses the differences between filmic representations of the First and Second World Wars, and the differences in the national experiences of war. It explores the role of the cinema in creating myths about war and in questioning some of those myths, and also considers how the representation of the past may be influenced by the concerns of the present.

The war film, as a genre, is characterized by its diversity, especially in respect of European cinema. First, we must make the important distinction between what are known as 'actuality' films (that is, films compiled from footage taken at the front line by camera operators attached to the armed forces) and narrative feature films (story films, made after the event, which may be either reconstructions of actual wartime incidents or entirely fictional). In the first category, for example, we would include *Battle of the Somme* (1916), the official film record of the British offensive of 1 July 1916 compiled by cameramen Geoffrey Malins and J. B. McDowell. In the category of narrative feature films we would include, among others, the American film version of *All Quiet on the Western Front* (1930), based on the novel by Erich Maria Remarque, which is a fictional story, and the British film *Regeneration* (1997), adapted from Pat Barker's historical novel, itself a semi-fictional account of the friendship between war poets Siegfried Sassoon and Wilfred Owen and psychologist Dr William Rivers, set in and around Craiglockhart military hospital. While these two films are both about the First World War and, in the case of *All Quiet on the Western Front* especially, have been acclaimed for their perceived realism and authenticity, they are reconstructions which do not have any value as primary sources for the war itself (even though clips from *All Quiet* ... have often turned up on television purporting to be actuality film of trench warfare). Within the category of narrative feature films, moreover, there is a great diversity of images and representations of war. We could draw distinctions between fictional and factually based films, for instance, and between films that depict major events (especially battles) and those that focus on stories of individuals set against the background of war. We should not assume that simply because a film is based on actual historical events or personages it is therefore a historically accurate representation of those events. Quite often the war film distorts historical 'truth' for its own ends – or rather those of its producers. There were outcries in the British press, for example, when Hollywood films showed the US army winning the campaign in Burma (*Objective: Burma!*, 1945) or the US navy capturing the German 'Enigma' code-making machine (*U-571*, 2000).

There are also differences in the style of war narratives. Both *Das Boot* (*The Boat*, 1981) and *Where Eagles Dare* (1969) are fictional stories, but whereas the former is a realistic account of the dangers of submarine warfare exploring the psychological make-up of its protagonists as they react to the stresses of war, the latter is a gung-ho *Boy's Own*-style adventure film offering an essentially comic strip representation of war that abandons any notion of psychological realism in favour of action and spectacle in the style of the James Bond films.

The majority of films discussed in this chapter are narrative feature films. There are two reasons for this: first because the majority of war films seen in cinemas are of this type, and secondly because you are more likely to be familiar with feature films than actuality films.

The First World War: from propaganda to anti-war cinema

The First World War marked an important watershed for the cinema. It was the first conflict to be recorded extensively on film, and the first occasion when governments took an active interest in the role that cinema could play in national propaganda. Previously despised by social and political elites as a low-brow, vulgar form of popular entertainment, cinema acquired a new status during the war, due to its role both in reporting events and in promoting support for the war effort to the public. '[F]or the first time', as film historians Furhammar and Isaksson note, 'the cinema managed to shake off its cultural inferiority complex. It was lifted out of the fairground and attained a significance beyond that of cheap entertainment' (Furhammar and Isaksson, 1971, p. 12). In Germany, no less a figure than General Erich Ludendorff, the deputy chief of staff, observed that 'The war has demonstrated the paramount power of images and of film as means of enlightenment and influence' (quoted in Jelavich, 1999, p. 42). The British government, initially resistant to allowing film camera operators access to the front line, relented in November 1915. Actuality film taken on the Western Front was used in a series of short topical films and in three longer works: *Battle of the Somme* (1916), *Battle of the Ancre and the Advance of the Tanks* (1917) and *The German Retreat and the Battle of Arras* (1917). But how were these films received at home? One view is given in the first reading, an extract from a review of the film *Battle of the Somme* by James Douglas in the *Star* newspaper.

The Somme pictures. Are they too painful for public exhibition?

The bravery of our boys is past our imagining. 'Every one of them,' said a wounded officer to me who fought on the First of July, 'every one of them is a hero.' His eyes filled with tears as he spoke. I thought of his words as I saw our soldiers bringing in a dying comrade under shell-fire. He died half-an-hour after he passed on the back of a soldier. I shall not soon forget his good English face. Nor shall I soon forget the face of the dead German soldier who is lying there waiting to be buried by the British soldiers who are digging the graves on the battlefield. These are dreadful sights, but their dreadfulness is as wholesome as Tolstoy's *War and Peace*. It shakes the kaleidoscope of war into human reality. Now I know why soldiers are nobler than civilians in their tenderness and their chivalry and their charity. They have seen war, and they hate it as we can never hate it.

Therefore I say these pictures are good for us. The dead on the battlefield, the drivers of the gun-teams steering the wheels clear of the corpse, the demented German prisoners, the kindly British soldiers showering cigarettes upon their captives, the mangled heap of anguish on the stretcher, the half-naked wounded men in the dressing-station – let our men and women see it all and vow that earth shall be delivered from it all. Dying men, dead horses, the dead dog lying beside his dead master – these vilenesses are war. War is the enemy, and Germany is its patentee, its idolater, its worshipper. It is our task to beat the German sword into a ploughshare so that the nations may learn war no more.

(*Star*, 25 August 1916, quoted in Reeves, 1999, pp. 36–7)

EXERCISE

Now consider the following questions.

1   How does Douglas respond to the film?

2   What do you think is the significance of the reference to Tolstoy's *War and Peace*?

DISCUSSION _____

1   Douglas's response illustrates his admiration for the British
     soldiers on the Somme and strongly indicates his underlying
     patriotism. His review gives an impression of the losses suffered
     by the British army but also asserts his clear belief in the justice of
     the British cause.

2   In comparing the film to a recognized literary classic, Douglas,
     albeit perhaps unwittingly, makes the case for the cultural
     legitimation of film as a consequence of the war.

Battle of the Somme is an example of an actuality war film; it was the
first major film to present an authentic picture of conditions on the
Western Front to the British public. While we cannot take one critic's
views as representative of the reaction of all cinema-goers, there is
evidence from other sources that this film was greatly admired by
British audiences. It 'did extraordinarily good business wherever it
was shown' (Reeves, 1997, p. 14). On the question posed by Douglas
as to whether the images of British casualties were 'too painful for
public exhibition', however, there were mixed views. The dean of
Durham wrote to *The Times* to decry the

> crowds of Londoners [who] feel no scruple at feasting their
> eyes on pictures which present the passion and death of
> British soldiers ... I beg leave respectfully to enter a protest
> against an entertainment which wounds the heart and violates
> the very sanctities of bereavement.
>
> (*The Times*, 1 September 1916)

This view was rebutted, however, by another correspondent who
wrote:

> I have lost a son in battle, and I have seen the Somme film
> twice ... I want to know what was the life, and the life-in-death,
> that our dear ones endured, and to be with them again in
> their great adventure.
>
> (*The Times*, 2 September 1916)

This sort of reaction suggests that watching the film may have been a
form of collective mourning and commemoration.

_____

Battle of the Somme is a propaganda film, yet it does not shy away from
picturing the human cost of war, as the reactions to it illustrate.
Although we know in hindsight that some of the battle sequences
were 'faked', the casualties were real enough. The other propaganda
films that followed it in 1917 were less well received, prompting film

historian Nicholas Reeves to the conclusion that 'film propaganda proved all but impotent in the face of the challenge posed by the disillusionment and war-weariness that became more and more evident'. *Battle of the Somme*, he suggests, was successful because it was 'screened at a time when public opinion was still broadly committed to the war' (Reeves, 1999, p. 38).

The suggestion that the reception of films is influenced, perhaps even determined, by the state of public opinion is an important consideration when we look at postwar films about the First World War. While the reaction to *Battle of the Somme* suggests that it was effective in promoting support for the war by asserting that it was being fought in a just cause, the next generation of First World War films were unequivocal in their view that the conflict had been a futile waste of life. In the immediate aftermath, however, there were very few films directly about the war; it was not until the late 1920s and early 1930s that it became a topical subject again in the cinema. Sorlin suggests that 'knowledge of the horrors of the war was a grim secret whose communication was delayed' (Sorlin, 1994, p. 360). The passage of time since the Armistice allowed a more detached and critical look at the war, which was reflected in the cycle of anti-war films made around the turn of the decade. These anti-war films were in large measure responding to the public mood at a time when pacifist sentiment was widespread. For example, the idealistic Kellogg-Briand Pact of 1928, a convention formally renouncing war as an instrument of foreign policy, was sponsored by France and the USA and signed by all the major powers. Moreover, Pierre Laval, who had narrowly escaped imprisonment for his anti-war stance in 1918, became French prime minister in 1931 and again in 1935. In Britain, meanwhile, the Oxford Union famously passed the motion that 'This House will in no circumstance fight for King and Country' in 1933, while the following year saw the formation of the Peace Pledge Union.

Perhaps the most significant point to note about the anti-war films appearing ten to fifteen years after the Armistice is that they were international in scope. Films questioning the ideology of war and critical of the conduct of the late conflict were produced in Britain (*Journey's End*, 1930; *Tell England*, 1931), France (*Verdun, visions d'histoire*, 1928; *Le Croix de bois/The Wooden Cross*, 1932) and Germany (*Westfront 1918*, 1930; *Kameradschaft*, meaning 'comradeship', 1931). This would seem to suggest that a belated reaction against the war occurred almost simultaneously in those countries which had witnessed its futility and brutality at close hand. The exception is the Soviet Union which, perhaps surprisingly, did not make any significant contribution to this anti-war cinema – the reason being that Soviet film-makers in the 1920s and 1930s were more concerned with mythologizing the Bolshevik Revolution in films such as *Battleship Potemkin* (1925) and *October* (1928) than with analysing the war.

Undoubtedly the most celebrated of this international cycle of anti-war films – and also the most famous of all films about the First World War – is *All Quiet on the Western Front.* Although it is an American film, made entirely in Hollywood by Universal Pictures, the fact that it was adapted from a German novel (Remarque's *Im Westen nichts Neues*, 1929) and has a German protagonist legitimates its inclusion here. Moreover, the film's producer, Carl Laemmle Jr, was a first-generation German-Jewish immigrant, while its director, Lewis Milestone, had been born Lev Milstein in Russia, so there was a strong European influence on the film. It is widely regarded as an early classic of sound cinema (talking pictures had arrived in the late 1920s) and has been acclaimed as the greatest anti-war film ever made.

> *Synopsis*: At the outbreak of the Great War a group of German schoolboys join the army, inspired by watching a parade of soldiers through their village and by the patriotic rhetoric of their schoolmaster. The central protagonist is Paul Bäumer (played by Lew Ayres), who goes through training with his friends and is then sent to the front. The boys' idealism is dented by the cynicism of the veterans they meet at the front and shattered by their first experience of battle. They share the terror and exhaustion of constant fighting in the trenches. Paul's first experience of close combat leaves him full of remorse after killing a French soldier. Paul is wounded and sent home on leave, but feels alienated from the false romantic ideals of war that still persist and by the belligerence of the old men in the beer cellars. He is almost relieved to return to the front, even though he finds many of his old friends have been killed. The film ends with Paul seeing a butterfly through an observation slit in his trench; when he reaches out to catch it he is shot dead by a sniper. The last shot of the film has a column of ghostly soldiers marching across an endless field of graves, including Paul.

All Quiet on the Western Front questions the patriotic sentiments that commentators like Douglas had expressed following *Battle of the Somme*. While the film's protagonist is German, this is of little consequence: he could just as easily have been French or British. The anti-war theme clearly appealed, for the film was well received in most countries, especially France and Britain. In Germany, however, where Remarque's book had provoked much controversy, the film version encountered censorship problems and was later denounced by the Nazis as 'a Jewish lie' and 'a hate film slandering the German soldier' (Kelly, 1998, pp. 123–4). It was also edited in other countries,

The Greatest War Picture Ever Made!

ALL QUIET ON THE WESTERN FRONT Ⓐ

starring LEW AYRES, LEWIS WOLHEIM, SLIM SUMMERVILLE

A UNIVERSAL-INTERNATIONAL PICTURE

Figures 5.1 and 5.2 *All Quiet on the Western Front.* Photos: Ronald Grant Archive

depending upon the censorship regulations in force – the Polish censors, for example, cut the scene of Paul's death. Sorlin argues that the acclaim heaped upon the film, and the controversy it attracted in some quarters, 'proves that the Europeans were ready to open a debate about the conflict' (Sorlin, 1999, p. 18).

Film historian Andrew Kelly, who has made a detailed study of the production and reception of the film, sums up its significance thus:

> There are many reasons why *All Quiet on the Western Front* retains its power and has continued to capture the imagination, despite the fact that few have seen a full version and that over half a century of cinema has passed since its first release. It brings together – indeed, helped establish – the classic themes of the anti-war film, book, play and poem: the enemy as comrade; the brutality of militarism; the slaughter of trench warfare; the betrayal of a nation's youth by old men revelling in glory; the incompetence of the High Command; the suffering at home, in particular by women; the dead, and the forgotten men who survived.
>
> (Kelly, 1998, p. 158)

All Quiet on the Western Front was the most successful and acclaimed film of the anti-war cycle of the late 1920s and early 1930s. But the filmic 'debate' about the First World War identified by Sorlin was short-lived. It was interrupted by the increasingly aggressive rhetoric of European politicians in the 1930s and by the international tensions of that decade. Films of the late 1930s exhibit a sense of belligerent nationalism and pride in national achievements. There was a vogue for displays of patriotic spectacle, often mobilizing the past to draw parallels with the present. Thus the British cinema presented Britain as a stalwart defender of democratic ideals against foreign tyrants (*Drake of England*, 1935 and *Fire over England*, 1937), while the German cinema turned to stories of national heroes (*Bismarck*, 1940 and *Der Grosse König*, meaning 'the great king', 1942). Meanwhile, one of the great epics of Soviet cinema, *Alexander Nevsky* (1938), seems to have anticipated the forthcoming 'battle of the century' with its inspiring reconstruction of the defeat of the invading Teutonic knights by the eponymous thirteenth-century Russian hero.

The outbreak of the Second World War in 1939 understandably focused attention on that conflict rather than the previous one. The great French film director Jean Renoir once suggested that the anti-war films of the interwar years must have failed because the Second World War followed:

> In 1936 I made a picture named *La Grande Illusion* in which I tried to express all my deep feelings for the cause of peace. This film was very successful. Three years later the war broke out.
>
> (Quoted in Kelly, 1998, p. 188)

Films about the First World War were thin on the ground during the 1940s and 1950s, partly because the Second World War was more immediate and recent, partly because the war against Nazism seemed morally justifiable in a way that the war against Wilhelmine Germany, in hindsight, did not.

Beginning in the late 1950s and continuing throughout the 1960s, however, there was a second cycle of films which 'reopened the debate about the Great War' (Sorlin, 1999, p. 22). Again this cycle was international in scope, including films from the United States (*Paths of Glory*, 1957), Britain (*King and Country*, 1964; *Oh! What a Lovely War*, 1969) and Italy (*The Great War*, 1959; *The Men Against*, 1970). The emphasis in these pictures is on class differences between officers and men, setting them apart from the earlier films in which the notion of a heroic, idealistic officer class still prevailed (this theme is explored in Renoir's *La Grande Illusion*, for example). But the way in which these films represent war as a futile, brutalizing experience is still very much in the tradition of *All Quiet on the Western Front*. In this respect little had changed since the 1930s.

EXERCISE

What international event do you think may have influenced the anti-war films of the 1960s?

DISCUSSION

The event was the Vietnam war, which provoked anti-war demonstrations in western Europe as well as the USA. Obviously this cannot have been a factor in the late 1950s or early 1960s, but I would suggest that films of the mid 1960s and later were strongly influenced by the international reaction against American involvement in Vietnam. The brutal conduct of the campaign, the revelation of atrocities committed by American soldiers and the consequent blurring of the distinction between 'good' and 'bad' all coloured attitudes towards war in general. This is evident in filmic representations not just of the First World War but of other conflicts too, as war films in the late 1960s became more brutal and morally compromised.

Filming the people's war

The Second World War has provided the subject matter for many more films than the First. In the context of British cinema especially, approximately 90 per cent of all war films have been about the Second World War. This section considers the dominant myths of that war as they have been constructed in British cinema. I make no apology for the focus on Britain. As the country, alone among the European allies, did not suffer Nazi occupation between 1939 and 1945, its experience of war, and thus the filmic representation of war, was significantly different from that of other nations. The narrative of heroic struggle that characterizes British popular historiography of the Second World War – focusing on events such as Dunkirk, the Battle of Britain and the Blitz, and privileging the North African campaign at the expense of other theatres, especially the Russian Front – owes much to films made in Britain both during and after the war.

The extent of popular support and participation in the war effort is one of the themes elaborated in the Open University course AA312, *Total War and Social Change: Europe 1914–1955*.

The dominant theme in British films of the Second World War is that of the 'people's war', with its connotations of participation and inclusivity. This myth – which has of course been questioned by historians – originates in propaganda films made during the war itself. Film propaganda in Britain was the responsibility of the Ministry of Information (MOI), which had a Films Division to devise official policy for the filmic representation of Britain and its people at war. The MOI sponsored documentary films, both through its own official production agency the Crown Film Unit (formerly the GPO Film Unit) and through independent documentary companies, and acted in an advisory capacity as far as commercial feature film-makers were concerned. It offered guidelines on what was considered good propaganda and provided practical assistance such as facilitating the release of personnel from the services to participate in productions (David Niven, for example, was allowed temporary release from the army to act in two feature films – *The First of the Few* and *The Way Ahead* – while Laurence Olivier was released from the Fleet Air Arm to direct and star in the patriotic *Henry V*). The MOI encouraged the production of films that presented images of national unity and social cohesion in the conduct of the war. This applied as much to pictures about the home front, such as *Millions Like Us* (1943) – note the sense of inclusivity in the title – as to those about the armed services, such as *In Which We Serve* (1942) and *The Way Ahead* (1944). Many people are likely to have seen *In Which We Serve*, Noël Coward's patriotic tribute to the Royal Navy. It has been interpreted as a metaphor for the British nation at war, with the ship HMS *Torrin* representing the country, united behind its Churchillian leader (though the role of the fictional Captain Kinross is also said to have been modelled on Coward's friend, the naval commander Louis Mountbatten) (Chapman, 1998, pp. 184–7).

The MOI was also concerned to encourage realism and authenticity in the representation of the war effort. Some early feature films, such as *Convoy* (1940) and *Ships with Wings* (1941), attracted criticism for presenting the war in melodramatic terms, full of unconvincing heroics and spectacular derring-do. Although these pictures were popular at the box-office in the early years of the war, the MOI – and the critics – preferred sober, realistic, unsensational narratives that focused on the role of ordinary men and women. This style became more prominent from the middle of the war onwards, exemplified by films such as *We Dive at Dawn*, *Nine Men* and *San Demetrio, London* (all 1943). The change in emphasis was partly due to an MOI policy directive of 1943 which declared that what it wanted were 'first class war subjects realistically treated, realistic films of everyday life, [and] high quality entertainment films'. It disapproved of

> war subjects exploited for cheap sensationalism, the morbid and the maudlin, entertainment stories which are stereotyped or hackneyed and unlikely because of their theme or general character to reflect well upon this country at home and abroad.

> (Quoted in Chapman, 1998, p. 80)

When it came to 'realistic films of everyday life', documentary film-makers were widely regarded as the most accomplished practitioners. The British documentary movement had acquired before the war a reputation for realism – or rather for what its influential father-figure, John Grierson, described as 'the creative treatment of actuality' – that was harnessed to the propaganda war by the MOI. The prevailing image of stoical Britons enduring wartime deprivations and German bombardment originates in short documentary films of 1940 such as *Britain at Bay*, *Britain Can Take It!* and *Christmas Under Fire*. The GPO/Crown Film Unit, which was responsible for these short works, also turned its hand to the production of longer narrative documentaries describing, in story terms, different aspects of the British war effort. These included *Target for Tonight* (1941), a reconstruction of an RAF bombing raid over Germany, and the celebrated *Fires Were Started* (1943), a tribute to London's auxiliary fire service during the Blitz that was much admired for its sober yet poetic treatment of the camaraderie and dangers faced by those men and women. Lindsay Anderson, who later became a film-maker himself, said of *Fires Were Started*,

No other British film made during the war, documentary or feature, achieved such a continuous and poignant truthfulness, or treated the subject of men at war with such a sense of its incidental glories and its essential tragedy.

(Quoted in Chapman, 1998, p. 176)

At this point, I should like you to turn to the second reading, an extract from an article published in the journal *Documentary News Letter* (*DNL*) in December 1941. *DNL* was the mouthpiece of the documentary film movement, regarded as the progressive sector of the film industry that was especially concerned with the representation of 'ordinary' people and their part in the war effort. The article was written by Jiri Weiss, a Czech documentarist who was exiled to and working in Britain during the war.

An Allied film unit

As the world settles to the greatest battle of all time, there is a chance to break the barriers which until now have stood between the peoples of Europe and forced them one by one into submission. The obstacles, and those who wished them and profited by them, have been smashed or exposed; moreover, many of the very interests which promoted isolationist feeling and tendencies in various countries, and opposed international collaboration, have been forced to change their mind; they now know that together we stand or together we perish.

Never in their history have the British been so much cut off from Europe as they are now; yet there was probably never less isolationist feeling in their hearts. The feeling of solidarity with other peoples is growing continuously. Even more is it growing in those lands which have been betrayed or conquered.

Like all mass feelings, this growing understanding of the fact of mutual dependence of all nations is essentially instinctive and vague. There is a danger that it may be forgotten once Nazism is defeated. Now is the moment to prepare the basis for maybe a better world. Human beings have been stirred as they can be stirred only by great crises or wars. The reality which people feel only vaguely must be interpreted clearly and understandably, as creatively as only film can do it – by documentary means.

British documentary film makers have given this country the best war films in the world. Technically extremely skilful, they have touched every subject with a breath of human feeling; they have introduced on the screen their people as the hero. We have seen in their films the real face of Britain: the miner, the seaman, the worker. We have seen people in shelters, the social services, the men and women in the Forces. We have had on the screen an exposition of the giant war-machine, that could not have been done better ...

But still, this is not enough. It is not enough to show on the screen the face of the man in the street or the man behind the lathe and for this man always to be a member of the same single country. *Reality*, as the documentary film desires to interpret it, is a vast and complex pattern where the destinies of human beings and nations are inextricably bound up in a common destiny. It is not sufficient to show the man in the street in Britain: *you must show the man in the street in Paris, in Prague, in Moscow, in Calcutta.* Documentary analysis must be extended to peoples of the world. The average Briton (and therefore, much more, the Neutral) is fed of course day by day with 'Allied' propaganda. But what does he know of the content of this word or of its significance?

The British Government which prepared the haven for so many refugee Governments in this country must have considered this step as one of great political significance; otherwise the whole thing is just a giant tragi-comic farce. The Government of Britain, by doing what it did, wanted to express its solidarity with the conquered peoples, and also it desired to indicate that it stands for the re-erection of the *status quo ante* 1938 (Munich), therefore, the stress on the word *Allied*.

But how are the 'Allies' presented on the screen to the British public? What do they hear and see of them? The Greeks are represented by King George [II]; the Poles by General Sikorski; the Czechs by [Edvard] Benes; the French by [General] de Gaulle; then there is [the Dutch] Queen Wilhelmina with her daughter and her baby ... and besides other notables there are rows of soldiers, flags, drums, tanks *ad infinitum*. But where are the peoples? It is important to acquaint the public with notable politicians, but it is much more important to tell them something about the 15, 30 or 40 million compatriots who stand side by side with them – not in security in the clubs of this island, but over there, at home, facing the terror of the enemy. It is they, and not the handful of politicians over here, with whom an understanding must be found. And it is they who will decide the fate of Europe. The British people, who for so long have lived in a splendid isolation on their island, must know about their real allies ...

The enlarging of the line of British film propaganda would certainly have a great effect not only overseas, but also in this country. It would show to the multi-national millions of the

Americas that Britain stands for much more than just the British Empire, that the word 'Allies' is not just a common denominator of yesterday's politicians in Sunday dress. British documentary has stirred the world by showing the face of Britain. But why not show also the face of Poland, of Holland, of Czechoslovakia? ... Peoples of this island, of the Dominions, of the U.S.A. would be stirred to greater efforts in the field of industrial production and elsewhere if they saw true stories of the multitude of nations which have forgotten the enmities of yesterday, and now stand side by side.

(Weiss, 1941, p. 233)

EXERCISE

Now consider the following questions.

1   What are Weiss's two principal complaints about the content of British film propaganda?

2   Can you identify the obvious problem with making the kind of films Weiss advocates?

3   What is the significance of the date of the article?

DISCUSSION

1   Weiss's first complaint is that British film propaganda has focused primarily on Britain at the expense of other nations. His second is that when other nations have been represented in films, they have been represented by prominent public figures (heads of state, politicians and generals) rather than by ordinary people.

2   The most obvious problem is that as most of continental Europe was occupied by the German army at this time, it would have been impossible to film on location in the traditional documentary style.

3   The significance of the date is that it was December 1941 when the USA entered the war on the Allies' side. (Following the Japanese bombing of Pearl Harbor on 7 December and the subsequent American declaration of war on Japan, Germany and Italy declared war on the USA on 10 December.) Weiss makes no mention of American involvement in the war, so it seems likely that the article was written before Pearl Harbor.

On re-reading this extract you might note the terms in which Weiss describes British documentary films – phrases such as 'the real face of Britain', 'their people as the hero' and so on are typical of the ways in which commentators have described wartime documentary films. But there is much truth in Weiss's point that, for all their realism, documentary film-makers focused on the British war effort at the expense of the efforts of their allies. This is not to say there were no films about these allies, but they were certainly in a minority. But perhaps this is only to be expected. For one thing, the sense of a commonality of interests and a community of nations advocated by Weiss was not always evident in Britain's relations with its allies. For example, the government had a rather strained relationship with Free French leader Charles de Gaulle (something that may well have influenced De Gaulle when he later vetoed the UK's application to join the Common Market in the 1960s), while the involvement of the Soviet Union posed problems for British politicians and film-makers alike in that they needed to express their support for the war effort of the Russian people without suggesting that they supported the communist political system. For this reason, the USSR was largely ignored in terms of film propaganda, with the MOI content simply to distribute some Soviet documentary films, re-edited and with an English commentary.

Weiss's suggestion that films could be made about the occupied countries, however, did not mean that film units should be sent to those countries. He suggested 'reconstructed' documentaries – in the manner of *Target for Tonight*, which had not sent camera operators to Germany but had used studio sets and facilities to convey its message, including the fuselage of a Wellington bomber and a reconstruction of the Bomber Command Operations Room. The problem here, however, was location. While some parts of the United Kingdom resembled parts of Europe – for instance, *The Silent Village* (1943), a film about the **Lidice massacre** in Czechoslovakia, was filmed in the south Wales mining community of Cwmgiedd – there were no UK cities that resembled Paris or Prague, and studio city sets always have an air of inauthenticity about them (you need only to watch Hollywood films about Britain at war, such as *Mrs Miniver* or *The White Cliffs of Dover*, to recognize the truth of this observation).

In June 1942 the Nazis massacred the entire population of the Czech village of Lidice, in reprisal for the assassination of Reichsprotektor Reinhard Heydrich by Czech agents trained in Britain.

Before moving on, I shall briefly note some more general points about Weiss's article which have nothing to do specifically with film but which do relate to some of the broader issues discussed here. You may have noticed Weiss's characterization of the British as living 'in a splendid isolation on their island'. How far do you think the British are insular and cut off from Europe? We might identify a paradox here during the Second World War, when Britain was militarily isolated from the rest of Europe but actually had greater common interests with the continent (namely the defeat of Nazism) than ever before. It is a question to ponder. In terms of cinema, certainly, there is little reason to disagree with Weiss's thesis. The Allied Film Unit he advocated never came to pass – indeed attempts at co-production were often hampered by political differences and national prejudices – and the filmic representation of the British war effort remained focused on the national experience. This insularity was to become even more apparent in postwar films about the Second World War, which marginalized the role of Britain's allies even further.

War films were largely absent from British screens in the late 1940s – this was probably a reaction to the glut of such films during the war itself – but they returned to prominence during the 1950s and early 1960s when these pictures became a staple of British cinema. The year 1950 marked a significant time for the revival of the genre, when two factually based war films – *Odette* and *The Wooden Horse* – were among the top ten attractions at the British box-office. For the rest of the decade war films were regularly among the box-office successes: *The Cruel Sea* (1953), *The Dam Busters* (1955), *Reach for the Sky* (1956) and *Sink the Bismarck!* (1960) were the biggest attractions of their respective years. While *The Dam Busters* was the most successful British film of the decade in the domestic market, the industry's greatest international success came with the psychological prisoner-of-war drama *The Bridge on the River Kwai* (1957), which was the leading money-maker in the North American market for the year 1958.

You may be familiar with some of these films, which crop up frequently on television – evidence of the enduring popularity and resonance of the images of war they present. When we look at them in closer detail, however, we find that, with only one exception, they all focus on stories about the British involvement in the war. They may be summed up as follows:

Odette: a biopic of Special Operations Executive agent Odette Churchill (a Frenchwoman by birth, though played in the film by the very English Anna Neagle).

The Wooden Horse: British prisoners escape from a German prison camp.

The Cruel Sea: a fictional account of a Royal Navy corvette crew in the battle of the Atlantic.

The Dam Busters: a factually based account of the invention of the 'bouncing bomb' by Barnes Wallis, and its use against the dams along the Ruhr in 1943.

Reach for the Sky: a biopic of the pilot Douglas Bader.

Sink the Bismarck!: a factually based account of the Royal Navy's destruction of Germany's most powerful battleship.

The exception is *The Bridge on the River Kwai*, which gives a prominent role to an American character (played by William Holden), though this is balanced by two British stars (Alec Guinness and Jack Hawkins). Indeed the vast majority of British war films of the 1950s focus on the home country's role. There was a particular trend for prisoner-of-war films – the cycle included *Albert, RN* (1953), *The Colditz Story* (1954) and *Danger Within* (1958) – in which plucky British officers escaped from their German (or Italian) captors, and an emphasis on events and areas where the British had been involved, such as *The Battle of the River Plate* (1956) and *Dunkirk* (1958). There are a few films which include the Americans, and a few which include the French Resistance, but – significantly – none which include the Soviet Union.

EXERCISE

How do you think we can account for the absence of the Soviet Union from British war films of the 1950s?

DISCUSSION

The Cold War made the Soviet Union an ideological enemy, so it was frowned upon to promote its role in winning the war. It is hardly surprising that the role of the USSR should have been omitted from the British cinema's reconstruction of the Second World War, just as its role was marginalized in the historiography of the war during the 1950s and 1960s. Moreover, successive British governments, both Labour and Conservative, actively sought to create an anti-communist, anti-Soviet consensus. One of the instruments they employed to this end was the cinema, encouraging the production of anti-communist films such as *High Treason* and *Secret People* (both 1951). In the prevailing climate of opinion it would have been contentious, not to mention poor commercial sense, to produce films promoting the Soviet contribution to the war.

The films that Mallory took particular objection to were *Reach for the Sky* ('Wing-Commander Kenneth More soaring through the blue with merry quip and jest'), *The Silent Enemy* ('Larry Harvey, as Commander Crabb, jousting mythically with handsome Italian frogmen in his latest underwater opera') and *Carve Her Name with Pride* ('two-fisted liberties taken with the Violet Szabo story').

While war films were popular with the British public throughout the 1950s, they had a mixed reception from the critics. One complaint was that such works made too many compromises with historical reality. Leslie Mallory, film critic of the *News Chronicle*, accused these films of 'the assassination of truth' and was astonished that fictional stories were lapped up by audiences: 'The most baffling attribute of the British picturegoer is his capacity for enjoying wide-screen war fables which he knows to be sacrilegious pantomimes of the conflict he personally lived through' (*News Chronicle*, 13 March 1958).

The next reading is an extract from an article by William Whitebait, film critic of the *New Statesman*. It was written on the occasion of the royal première of the film *Dunkirk*.

Bombardment

It is both tedious and disquieting, our addiction to war films. Not many days ago in Leicester Square, where snowflakes mingled with the lime fluff, I happened to look up through the trees at the cinemas beyond: one by one boasted war films; to the north *The Safecracker* (Crook Does his Bit, Croaks), to the east *The Silent Enemy* (With Crabb in the Underwater Ballet), to the south *Carve Her Name With Pride* (Woolworth's to Resistance). Since then *The Safecracker* has been relieved by *Dunkirk*, with *The Bridge on the River Kwai* on its flank. And elsewhere, down Haymarket and on the circuits, there are similar concentrations and replacements.

A dozen years after World War II we find ourselves in the really quite desperate situation of being, not sick of war, but hideously in love with it. Not actively fighting, we aren't at peace. The H-bomb looms ahead, and we daren't look at it; so we creep back to the lacerating comfort of 'last time'. No old general preparing to lose the next war could dream more disastrously. And I think that war films, nearly all of which hark back, emotionally as well as factually, contribute more than any other source to this daydream; because if the horror of war strikes the eye more than in any other way, so does its glossing-over lull fears and angers, and creates an imaginary present in which we can go on enjoying our finest hours. That is a price paid for victory.

So while we 'adventure' at Suez, in the cinemas we are still thrashing Rommel – and discovering that he was a gentleman! – sweeping the Atlantic of submarines, sending the few to scatter Goering's many. The more we lose face in the world's counsels, the grander, in our excessively modest way, we swell in this illusionary mirror held up by the screen. It is less a spur to morale than a salve to wounded pride; and as art or entertainment, dreadfully dull.

(*New Statesman*, 5 April 1958)

EXERCISE

How does Whitebait account for the British obsession with war films?

DISCUSSION

Whitebait's argument is that war films provide a degree of comfort and certainty (audiences know what their outcome will be) missing from the present. He suggests that reliving the war is a way of coming to terms with Britain's postwar decline. The reality of the country's decline as a world power was rudely demonstrated by the Suez crisis of 1956, to which Whitebait refers. (When Egypt's Colonel Nasser nationalized the Suez Canal, Britain and France sent troops there to protect their interests, only to be forced into a humiliating climb-down when their action was condemned by the United Nations and was not supported by the United States. This episode brought home to Britain that it was no longer capable of asserting its global military and economic interests without American support.) Moreover, the late 1950s and early 1960s witnessed the 'retreat from empire', as most of Britain's former colonies won their independence. Reliving the Second World War – and privileging Britain's role in winning it – was one means of reasserting national pride in the face of decline. Other commentators as well as Whitebait recognized this. The American film critic Arthur Knight, for example, observed:

> For the past few years, the British filmmakers have been making stabs at a kind of national epic. They have been going back to events in their recent past – and particularly back to World War II – as if intent on discovering, in this day of uncertainty and confusion, those values that once spelt survival.
>
> (*Saturday Review*, 20 September 1958)

The British war films of the 1950s, in short, were as much responding to postwar conditions as they were revisiting the events of the war itself.

Nazis and 'good Germans'

Germany's experience of the Second World War was obviously very different from Britain's. Quite apart from the outcome of the war, the legacy of the Nazi period left psychological scars on German society that have been discussed elsewhere in this book. We would not, therefore, expect German cinema to propagate a heroic myth of the war in the same manner as British cinema. But this is not to say that the war has been absent from German cinema. In the 1950s, for example, war narratives were prominent in West German cinema alongside the more traditional *Heimat* films (focusing on home and family life). Productions such as *Canaris* (1954), *The Jackboot Mutiny*

(1954) and *The Devil's General* (1955) dramatize stories of internal German resistance to the Nazi regime. There was a political agenda at work here that arose from West Germany's situation in the 1950s, as Sorlin identifies:

> The German studios were in a position to fill the gap in the mid-1950s, but their series of resistance films was uniquely a commercial attempt intended to exploit the situation. Defeated Germany was being progressively reintegrated into the concert of western nations in the 1950s, first by entering the European Coal and Steel Community, by experiencing the end of the Allied occupation and finally by becoming a member of NATO. During this period the Germans were anxious to prove they had not been entirely infected by Nazism, and in this respect films celebrating the persistence of a strong individual opposition to Hitler were apt to please domestic opinion as well as those foreigners who did not conceive of a European future without the integration of Germany. The films made in 1954–57 were not blatant propaganda but were merely adapted to the circumstances. Once Germany was rehabilitated the producers abandoned the field.
>
> (Sorlin, 1991, pp. 76–7)

We might say that in focusing on the German resistance to Hitler (such opposition did exist, historians have suggested, but was centred on the efforts of individuals and small groups who did not command much popular support; see for example Fest, 1996) West German cinema was simply creating its own myths of the war in a manner not dissimilar to British cinema of the time. But there are some similarities in the German and British representations of the war. British films of the 1950s also make a distinction between Nazis (characterized as cruel, ruthless, ideological automatons) and 'good Germans' (characterized as basically decent, honourable soldiers who disliked the excesses of Hitler). British films notable for their humanization of the enemy include *The Battle of the River Plate* (1956), *The One that Got Away* (1957) and *Ice Cold in Alex* (1958).

The theme of Nazis and good Germans is evident in what is undoubtedly the most acclaimed West German war film, *Das Boot/The Boat* (1981) (Plates 12 and 13). This was a major box-office success both in Germany and abroad; it brought director Wolfgang Petersen to the attention of Hollywood; and an expanded version of the film was shown as a television mini-series. It is an important film that is worth considering in more depth.

Figures 5.3, 5.4 and 5.5 *Das Boot.* Photos: Ronald Grant Archive

Synopsis: The battle of the Atlantic, 1941. A war correspondent, Werner (played by Herbert Grönemeyer), joins the crew of the submarine U-96. The vessel's captain (played by Jürgen Prochnow) gets his men drunk to alleviate their fears. U-96 leaves on a patrol and has a narrow escape from a British destroyer when it attacks a convoy. Another convoy is sighted and this time the submarine successfully torpedoes a merchant ship. As U-96 is attacked with depth charges, the captain is forced to take the submarine to unprecedented depths. The chief mechanic (played by Erwin Leder) becomes unhinged and deserts his post; the captain threatens him with court-martial but later rescinds this. The submarine surfaces and finishes off a damaged merchant vessel, though it is unable to rescue the survivors. U-96 is then ordered to proceed to Italy for repairs and stops off in neutral Spain, where the crew attends a Christmas banquet. Proceeding through the Straits of Gibraltar the submarine is bombed by enemy aircraft and goes into an uncontrollable dive. With the oxygen running out the crew manage to bring the vessel to the surface and reach port in La Rochelle. They are welcomed back as heroes, but an air-raid destroys the docks, sinks the submarine and kills most of the crew, including the captain. The film ends with Werner kneeling next to the captain's body.

Das Boot was acclaimed for its realistic representation of the psychological effects faced by men at war. But is it an 'anti-war' film? To some extent, its narrative structure is similar to that of *All Quiet on the Western Front*: the war is seen through the eyes of a newcomer (Paul/Werner) who is shocked by his first experience of combat; the battle sequences are punctuated by a brief respite (Paul's leave/the Christmas dinner); and both films end with the death of a central protagonist. You will have to watch the film yourself to decide whether it is making a statement about the futility of war. But what about its representation of Germans and Nazis? One view is given in the fourth reading, an extract from a review of *Das Boot* by film critic Richard Combs, which appeared in the British film magazine the *Monthly Film Bulletin* in 1982.

Das Boot (The Boat)

The predictable stiltedness of the dubbing of this, West Germany's most expensive film and probably its biggest box-office smash at home and abroad, only emphasises what might have been obvious anyway. To wit, that the Germans have produced, out of their side of the last conflict, a film acceptable to their ex-foes by playing into the values and stereotypes of something like the 1950s British model. To avoid dealing with the specifics of who was a Nazi and what constitutes Fascism, the film makes do with an old-fashioned adventure yarn about the exploits of a U-boat over which hangs the pall of sacrifices nobly made and the ultimate futility of war. Heroism in the grand, war-winning manner is of course ruled out, but equally unregenerative heroics-for-the-good-of-the-group are the order of the day (the film not only isolates these submariners from the conduct of the war in general, but doesn't provide much information about the submarine service itself). There is some de rigueur decrying of Hitler and the villains at the top, which seems both strangely detached and disingenuous (the Captain and his older alter ego, the drunken, decorated veteran Thomsen, are allowed – rather unconvincingly – to make speeches on the subject). The one avowedly Nazi crew member of U-96 is easily recognised because he is fastidiously neat about his food; the sloppiness of the others is proof not just that the film is scrupulously realistic but that they are politically okay. What all this suggests is that Wolfgang Petersen and his collaborators are so busy looking over their own shoulders – 'dealing' with the problem of German guilt by luxuriating in a sense of doom about the enterprise of U-96 and its crew – while looking towards those ex-Allied markets, that they can't begin to investigate the subject in a more honest way. Even the character who traditionally should have provided some objectivity, the war correspondent Werner, is simply absorbed in the crew. In this context, the vaunted realism of the production, with Rolf Zehetbauer's no-expense-spared submarine facsimiles, becomes tediously beside the point. The steadicam zipping through the claustrophobic cabin in moments of crisis turns into a cliché before it makes much dramatic or visual impact (likewise the disembodied aural effects, courtesy of Dolby, as the submariners listen nervously to the groanings of the sub as it dives ever deeper). Style and tone overall is very roughly cobbled-together rhetoric, veering from comic-strip and *Boy's Own* to painterly moments (Bosch, perhaps, for the huddle of faces in the submarine's hellish twilight as the enemy circles overhead) and even designs that look rather operatic (though this may have something to do with the sense of dislocation caused by poor optical and miniature work). *The Boat* ends up making less impression as a German history of the war than *Cross of Iron* and, as sea stories go, *The Battle of the River Plate*.

(Combs, 1982, p. 81)

EXERCISE _____

Now consider the following questions.

1   What are Combs's main complaints about the film?

2   What external constraints does he imply influenced the representation of Germans in the film?

DISCUSSION _____

1   Combs complains that the film side-steps the wider political issues arising from Nazism because of its stereotyped characterization, and that, for all the realism of its setting, it is essentially an adventure story rather than an anti-war statement.

2   He implies that, as the film was made with an eye on non-German markets, it has been compromised by the need to make story and characterization acceptable to those markets.

This particular review is not representative of critical reaction to the film, but it provides an interesting corrective to the assumption that because a film portrays war as an unpleasant, frightening and horrific experience it is therefore an anti-war statement. (This is also apparent in the responses to Steven Spielberg's Hollywood epic _Saving Private Ryan_, 1998, which begins with a harrowing depiction of the Omaha beach landings on 6 June 1944 but then settles into a traditional dramatic war narrative.) I would argue that _Das Boot_ is examining the psychological effects of war rather than making a case for or against its conduct. I would take issue with Combs, who criticizes the film for not '"dealing" with the problem of German guilt', as this does not seem to me to be the point of the film. Indeed I would go so far as to suggest that the fact that the protagonists of the film are German is almost irrelevant – they could equally have been British or American, and much the same incidents and experiences could have been portrayed in either case. In this context, _Das Boot_ might be compared to British submarine films such as _We Dive at Dawn_ (1943) and _Morning Departure_ (1950). Moreover, the incident of the engineer who panics and deserts his post recalls a similar episode from _In Which We Serve_. The battle of the Atlantic was equally harrowing for German and Allied submariners. We would not expect British films on the subject to examine the question of war guilt; should we necessarily expect a German film to do so?

_____

Resistance and collaboration

A different type of war guilt can be discerned in films made in those countries which suffered German occupation. The French and Polish cinemas make an interesting comparison in this regard, because of the different ways in which they explore the legacies of resistance and collaboration. They also demonstrate the politics invested in narratives of resistance. Just as the German resistance films of the 1950s can be seen as a response to broader political issues of the time, so film-makers in France and Poland have used the resistance film both as a vehicle for re-examining their national pasts and as an allegory of present circumstances.

The heroic resistance film became a popular genre of French cinema in the late 1950s, coinciding with the establishment in 1958 of the new Fifth Republic under the leadership of wartime hero **Charles de Gaulle**. The historical significance of these films is explained by French cinema specialist Susan Hayward:

> During the de Gaulle era, some sixty feature films about the Occupation period were made (compared with only eleven under **Giscard**). The peak years were 1958–62 when thirty films were produced, half of which were either specifically about the Resistance (nine in all) or directly referred to it through their narrative (six). This exaltation of the Resistance is hardly surprising given de Gaulle's prominent role as leader of the Free French during World War II. This time, of course, the resurrection of the Resistance 'as a good thing' was once again not without its political expediency. De Gaulle's designation of power in 1958 was a popular decision, but he still had to convince the electorate to vote for his constitutional reforms and consolidate his own legitimacy (through universal suffrage). There is no intention to point to a propaganda conspiracy here, but it is clear that, with pre-censorship still in effect, scenarios not extolling the Resistance would be unlikely to get past the final post of censorship. Whatever the case, the indications are that producers had seen a winner in cashing in on de Gaulle's iconographic prestige and milked it for what it was worth. Post-1962, the genre started its move back towards the periphery. But by then de Gaulle had the cachet of legitimacy and television too – the medium he was henceforth to exploit as his propaganda sheet.

> (Hayward, 1993, p. 250)

De Gaulle was the first president of the Fifth French Republic (1958–69); Giscard d'Estaing was the third president (1974–81).

French cinema promoted a national myth of the Resistance – exaggerating the extent of active participation and marginalizing incidences of internal dissent within the movement – in much the same way as British cinema promoted the myths of Dunkirk and 'the Few'. It was not until the 1970s that a film dared to question the dominant myths and to tell the 'truth' about the Resistance (the inverted commas here indicate that we should not necessarily equate the questioning of myths with some kind of historical truth). This film was *Lacombe, Lucien* (1974) (Plates 14 and 15), the work of the critically acclaimed director Louis Malle, which proved so controversial that Malle was forced to leave France to work in America for the next decade.

> *Synopsis*: The film begins in June 1944, shortly after the Allies have landed in Normandy. In a village in southwest France 17-year-old Lucien Lacombe (played by Pierre Blaise) works as an orderly in a nursing home. Lucien approaches a schoolmaster whom he knows to have contacts with the Resistance and asks to join the group; he is rejected. Cycling home, he has a puncture and is arrested for breaking curfew. He is treated in a friendly manner by Gestapo agents and after being plied with drink he talks about his village. The next day the schoolmaster is arrested. Lucien falls under the spell of the Gestapo and its French collaborators, including the aristocratic Jean-Bernard de Voison (played by Stéphane Bouy) and his mistress Betty (played by Loumi Jacobesco). Lucien becomes a collaborator, is given a pistol and money that he spends on clothes and in pursuit of France (played by Aurore Clément), daughter of a Jewish tailor hiding from the Gestapo. As the Allied forces move south, Resistance activity increases; Jean-Bernard and Betty are killed. Lucien is sent with a German NCO to arrest France and her grandmother, but he kills the soldier and hides the two women in the countryside. They enjoy an idyllic rural lifestyle on a farm, but a closing caption reveals what lies in store for Lucien: 'Lucien Lacombe was arrested on 12 October 1944. Tried by a military court of the Resistance, he was sentenced to death and executed.'

The subject of collaboration was obviously a difficult issue for French society to address, even thirty years after the war, and this accounts to a large extent for the hostility that greeted the film. Malle's intention had been to expose some of the myths surrounding the occupation: 'What they teach French school-children about the Occupation is a bunch of lies' (Austin, 1996, p. 30). This is what he said about the controversy surrounding the film:

> What makes *Lacombe, Lucien* strong and what made the controversy somewhat a series of misunderstandings is that in its description of characters and events the film exposes all the ambiguities and contradictions in behaviour that

Figures 5.6 and 5.7 *Lacombe, Lucien*. Photos: Ronald Grant Archive

belonged to that period. For instance, in this part of France where Resistance and collaboration had been facts of life, the film was completely accepted. People who had lived through that period knew that this film was completely true and honest about what actually happened. And people who were not French took it for what it was: a reflection on the nature of evil. The controversy was between French intellectuals and politicians. Those who attacked it did it on the grounds that it was fiction; we had invented and put on the screen a character who was complex and ambiguous to the point where his behaviour was acceptable. For them, it justified collaboration – which certainly is not what I was trying to do.

(Quoted in French, 1993, p. 103)

Malle's remarks seem as ambiguous as the film itself – note how he talks about the film being both 'completely true and honest' in one breath and then 'fiction' in another. The character of Lucien is fictional, but to my mind the suggestion that Malle invented a story of collaboration does not fully explain the controversy. It is not merely that the film suggests that some French people may have collaborated with the Gestapo (this is a matter of historical record), but also that it presents fascism as an attractive and seductive idea. Lucien does not become a collaborator through political or ideological commitment, but is lured by the promise of money, a gun and women. Significantly, the press release for the film described Lucien as 'un jeune d'aujourd'hui' (a youth of today). Do you think that Malle was suggesting that contemporary French youth might also be attracted by fascism? Obviously, you will need to watch the film yourself to answer that question.

Other French films of the Resistance have been much less controversial than *Lacombe, Lucien*. They tend to leave politics aside and focus instead on personal narratives – François Truffaut's *Le Dernier Métro/The Last Metro* (1980), for example, is really a star vehicle for Catherine Deneuve and Gérard Depardieu. After a decade in Hollywood, Louis Malle returned to French cinema and to the subject of the occupation with *Au revoir les enfants* (1987), which was a major critical and commercial success: it won seven Césars (the French equivalent of Hollywood's Oscars), suggesting that Malle was now welcomed back into his native country. The film explores the friendship between the boy Julien (purportedly based on Malle's own wartime memories) and a Jewish boy. Guy Austin considers that, in contrast to *Lacombe, Lucien*, 'this is a positive portrayal of the French during the Occupation, especially the priests who – in contrast with the complicity of the Catholic Church in the Vichy regime – shelter Jewish boys in their school' (Austin, 1996, p. 32). Similarly, Claude Berri's *Lucie Aubrac* (1997) is based on the true story of the wife of a

Resistance fighter who organizes his rescue after he is captured by the Gestapo and escapes with him to Britain. Again, the national story of resistance here becomes the personal narrative of a romantic couple, played by leading French stars Carole Bouquet and Daniel Auteil. The effect of the film, as one critic put it, is 'to generate the oceanic feeling of the French as one big anti-Nazi family' (Darke, 1998, p. 47).

With the notable exception of *Lacombe, Lucien*, therefore, French cinema has portrayed wartime resistance in terms which emphasize national unity. The internal divisions within the Resistance are barely alluded to and, significantly, the role of the communists is largely written out of the cinematic historiography. In eastern European cinemas, however, a rather different picture of internal dissent and disillusionment characterizes the cinema of resistance. Eastern European cinema is still relatively unknown in the west, even after the collapse of communism, but one film-maker who has received international recognition, and whose films engage explicitly with the subject of resistance, is the Polish director Andrzej Wajda. His war trilogy – *Pokolenie/A Generation* (1954), *Kanal* (1956) and *Popiól I Diament/Ashes and Diamonds* (1958) – represents a rather different use of the resistance narrative compared with French cinema.

Wajda had served in the (non-communist) Home Army during the war and his experiences have undoubtedly influenced his films. It is tempting, given the political situation in Poland after 1945, to interpret films about resistance to the Nazis as straightforward allegories of resistance to Soviet communism. But there is little that is straightforward about Wajda's films. 'In the course of the trilogy', write film historians Thompson and Bordwell,

> [Wajda's] representation of the underground evolves from ideologically correct criticism of the army (*A Generation*) through a grim celebration of its stubborn heroism (*Kanal*) to an ambiguous affirmation of the non-Communist Resistance (*Ashes and Diamonds*).

> (Thompson and Bordwell, 1994, p. 475)

A Generation bears a superficial similarity to *Lacombe, Lucien* in that it features a protagonist who joins the Resistance not because of political or national sentiment but because he is attracted to the woman who leads an underground group. Stach and his teenage friends initially treat fighting the German occupation forces as a cat-and-mouse game and engage in spontaneous acts of defiance that are of no military value. Stach then takes up an apprenticeship and begins to learn basic Marxist economics from a shop steward. He volunteers for the Resistance when he meets the beautiful underground leader Dora and recruits his friends into the group. The film suggests that Stach finds maturity through suffering loss (several of his friends are killed) and by accepting left-wing political thought. In this sense it endorses the political system under which it was made and provides an ideologically 'correct' view of the Resistance in which it is the communists who are shown to have a political and social agenda committed to reconstruction and anti-fascism.

The post-Stalinist 'thaw' in eastern Europe, which saw the relaxing of doctrinaire communism, had only just begun when Wajda made *A Generation* in 1954 and the film is therefore not inclined to question the party line, though it does hint at the differences between the communists and the Home Army (which was loyal to the Polish government in exile in London). In 1956, when Wajda made *Kanal*, the thaw had reached its fullest extent and he took advantage of the conditions to make a film that was more sympathetic to the non-communist Resistance than its predecessor. *Kanal* celebrates – even mythologizes – the Warsaw uprising of 1944 through its narrative of a platoon of Home Army partisans who fight to the bitter end. When they finally realize the uprising has been defeated, they attempt to escape through the sewers and are killed off one by one. The partisans' descent into the sewers has been interpreted as a psychological descent into the minds of a defeated people: in the longer term the defeat of the Home Army by the Nazis also removed the main source of Polish opposition to communism.

Ashes and Diamonds, the third film of the trilogy, is even more explicitly anti-communist. It is set at the very end of the war and explores how the generation of young men who served in the Resistance came to reconcile themselves to communist rule. Maciek, a disillusioned partisan, is ordered to assassinate Szczuka, a communist district leader. Maciek is uneasy about the mission, as Szczuka is a fellow Resistance fighter. Thus the unity forged in the struggle against Nazism has now disintegrated; Pole turns upon Pole and former comrades in arms become sworn enemies. The film has a bitterly ironic resolution: Maciek reluctantly goes through with his mission and kills Szczuka, only himself to be shot accidentally by a policeman and die on a garbage heap while fireworks signal the end of the war.

Wajda's films have been acclaimed for their combination of 'gritty realism' and 'poetic vision'. He uses the resistance narrative to question official histories of the war. What makes his films different from *Lacombe, Lucien*, however, is that they engage directly with political issues and highlight the differences between communists and non-communists – a remarkably bold theme, given the prevailing political circumstances. Wajda's films are not typical of eastern European cinema at the time – they were denounced by a conference of communist film-makers held in Prague in 1957 who called for war films to adhere more closely to the party line – but they made Polish cinema visible in the west, where they won various awards (*Kanal*, for example, won a special prize at the Cannes Film Festival).

Conclusions

This chapter has offered you a necessarily selective and much condensed discussion of the representation of war in different European national cinemas. There is of course no substitute for actually watching the films themselves, and I suggest you do that now, using the Select filmography at the end of the chapter as a guide. In general, however, I would suggest that the cinematic representation of war is characterized by three general features which are present in most films and most national cinemas.

1   *War as a national experience.* On the whole each country tells its own past through its own films. Moreover, it usually tells a version of its own past that it is comfortable with, rather than one that necessarily represents the historical actuality. There are, admittedly, a number of films made as international co-productions which attempt to show different sides of the war – films such as *Cross of Iron* (1977), for example, an Anglo-German co-production with an American director (Sam Peckinpah), or, to take a film that is showing in cinemas at the time of writing, *Enemy at the Gates* (2001), an epic of the battle of Stalingrad which casts British actors (Joseph Fiennes, Jude Law) as Russians and an American (Ed Harris) as a German, and is directed by a Frenchman (Jean-Jacques Annaud). But such films are exceptional rather than typical. Most war films, produced within the context of particular national cinemas, focus on the war experience of their own country. This is especially apparent in the British films of the 1950s, which focus almost exclusively on the British war effort, but French and Polish resistance films are no less concerned with their own national experience.

2   *War as a personal narrative.* Feature films tell stories, even when based on real events; these stories are taken forward by characters, usually played by stars who provide points of identification for the audience. Films deal with the specific rather than the general, and with the individual rather than with the mass. War films typically focus on stories of individuals or small groups – a platoon rather than an entire army, one U-boat crew rather than the entire navy, one resistance cell rather than the entire movement. The experience of war is personalized for audiences, who can identify with individual characters. The tendency of the war film to reduce complicated historical events to personal stories is perfectly exemplified in a line from the

cinema trailer for *Enemy at the Gates*: 'A war between two nations became a battle between two men.' If it did, then it was only in the cinema.

3   *War as allegory.* The war film does more than merely relive battles and campaigns and dramatize stories of heroism and suffering. It is often (though not necessarily always) invested with an allegorical meaning. This means that war films may be as significant in terms of what meaning they have for the present as in what they have to say about the past. Films about the First World War, for example, have since the late 1920s generally been invested with an explicitly anti-war message. Films about the Second World War have been put to a wide array of uses: reliving the past as a national epic in the face of imperial decline and Cold War uncertainty (Britain), exorcizing the memory of Nazism (Germany) and collaboration (France), or interpreting the resistance to Nazism in the light of present political circumstances (Poland). In short, there is more at stake in the war film than just the memory of war itself.

References

Austin, Guy (1996) *Contemporary French Cinema: an Introduction*, Manchester, Manchester University Press.

Chapman, James (1998) *The British at War: Cinema, State and Propaganda, 1939–1945*, London, I. B. Tauris.

Combs, Richard (1982), 'Das Boot (The Boat)', *Monthly Film Bulletin*, vol. 49, no. 580, May, p. 81.

Darke, Chris (1998) review article, *Sight and Sound*, new series, vol. 8, no. 2, February, pp. 46–7.

Fest, Joachim (1996) *Plotting Hitler's Death: the German Resistance to Hitler 1933–1945*, transl. Bruce Little, London, Weidenfeld & Nicolson.

French, Philip (1993) (ed.) *Malle on Malle*, London, Faber & Faber.

Furhammar, Leif and Isaksson, Folke (1971) *Politics and Film*, transl. Kersti French, London, Studio Vista.

Hayward, Susan (1993) *French National Cinema*, London, Routledge.

Jelavich, Peter (1999) 'German culture in the Great War', in Aviel Roshwald and Richard Stites (eds), *European Culture in the Great War: the Arts, Entertainment and Propaganda, 1914–1918*, Cambridge, Cambridge University Press.

Kelly, Andrew (1998) *Filming 'All Quiet on the Western Front'*, London, I. B. Tauris.

Reeves, Nicholas (1997), 'Cinema, spectatorship and propaganda: *Battle of the Somme* (1916) and its contemporary audience', *Historical Journal of Film, Radio and Television*, vol. 17, no. 1, pp. 5–28.

Reeves, Nicholas (1999), *The Power of Film Propaganda: Myth or Reality?*, London, Cassell.

Richards, Jeffrey (1997) *Films and British National Identity: from Dickens to 'Dad's Army'*, Manchester, Manchester University Press.

Sorlin, Pierre (1991) *European Cinemas, European Societies 1939–1990*, London, Routledge.

Sorlin, Pierre (1994) 'War and cinema: interpreting the relationship', *Historical Journal of Film, Radio and Television*, vol. 14, no. 4, pp. 357–66.

Sorlin, Pierre (1999) 'Cinema and the memory of the Great War', in Michael Paris (ed.), *The First World War and Popular Cinema: 1914 to the Present*, Edinburgh, Edinburgh University Press.

Taylor, Philip M. (ed.) (1988) *Britain and the Cinema in the Second World War*, Basingstoke, Macmillan.

Thompson, Kristin and Bordwell, David (1994) *Film History: an Introduction*, New York, McGraw-Hill.

Virilio, Paul (1989) *War and Cinema: the Logistics of Perception*, transl. Patrick Camiller, London, Verso.

Weiss, Jiri (1941) 'An Allied film unit', in *Documentary News Letter*, vol. 2, no. 12, December, p. 233.

Select filmography

All Quiet on the Western Front. USA. 1930. *Director:* Lewis Milestone. *Producer:* Carl Laemmle Jr. *Screenplay:* Del Andrews, Maxwell Anderson and George Abbott. Based on the novel *Im Westen nichts Neues* by Erich Maria Remarque. *Cast:* Lew Ayres, Louis Wolheim, John Wray, George 'Slim' Summerville, Raymond Griffith, Ben Alexander.

Au revoir les enfants. France. 1987. *Director, producer and screenplay:* Louis Malle. *Cast:* Gaspard Manesse, Raphaël Fejtö, Francine Racette, Stanislas Carré de Malberg, Philippe Morier-Genoud, François Berléand, François Négret.

Battle of the Somme. UK. 1916. *Producer:* William F. Jury. *Camera operators:* Geoffrey Mahlins, J. B. McDowell.

Das Boot (*The Boat*). FDR (West Germany). 1981. *Director and screenplay:* Wolfgang Petersen. *Producer:* Gunter Rohrbach. *Cast:* Jürgen Prochnow, Herbert Grönemeyer, Klaus Wennemann, Hubertus Bengsch, Martin Semmelrogge, Erwin Leder.

The Bridge on the River Kwai. UK. 1957. *Director:* David Lean. *Producer:* Sam Spiegel. *Screenplay:* Michael Wilson (uncredited) and Pierre Boulle. Based on the novel of the same name by Pierre Boulle. *Cast:* Alec Guinness, William Holden, Jack Hawkins, Sessue Hayakawa, James Donald.

A Bridge Too Far. USA/UK. 1977. *Director:* Richard Attenborough. *Producer:* Joseph E. Levine. *Screenplay:* William Goldman. Based on the book of the same name by Cornelius Ryan. *Cast:* Dirk Bogarde, James Caan, Michael Caine, Sean Connery, Edward Fox, Elliott Gould, Gene Hackman, Anthony Hopkins, Hardy Kruger, Laurence Olivier, Robert Redford.

Fires Were Started. UK. 1943. *Director and screenplay:* Humphrey Jennings. *Producer:* Ian Dalrymple. *Cast:* George Gravett, Fred Griffiths, William Sansom, Johnny Houghton, Philip Wilson-Dickson, T. P. Smith, Joe Barker, Loris Rey (all members of the National Fire Service).

In Which We Serve. UK. 1942. *Directors:* Noël Coward and David Lean. *Producer and screenplay:* Noël Coward. *Cast:* Noël Coward, Bernard Miles, John Mills, Celia Johnson, Joyce Carey, Kay Walsh, Richard Attenborough.

Kanal. Poland. 1956. *Director:* Andrzej Wajda. *Producer:* Stanislaw Adler. *Screenplay:* Jerzy Andrzejewski and Andrzej Wajda. Based on the novel of the same name by Jerzy Andrzejewski. *Cast:* Zbigniew Cybulski, Ewa Kryzewska, Waclaw Zastrzezynski, Adam Pawlikowski, Bogomil Kobiela.

Lacombe, Lucien. France. 1974. *Director and producer:* Louis Malle. *Screenplay:* Louis Malle and Patrick Modiano. *Cast:* Pierre Blaise, Aurore Clément, Holger Lowenadler, Thérèse Gieshe, Stéphane Bouy, Loumi Jacobesco.

Lucie Aubrac. France. 1997. *Director and screenplay:* Claude Berri. *Producer:* Patrick Bordier. Based on the book *Ils partiront dans l'ivresse* by Lucie Aubrac. *Cast:* Carole Bouquet, Daniel Auteil, Patrice Chérau, Eric Boucher, Jean-Roger Milo, Heino Ferch.

Pokolenie (A Generation). Poland. 1954. *Director:* Andrzej Wajda. *Screenplay:* Bohdan Czesko, based on his own novel of the same name. *Cast:* Tedeusz Lomnicki, Urszula Modrzynska, Tadeusz Janczar, Roman Polanski.

Popiól I Diament (Ashes and Diamonds). Poland. 1958. *Director:* Andrzej Wajda. *Screenplay:* Jerzy Andrzejewski and Andrzej Wajda. Based on the novel of the same name by Jerzy Andrzejewski. *Cast:* Zbigniew Cybulski, Ewa Kryzewska, Waclaw Zastrzezynski, Adam Pawlikowski, Bogomil Kobiela.

1 British trenches at Sanctuary Wood in the Ypres salient. Trenches like this were initially preserved for visitors in the 1920s, particularly for families wishing to see where their loved ones had died. Few of these survive because of the effects of the weather, which tends to cause them to collapse. But the trenches in Sanctuary Wood have been re-excavated and maintained as they were in late 1916. They continue to be the site for visitors today. Entry, as in the 1920s, is for a fee through a small cafe with an attached museum based on artefacts dug up from the district. Photo: Gerard Oram

2 Paul Nash (1889–1946), *We are Making a New World*, 1918, oil on canvas. Photo: Imperial War Museum, London/Bridgeman Art Library

3 Georges Paul Leroux (1877–1957), *L'Enfer* (Hell), 1916. This is not one of the greatest paintings of the First World War, but it is commonly reproduced on book covers and in magazines as a colour image of the war and, particularly, of the fighting around Verdun in 1916. Photo: Imperial War Museum, London/Bridgeman Art Library

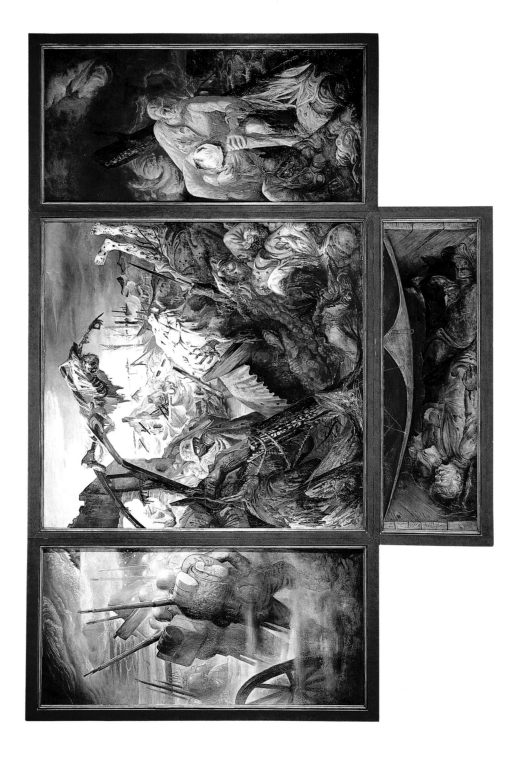

4 Otto Dix (1891–1969), *Triptychon Der Krieg* (War Triptych), 1929–32, tempera on wood, central panel 204 x 204 cm, side panels 204 x 102 cm each. Photo: Gemäldegalerie Neue Meister, Dresden

5 Käthe Kollwitz, *Die Eltern* (The Parents). Kollwitz's statues were completed in 1931, exhibited in Berlin and moved, later that year, to the German military cemetery at Vladso in Belgium. Photo: Clive Emsley

6 The German military cemetery at Langemarck, a few kilometres south of Vladso and in the Ypres salient in Belgium. In the background are statues of four German soldiers looking over their fallen comrades. The clusters of crosses are a mixture of both Iron Crosses and Calvarys. The slabs set in the grass contain the names of men buried in the cemetery. Photo: Clive Emsley

7 The Thiepval memorial on the Somme battlefield in France. This was designed by Sir Edwin Lutyens, also responsible for the Cenotaph in London's Whitehall, and erected in 1932. It contains the names of 73,000 British empire war dead from the Somme battles who have no known grave. Every British war cemetery has the 'cross of sacrifice' with the sword embedded within it, as can be seen here in the foreground. The memorial site at Thiepval comprises the monument and French graves as well as British (all unknown soldiers). On the monument itself fly both the French tricolour and the British union flag to symbolize the shared sacrifice (the battle of the Somme was a joint Franco–British offensive). Photo: Gerard Oram

8 The Menin Gate memorial at Ieper (Ypres), Belgium. This was designed by Sir Reginald Blomfield and officially unveiled in 1927. It contains the names of 54,000 British empire war dead with no known grave from the salient. Photo: Gerard Oram

9 The French war cemetery at Neuville St Vaast. The French government opted for crosses to commemorate its dead, except for the graves of Jewish soldiers or Muslim troops from North Africa who were commemorated with a tablet topped with merlons. The British always opted for a single slab/tablet. Photo: Gerard Oram

10 The gravestone of a German-Jewish soldier in a German military cemetery at Rancourt on the Somme battlefield in France. German cemeteries generally opted for crosses, like the French. Photo: Gerard Oram

11 A Soviet war memorial in Berlin. Note the kneeling soldier with his sub-machine gun and helmet. For all that it is 'Soviet' the iconography here seems very similar to the idea of a medieval knight, with sword and helmet, kneeling and giving thanks for victory. Photo: AKG/Erik Bohr

12 and 13 *Das Boot*. Photos: Ronald Grant Archive

14 and 15 *Lacombe, Lucien*. Photos: Ronald Grant Archive

16 Max Beckmann (1884–1950), *Night*, 1918–19, oil on canvas, 133 × 154 cm. Photo: Kunstsammlung Nordrhein-Westfalen, Dusseldorf

17 Fernand Léger (1881–1955), *The Card Game*, 1917, oil on canvas, 129 x 193 cm. Photo: Collection Kröller-Müller Museum, Otterlo, The Netherlands

18 Pablo Picasso (1881–1973), *Guernica*, 1937, oil on canvas, 349.3 x 776.6 cm. Photo: Museo Nacional Centro de Arte Reina Sofia, Madrid, Spain

19 Museum postcard showing Maximilian Kolbe's cell, in Block 11 of Auschwitz. Photo: Adam Bujak

HOLOCAUST EMLÉKMŰ

20 Postcard showing Imre Varga's 1990 'Memorial of the Hungarian Jewish Martyrs', Budapest. Photo: Zsolt Szaboky

21 The Voices Foundation Children's Choir performing 'In Memoriam Anne Frank' at the ceremony held in London to mark Britain's first official national Holocaust Memorial Day, 27 January 2001. Photo: PA Photos

22 and 23 Jessica Rost, *Ilfie*, 2001, brown paper and photographic transfers, 105 x 35 x 30 cm. Photo: Maria Barry

This sculpture is a commentary on the memory of persecution and how it has been carried through family memory. The piece is the work of a young British sculptor whose father's family emigrated from Germany in 1937 to escape Nazi persecution of the Jews. It is a portrait of Rost's aunt, aged 3 when the family emigrated from Berlin to England. The images on the surface of the figure have been transferred from family archive material, photographs, newspaper articles, stamps and old money, all describing the first three years of her life in Germany before she was uprooted to start a new life in England. The label attached to her wrist illustrates the parcelling and posting of children across Europe at that time. The sculpture has been shown in both England and Germany

24 Ilfie, aged 3, Berlin, 1937. It was this photograph, found in a family album, that led Jessica Rost to investigate her family history and that inspired her to make the sculpture

25 Jessica Rost's father, Berlin, 1936. As a 7-year-old schoolboy he was, by necessity, a junior member of the Hitler Youth. This image is one of the many contemporary artefacts the artist used to cover the surface of the sculpture

26 Gift shop at the entrance to the Statue Park, Budapest. Photo: Mark Pittaway

27 The Ostapenkó statue. Photo: Mark Pittaway

28 Nineteenth-century painting illustrating 'The Maid of Kosovo'. Photo: National Library of Serbia

6

Two total wars, the Cold War and postmodernism:

the arts in Europe, 1910–2000

ARTHUR MARWICK

Introduction

I believe it is essential that I provide a detailed example of how a cultural *historian* deals with a topic, such as the First World War and the arts in Europe, embracing two vital activities:

1   Presenting some of the primary sources one uses, and taking up the time and space to analyse these.

2   Introducing you to a major controversy among historians over the effects of war on the arts.

Unfortunately, having done that, I did not have nearly enough space to treat the two other topics allocated to me in similar detail. I have therefore written much more schematic treatments of 'The Second World War and the Cold War' and 'The cultural revolution and postmodernism' – each, in itself, a pretty capacious topic. I am clear nonetheless that these 'schematic treatments' provide the essential information and concepts for you to grasp the vital points about these two topics. If, for your own personal interest, you want more detail on the second and third topics, you could read my *Arts in the West since 1945* (Marwick, 2002).

EXERCISE _____

Imagine you are back in 1910, an educated person, moderately interested in the arts, about 30 years old. You pay a visit to one of the better-known private art galleries in the Leicester Square and Charing Cross Road area of London. On a whim, you make a trip to Paris and visit a gallery of similar status in the Montparnasse quarter. Then (let us have fun while there is yet time) you are whisked off for a piece of time travelling to arrive at one of the avant-garde galleries in London at the beginning of the twenty-first century.

What would have shocked you most: what you saw in Paris 1910 after London 1910, or what you saw in London 2001 after what you saw in Paris 1910? Give reasons for your answer – the reasons, of course, being much more interesting than the actual answer.

DISCUSSION

Well, obviously, you'd have to have a clear idea about what sorts of art you would see in the different galleries. Perhaps you do know something about current 'Britart', with its pickled animals, its heavily sexual subject matter – from filthy unmade beds to multiple models of human creatures, all with genitals poking out everywhere – and its use of elephant dung (incidentally, the notion of an exclusive Britart is merely an advertising scam: art as challenging and shocking can be found all over Europe). You could probably lodge a safe answer by saying the most shocking move was from France 1910 to London 2001. To go any further much depends on what you think you would have seen in Paris, and how that would compare with what you had seen in London 1910. Perhaps you know that when a post-Impressionist exhibition came to London at this time it was scorned and derided, whereas the works of the great post-Impressionists – Cézanne, Van Gogh, Gaugin – were already accepted in Paris, along with those of the Fauves (which means 'wild animals') and the Cubists. In Britain at this time painting was very largely representational, the Scottish 'colourists' perhaps being among the most imaginative artists, and the 'Camden Town School' being rather parochial. So seeing the work of the latest French artists might have been quite a shock. The French works contained greater or lesser degrees of abstraction and were, in part at least, non-representational. Maybe, with that shock digested, Britart would not have seemed so shocking? After all, the fundamental ties of naturalism, of representationalism, had already been cut by 1910. One could make that argument, though I suspect that Britart would still have come as a severe shock. We could indeed use the 2001 exhibition as a measure of the enormous changes in art which took place between 1910 and 2001. We could perhaps see the English exhibition of 1910 as trying to cling on to a mode of art which was passing, while we could see the French one as looking forward to what was yet to come.

Between 1910 and 2001 there were many other changes, perhaps rather more important than those in the arts: the introduction of television, transport systems, votes for women, welfare services, an ostensible concern for the 'common man' and, with many ups and downs, the general establishment of parliamentary democracy. In any of these matters, including the arts, are the two total wars of relevance?

EXERCISE _____

Whether or not we see the direction taken by the arts as being influenced by the wars, we all have to accept that a crucial influence, quite independent of the wars, was a great aesthetic and intellectual movement. What is that movement called? When did it begin? Try to pin down some of the most distinctive features of this movement.

DISCUSSION _____

The movement is Modernism.

With regard to when it began, the crucial point for our purposes is that it had already begun well before the First World War. 'The late nineteenth century' – post-Impressionism, post-Wagnerian music, Symbolism (mainly in poetry) and brutally realistic novels – would probably be the safest dating, though the most extreme experimental music of, say, Schoenberg or Stravinsky, the avant-garde painting of Pablo Picasso or Filippo Marinetti, and the truly Modernist literature of James Joyce did not come until the early twentieth century.

With regard to the characteristics of Modernism, congratulations if you said things like: abandonment of realism, naturalism, representationalism (though uncompromising realism can be regarded as a component of one type of Modernism in literature); abstraction; experimentation and the privileging of theory; abandonment of traditional harmonies, of the pretty, the appealing, the romantic.

EXERCISE _____

I have referred to post-Impressionism in art. Already by 1914 there were a number of separate artistic movements, all part of Modernism. Can you name these movements? If you can't, no sweat, just go on to my answer. But if you can, see if you can also briefly note down the distinguishing features of each of the movements.

DISCUSSION _____

Well, I have actually already mentioned two such movements: that of the Fauves (using strong, naturalistic colours, with the paint looking as if it has been applied with some violence), and Cubism (where objects – inanimate or human – have the appearance of being made up of cubes; the attempt to represent three dimensions on a flat surface is made in an openly contrived way, as distinct from the illusionism of Renaissance perspective and *chiaroscuro*). The other movements which I think are of major significance, particularly when we are going on to estimate the effects, if any, of the war (but all credit to you if you noted down other movements as well), are Futurism and Expressionism (mainly represented by the German movement known as *Der blaue Reiter*, or The Blue Rider). Expressionism is characterized by exaggeration, distortion and the use of unrealistic colours to heighten effects, while still retaining substantial representational elements. Futurism is much more abstract, incorporating zigzag patterns, lines of force and circles – all designed to give a sense of dynamism and speed. You might well have separately mentioned Abstraction, the reduction or abolition of representational elements which to some degree can be seen in all Modernist movements, but most strongly in Cubism and Futurism: it is a mistake to believe that Modernism entails complete abstraction and/or the abandonment of all human subject matters.

The First World War

The controversy

The issue of the First World War and Modernism, and the artist's representation of war, is discussed in a rather broader context by Clive Emsley in Chapter 2 (pp. 43–56).

Over many years I personally have developed strongly held views over the far from simple topic of the effects of the war experience on developments in the arts. It is impossible for me to conceal that, while I have immense admiration for Richard Cork (art critic of *The Times* who once, at my invitation, gave a brilliant lecture at an Open University summer school) and Professor Jay Winter (of Columbia University in New York), I believe their arguments that responding to the war resulted in avant-garde artists returning to traditionalism to be profoundly misconceived. Part of the difference of opinion can be explained by the fact that I ask rather different questions from them; but then I have to say that I think my questions are the right ones. Taking all the complexities into account, the inevitable movements 'backwards' and 'sideways' as well as 'forwards', I believe that if we look at the situation as it settled down in the interwar years (which I think is the right approach for historians to take) we can see both that there were significant new developments in Modernism and that Modernism was widely accepted in a way that it simply was not before 1914. What I am going to do is to quote (absolutely honestly and fairly) the key statements by Cork and Winter (and you can adhere to them, and follow them up if you so choose), and then show briefly why I think they are misguided. I shall then go on to summarize what I take the critical developments to be.

Richard Cork's *A Bitter Truth: Avant-Garde Art and the Great War* (Cork, 1994) is a magnificent book, which I commend to you very heartily. It contains over 300 reproductions, a fact which in itself supports the case that the Great War was a total war, permeating every corner of life, including the arts, in a way which was simply not true of previous wars (try listing the paintings relating to earlier, 'limited' wars – one thinks of the battle scenes of Paolo Uccello (1397–1475) and Salvator Rosa (1615–73), the seventeenth-century etchings of Jacques Callot (1572–1635) and *The Disasters of War* by Goya (1746–1828) – and a point is made). Cork's fundamental argument is that to engage with the war, artists who had previously been avant-garde or Modernist had to return to traditionalism or representationalism. He writes:

> Throughout Europe ... artists who had earlier been identified in differing ways with the innovative cause found themselves adopting less hermetic approaches ... Even [Fernand] Léger, whose active service did not prompt him to repudiate his previous affiliations, began to evolve a more plain-spoken, figurative idiom shorn of arcane pre-war complexities.
>
> (Cork, 1994, p. 10)

Cork adds, 'the later stages of the conflict proved so repugnant that more and more artists turned to representational imagery fired by a protesting vehemence' (Cork, 1994, p. 10).

My problem with Cork is that he seems to be treating artists simply as reporters or journalists, *illustrating* the horrors of war, or *expressing* their bitterness. Serious artists actually have far more profound things to say about war than simply to illustrate it, or make political comments.

'[R]epresentational imagery fired by a protesting vehemence' is a magnificent phrase (Cork is a journalist) but does scant justice to work being produced by a range of artists, from Dada to Max Beckmann, and perhaps refers most accurately to the work being produced by the Weimar artists *after* the conflict. The limitations of Cork's otherwise brilliant study are brought out in his not very well-chosen words: 'The reality of war, and the need to define it in images conveying a "a bitter truth", would have to be discovered all over again' (Cork, 1994, p. 10). This again is to present artists as reporters with very specific briefs. In fact the manifold responses to the war were absorbed into an expanded, a developing Modernism; and the Modernism of 1939 (which is what Cork is referring to) was manifestly different from that of 1914 or 1918.

In his justly praised *Sites of Memory, Sites of Mourning: the Great War in European Cultural History* (Winter, 1995), Winter starts by making the valuable point that it is wrong to see 'traditional' and 'modern' as two absolute opposites. This is entirely in keeping with my own point that artists often swing between different styles and, more important, generally incorporate many different elements into their major works. But this very truth, it seems to me, makes it much more difficult to claim that during the war artists swung from the avant-garde to traditionalism. Winter writes:

> This book attempts to go beyond the cultural history of The Great War as a phase in the onward ascent of modernism. This now fashionable and widely accepted interpretation will not stand scrutiny, primarily for two reasons. First, the rupture of 1914–18 was much less complete than previous scholars have suggested ...
>
> Secondly, though, the identification of the 'modern' positively with abstraction, symbolic representation, and an architectural exploration of the logical foundations of art, and negatively through its opposition to figurative, representational, 'illusionist', naturalistic, romantic, or descriptive styles in painting and sculpture, is so much a part of cultural history, that it is almost impious to question it. But question it we must. What is at issue is both whether such a distinction is accurate and whether it contributes to an understanding of the cultural consequences of the Great War. On both counts, I dissent from the 'modernist' school.
>
> Equally sacrosanct is the view that there was a 'modernist' moment in literary history, beginning in the 1860s, maturing before 1914, but coming of age after the Great War ... Once again, this book offers a dissenting point of view on these widely held convictions about the location of the 1914–18 war within European cultural history ...
>
> It is the very teleology of this position – the search for precursors or exponents of what later critics have admired or rejected – which makes the 'modernist' hypothesis about the cultural history of the early twentieth century just as misleading as other tendentious interpretations of recent or not so recent history. To array the past in such a way is to invite distortion by losing a sense of its messiness, its non-linearity, its vigorous and stubbornly visible incompatibilities ...
>
> The history of the Great War and its aftermath is full of them, and one purpose of this book is to go beyond the so-called modernist/traditionalist divide to a more sophisticated appreciation of the way Europeans imagined the war and its terrible consequences. I do so by concentrating primarily on aspects of one particular theme within the cultural history of the war: the theme of mourning and its private and public expression.
>
> (Winter, 1995, pp. 2–5)

With most of that, I do not disagree (though I detest the pompous, very American style). Winter does not refer to any of my own books or articles touching on these subjects which certainly do not contribute to the 'fashionable', 'sacrosanct', or 'teleological' position he identifies here: his quarrel is entirely with a group of equally pompous American literary scholars. 'Try reading historians' would be my advice to Winter. The final sentence quoted here is the one which exposes the fundamental weakness in Winter's arguments. Artists are concerned with many, many more issues than 'mourning': to concentrate on that topic is to give a most peculiar version of the 'cultural history' about which Winter makes so many pretentious utterances. You have to read to the end of the book before realizing that Winter is preparing the ground for arguing how important the Second World War (in contrast to the First) was in 'cultural history'. In assessing Winter's arguments about the unimportance of the Great War in the evolution of Modernism his determination to make the case for the Second World War must always be borne in mind.

The First World War and the arts: a schematic list of key points

As space is limited, I am simply going to provide a schematic list of what I regard as key points. To give some sense of the primary source materials on which such arguments are based, I shall include a few detailed exercises.

1 Different artists responded in different ways to the war. Some (I am speaking solely of their art, of course) appear to have been unaffected by it. I believe this is true of Pablo Picasso, whose genius was so secure that he does not seem to have been affected by external events, until he was profoundly touched (in 1937) by the Spanish Civil War. Of course, as a Spanish citizen he was not conscripted into the services and remained in Paris throughout the war. Whether or not this is critical, I am not sure, as you will see in a moment. Georges Braque, Picasso's partner in the creation of Cubism, was similarly unaffected, though he served heroically in the front line, being much decorated and, on one occasion, left for dead in no man's land.

2 A remarkable number of leading artistic figures *did* serve in the war and we do have plenty of evidence of both the traumatic and the constructive effects the war had on them (as you will see from several of the readings below, a minute selection from the many collections of letters from the front). Yet the fact is that the most radical responses to the war (in the fullest sense) were those of the Dada movement set up in Switzerland by young men escaping from conscription (and I'd say the same of the musician Igor

Stravinsky, who also spent the war in Switzerland). My point is that we have to consider artists reacting to the complexities of total war, to war as crisis in civilization, to war as beginning a new era, and not just the rather literal matters of protest or mourning.

3   It is important to establish whether it was only the art of individuals which was affected by the war or whether whole artistic movements were created or transformed by the experience. The distinction is not quite clear-cut, since when the work of talented individuals is altered that often has an effect on lesser artists. The classic case here is that of the German Max Beckmann, who before the war was rather hostile to the post-Impressionists, but who during the war (and after it) forged an entirely new and personal Expressionism, as best represented in his painting *Night* (1919) (Plate 16). Beckmann had hosts of imitators, so we are justified in identifying what we might call Weimar Expressionism as a new movement very largely arising from the war experience. Dada scarcely survives the war, but it is a very important component of what is essentially the new and dominant Modernist movement of the interwar years, Surrealism (and Dada suddenly appears again in the 1960s). Another influence is an intensified emphasis on the importance of the unconscious – not, as is almost always assumed, because of the works of Sigmund Freud, but directly attributable to the war and to the work done by the French sponsor of Surrealism, André Breton (1896–1966), who worked during the war at the psychiatric centre at Saint-Dizier, treating 'shell shock' victims, mainly through helping them analyse their dreams. Breton and his associates could not read German. It is particularly true, I think, that the war affected musicians as individuals (I think of both relative traditionalists such as Edward Elgar and Modernists such as Alban Berg). Later, I shall look in greater detail at one musician (Paul Hindemith), one novelist (Henri Barbusse) and one painter (Fernand Léger).

4   We have to distinguish, too, between the war experience (in all its ramifications) affecting the content and philosophy of different art forms, and the rather more complex and profound issues of its effects (if any) on style and language. Edward Elgar's *The Spirit of England* (1917), a great choral work based on the war poems of Laurence Binyon, clearly had its content (celebrating the heroism of the fallen and also of the women serving at the home front) and philosophy (no patriotic bombast, but a profound sense of elegy and epic tragedy) determined by the war. But, technically, there is no change in Elgar's musical language. The big question is whether the war affected style and language in the arts, creating, in effect, new types of Modernism. My answer is that we

have a mix of: no change; immense changes in personal styles; and the two major artistic movements I have just mentioned. In addition I make what is to me a crucial point, that before the war Modernism is limited, experimental and not widely accepted; after the war, whether people liked it or not, it is recognized as *the* mode of what is perceived as a new era.

5   This leads to the vital point, but one rather neglected by Cork and Winter, that if we are to make a proper assessment of the significance of the war we have to consider the arts not just during the war, but as they settled down *after* the war. It is, I think, beyond question that postwar works have an intensity, a variety, a humanity, a sense of contemporary relevance (while at the same time being indisputably Modernist) which sets them apart from the more tentative, the more experimental works of before the war.

Paul Hindemith

The arts, more than any other human activity save perhaps sex, are, in their very nature, international (trans-European). It was politicians, not artists, who proposed banning German music, for instance. It is true there was a strong movement in France, supported by some older musicians, in favour of 'purity' and against what was represented as German decadence. But we get a clearer picture of the real situation from, for instance, this letter of 7 June 1916 written by the young composer Maurice Ravel:

> It is of little importance to me that M. Schoenberg, for example, is of Austrian nationality. This does not prevent him from being a very fine musician, whose very interesting discoveries have had a beneficial influence on certain allied composers, and even our own. Moreover I am delighted that M. Bartok, Kodály and their disciples are Hungarian and show it unmistakably in their music.
>
> In Germany, apart from M. Richard Strauss, there appear only to be composers of secondary rank, whose equivalent could easily be found within France. But it is possible that some young artists may soon be discovered, whom we would like to know more about here.
>
> (Quoted in Orenstein, 1975, p. 74)

And here is something the German composer Paul Hindemith wrote in his brief collection of pictures and reminiscences, *Zeugnis in Bildern* (*Testimony in Pictures*, 1975):

During my time as a soldier in World War One, I was a member of a string quartet that served our commanding officer as a means of escape from the miseries of war. He was a great music-lover and a connoisseur and admirer of French art. It was no wonder, then, that his dearest wish was to hear Debussy's String Quartet. We rehearsed the work and played it to him with much feeling at a private concert. Just after we had finished the slow movements the signals officer burst in and reported in great consternation [that] the news of Debussy's death [on 25 March 1918] had just come through on the radio. We did not continue our performance. It was as if the spirit had been removed from our playing. But now we felt for the first time how much more music is than just style, technique and an expression of personal feeling. Here music transcended all political barriers, national hatred and the horrors of war. Never before or since have I felt so clearly in which direction music must be made to go.

(Quoted in Skelton, 1975, p. 49)

This is an immensely rich passage. Take a few minutes to ponder it and its relevance to such issues as: the Cork and Winter view of the arts; war, the arts, and nationalism and internationalism; the effects of the war on one particular artist (i.e. this musician).

Turn now to the first two readings, which are both extracts from letters from the front written by Hindemith. (You should be aware that Hindemith, who was only 18 years old at the time, occupied a position well to the rear of the front, and never served with those he refers to as the 'conscripts in the trenches'.)

Letter from Paul Hindemith to Emmy Ronnefeldt, from the Western Front, 28 September 1918

It's not easy writing in a dugout, it's too cramped and too wet, and all day long one's ears are ringing with the sound of eternal gunfire. Outside, shells are flying around our heads. Mornings and evenings we go to Douai to play to whichever of our regiment's companies is taking a rest. We have to march at the double, since the street is under constant fire. Everything gets shot at here, nowhere can one live for 2 or 3 days in the blissful knowledge of not hearing this beastly noise. In fact we're no better off than the conscripts in the trenches. You can't imagine how sick and tired I am of this life. How long does this wretched existence have to go on? Will this stupid breed of idiots never put an end to this devilish war? A pity I'm not religious, or I should long ago have declared war on God. These damned people who keep the war going should be out here for a few weeks' summer holiday, then they would soon learn.

But enough of this grumbling, it won't do any good ... Recently I have got back again to composing, after having had absolutely no ideas since June. The day before yesterday I completed the first movement of a sonatina for violin and piano and am now working on the last, but I haven't got the middle movement yet. The piece will sound very alfresco. Very big and thick, sweeping broad strokes. The other sonatina, on which I was working during my leave, is also not quite finished; it's just that I can't find the right approach to this interrupted work.

(Hindemith, 1995, pp. 21–2)

Letter from Paul Hindemith at the front to Frieda and Emma Lubbecke, 5 November 1918

Our present way of life has of course many advantages: one travels the world free, one sees and experiences splendid things, one 'learns to be tough,' and, above all, one is part of the so-called Great Times. But why is one never satisfied? Many a conscript in the trenches – though there are not many in the trenches now – envies us on account of our comfortable life. But, wait a while, soon – ! In the coming days our band is to be reduced in numbers. The reduction, as all of us fairly confidently predict, is almost certainly the prelude to a complete dissolution before long, and then we should be setting out *in corpore* to meet the Tommys. My intention at the moment is to make a smart 'about turn' halfway. I can only hope that the armistice for which we all (and particularly I) long will prevent me from doing that ... By rights the eager warmongers and Vaterland party members should now be sent to hold the front themselves for a change. Of course I know nothing at all about politics, and for that reason have in the last few days become a keen social democrat. When the war ends I shall be inscribing Liberté, Egalité, Fraternité on my banner ... Infested by the democratic bug, I shall from now on compose only bright red pieces. I have now completed a sonatina (yet again), the first movement of which is so left-wing and radiates so much bolshevism that on listening to it the whole right-wing loudly cries 'shame' and rises from its seats, but that does not worry the composer Hindemith.

(Hindemith, 1995, p. 22)

EXERCISE

Now consider the following questions.

1 What are Hindemith's reactions to the physical conditions he is enduring?

2 What hints does he give of the effects of his experiences on his music?

3 Using the quotation from the reminiscences given above, as well as these two letters, explain as fully as you can how Hindemith's attitudes, politics and general philosophy towards the arts were affected by his war experience. How would you describe the tone of his letters?

DISCUSSION

1 The fundamental point is that even if you were not in the front line you were at the total mercy of artillery and high explosives (this is a point, incidentally, that comes through very strongly in Barbusse's pioneering novel *Le Feu* (*Under Fire*, 1916), just as much as soldiers in the front line where: 'one's ears are ringing with the beastly noise of eternal gunfire'. Marching from one place to another, as Hindemith has to do every morning and every evening, is particularly dangerous, since the street is under constant fire. His dugout is cramped and wet, not all that different from a front-line trench, as he remarks. It is a wretched existence of which he is sick and tired. (In case you don't understand what he is saying in the second letter, he expects the group of musicians soon to be disbanded so that *they* can be sent to the front line, where he will engage directly, 'bodily' [*in corpore*], with the British soldiers – 'the Tommys'.)

2 The first description Hindemith gives of the music he is composing is that it will 'sound very alfresco', or as if composed in the open air, and he explains this further by saying it is '[v]ery big and thick', with 'sweeping broad strokes'. Whether we can see this as specifically Modernist is unclear; but manifestly Hindemith does see himself as breaking the stricter conventions by which he had previously been constrained. One imagines that his tongue is somewhat in his cheek when he talks about composing 'only bright red pieces' and describes the first movement of his new sonatina as 'so left-wing' and radiating 'so much bolshevism that on listening to it the whole right-wing loudly cries "shame" and rises from its seats'. Presumably what he is referring to is an intensification of his 'alfresco', unconventional non-academic style. I hope you picked up these points. These letters are typical in giving us hints of the way in which the war affected

Hindemith's music, without giving the full technical detail we would need to make a proper assessment.

3   Disillusionment with the war, hostility to it, total lack of enthusiasm for the German cause: these are the attitudes that come through most strongly in these two letters. There are echoes of the 'protesting vehemence' which Cork finds in paintings of this period – give yourself a special pat on the back if you made this cross-reference: 'this stupid breed of idiots' with their 'devilish war'; '[t]hese damned people who keep the war going'; the eager warmongers and members of *Vaterland* (the patriotic extreme right-wing party); the enmity Hindemith would have felt for God had he been religious; his desire for an armistice and his readiness to turn round and go home rather than face the enemy. More than that, Hindemith has become a social democrat (a reference to the main socialist party in Germany), supporting the French revolutionary ideals of 'Liberty, Equality, Fraternity'. These can be described as matters of politics.

For general philosophy, we need to turn to the extract from the reminiscences. Here Hindemith is suggesting that, because of the immensely powerful experiences of the war, he sees music as going well beyond style, technique and (particularly relevant to my little controversy with Cork and Winter) the expression of personal feeling. That is what I had in mind in referring to these two scholars. You may well feel that I am prejudiced, but I think they have the too simplistic idea of art simply being an expression of personal feeling (while of course Hindemith is saying that it is much, much more). In particular Hindemith sees music as not being purely nationalist: it transcends all political barriers, national hatred and the horrors of war. Again (sorry if I am belabouring this), Cork and Winter seem to think that it is the sole duty of artists to express the horrors of war, while Hindemith (who is only one among many) sees the artist's role as going far beyond that. The last sentence of the autobiographical extract suggests that, as a consequence of his war experiences, Hindemith now sees music as having a clear philosophical/political purpose. The idea seems to be that music should be an instrument of international reconciliation. That is very much in tune with what I have referred to as the constructive effects of war.

Dada

Now turn to the next three readings, which come from the writings of three of the founders of Dada. The first is an extract from the first Dada publication, Hugo Ball's *Cabaret Voltaire*, published in Zurich on

15 May 1916; the second is taken from Tristan Tzara's Dada manifesto, dating from 1918; the third is from Jean (or Hans) Arp's *Dadaland*, which first appeared in Paris in 1938.

Cabaret Voltaire

When I founded the Cabaret Voltaire, I was sure that there must be a few young people in Switzerland who like me were interested not only in enjoying their independence but also in giving proof of it ... So on 5th February we had a cabaret. Mademoiselle Henings and Mademoiselle Leconte sang French and Danish chansons. Herr Tristan Tzara recited Rumanian poetry. A balaika orchestra played delightful folk-songs and dances.

I received much support from Herr M. Slodki, who designed the poster, and from Herr Hans Arp, who supplied some Picassos, as well as works of his own, and obtained for me pictures by his friends O. van Rees and Arthur Segal. Much support also from Messrs. Tristan Tzara, Marcel Janco and Max Oppenheimer, who readily agreed to take part in the cabaret. We organised a Russian evening and, a little later, a French one (works by Apollinaire, Max Jacob, André Salmon, A. Jarry, Laforgue and Rimbaud). On 26th February Richard Huelsenbeck arrived from Berlin and on 30th March we performed some tremendous Negro music ... Herr Tristan Tzara was the initiator of a performance by Messrs. Tzara, Huelsenbeck and Janco (the first in Zurich and the world) of simultaneist verse by Messrs. Henry Barzun and Fernand Divoire, as well as a *poème siumultané* of his own composition ... The present booklet is published by us with the support of our friends in France, Italy and Russia. It is intended to present to the Public the activities and interests of the Cabaret Voltaire, which has the sole purpose to draw attention, across the barriers of war and nationalism, to the few independent spirits who live for other ideals.

(Hugo Ball [1916], quoted in Richter, 1997, pp. 13–14)

Dada manifesto

DADA MEANS NOTHING

We see by the papers that the Kru Negros call the trail of a holy cow: Dada. The cube and the mother in a certain district of Italy are called: Dada. A hobby horse, a nurse both in Russian and Rumanian: Dada ...

A work of art is never beautiful by decree, objectively and for all. Hence criticism is useless, it exists only subjectively, for each man separately without the slightest character of universality ... How can one expect to put order into the chaos that constitutes that infinite and shapeless variation: man? The principle: 'love thy neighbour' is a hypocrisy. 'Know thyself' is utopian but more acceptable, for it embraces wickedness. No pity. After the carnage we still retain the hope of a purified mankind. I speak only of myself since I do not wish to convince, I have no right to drag others into my river, I oblige no one to follow me and everyone practices his art in his own way ...

And so Dada was born of a need for independence, of a distrust toward unity. Those who are with us preserve their freedom. We recognise no theory. We have enough cubist and futurist academics: laboratories of formal ideas. Is the aim of art to make money and cajole the nice bourgeois? ...

Let each man proclaim: there is a great negative work of destruction to be accomplished. We must sweep and clean. Affirm the cleanliness of the individual after the state of madness, aggressive complete madness of a world abandoned to the hands of bandits, who rend one another and destroy the centuries.

(Tristan Tzara [1918], quoted in Lippiard, 1971, pp. 14, 15, 19)

Dadaland

In Zurich in 1915, losing interest in the slaughterhouses of the world war, we turned to the Fine Arts. While the thunder of the batteries rumbled in the distance, we pasted, we recited, we versified, we sang with all our soul. We searched for an elementary art that would, we thought, save mankind from the furious folly of these times. We aspired to a new order that might restore the balance between heaven and hell. This art gradually became an object of general reprobation. Is it surprising that the 'bandits' could not understand us? Their puerile mania for authoritarianism expects art itself to serve the stultification of mankind.

(Jean (or Hans) Arp, *Dadaland* [1938] quoted in Lippiard, 1971, pp. 23–4)

You can immediately spot the differences between the three: Hugo Ball was a level-headed organizer; Tristan Tzara was an extreme and rather incoherent theoretician; Jean (or Hans) Arp was clear and rational. Note the references to the war: in the last sentence of the extract from Ball; in the last sentence of the piece by Tzara ('a world abandoned to the hands of bandits'): and in the first three sentences of the excerpt from Arp (note the phrase 'the furious folly of these times').

Barbusse and Léger

I do not wish to deny for one moment that much art during and after the war expressed a sense of horror, tragedy ('mourning', if you like), catastrophe. But it seems to me that we miss much if we do not also bring out the sense – in some works, but obviously by no means all – of the heroism of ordinary men and women, of the reconstructive elements, of there being possibilities for the building of a better world. These aspects are well represented in the work of Henri Barbusse and Fernand Léger, so I must make it clear that while I do think they represent important currents arising from the war I do not for a moment claim that they encompass all the important responses that there were to the war.

Once again, space being short, I set my points out schematically.

1   *The careers of Barbusse and Léger.* Both Barbusse and Léger were what Winter and Cork would call avant-garde figures, Léger most obviously so. Barbusse, aged 41 in 1914, was an upper-class member of the Parisian intellectual establishment. As a Modernist he was not quite in the same advanced category as James Joyce, though in its sexual frankness his *Hell* (1908) was as shocking as the latter's *Ulysses*. Léger, 33 years old in 1914, was a reasonably well-off provincial, beginning to make his way in the Cubist circles of Picasso and Braque. Though a socialist and pacifist who through age and position could certainly have avoided military service, Barbusse volunteered on the outbreak of war – even in the midst of the slaughter he likened this war to the one of 1792 which revolutionary France waged against the rest of Europe. Léger was conscripted. Both men served in, and mostly out of (horrific enough), the front line. Barbusse served with great bravery (as a rifle-carrying stretcher-bearer), until invalided out in the summer of 1916. In hospital he wrote *Under Fire*, which was published that November. He did not return to the front. Léger was invalided out in the autumn of 1917, and painted *The Card Game* (Plate 17) while in hospital. He did not return to active service either.

2   *Sources for their lives and work during and after the Great War.* We have some rich primary sources. While in the trenches and various billets, Barbusse kept regular notes, the *carnet de guerre*; comparing this with *Under Fire*, we can see how some episodes he

noted down went practically straight into the novel, and how, in regard to the organization of the book, he changed his mind. All of this is reinforced, and amplified, by the collection of letters he wrote to his wife, to whom he was devoted. As with Léger, we have his drawings and sketches which show, in particular, the way in which *The Card Game* was constructed. We also have his later statements (some from the 1930s, some from after the Second World War) and interviews explaining the effects of the war on his painting. These have to be balanced against the letters he wrote at the time to a friend who was an influential civil servant (see Léger, 1997).

3   *The effects of the war on their attitudes and their art.* It is not terribly difficult to perceive what it is that Barbusse is saying in his novel, which takes the form of a series of separate episodes, most bringing out the horrific nature of the war (we are constantly encountering dismembered and rotting corpses), and some the alienation the servicemen feel from the civilian population. Barbusse makes great efforts to represent the crude language of his fellow soldiers. But the first chapter is not naturalistic; it is printed in italics to draw attention to this. We meet disembodied, almost God-like representatives of the main countries, looking down on the world 'as if they were already of the Future' (Barbusse [1917] 1965, p. 2). The purpose of this chapter, clearly, is to express pretty directly the author's own view of the significance of the war: the soldiers (in the final sentence of the chapter) are slaves who have suffered infinitely, but (as in Marxist prophecy) they will (specifically as a result of this war experience) 'transform the old world' (Barbusse [1917] 1965, p. 4). Here, and throughout the book, Barbusse obviously identifies very closely with his working-class and peasant fellow soldiers, people he would not normally come into contact with in peacetime. The final chapter seems at first to be in the realistic idiom of all of the other chapters except the first. But we find the soldiers speaking in a more philosophical and rhetorical manner than would be natural and we begin to realize that the title of the chapter, 'The Dawn', is to be taken symbolically as well as literally. The soldiers are expressing the views of the first chapter, that however horribly they have suffered, and however much they have borne the entire burden of the conflict, while the civilians have escaped, it will all lead to a better world. The final words of the book are spoken by an ordinary soldier: 'If the present war has advanced progress by one step, its miseries and slaughter will count for little' (Barbusse [1917] 1965, p. 342). The book, then, combines the sense of the utter and almost unimaginable horror of the war as experienced by ordinary soldiers, with the sentiment that the war is for a

purpose and will lead to a better world. Clearly the influence of the war is almost exclusively on content and philosophy. The novel is modernistic in its two non-naturalistic episodes, particularly Chapter 1. But I would not say that this is a great advance on *Hell*. What Barbusse has done is to create a completely new genre, unique to the twentieth century: the war novel (of which Erich Maria Remarque's *All Quiet on the Western Front*, 1929, is another example). Barbusse wrote nothing else of significance and became something of a stooge of international communism, dying in Moscow in 1935.

The next two readings are both extracts from statements by Léger. The first is about *The Card Game* and was made after the First World War. The second, a statement about the 1914–18 conflict, dates from after the Second World War.

The Card Game

It was during the war that I got my feet on the ground ... Ah, these big lads! I was also strong, and I did not suffer from fear. I became their comrade. Even when it was proposed that I should join the camouflage unit far from the front I did not want to leave them; 'I shall remain,' I said. While the lads were playing at cards, I remained by their side, watching them, and I made drawings, sketches, because I wanted to seize hold of them. I was very impressed by the lads and the desire to draw them came to me spontaneously. It was from them that later there emerged *The Card Game* ... I was drawn into things in 1917, in *The Card Game*, the first painting in which I had deliberately chosen a contemporary topic. I worked on it, I recall, at the hospital where I found myself because I had been gassed. I also had been affected by the gas.

(Quoted in Néret, 1990, p. 70)

The First World War

The war was an enormous event for me. At the front was this super-charged [*surpoétique*] atmosphere which stirred me to my depths ... Paris, when I left, was in an epoch of artistic liberation, and I was totally absorbed in abstract painting. Without warning, I found myself on a level with the entire French people ... my new comrades were miners, labourers, artisans who worked in wood or metal. I discovered the people of France. And at the same time I was suddenly stunned by the sight of the open breech of a .75

cannon in full sunlight, confronted with the play of light on white metal. It needed nothing more than this for me to forget the abstract art of 1912–15. It came as a total revelation to me, both as a man and as a painter.

(Quoted in Derouet, 1997, p. 762)

EXERCISE _____

What is Léger saying about the effects of the First World War on his paintings, compared with what I have said above about the effects of the war on Barbusse's novel?

DISCUSSION _____

Like Barbusse, Léger, it seems, identified very closely with his fellow soldiers, expressing great admiration for them. It was during the war that he 'discovered the people of France'. And with regard to artistic language, Léger specifically mentions the impact of large-scale artillery, particularly 'the play of light on white metal'. What he saw in the war, he says, 'came as a total revelation' to him, 'both as a man and as a painter'. The general impact on Léger is perhaps even stronger than that on Barbusse.

_____

However, the expert on Léger at the Pompidou Museum in Paris, Christian Derouet, having published a collection of Léger's wartime letters to Louis Poughon, an influential civil servant friend in Paris, has suggested that these letters cast great doubt on the validity of what Léger says in these later statements. Derouet considers Barbusse a great hero and a great man. He does not think the same of Léger, whom, among other things, he accuses of being more interested in selling his drawings and paintings than in his fellow soldiers.

At this point you should refresh your memories of Léger's statements in the two previous readings and then turn to the next four readings, which are all extracts from letters that Léger wrote to Poughon during the war.

Letter from Fernand Léger from the front line (Argonne) to Louis Poughon, 12 August 1915

I didn't manage to remain in the attack of the 14th. I was half asphyxiated by these German pigs and a piece of shrapnel in my thigh, which to my regret was not sufficient to get me sent to the rear. A 14th which I shall continue to remember! What an episode, five hours of non-stop bombardment. I had had a lovely arbour where I wrote, which totally disappeared, being replaced by a hole 210 metres deep. With that, wintry weather, two whole days in the blood and the mud, the two hardest days I have suffered, you had to have your head screwed on to make sure that it didn't just take off. And the details? I was obliged to burrow into the grave of a fellow I had just buried in order to evade the shells. I was flat on my stomach on top of him. Infantrymen told me more; while they were eating behind a wall, a shell sent a piece of head straight onto their plate. It had been a fortnight that they were stuck in a pathetic cemetery which had been abandoned for a month in which there were at least 100 killed during the month of December. Everything was returned there by the shells! These poor devils lived in an appalling charnel house and they had to stay there. It's a terrible war ... Half of the Germans had lost their gas masks, their eyes were coming out of their heads, and they could no longer see where they were going. I took part in that whole action by the reserves; it was fantastic. And there it was, our infantrymen had managed to make the 3 kilometres and they had found the legs to overwhelm the Boches and thrust them back to where they had come from. What a strange fellow a Frenchman is! In their billets, they didn't want to know anything. They were fed up, disgusted with it all. A hard blow, and you find them still apparently a disorderly rabble, but one which immediately sorts itself out ...

Ah! If the Germans had known it and what they see now, perhaps they would have understood what it is to be a Frenchman of 1915 and they would not have dared start the war.

(Letter 15 in Léger, 1997, pp. 41–2)

Letter from Fernand Léger from the front line (Verdun) to Louis Poughon, 25 October 1916

It is formidable, the number of cannons involved in that attack. But that is nothing. The orchestra is complete. To judge the entire thing, you have to go into the suburbs of Verdun where the heavy guns were lurking. There, it was truly infernal. Note that I came down with a heap of prisoners (the first taken). Boches and French mixed, we had taken part in one of the most potent artillery attacks of Verdun. The artillery men were like madmen. They yelled like fanatics. Think about it; they had ordered an increased rate of firing. I saw officers in shirt sleeves passing shells by hand to speed things up. I was completely taken by all that, the Boches as well. These poor devils who were dying of hunger couldn't even manage to devour the bits of bread we gave them. I saw the moment when our men even went to the assistance of the artillery men. And what a state they were in. For four days the constant barrages prevented any food getting through. They were all pretty big and pretty young. It was a procession I will remember forever, these lumps of mud on gaunt faces with dead eyes. For destitution, moral and physical suffering, that could not be exceeded. However, in the face of such spectacles we knew how to behave. Among us, I did not see one word or gesture out of place ... Oh! the infantrymen, we never have any rest, who, after having passed the days in the line, pass to the rear and work day and night to dig more lines. What genial sculptor will fashion and immortalize forever the infantrymen? One needs a cataclysm like that one to judge fully their values; the value of these men is prodigious. These characters are lively and blunt. Goodbye my old friend ... [our friend Dangel] tells me not to despair, but I will be taken by the air authorities as a camouflage artist. Certainly he is concerned about me, but everything depends, I guess, on the Commander of the Engineers.

(Letter 27 in Léger, 1997, pp. 63–4)

Letter from Fernand Léger from Verdun to Louis Poughon, 23 November 1916

I adore Verdun. I think I have already told you that. This old town, totally ruined, with its impressive calm. I adore spending afternoons here. I have made numerous drawings, all of which I have sent to Paris. I hope later to have an exhibition of my drawings of the Front. At Verdun there are totally unexpected subjects to rejoice my Cubist soul. For example, one discovers a tree with a chair perched in it. People thought sensible would treat you as mad if you presented them with a painting composed in that fashion. Nonetheless, there is nothing to do but copy. Verdun authorizes every pictorial fantasy. That is why I am so pleased. *Le Matin* [the newspaper] has informed me of the nomination of a substitute Granié as procureur general at Toulouse. Naturally I have sent him a letter of congratulations (do you know that he was the first person to buy one of my paintings?) and I have told him about the oddities of the Verdun academy of Cubism! That will amuse him. The [river] Meuse is very pretty with its grand poplars spurned by the shells. I am sure it would provide delight for a fisherman with a rod. From time to time several shells but so few, so that one can appreciate the calm and serenity of this great cemetery!

(Letter 30 in Léger, 1997, p. 72)

Letter from Fernand Léger from Paris to Louis Poughon, 7 December 1917

I must thank you for facilitating my interview with Fournery [brother-in-law of Poughon, and a painter and decorator employed during the war remodelling hospitals], who is a charming man and who was fully disposed towards receiving me and taking trouble over me. Perhaps I shall go there; in any case I can enter tomorrow or the day after into the Italian Hospital, a fine hospital in the centre of Paris run by the Italian government [Léger had previously been in the Hospital St Joseph in Paris]. I am always rather tired and as my convalescence is coming to an end I have easily been able to hospitalize myself once more ... The chief doctor at the Italian whom I know also knows Fournery and if I wish to go to Auteuil [outside Paris] he will send me there. You can see that it is all for the best. There I can try for a temporary discharge or a non-combatant posting. I don't know, we will see. On the other hand, I have a good chance of joining the camouflage [unit] and perhaps that would enable me to remain in Paris thanks to Rosenberg [a leading Parisian art dealer] who would arrange for me to remain here to work [i.e. to paint]. Rosenberg is that dealer in paintings with whom I have been having business dealings for nearly two months. We are finally about to conclude a contract which I consider to be advantageous. But it has not been without struggle; these Jews are terrible. Finally, I imposed my conditions on him, and I am happy. It is an agreement for three years directly the war is finished or from when I am discharged. There is a payment for me of 20,000 to 25,000 francs a year, so you can see that it would be worthwhile for me to remain in Paris during my convalescence. He has just bought an important painting from me [*The Card Game*] which I have been able to do here in a month and which forms the basis of the contract. This makes me relaxed for the postwar years ... Do not think that I am very ill ... No, I am in a state of general depression and, with all the sympathy I am receiving, I hope to escape from it.

(Letter 42 in Léger, 1997, pp. 84–5)

EXERCISE _____

Now consider the following questions.

1   Leaving aside for the moment the question of Léger's art, which two assertions in the earlier reading, giving his statement on *The Card Game*, are revealed to be untrue?

2   Is there evidence in the letters of Léger developing a great admiration for his working-class comrades?

3   What evidence, if any, is there in the letters of the war experience affecting Léger's art?

4   In the fourth letter to Poughon reproduced above (the one dated 7 December 1917), we learn about the painting and the sale of *The Card Game*. With regard to the main topic of this chapter, what significance, if any, do you attach to this information and also to the evidence about Léger not telling the truth? Do you have any comments to make on the third letter quoted here (dated 23 November 1916), sentences five ('I have made ...') and seven ('At Verdun ...')?

DISCUSSION _____

1   The statement 'Even when it was proposed that I should join the camouflage unit far from the front I did not want to leave them; "I shall remain," I said' is clearly untrue. The second last sentence of the letter written on 25 October 1916 ('[Dangel] tells me ...'), and the sentence in the middle of the letter dated 7 December 1917 ('On the other hand ... '), indicate clearly that Léger was trying very hard to get away from the front to a camouflage unit (and, in fact, though you don't know this, pretty well every second letter printed in the collection has some reference to getting away from the front).

The fourth letter here (7 December 1917), when Léger is moving from one hospital to another, makes no mention of his having been gassed – if he had been he would have been in a much more serious condition. It seems that Léger's later statement that he was gassed (as distinct from suffering from general exhaustion and various minor ailments) was also untrue.

2   Evidence of Léger's admiration for his working-class comrades occurs towards the end of the first letter quoted here ('And there it was ... ') and again about halfway through the second letter ('However, in the face of such spectacles ... lively and blunt').

There are similar references in other letters too. Judge for yourself, but my view is, when taking the drawings and paintings into account, that Léger was genuine enough in expressing admiration for his fellow soldiers. These are more directly and subtly expressed than the almost propaganda-like statements of much later.

3   There is plenty of evidence in the letters about the horrific, traumatic conditions of the war (particularly Verdun), but though one might make guesses there is little to connect this directly with Léger's art (some of the other letters – you would not know this – speak of the war experiences as being the most powerful in his life). The one definite statement comes in the third letter cited here (dated 23 November 1916), in the passage 'At Verdun ... every pictorial fantasy'. The information is perhaps not very precise, but to me suggests an extension in range and in imagination.

4   Léger was *an artist*. To me it does not seem particularly reprehensible that he should have been concerned to sell his work and establish himself as a successful artist. He did serve for three years in the most appalling conditions. No doubt he was less heroic than Barbusse, but I for one cannot blame him for wanting to get away from the front into a posting which would have enabled him to use his talent as an artist. With regard to his 'telling lies' he may not, thirty or forty years later, even have been aware that he was doing so – what old soldier does not embellish the truth? For myself, I am less inclined than Derouet to be censorious. I believe the broad picture of the effects of the war on Léger's art, as conveyed in the two statements written so much later, remains broadly accurate. However, your own thoughts here are particularly important. I just wanted to demonstrate that historical evidence is seldom either absolutely consistent or absolutely watertight.

Summing up – we have to establish a balance between the Modernist techniques which both Barbusse and Léger had acquired before the war and new elements (content, philosophy and also style and language) which came through war experiences. Barbusse produced what has been claimed as perhaps the greatest war novel of all time, and he certainly created the new genre of the modern war novel. But even if Barbusse is the greater hero, I have to say Léger is the greater artist. He went on to produce a series of masterpieces, distinctively different from the works he was producing before the war.

The Second World War and the Cold War

It is legitimate to say that the Cold War sprang directly out of the circumstances in which the Second World War ended, with the Soviet army physically in occupation of eastern Europe and the first to reach Berlin, and with both America and the Soviet Union (for the time being) as superpowers, holding diametrically opposed ideologies. With regard to developments in the arts the Second World War has far greater significance than the Cold War. True: for Marxists hostile to America, and the consumerism it stood for, the Cold War intensified their hostility. But as far as the new fear of nuclear annihilation was concerned, this was essentially an intensification of the despair and pessimism already engendered by the destruction and brutality of the war and, above all, by the Holocaust which accompanied the war. In my view what had a really important effect on the arts was the eventual ending of the Cold War, not the Cold War itself.

But how with regard to influences on the arts did the Second World War compare with the first war? At the time of writing (spring and early summer 2001) Professor Winter had not gone beyond the few sentences I have already referred to (in the section 'The First World War'), suggesting that while the First World War had brought a restoration of traditionalism, the second war really did have a transforming effect on the arts. Personally I think that both wars, being total wars, had largely similar effects, but that because Modernism had been in existence since before the Great War, and as the Great War broke upon a relatively naive and unsuspecting world, there was in fact less scope for change as a result of the Second World War. To me the crucial point about the First World War is that it coincided with the first phase of Modernism. The two reacting together produced immense changes in the arts, echoed, with many differences of detail and on a lesser scale, in the Second World War.

Effects and non-effects of the war

Picasso

Let us look first at Picasso. His *Guernica* (1937) (Plate 18) is the best known of all twentieth-century artistic statements on war (in this case, the destruction by German bombers of the Basque town of Guernica during the Spanish Civil War). *Guernica* – not, of course, a direct response to either of the total wars – is immensely powerful in its presentation of Nazi brutality and of the terror and suffering of civilians, but given the immense variousness of Picasso's work in any case it is not particularly new in style and language. At the end of the war, when news was coming through about the Nazi concentration camps, Picasso began a work of considerable stylistic similarities, *The Charnel House*, another protest against Nazi atrocities. Picasso, who suffered the unpleasantness of living in occupied Paris when he could easily have escaped to America, said himself that he was sure that the war had affected his art, though it would be for others to discern this. Personally I think that what most influenced Picasso's painting was his joining the Communist party at the end of the war and his being swept up into the ideological conflict of the Cold War: at this time, he painted some of his worst works ever, little more than crude communist propaganda.

Boulez, Shostakovich and Britten

I do not have the space to do justice to the great French composer Pierre Boulez. If, by any chance, you are interested in my views that Boulez, reacting to the war and what he saw as a decadent society which preceded it, pioneered a new musical language, turn to Chapter 3 of my *Arts in the West since 1945* (Marwick, 2002). For works which in content and philosophy are manifestly responses to the war, but which do not really show any innovation in musical language, turn to the Leningrad Symphony by **Dmitri Shostakovich** (première in Moscow in March 1942) and **Benjamin Britten**'s *War Requiem* (première in 1962 in the new Coventry cathedral, which replaced the one destroyed in the war). Shostakovich wrote the first movement of the Leningrad Symphony while he was in Leningrad (now St Petersburg), where over a million people were killed or died from starvation while under siege by the Germans. Shostakovich himself said of the first movement, 'It tells how our pleasant and peaceful life was disrupted by the ominous forces of the war.' He also explained that he deliberately avoided naturalism and 'battle music' (quoted in Blokker, 1979, p. 82). What we have throughout the symphony is a relentless but subtly understated communication of the barbarity of war, blended with a statement of passionate defiance and belief in ultimate victory. And this is what the symphony has come to represent. Played in New York (and later in London), it symbolized the Grand Alliance between the west and communist Russia.

In his choral work *The War Requiem* Britten ingeniously weaves together two separate texts: one is the 'Dies irae', the traditional setting of the Latin mass for the dead; the other is made up of nine First World War poems by Wilfred Owen. By bringing in these poems, Britten is clearly linking the First World War to the Second. His work is about twentieth-century war in general, about its terrible cost to humanity and, beyond that, about reconciliation – particularly between Britain and Germany.

Shostakovich and Britten are discussed in more detail by Robert Samuels in Chapter 4.

222

Fautrier, Informal Art

The predominant movement in art after the First World War was Surrealism, while after the Second World War it was Abstract Expressionism – though the latter was very much an American creation. The parallel movement in Europe was Informal Art (meaning not 'casual art', but 'art without form') which embraced *Art Brut* (unrefined art), whose principal exponent was Jean Dubuffet, and *Tâchisme* (a *tâche* being a blob of paint), whose principal exponent was Nicolas de Staël. By the 1930s Jean Fautrier (1898–1964) had given up the attempt to make a career out of painting. Then, in 1940, he began to perfect a distinctive new method, paper placed on canvas, with *grumeaux* (clots) and *magmas* (heaps) of oil paint (in delicate tints, blues, orange, or green) built up on the paper, and ink drawings scratched on these clots. Fautrier, resident in France throughout the German occupation, was deeply affected by the wartime atrocities, as is demonstrated by the titles of his works, such as *Le Fusillé* (*Shot* [by firing squad]), *La Juive* (*The Jewess*), the series *Les Otages* (*Hostages*), and *Oradour-sur-Glane* (after the village in west central France that was destroyed by the Nazis in 1944 (see p. 27 and Figure 1.4); the men were shot, the women and children burned to death in the church). At first sight these paintings appear charming; then one perceives the lifeless faces inscribed upon the clots of paint – 'hieroglyphics of suffering', as they have been termed by the critic Maurice Fréchuret. Fréchuret has also commented on these apparently gentle, but manifestly deeply felt paintings: 'Is not this the only response possible to a world become mad upon which a version which is merely horrified would exercise no grip ... ?'(Fréchuret, 1987, p. 166). Quite clearly what is important here is the new style, which in turn feeds into the postwar movement of Informal Art.

The cultural revolution and postmodernism

What I, and others, term the 'the cultural revolution' fell within the period of 'the long 1960s', from around 1958 to around 1974, though the transformations of this revolution continued right through to the end of the twentieth century and afterwards. The dominant influence on the arts from the mid 1970s to the end of the century was postmodernism, itself largely a product of the new intellectual movements of the 1960s. I'll first list some of the main features of the cultural revolution and after, then five key concepts of postmodernism, connecting this section with the names of some of the leading European practitioners in the arts in this period from the end of the 1950s to the beginning of the twenty-first century.

Features of the cultural revolution and after

1   The first feature is the thaw in, and then the ending of, the Cold War. Though there were severe interruptions in these processes (such as the building of the Berlin Wall in 1963, and the brutal repression of the Czech bid for freedom in 1968), a general improvement in the international climate did lead to a relaxation in the extremely authoritarian and narrowly conventional attitudes which prevailed in the west during the height of the Cold War period. The collapse of the Soviet empire in 1989 was particularly important in that it permitted the release, particularly in music, of Russian and east European influences. This music is also postmodernist in that it is highly eclectic, containing a large proportion of traditional (in this case, particularly, religious and nationalist) influences. I am thinking of such composers as the Pole, Henryk Górecki (born 1933), the Estonian, Arvo Pärt (born 1935), and the Russians, Alfred Schnittke (1934–98) and Sofuga Gubaydulina (born 1931).

2   Returning to the cultural revolution itself, consumerism has been a very important influence here, both in the way in which some artists rejoice in it and in the way in which others are very hostile to it. Both reactions can be seen in the most characteristic artistic movements of the long 1960s, Pop Art and (in France) *Nouveau Réalisme.*

3   It is a cliché that the cultural revolution is characterized by a 'youth revolution', or at least that in many artistic activities standards were set by people who, by traditional criteria, were remarkably young. Perhaps all this is best seen as part of a general challenge to older authorities and a general shake-up in human relationships, affecting both young people and adults, men and women, blacks and whites, and giving rise to movements which had strong effects on the arts: feminism, gay liberation and postcolonialism.

4   Among other influences within the cultural revolution I would single out the revival of the basic ideas of Dada – notions of anti-art, of art as challenging respectable society.

5   For the earlier eras of Modernism it is possible to speak of the 'shock of the new'. By the 1960s, the new was not shocking enough in itself and the dynamic becomes that of the ever-more-shocking. In the arts, and in philosophy, ever more extreme views are put forward, ever more extreme methods deployed. Nowhere is this more true than in the replacement among Parisian intellectuals of existentialism by, first, structuralism, and next post-structuralism, which then merge into postmodernism.

Five key concepts of postmodernism

1   *The transgression of boundaries.* The structuralists and their
    associates, often in an exhilarating way, work outside and across
    conventional disciplines. Michel Foucault, for example, moved
    from psychiatry into medical history, into what he called 'the
    archaeology of knowledge', into language, into the history of
    crime and punishment, into the history of sexuality. Roland
    Barthes and Jacques Derrida, meanwhile, have worked in
    literature, language, grammar, with Barthes concentrating more
    and more on the signs, symbols and representations (in the form
    of both language and visual imagery) by which we are
    surrounded, developing the new subjects of semiology and
    semiotics. All around, in the creative arts, the distinctions
    between painting and sculpture, between words, images and
    music, between poetry and solid form, between popular and elite
    culture, have been broken. The postmodernists see no distinction
    between the imaginative arts and evidence-based scholarship –
    everything is interpretation, or ideology, or text.

2   *De-centring of the human subject.* The theory here is that our lives
    are governed by structures and codes, in which individual human
    agency plays no part, and that the proper focus for attention,
    whether in works conventionally seen as scholarship or as art, is
    the system of inter-relationships, not the individual human
    subject.

3   *The centrality and the indeterminacy of language.* The full
    postmodernist position is that nothing has reality outside of
    language, everything being constructed *within* language. This
    position is stated by different authors to different degrees. At the
    very least, the contention is that there is no secure
    correspondence between any actual reality and the attempt to
    represent that reality in language. One argument (which does
    have a good deal of plausibility) is that it is impossible for one
    human being to communicate one exact meaning to another
    human being. Everything that is written or spoken will contain
    several possible meanings. This is what is meant by 'the
    indeterminacy of language'. Much attention has been paid to the
    nature of literary forms, and theories developed about the rules
    governing 'narrative', 'developing plots' and so on.

4   *Discourse and the discursive.* These concepts concern the
    relationship between knowledge and power, whether that power
    resides entirely in some impersonal structure, or whether it is in
    the hands of the bourgeoisie. Discourses are cultural formations
    related to particular structures of power obtaining at particular
    points in time. The word 'discursive' refers to the way in which all

cultural products, knowledge, texts and so on are embedded within the prevailing power structure. The basic notion that in any historical period there are clear limits to what can be known or believed is one which would find broad sympathy with professional historians. The conclusion to which theories of the discursive tend to reach, however, is that of the relativity of all knowledge: postmodernist theory rejects the belief that there can be any objective science, or any objective history.

5 *The death of the author.* This slogan is very much in keeping with the notions of the indeterminacy of language and the relativity of cultural forms. This is evident in the final reading, an extract from Barthes's essay of the same name, first published in 1968.

The Death of the Author

The author is a modern figure, a product of our society insofar as, emerging from the Middle Ages with English empiricism, French rationalism and the personal faith of the Reformation, it discovered the prestige of the individual, of, as it is more nobly put, the 'human person'. It is thus logical that in literature it should be this positivism, the epitome and culmination of capitalist ideology, which has attached the greatest importance to the 'person' of the author ...

Once the Author is removed, the claim to decipher a text becomes quite futile. To give a text an Author is to impose a limit on that text, to furnish it with a final signified, to close the writing. Such a conception suits criticism very well, the latter then allotting itself the important task of discovering the Author (or its hypostases: society, history, psyché, liberty) beneath the work: when the Author has been found, the text is 'explained' – victory to the critic. Hence there is no surprise in the fact that, historically, the reign of the Author has also been that of the Critic, nor again in the fact that criticism (be it new) is today undermined along with the Author. In the multiplicity of writing, everything is to be *disentangled*, nothing *deciphered* ... In precisely this way literature (it would be better from now on to say *writing*), by refusing to assign a 'secret', an ultimate meaning, to the text (and to the world as text), liberates what may be called an anti-theological activity, an activity that is truly revolutionary since to refuse to fix meaning is, in the end, to refuse God and his hypostases – reason, science, law ...

> Classic criticism has never paid any attention to the reader; for it, the writer is the only person in literature. We are now beginning to let ourselves be fooled no longer by the arrogant antiphrastical recriminations of good society in favour of the very thing it sets aside, ignores, smothers, or destroys; we know that to give writing its future, it is necessary to overthrow the myth: the birth of the reader must be at the cost of the death of the Author.
>
> (Barthes [1968] 1977, pp. 142, 147–8)

EXERCISE _____

Now consider these questions.

1   What indicates that Barthes is fundamentally Marxist?

2   What, from his point of view, makes what he is saying liberating, anti-authoritarian, revolutionary?

3   What is meant by 'the birth of the reader must be at the cost of the death of the Author'?

DISCUSSION _____

1   Barthes regards the view of literature giving prestige to the individual author, which he is attacking, as the 'culmination of capitalist ideology': a fundamentally Marxist idea.

2   He is challenging the authority of the author and of the critic, who, he says, defines the author and explains the text, laying down a secret or ultimate meaning in the manner of theology. In this way, the reader is being liberated, and in a manner which is truly revolutionary since in doing this Barthes is also rejecting reason, science, law (the imperatives, as he would put it, of bourgeois society).

3   '[T]he birth of the reader' means recognizing the right of the reader to give any text whatever meaning he or she likes. In doing so, this is overthrowing the myth that it is the author who determines the meaning of the text, and once that power is removed from the author, this is tantamount to the death of the author.

Some leading figures in the arts in Europe, 1950s to the turn of the century

The French *nouveau roman* (whose foremost practitioner is Alain Robbe-Grillet) actually appears in the 1950s and develops, during the cultural revolution, into the more extreme *nouveau nouveau roman*. The critical point about the new novelists (and still more the 'new new novelists') is that their driving force is radical hostility, Marxist or neo-Marxist, to existing society: the enemy is the bourgeosie, bourgeois 'liberal humanism' and, in this particular case, the bourgeois novel, which is seen as having achieved its apogee in the mid nineteenth century. The fundamental aim of the new novel is to deny everything that went to make up the traditional novel: there should be no linear narrative, no plot, no suspense, no characters with defined identities; events are to be recounted in the arbitrary mode of the human mind, stretched, abridged, repeated; meaning will come not from individual passages of realism, but from the work as an entity. The new novel, in effect, is an artefact of postmodernism.

The British artist David Hockney, who achieved fame while still a student, can be taken as symbolic both of the power of youth and of a highly personal Pop Art which denies allegiance to any of the Modernist movements; some of his works are openly homosexual in content and philosophy.

From the end of the cultural revolution onwards the most distinctive medium in art is assemblage, often incorporating technological elements such as television sets or computers. Leading figures in the first wave of assemblages are the German, Josef Beuys, something of an impresario for early postmodernist exhibitions and 'happenings', and the Italian, Michelangelo Pistoletto, one of the first to incorporate mirrors in his installations.

Conclusion

Go back to the exercise you did at the very beginning of this chapter. Would you like to change your answer? How far *have* the arts come since 1910? What is genuine change, what is really continuity? What part *have* the wars played?

References

Barbusse, Henri [1917] (1965) *Under Fire*, transl. W. Fitzwater Wray, London, Dent (first published as *Le Feu*, 1916).

Barthes, Roland [1968] (1977) 'The death of the author', in Barthes, *Image Music Text*, selected and transl. Stephen Heath, London, Fontana.

Blokker, Roy (1979) *The Music of Dmitri Shostakovich: the Symphonies*, London, Tantivy.

Cork, Richard (1994) *A Bitter Truth: Avant-Garde Art and the Great War*, New Haven, CN/London, Yale University Press.

Derouet, Christian (1997) *Fernand Léger*, Paris, Centre Pompidou.

Fréchuret, Maurice (1987) 'L'impossibilité de peindre', in Bernard Ceysson and Jacques Beauffet (eds), *L'Art en Europe: les anneés décisives, 1945–1953*, Geneva, Skira.

Hindemith, Paul (1995) *Selected Letters of Paul Hindemith*, ed. and transl. Geoffrey Skelton, New Haven, CN/London, Yale University Press.

Léger, Fernand (1997) *Fernand Léger: Un Correspondence de guerre à Louis Poughon, 1914–1918*, transl. Christian Derouet, Paris, Les cahiers du Musée National d'Art Moderne.

Lippiard, Lucy R. (ed.) (1971) *Dadas on Art*, Englewood Cliffs, NJ, Prentice-Hall.

Marwick, Arthur (2002), *The Arts in the West since 1945*, Oxford, Oxford University Press.

Néret, Gilles (1990) *Léger*, Paris, Casterman.

Orenstein, Arbie (1975) *Ravel: Man and Musician*, New York, Columbia University Press.

Richter, Hans (1997) *Dada: Art and Anti-art*, transl. David Britt, London, Thames & Hudson.

Skelton, Geoffrey (1975) *Paul Hindemith: the Man behind the Music*, London, Gollancz.

Winter, Jay (1995) *Sites of Memory, Sites of Mourning: the Great War in European Cultural History*, Cambridge, Cambridge University Press.

Europe and the cultural impact of the Holocaust

TIM COLE

Introduction

The year 1993 was dubbed in America 'the year of the Holocaust'. It was then that a national Holocaust museum – the United States Holocaust Memorial Museum (USHMM) – opened in the heart of the nation's capital, and the Holocaust movie *Schindler's List* opened at American box-offices. Both were immediate hits, with the museum in Washington, DC, attracting 2 million visitors annually and Steven Spielberg's film receiving both popular and critical acclaim. This single year was seen as simply the high point in a longer history of the emergence of the Holocaust as a central icon in the United States during the course of the 1980s and 1990s. That history has been told by – among others – Peter Novick, who contrasts the relative silence about the Holocaust within America in general (and the American Jewish community in particular) during the late 1940s and 1950s with the more recent 'Holocaust fixation' in the United States (Novick, 1999, p. 10). The irony is of course that the Holocaust has assumed a central place in American consciousness despite, or perhaps precisely because of, the fact that it took place many thousands of miles away.

The exporting of this European event to the United States, in the 1980s and 1990s in particular, has been termed the 'Americanization of the Holocaust'. Although there have been a number of different takes on what this amounted to, in general it has been seen as the nationalization of Holocaust memory in the American context, resulting in universalization at best and trivialization at worst. To Michael Berenbaum – himself involved in the early years of the USHMM – Americanization of the Holocaust has involved reshaping the memory of this event into a story which fits with 'the fundamental tale of pluralism, tolerance, democracy, and human rights that America tells about itself' (Berenbaum, 1990, pp. 40–1). Within this bigger tale of what it means to be American, the Holocaust tends to function as the antithesis of all that America holds dear. It is the example *par excellence* of intolerance and dictatorship, of racism and the denial of human rights. In short, it is the 'other' against which America can define itself.

I think a clear example of this can be seen in the USHMM itself. Entering the museum from Raoul Wallenberg Place (the street was renamed after the Swedish diplomat who issued safe passes to Jewish people in Budapest in 1944), the visitor encounters two famous quotations. One is an extract from the Declaration of Independence of 1776, with its promise to all citizens of the right to 'life, liberty and the pursuit of happiness'. The other is taken from George Washington's words to a Jewish congregation in Newport, Rhode Island, in 1790, assuring them that 'the government of the United States ... gives to bigotry no sanction, to persecution no assistance'. It is these words which frame the visitor's experience of the historical narrative of the Holocaust that is expertly laid out over three floors in the permanent exhibition. And so the Nazi German prosecution of the Holocaust is framed as the most un-American of all crimes, because here was a regime that took away 'life, liberty and the pursuit of happiness' from millions of European Jews, and gave 'bigotry' full sanction and 'persecution' every possible assistance.

Now, arguably, such a telling of the Holocaust can work in a removed environment like Washington, DC, but it is more problematic in the areas where the historical events themselves took place. This suggests that we can expect American memory of this event to differ somewhat from European memories. But can we talk of the 'Europeanization' of the Holocaust in the same way that we can talk of its 'Americanization' or 'Israelization' (Cole, 1999, p. 135)? Is there a shared European memory of the Holocaust, or have there been distinct national memories? To what extent did the Cold War divisions within Europe create essentially two different traditions and narratives of Holocaust memory? These are just some of the questions that I hope to explore in the course of this chapter by thinking about three places of memory: the former death and concentration camp at Auschwitz, Poland; the memorial spaces of Budapest, Hungary; and the capital of the Third Reich and new German capital, Berlin.

Besides thinking about whether there are shared or divided memories in Europe, I think it is also important to ask more fundamental questions about memory itself. How useful is it to think at the level of national and supranational memory? Do we need to think at the level of the individual? To what extent do we need to explore the intersections between national and public memory and individual memory (Cole, 2002, pp. 131–4)? How does memory work

– from the top down, or the bottom up? To ask these questions is to address fundamental issues not simply about memory, but also about identity.

Auschwitz

I start with Auschwitz, a place that has become synonymous with the Holocaust. Of all the former concentration and death camps in Europe, it is this site in southern Poland which has emerged as representative of the industrialized mass killing of the Holocaust, and a – if not the – symbol for evil. And yet that was not always the case. In the immediate postwar context it was not Auschwitz but the concentration camp at Bergen-Belsen which resonated in Britain. Belsen was liberated by British troops on 15 April 1945, and the harrowing film footage shot in the days after liberation had an impact upon British cinema audiences. These images came to represent the nature of Nazi brutality to an entire generation; so it was Belsen – not Auschwitz – that emerged in British popular consciousness in the late 1940s and 1950s as the definitive concentration camp. Thus the infamous SS guards Irma Grese and Josef Kramer who had served at both Auschwitz and Bergen-Belsen were nicknamed at the time of their postwar trials 'the bitch of Belsen' and 'the beast of Belsen', respectively. And in postwar Britain it was the phrase 'looking like someone out of Belsen' that was applied to the skinny kid in the class (Stratton, 2000, p. 243). Auschwitz remained relatively unknown in Britain and much of western Europe, given that it had been liberated not by British or American troops, but by Soviet troops on 27 January 1945.

Within a divided Europe, a divided memory of Nazi atrocities emerged, with Auschwitz playing a central role in memory in the east, but not in the west. As early as 1947, the former concentration camp at Auschwitz was turned into a memorial museum by the newly formed Polish government and visits here became compulsory for Polish schoolchildren. There were also busloads of visitors from the other communist-bloc nations. However, the site of Auschwitz played little part in western European memory until the 1960s. That decade can be seen more generally as a period of increasing focus on the Holocaust as a distinct event, and in that context Auschwitz began to emerge as the representative site of this event. The historian Tony Kushner has pointed to Sylvia Plath's 1965 poem 'Daddy', which mentions both Belsen and Auschwitz, as an 'important cultural guide in which Belsen and Auschwitz are accorded equal weight' (Kushner, 1997, p. 195). His suggestion is that prior to the 1960s references would be made to Belsen alone – in the British context – while after the 1960s references would increasingly be made to Auschwitz alone.

Certainly there does seem to be a sense in which the divided memorial geography of the immediate postwar period was increasingly replaced by a greater consensus that Auschwitz was the definitive site of Holocaust memory. However, the legacy of the divided memory remained, with Auschwitz being interpreted very much within a Cold War frame of reference well into the 1970s and 1980s.

The first reading is an extract from the fifth edition of the Auschwitz museum guidebook, published in 1974. You should read it now.

WE REMEMBER

In spite of the fact that, according to the Potsdam Agreement [of 1945], Germany was to be entirely demilitarized, there exist quantities of *'Soldiers' Unions'* in the German Federal Republic. Congresses of former SS [members] take place and revisionist slogans are heard at them, together with the Nazi song *'Horst Wessel-Lied'*. A new army[, the] *'Bundeswehr'*, has been organized and is continually increasing in numbers.

All peace loving nations are protesting against the violation of the Agreement, fearing the possibility of a new war scourge, which could prove to be even more disastrous in its results than the last war. We should keep this in mind when [walking] along the streets of the former concentration camp in Ausch[w]itz-Birkenau, where, not so many years ago, lorries had passed, loaded with the corpses of prisoners, both of those who had died in the camp and of those who had been shot in the yard of Block 11; their blood had soaked into the road leading to the crematorium.

Our duty is to honour the memory of those who had perished here, those whose ashes were scattered over the fields of Birkenau or were thrown into the adjoining ponds.

To remember and to honour them is the aim of the Museum, established here by the decree of July 2, 1947, which states: *'on the site of the former Nazi concentration camp a Monument of the Martyrdom of the Polish Nation and of Other Nations is to be erected for all times to come.'*

(Smolen, 1974, pp. 113–14)

EXERCISE

On the basis of this extract, what is the museum self-consciously seeking to remember, and why?

DISCUSSION

You might have been struck by the lack of mention of 'Jews' in this text. Rather than specifically highlighting the memory of Jewish victims of the Nazis, a general reference is made to 'those who had perished here'. Such non-specific references were the norm within the Soviet Union and communist-bloc countries. It is clear from the museum's aims, as stated at the end of the reading, that the victims who are remembered came from both Poland and 'Other Nations', but we aren't given much of a sense of why they were killed here. We are given a sense of why we should remember them, though. In particular, contemporary events to the west – that is, in West Germany – are flagged as the context to remembering what occurred in this place. There is a clear suggestion of a continuity between Nazi Germany, which created this camp, and West Germany, which is seen to be re-arming. The subtext seems to be that the threat in the past came from the west, and that the threat in the present also comes from the west.

This passage – as you might have assumed – has been omitted from the later version of the guidebook that appeared after the fall of communism. The earlier spelling out of the museum's aims contrasts markedly with the edition published just under twenty years later, which simply reports in a matter-of-fact manner that 'The camps in Oswiecim (KL Auschwitz I) and in Brzezinka (KL Auschwitz II – Birkenau) are now maintained as museums open to the public' (Smolen, 1993, p. 4).

It is interesting to compare these two guidebooks, the first published in the communist era and the second in the post-communist era (1974 and 1993, respectively). The next reading highlights their different descriptions of the exhibition in Block 4 of the museum.

Block 4. Room 4.

4 million persons perished in the '*Konzentrationslager Auschwitz-Birkenau*'; 4 million persons from all the countries under Nazi occupation. This number was arrived at as the result of computations made after surveying the terrain, the installations of destruction and the documents of the Auschwitz camp; it is also based upon the evidence of hundreds of surviving prisoners and upon the opinion of experts.

The Soviet State Extraordinary Com[m]ission for the Investigation of Nazi Crimes stated that *'no less than 4 million people perished in Auschwitz.'* The Supreme National Tribunal in Poland stated that *'about 4 million persons perished in Auschwitz.'* According to the international Military Tribunal in Nuremberg *'more than 4 million persons perished in Auschwitz.'*

The urn with a handful of ashes, collected in the Birkenau terrain, commemorates *'4 million of those'* who had perished there.

(Smolen, 1974, p. 19)

Block 4.

Room 1.

Auschwitz was the biggest Nazi concentration camp for Poles and prisoners from other countries. They were condemned by the hitlerite fascism to isolation and slow extermination by hunger, exhausting work, criminal experiments, or to a quick death as a result of individual and mass executions.

Since 1942 Auschwitz became the biggest center for the mass extermination of European Jews. The majority of Jews deported to Auschwitz were killed in gas chambers immediately on arrival, without registration and without identification with the camp numbers. Therefore it is very difficult to determine precisely the number of people murdered there. For many years this problem has been debated by historians from various countries. They give different numbers, most often [up] to 1.5 million victims. The search for additional documentation is under way to find a more precise number.

The urn containing a handful of human ashes, gathered from the territory of Birkenau, commemorates the dead.

(Smolen, 1993, p. 6)

EXERCISE _____

What differences strike you between these extracts from the two guidebooks?

DISCUSSION

You will no doubt have noticed the absence of reference to Jewish people in the first extract, compared with the specific references in the second one. As well as Jews, the second extract also explicitly mentions Poles. These references make sense both in the context of the increased international recognition of Auschwitz as the definitive symbol of the Jewish Holocaust, and in the post-communist Polish nationalist context, where Auschwitz is seen as a site of specifically national martyrdom. The sense of distinct Jewish and Polish memories of this place is something which we will think about some more.

The other thing which is striking concerns the differing numbers of dead offered in the two extracts. The inflated figure of 4 million is replaced in the later guidebook with an estimate of 1.5 million. And that latter figure is revealed as problematic given the nature of the sources. It is interesting that in the earlier guidebook the figure is stressed as accurate and shown to be supported by official 'experts'. In the later version the figure is emphasized as an estimate drawn from the work of historians.

I don't know if you thought about the use of the German word for concentration camp – *Konzentrationslager* – when referring to Auschwitz-Birkenau in the first extract. Do you think that the use of a foreign term, and specifically a German term, was a conscious choice? If you think back to the earlier extract from this 1974 guidebook the link is clearly made between Germany in the past and Germany in the present. Is there a sense that in using this German term the writers of the guidebook are suggesting that concentration camps were foreign – German – inventions brought into Polish territory, and that Germany is still the potential threat?

As can be seen in the extract from the second guidebook, Auschwitz has emerged as a site of both Jewish and Polish memory. One element of the Polish commemoration of Auschwitz as a site of specifically national martyrdom has been an increasing Polish Catholic memory of the camp. Indeed for the historical geographer Andrew Charlesworth, the last couple of decades have seen attempts to 'Catholicize' Auschwitz (Charlesworth, 1994, p. 585). This has been centred around the person of Maximilian Kolbe, a Polish Catholic priest who gave up his own life in place of another prisoner who was to be executed. This act of self-sacrifice, with its Christological overtones, resulted in Kolbe being beatified in 1971 and canonized in 1982. His cell in Block 11 (Plate 19) has emerged as a site of Catholic pilgrimage, especially on All Saints' Day

(1 November) when candles are lit and prayers said in Kolbe's memory. Kolbe's memory was also invoked when Pope John Paul II celebrated mass at Auschwitz-Birkenau in 1979. Hanging from the cross erected for the mass was a symbolic prisoner's uniform with Kolbe's prison number – 16 670 – written on it. Clearly a parallel was being drawn here between Kolbe's self-sacrificial act and Christ's.

These acts of 'Catholicization' were challenged in particular by Jewish groups, who saw Auschwitz not only as the site of around 1 million Jewish deaths, but increasingly as the central symbol of the Holocaust. It was pointed out that Kolbe was a controversial figure, as both the pre-war editor of an anti-semitic newspaper and a member of an organization committed to seeking the conversion of Jews. The appropriateness of erecting a cross in Auschwitz was also questioned, given the Jewishness of the majority of the victims there and the problematic history of Christian anti-semitism. During the 1980s Catholic and Jewish groups frequently contested the meaning of the site at Auschwitz. This conflict culminated in July 1989 with a group of protesters, led by the American Orthodox Jewish Rabbi Avraham Weiss, breaking into the grounds of a Carmelite convent which had been controversially established just outside the perimeter fence of the main camp at Auschwitz. Ultimately the Vatican intervened and the convent was relocated. However, contestation continued into the 1990s, and questions still remain over the compatibility of specifically Catholic and Jewish memories at this one site.

That Weiss is an American Jewish rabbi reflects, I think, the increasing international symbolism of Auschwitz. From being primarily a site of memory within eastern Europe, it has become not simply a broader European site of memory, but an – if not the – international site of memory. In particular, it has assumed a central place in American memory of the Holocaust. Thus in the United States Holocaust Memorial Museum it is Auschwitz that is used to represent all of the concentration and death camps. At the climax of the permanent exhibition at the USHMM, visitors are taken under a casting of the *Arbeit macht frei* (work makes you free) gateway from the main camp at Auschwitz and into part of an original wooden barracks from Auschwitz-Birkenau which houses a model of the gas chambers and crematoria.

The route from the original *Arbeit macht frei* gateway to the gas chambers of Auschwitz-Birkenau is one re-enacted annually by some 700,000 tourists and pilgrims to the museum at Auschwitz. And each year it is walked by the thousands of Jewish teenagers who take part in the March of the Living. Started in 1988, this march takes young Jews from the United States and a host of other countries on what can best be described as a pilgrimage to Poland and Israel. A ritualized journey of around one and a half kilometres from the main camp at Auschwitz to the death camp of Auschwitz-Birkenau, the March of the Living lies at the very heart of this pilgrimage.

The march takes place on Israel's Holocaust Memorial Day (the precise date of which varies according to when Passover falls), making it a self-conscious act of shared remembrance with the Israeli nation. A week or so later the marchers are in Israel engaged in another shared act, this time one of celebration on Israel's Independence Day. The aim of the march is clear. Auschwitz in particular (but also Poland and indeed Europe more generally) is seen as the place of destruction for Jews. In contrast, Israel is seen as the place of their salvation.

The following accounts of the march were written by two young participants – both 15-year-olds from Toronto, Canada.

Leigh Salsberg ...

A *shofar* (horn) was blown in Auschwitz. We stood between the red barracks, thousands of people from Canada to Israel to South Africa to India, all wearing blue jackets and waving Israeli flags, and a *shofar* was blown in Auschwitz. I have never heard a more powerful sound. All of humanity might have swelled with pride at that moment. I don't know exactly what I was feeling proud of, nor exactly why my eyes were tearing. But the sound of the *shofar* in the nethermost depths of the netherworld, the presence of life in the valley of the shadow of death, was both painful and comforting, terrible and magnificent. Then, chins up, holding hands, in silence, we began to walk towards Birkenau ...

Jillian Moncarz ...

As I walked around Birkenau, my only sense of security (the Jews who died there didn't have this comfort) was the fact that I was carrying the Israeli flag with me. There's something so special about that flag. By carrying the Canadian flag, you show the world that you are Canadian ... but by carrying the Israeli flag, you show the world that you are Jewish, and in a world like the one over here, where Jews are spat upon, the Israeli flag also shows the world that you are proud to be Jewish.

(Rubenstein, 1993, pp. 56, 113)

238

EXERCISE _____

What do you make of the nature of these young people's March of the Living memory of Auschwitz?

DISCUSSION _____

The memory of Auschwitz which these two teenage marchers articulate is perhaps not what you might expect. Both write of a sense of pride when walking from the main camp at Auschwitz to the death camp at Auschwitz-Birkenau. In large part that sense of pride seems to be tied in with the presence of Israeli flags in this place – with all that they see these flags as symbolizing (the survival of the Jews, the security of the Jews). The linking of Jewishness and Israel clearly suggests that the march aims at an explicitly Zionist memory of Auschwitz. The first marcher is interesting in stressing the experience as a march of the living in this place of mass death. The second marcher is interesting in speaking of Europe in general and Poland in particular as essentially places of anti-semitism – places where you end up with somewhere like Auschwitz in the past and Jews being 'spat upon' in the present.

_____

The feelings of the marchers remind us that we should be aware of the importance of rituals in giving significance to sites of memory. Such sites are animated through the rituals which take place there. These two marchers' memories of Auschwitz are characterized by pride, but different people enacting different rituals may well remember Auschwitz rather differently. When reflecting upon memory it is important to consider the nature of individual responses. So even a place with an apparently 'simple', single memory may be interpreted rather differently by different people. Now Auschwitz is a place around which, I have suggested, there is no 'simple', single, uncontested memory. Rather, around it has gathered a complex history of competing memories – communist, Polish nationalist, Catholic, Jewish. But even so we cannot assume that all Catholics, or all Jews, have common memories of the site. The two Jewish teenagers who visited Auschwitz to participate in the March of the Living have a memory which differs markedly from, say, that of a Jewish survivor returning to Auschwitz to say *kaddish* (prayers for the dead). And, arguably, for a large number who visit the site, Auschwitz is less a place of memory than a place of tourism: a site to be consumed on a demanding itinerary of 'must visit' places. It is, after all, one of Poland's top tourist attractions.

The next reading comprises two extracts from the historian Paul Levine's comments on visiting Auschwitz – first his reflections on what he overheard there, and then his own reflections on his visit.

To choose to go to Birkenau: reflections on visiting a death camp, August 1996

Walking alongside a grandfatherly type, I heard him ask his fellow tour members if they thought the day's schedule permitted shopping that afternoon. His companions seemed equally concerned about the time – and my mind reeled. Is that what most concerns the average visitor at the end of their visit? How, why, do normal people contemplate the importance of buying souvenirs for their grandchildren back home while still in the shadow of Auschwitz? Didn't the place shock them out of their usual thought processes – and if that place didn't, what could? Is this blasphemous, a surely unintended sign of disrespect to the victims? Or is such a mundane response, perhaps reassuredly, a normal reaction to something impossible to understand. The question is compelling – what should a visitor to Auschwitz think and feel? ...

I was overwhelmed by a feeling of futility. My job is to educate people about the facts of [the] Holocaust and what it means in the world today. But now and here, seeing and feeling this place, such a goal seemed bitterly futile, even desperately useless. How does one teach horror? What can possibly be said to students which will make some sense to them about such a place? Walking there made me feel useless, deflated, doubting the value of my life's work.

(Levine, 1996, pp. 8, 10)

EXERCISE

Try to contrast Levine's thoughts, and the words of the 'grandfatherly type' he encountered, with those of the two young Canadian Jewish marchers quoted above. Are all four of them engaging in an act of memory when visiting Auschwitz?

DISCUSSION

Comparing these comments from Levine with the thoughts of the marchers, it appears that this place engenders a range of emotions – from pride, through concerns about consumption, to feelings of futility and even desperation. You might feel that all of these are expressions of memory, or that the marchers are engaged more in a contemporary ritual rather than memory, the grandfather in an act of

tourism, and Paul Levine in an act of reflection about being a
historian and teacher. Memory is a notoriously slippery concept –
especially when we start to talk about 'collective' or 'public' memory,
not simply 'individual' or 'private' memory.

It is clear that the Holocaust plays a central role in contemporary
European popular culture. Indeed given Levine's use of the word
'blasphemous' in the extract above – a term generally associated with
God – it seems fair to suggest that the Holocaust has a quasi-religious
status in contemporary culture, with Auschwitz as the most sacred
space and pilgrimage site in that 'religion'. But it is one thing to
accept the iconic status of the Holocaust, and another to regard it as
central to a shared European memory or identity. As I've suggested, if
there are collective memories of Auschwitz then these are multiple
and contested memories, rather than single monolithic memories.
And therefore it is important to think about memory not simply from
the top down (such as the communist Polish state creating a
particular history of Auschwitz) but also from the bottom up (for
example, how an individual visiting Auschwitz interprets the site). It
doesn't seem to be just a case of a state or organization creating a
collective memory which people then simply buy into. Rather,
individuals buy into, appropriate, subtly change, question, contest
and challenge the whole notion of 'collective memory'. So, in the
case of Auschwitz, I think we can safely say that during the
communist period there were attempts to utilize the memory of the
site within the context of the Cold War division of Europe, and that
there have also been attempts to 'Catholicize' the site, which have
been contested by Jewish groups arguing for a 'Jewish' memory of the
site. But it is harder to say how successfully those memories have been
passed on to the individuals who visit. There seem to be multiple ways
in which individuals may interpret the site, depending on their own
particular biographies and contexts.

This sense of thinking about memory from the top down and the
bottom up is something that James Young is sensitive to in his study
of Holocaust memorials. He writes of 'the constant give and take
between memorials and viewers' (Young, 1993, p. ix), suggesting that
if we want to understand memorials then we do well to ask questions
not simply about who is creating them and why, but also about who is
visiting them and what meanings they bring to and derive from them.
These two sets of questions are important, I think, although it is
generally easier to find answers to the first set than the second. We
can ask who commissioned the memorial, what they remembered
(and by implication what they forgot), when and where they did that
remembering, and how that memory was articulated aesthetically. But

then we need to go further and address a whole series of other issues. As Young notes,

> by themselves, monuments are of little value, mere stones in the landscape. But as part of a nation's rites or the objects of a people's national pilgrimage, they are invested with a national soul and memory.

(Young, 1993, p. 2)

So we need to ask how these memorials are used within public ritual. For example, the March of the Living is an obvious example of a particular meaning being given to Auschwitz through a ritual act.

It is easy to assume that a memorial, once created, means exactly the thing which was originally intended. But the kinds of ritual that are enacted can add layers of meaning to those originally intended. And as Young suggests,

> the relationship between a state and its memorials is not one-sided, however. On the one hand, official agencies are in a position to shape memory explicitly as they see fit, memory that best serves a national interest. On the other hand, once created, memorials take on lives of their own, often stubbornly resistant to the state's original intentions. In some cases, memorials created in the image of a state's ideals actually turn around to recast these ideals in the memorial's own image. New generations visit memorials under new circumstances and invest them with new meanings. The result is an evolution in the memorial's significance, generated in the new times and company in which it finds itself.

(Young, 1993, p. 3)

What Young is pointing to is – I think – a need for the anthropological and ethnographical study of memorials, not simply the study of their form and text. In short, we need to consider not just what memorials say, but how they are interpreted by viewers.

Budapest

I was struck by this need to think about what the viewer (or user) makes of a memorial when walking one summer in the section of Budapest where the Jewish ghetto was located during the Second World War. There are a number of memorials here which commemorate various aspects of the Holocaust in Hungary in general and in Budapest in particular. One of these is dedicated to Carl Lutz, a Swiss official involved in the rescue of Jews in Budapest in 1944–5. It is a striking memorial. When I came across it, a bunch of kids were playing on it. It makes a perfect slide to slither down, or

CARL LUTZ EMLÉKMŰVE

Figure 7.1 Postcard showing Tamás Szabó's 1991 memorial to the Swiss diplomat Carl Lutz, erected in the former Jewish ghetto area, Budapest. Photo: Szaboky Zsolt

beam to hang off. I asked them if they knew why their 'slide' was there, and who was the man it commemorated. They didn't. I wonder if their relationship with this particular material form of Holocaust memory in Budapest was not that dissimilar from the grandfather's relationship with the material form of Holocaust memory in Auschwitz, mentioned by Levine in the fourth reading above. We need to think about what is intended by Holocaust memorials, but we also need to ask how they are then interpreted and used by those who view them.

Figure 7.2 Wall plaque erected in the late 1940s close to one of the gateways into the former Jewish ghetto, Budapest. Photo: Tim Cole

Having said all that, however, I do think it is possible to identify broad memories of the Holocaust, at a level other than that of the individual. And exploring the Holocaust memorials established in and around the Budapest ghetto is one way into thinking about the nature of those memories. The very first Holocaust memorial set up in the former ghetto area is perhaps the best place to start. It takes the form of a simple wall plaque, set up at the edge of the former Pest ghetto at the end of the war.

EXERCISE _____

Look at the plaque pictured in Figure 7.2. The inscription on it reads, in translation:

> In the fascist period one of the gates to the Budapest ghetto stood here. The liberating Soviet army broke down the ghetto walls on 18 January 1945.

Think about what is being remembered here and, by implication, what is being forgotten.

DISCUSSION _____

You might have been struck by some similarities with the early texts from Auschwitz that we have already looked at. As with the 1974 guidebook (which also originated in the communist bloc), the word

'Jew' is noticeable by its absence here. Although the Budapest ghetto was specifically 'Jewish', there is no mention of this in the words on the plaque. And it's not just that the text doesn't specify the Jewishness of the victims: it doesn't actually mention the victims at all. As you can see from the inscription, the largest type and most prominent position are reserved for the liberating Soviet army and the date of liberation. In essence the plaque seems to be less about the ghetto itself than about its liberation and the liberators. This makes sense if you think of the immediate postwar context. The Soviet army is being celebrated more than the Holocaust is being remembered. The central actors being remembered are the liberators, with no explicit reference to the victims and only general reference to the perpetrators. The broad term 'the fascist period' does not raise questions about native collaboration which are so pertinent in the Hungarian context: the Budapest ghetto was, after all, established in late November 1944 by the Hungarian *Nyilas* (Arrow Cross) government. (The *Nyilas* – a native Hungarian fascist party – had come to power in October 1944 as a pro-Nazi puppet government.)

Within the area of the former Pest ghetto, the only Holocaust memorial for some forty years was this plaque commemorating the Soviet liberators. The memory of the Jewish victims was pushed to the periphery, with the creation of a memorial in 1949 in the central Jewish cemetery on the outskirts of the city. This takes the form of a wall of names and a symbolic tomb, remembering all of the Hungarian Jews murdered during the Holocaust, in the traditional memorial space of a Jewish graveyard. It is clear that the monument has been interpreted by some visitors as a virtual tombstone for the dead, with some following the traditional Jewish ritual act of laying a stone on the tomb as an act of remembrance.

These stones have been joined by flowers – an act of Christian rather than Jewish remembrance. Such acts point to that sense of 'give and take' mentioned earlier in the quote from James Young. The memorial is being reinterpreted by visitors, and in particular being reinterpreted as tombstone rather than memorial. The act of reinterpretation is not simply restricted to the leaving of a stone or flowers. Rather, names have been repainted as both an act of memory and a safeguard against forgetting and obliteration, and additional names have been pencilled in. This memorial is therefore striking for the sense in which it continues to be created and re-created by those who visit, especially as names continue to be added. In short, it is not fixed memory, but very much memory in flux which is being re-created from the bottom up here.

Figure 7.3 Flowers and stones left at the wall of names at the Holocaust Memorial in the central Jewish cemetery, Budapest. Photo: Tim Cole

Names also play a central part in a memorial to the Jewish victims – once again from the entire country, not simply Budapest – officially unveiled on 8 July 1990. Erected in the courtyard of the city's main Dohány Street synagogue, this 'Memorial of the Hungarian Jewish Martyrs' brought the first explicit memorial reference to the Jewishness of the victims to the area of the former Pest ghetto (Plate 20). The text on it reads, in translation:

> The Emmanuel Foundation set up this memorial in memory of the 600,000 Hungarian Jewish martyrs who can never be forgotten, who were innocent victims of an evil unparalleled in history.
>
> 8 July 1990, in the period of László Keller's presidency

The erection of this memorial to Jewish victims marked a radical shift. A mere five years earlier, in 1985, a memorial plaque had been erected on a neighbouring stretch of reconstructed ghetto wall. It made no mention of the Jewishness of the victims, focusing instead on the Soviet liberators. The shift in attitude that occurred at the end of the 1980s, with the acknowledgement of the memory of the Jewish victims of the Nazis, was a reflection of the broader political changes taking place in Hungary with the loosening of Soviet influence on the country. The memorial – a weeping willow reminiscent of an upturned menorah – has the names of individual victims etched on to the underside of its many leaves. However, the act of etching on

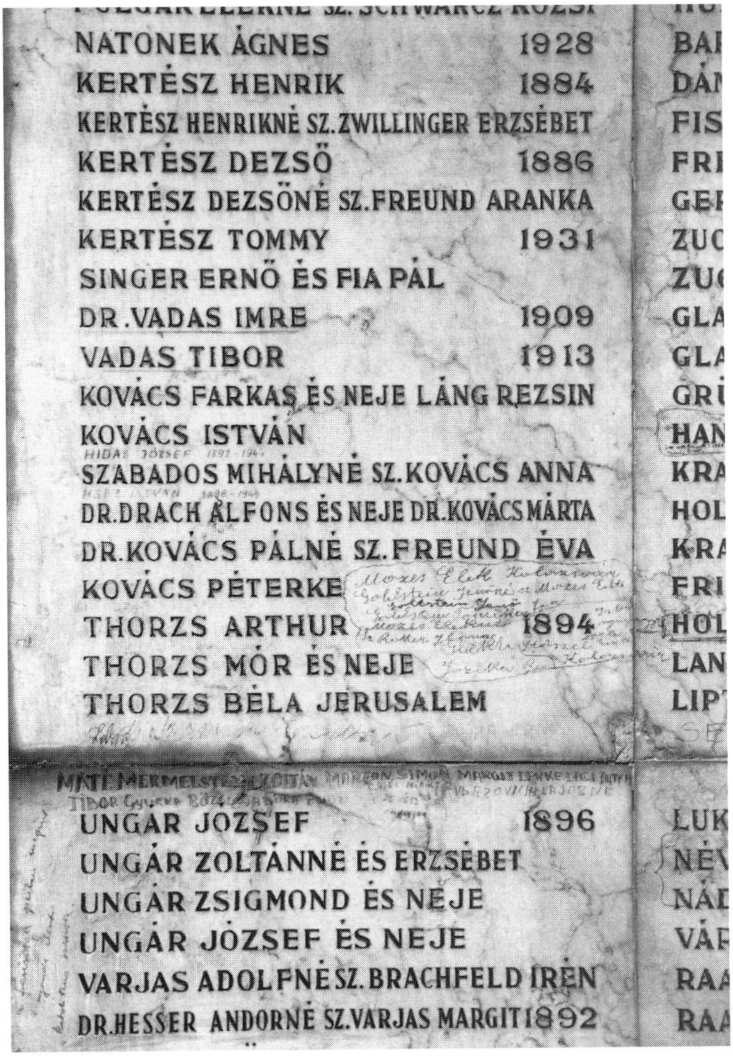

Figure 7.4 Evidence of the repainting and addition of names to the wall of names at the Holocaust Memorial in the central Jewish cemetery, Budapest. Photo: Tim Cole

any additional names is effectively policed. Unlike in the Jewish cemetery where visitors have continued to pencil in names, here names are added at the rate of $125 a time. Moreover, when reading the inscription one does have to question whether the memorial is not simply remembering Hungary's Holocaust victims, but also those who set it up.

This is not the only Holocaust memorial to be erected in the area of the former Budapest ghetto. As I mentioned earlier, there is also a memorial to Carl Lutz, a Swiss rescuer who in some ways parallels the Swedish rescuer Raoul Wallenberg, who has been remembered elsewhere in the city. Set in a prominent spot on one of the main streets of the former ghetto, this memorial was erected in the post-communist period when there was a relative freeing up of state control over memory. The inscription on it reads, in translation:

> Who saves a single life, is like one who saves the whole world.
>
> (Talmud)

> In memory of those thousands of Nazi persecuted saved through the leadership of Swiss consul Carl Lutz in 1944.
>
> Swiss Carl Lutz Board, Budapest meeting, 1991

EXERCISE

With regard to the text on the memorial, think about what is being remembered and what is being forgotten here, and by whom.

DISCUSSION

You might have been struck by the lack of explicit reference to Jews in this inscription – like so many others that we have looked at. The quote from the Talmud does suggest Jewishness implicitly, but not explicitly. This lack of specific reference to the Jewish people is striking given that the text does not come from the communist period, when the Jewishness of the Nazis' victims was downplayed, but from the post-communist period. The language used – the 'Nazi persecuted' – tells us little about the specifics of who these victims were and why they were being persecuted. That phrase, 'thousands of Nazi persecuted', is interesting in that it presents the perpetrator as Nazi Germany, but makes no reference to the historical realities of native Hungarian complicity in the Holocaust: in particular, in the case of Budapest, the collaboration of the *Nyilas* government. Ultimately of course the memorial is not really about either victims or perpetrators but rescuers, and one particular rescuer: Carl Lutz. Above all, this is a commemoration of Lutz's acts of rescue, set up by an organization dedicated to his name and memory.

It has become increasingly commonplace to remember the rescuers. One needs only to think of the film *Schindler's List* to find an example of the way in which Holocaust rescuers have been accorded increasing attention in recent years. And Wallenberg, Lutz and Schindler are not the only ones. Miep Gies, for example, has emerged as the – ultimately unsuccessful – rescuer of the most famous Holocaust victim of them all, Anne Frank. There has been, Alvin Rosenfeld suggests, 'a paradigm shift of significant proportions' (Rosenfeld, 1997, p. 140) away from the categories of perpetrators, victims and bystanders to those of rescuers and survivors. To all these categories, we need to add that of the 'liberators' which, as we've discussed in the context of Hungary, played a central role in the early memory of the Budapest ghetto.

If there is a need to think both chronologically and geographically about Holocaust memory – when and where are events being remembered? – and about memory from above as well as below – what do those who visit make of these sites of memory? – there is, too, a need to think about who is being remembered. After all, as we have seen there is a plethora of categories to choose from: perpetrators, victims, bystanders, liberators, rescuers and survivors. All this suggests that there are real problems in trying to think about Holocaust memory as a single entity. Rather we should think of it as contested, and as having both a history and a geography. Perhaps nowhere is this more relevant than when thinking about Holocaust memory (or 'anti-memory') in Germany. How the nation of the perpetrators has remembered this event raises questions peculiar to that nation.

Germany

The broad divisions between eastern and western European memories of the Holocaust were exemplified within the postwar divided nation of Germany. In the east the 'Jewishness' of the victims was downplayed (as elsewhere in eastern Europe), with the stress placed upon the political victims of Nazism. The East German Communist party could portray itself not only as the first victim of Nazism, but also as the well of resistance to Nazism and ultimately the self-liberator of the Buchenwald camp. This anti-Nazi past was stressed as a line of continuity within the anti-fascist state of the GDR. In the west the picture was not as simple as a memory of anti-fascist resistance. Rather there was a mixture of silence and of emotional and contested attempts to remember a troubling past. Historian Mary Fulbrook contrasts the two responses during the 1950s as a period when 'in the West there was an incorporation of collective penance into public political culture; the counterpart in the East was a form of official heroism' (Fulbrook, 1999, p. 50).

In essence, memory in the GDR was more monolithic and, given the twist of resistance against Nazism, was also – to cite Fulbrook again – 'always both positive, and consciously produced with specific political intent'. By contrast, she notes that 'in the Federal Republic, all public representations were fraught with taboos, surrounded with controversies, subjected to acute debate, analysis and critique' (Fulbrook, 1999, p. 79). This contrast between a more singular memory in the east and a more contested memory in the west reflects the differences in who was doing the remembering. Whereas in the east memory was state-sanctioned and very much from the top down, in the west it came much more from the bottom up and was the result of initiatives by individuals and local organizations. For example, in 1985 a small independent group called the Active Museum of Fascism and Resistance in Berlin began an unofficial excavation of the cellars next to the former Gestapo headquarters in the centre of Berlin, a central site of the perpetrators. The impetus for this literal digging up of the past was very much bottom up rather than top down – in contrast to, say, the state-sanctioned transformation of Buchenwald into a memorial site of anti-fascist struggle in the east.

This contrast between top-down and bottom-up approaches is something that the historian Rudy Koshar suggests – on the whole rightly, I think – was characteristic not simply of East *vs.* West Germany, but more generally of east *vs.* west Europe during the Cold War era. Koshar writes of 'the contrast between a centrally organized, ideologically focused memory of Nazism and a more local and discordant public memory in the West' as 'not a specifically German pattern'. He notes that

> Eastern European governments directed Holocaust memorialization on the basis of socialist principles while in the West the memorials were usually left to a memory marketplace shaped by a combination of official agencies, private and local initiatives, tourism, and pilgrimages.
>
> (Koshar, 2000, p. 218)

The result was that in the east a relatively simple, unified story could be told, whereas in the west there was greater complexity and contestation.

In the aftermath of reunification, it tended to be these earlier western traditions of complexity and contestation which carried over into the new Germany. Rather than a distinctive eastern German approach developing after 1990, memory of this past continued along the lines developed in the western area. The fact that debates around the subject of how to remember this past persisted in the new Germany is clearly demonstrated by two controversial memorial projects in Berlin, *Die Neue Wache* and the Holocaust memorial.

Debates around *Die Neue Wache*

On 14 November 1993 the then German chancellor, Helmut Kohl, inaugurated a national monument 'to the victims of war and tyranny' in *Die Neue Wache* (the new guardhouse) in Berlin. As Clive Emsley notes in Chapter 2, this early nineteenth-century building has a complex history of use. It was first used as a memorial site to remember those who died in the First World War, with subsequent layers of memory added by the Nazi and East German governments. In the aftermath of reunification Kohl ushered in a new history for the memorial, with a reproduction of Käthe Kollwitz's *pietà* taking the place of the hammer and compass in a united national memorial to all of 'the victims of war and tyranny' in Germany's troubled twentieth century.

In choosing to adopt the *pietà* here, a gendering of memory was taking place. The very nature of the memorial sculpture – a mother holding her dying son – cast women in the role of the mothers of male victims, and thus suggested a female experience of victimhood at a remove. In reality of course, as a number of commentators pointed out, women were victims themselves and not simply the mothers of victims (Till, 1999, p. 270). However, it was not the gendering of memory associated with the choice of the *pietà* which aroused the most controversy. Rather it was the question of whether this form of memorial effectively excluded not only women, but also Jews. This sculptural form has a long Christian tradition, and thus its use was seen to amount to an undermining of the Jewish specificity of the Holocaust by drawing upon Christian symbols.

Ultimately the entire memorial project – not simply the choice of sculpture – was criticized for what was perceived to be an effort to merge the distinctive categories of victims and perpetrators. Here, as was quickly pointed out, was an attempt to include both perpetrators and victims of the Holocaust in one memorial space. The result was that victims of the Holocaust were subsumed within a much broader category – that of 'the victims of war and tyranny', as the inscription on the floor of the memorial phrased it – spanning the political twists and turns of the twentieth century. The specificity of the Holocaust was being fitted within a much broader German history, raising parallels with the so-called **Bitburg Affair** and the *Historikerstreit* (historians' controversy) of the mid to late 1980s (Maier, 1988, pp. 9–33). Those two controversies highlighted the questions of whether German soldiers could be seen as co-victims of the Second World War and whether it was possible and appropriate to 'normalize' the German past. The same questions were raised again in 1993, with the inauguration of the national memorial 'to the victims of war and tyranny'.

Clive Emsley discusses both the Bitburg Affair and the *Historikerstreit* in Chapter 1 (pp. 16–17).

During the inauguration ceremony itself, protestors made their feelings known through slogans such as 'German murderers are not victims!' Prior to the inauguration a group of prominent intellectuals signed a petition that asked, 'Should it now be considered in Germany that those who voluntarily wore the swastika were equal to those who were forced to wear yellow stars inscribed with the word "Jew"?' (Wiedmer, 1999, p. 118). And the feelings of the president of the Jewish community of Germany, Ignatz Bubis, were made plain to Kohl when he threatened to boycott the ceremony. In the end a compromise of sorts was reached, with Kohl promising to support a proposal for a distinct Jewish memorial in Berlin and agreeing to a bronze plaque being placed to the right of the entrance to the interior room of the *Neue Wache* memorial, listing the groups of victims – including Jews – who had been persecuted by the Nazis. This plaque carried an inscription in eight languages; the English version is given in the next reading.

> We honour the memory of the peoples who suffered from the war.
> We remember their citizens who were persecuted and who lost their lives.
>
> We remember those killed in action in the World Wars.
> We remember the innocent who lost their lives in war and as a result of war in their homeland, in captivity and through expulsion.
>
> We remember the millions of Jews who were murdered.
> We remember the Sinti and Roma who were murdered.
> We remember all those who were killed because of their origin, their homosexuality or because of sickness and weakness.
> We remember all who were murdered, whose right to life was denied.
>
> We remember the people who had to die because of their religious or political convictions.
> We remember all those who were victims of tyranny and met their death, though innocent.
>
> We remember the women and men who sacrificed their lives in resistance to despotic rule.
> We honour all who suffered death rather than act against their conscience.
>
> We honour the memory of the women and men who were persecuted and murdered because they resisted totalitarian dictatorship after 1945.
>
> (Quoted in Till, 1999, p. 273)

EXERCISE _____

Think about how the text on the plaque breaks down the original group of 'victims of war and tyranny' into specific categories. Who is mentioned by name?

DISCUSSION _____

In a chronological roll-call of victims, the plaque's text runs through the victims of the wars, the Nazi regime and the East German government. While all are seen to have suffered through 'war and tyranny', you will no doubt have noticed that not only are Jews explicitly mentioned as a distinct victim group, but women too are highlighted as victims – and not just the mothers of victims as the *pietà* suggests. However, these are not the only groups identified. In the listing of victims of the Nazi period, the Sinti and Roma (these groups together are usually known as Gypsies), homosexuals, those who were regarded as mentally or physically 'sick' or 'weak', and the political and religious opponents of Nazism are specifically named alongside Jews. Jews are given first place in this listing of Nazi victims, but the language used to refer to them is – aside from numbers – identical to the language used to refer to Sinti and Roma victims.

The plaque's explicit references to victims of Nazism other than Jews raises the critical issue of defining the Holocaust. There is considerable debate as to whether this term should refer to the Nazi extermination of European Jews alone, or whether it should also include other groups persecuted by the Nazis, including the Sinti and Roma, Poles, Soviet prisoners of war, homosexuals, Jehovah's Witnesses, those with learning or physical disabilities, and those regarded as 'a-social'. As Peter Novick points out, the tendency has been to talk of 11 million victims of Nazism: 6 million Jews and 5 million others. In such a definition (whose historical basis Novick questions) it is only Jewish people who are a named victim group. All the others are subsumed into the category 'others' (Novick, 1999, pp. 214–26).

Such a definition was essentially the one adopted by the United States Holocaust Memorial Council in 1980 after considerable internal debate (Linenthal, 1997, pp. 36–51). The Council, which was mandated to establish a memorial to the Holocaust, decided to describe the victims of the Holocaust as 'six million Jews – and the millions of other Nazi victims in World War II'. This description differs from the subsequent definition adopted by the museum in its mission statement, as well as from the words on the plaque erected in Berlin. In both of those cases a number of distinct groups are explicitly identified by name. The museum defines the Holocaust as

> the state-sponsored, systematic persecution and annihilation of European Jewry by Nazi Germany and its collaborators between 1933 and 1945. Jews were the primary victims – six million were murdered; Gypsies, the handicapped, and Poles were also targeted for destruction or decimation for racial, ethnic, or national reasons. Millions more, including homosexuals, Jehovah's Witnesses, Soviet prisoners of war, and political dissidents also suffered grievous oppression and death under Nazi tyranny.

> (USHMM, 2002)

On the Berlin plaque, as we know, Jews are given primacy as one of a number of named victim groups, although Soviet prisoners of war, for example, are not referred to explicitly by name.

The text of the Berlin plaque has its own history, which draws upon earlier debates over Holocaust remembrance. It is adapted from a speech delivered in 1985 by the then West German president, Richard von Weizsäcker, in the aftermath of the Bitburg Affair (Till, 1999, p. 273). Thus there is a sense in which the words attached to the 1993 memorial are themselves words with their own memory – that of political discourses of the Holocaust in 1980s western Germany. In choosing these words, the *Neue Wache* memorial references a more recent (West) German history of how this troubling past should be remembered as well as offering itself as a site of memory.

A Holocaust memorial in Berlin

The kinds of question centring on who exactly the victims of Nazism were, and to what extent Jewish groups have a 'privileged' place in a sort of hierarchy of Holocaust victims, also featured in discussions over the building of a Holocaust memorial in Berlin.

The proposal was first raised in 1988 by the TV chat-show host Leah Rosh. It received fresh impetus when on 30 January 1989 an open letter addressed to the federal government, the Berlin senate and the federal states was published as an advertisement in several German newspapers. The next reading reproduces the text of this letter.

Open letter, 30 January 1989

A half century has passed since the Nazis came to power and since the murder of the Jews of Europe. But on German soil, in the country of the perpetrator, there is still no central site of remembrance to recall this singular genocide, and no memorial that remembers the victims. This is shameful.

Therefore we demand that a clearly visible memorial for the millions of murdered Jews be erected in Berlin. Furthermore, we call for the erection of this memorial on the former GESTAPO site, the seat of the SS headquarters, the murder centre of the capital. The erection of this memorial is an obligation for all Germans in East and West.

(Quoted in Wiedmer, 1999, p. 143)

EXERCISE

Think about what this open letter called for – and, by implication, what it did not call for.

DISCUSSION

It is striking that the memorial demanded was to be specifically for the Jewish victims of Nazism, rather than the more general category of all victims of Nazism. This specificity raised controversy, with suggestions that other victim groups, in particular the Sinti and Roma, would effectively be ignored. Indeed the head of the Central Council of the Sinti and Roma, Romani Rose, suggested that the proposed memorial was tantamount to 'differentiating between first- and second-class genocide victims' (Wiedmer, 1999, p. 144) And the focus on Jewish victims was criticized all the more because of the proposal to build the memorial at the former Gestapo site. It was pointed out that groups other than Jews had been targeted for persecution by members of the Gestapo, and thus the memory articulated at that location should be inclusive. Indeed, for the historian Reinhard Rürup who had overseen the earlier unofficial excavation of the place, this was a site that should be focused on remembering 'the deeds of the perpetrators, and to revealing the structures in which they operated, and the manner in which these structures continue to operate to this day' (Wiedmer, 1999, p. 143).

If you think of the date of this appeal for a memorial, it is striking that it was prior to reunification, and yet the appeal was self-consciously seeking a national memorial for both East and West Germany. Ultimately reunification in one sense resolved the impasse, by offering up other potential sites for a national Holocaust memorial in Berlin. Rather than building it where the Gestapo headquarters had been, the decision was made to situate the memorial in the centre of Berlin, on the site of the former Ministerial Gardens. It was also decided that this memorial would be specifically for the Jewish victims of the Holocaust, and that another memorial could be erected for the Sinti and Roma victims. However, this was in many ways only the beginning of the controversy. The first competition to find a suitable memorial design, held in 1995, did result in the awarding of a joint first prize to two proposals, but then disintegrated into wrangling. Finally a second competition, held in 1997, produced a winning design, which was subsequently reworked, accepted, but then put on hold because of the upcoming elections.

Ultimately, on 25 June 1999, the fate of the prize-winning design was handed to the German parliament, which was presented with the following motion:

(1) The Federal Republic of Germany will erect in Berlin a memorial for the murdered Jews of Europe on the site of the former Ministerial Gardens in the middle of Berlin;

(2) The design of Peter Eisenman's field of pillars will be realized, as well as a small place of information that will detail the fate of the victims and the authentic sites of destruction; and

(3) A public foundation will be established by the *Bundestag* [West German parliament] to oversee the completion of the memorial. It will be composed of representatives from the *Bundestag*, the city of Berlin, and the citizens' initiative for the establishment of the memorial, as well as the directors of other memorial museums, members of the Central Committee for the Jews of Germany, and other victim groups. The foundation will begin its work with the memorial's groundbreaking in the year 2000.

(Quoted in Young, 2000, pp. 222–3)

After five hours of debate, the motion was passed by a vote of 314 for and 209 against, with 14 abstentions. What had started as the initiative of a small group of west Berliners had – after a decade of acrimonious debate – received official state sanction. But even so the debate was not yet over. As Young points out, the issues of what the text would say, and who would write it, still remained. And of course the ultimate questions of how visitors would perceive and use this memorial site once it is finally constructed are still unanswered.

Conclusion: 27 January – a European Holocaust Memorial Day?

Although much delayed, the breaking of the ground for the Berlin memorial finally began on 27 January 2000. This date was chosen not simply because it is the anniversary of the liberation of Auschwitz – the definitive death camp, as I have suggested – but also because it has become something of a European Holocaust Memorial Day. By breaking the ground on this day, therefore, the Berlin memorial was positioned within a wider shared remembrance of the Holocaust.

Immediately after being involved in these proceedings in Berlin, the German minister of state for cultural affairs, Michael Naumann, hot-footed it to Stockholm to take part in the Stockholm International Forum on the Holocaust. Bringing together high-ranking politicians and educators from forty-eight countries, this three-day conference drew up a declaration which stressed both the 'unprecedented character' of the Holocaust, and the imperative to remember and teach about it. One of the commitments made was to 'encourage appropriate forms of Holocaust remembrance, including an annual Day of Holocaust Remembrance, in our countries'. In the aftermath of this conference, the British parliament pledged to make 27 January an annual Holocaust Memorial Day, joining Germany, Italy and Sweden in this 'European' day of remembrance.

However, while in some ways the designation of 27 January as a European remembrance day of sorts suggests the emergence of a form of shared European remembrance in the post-Cold War era, there remain strong alternative national traditions of remembering. Rather than 27 January, other dates with national resonances have been adopted elsewhere in Europe as Holocaust memorial days. In the Czech Republic, for example, the date is 3 May; in Latvia it is 4 July; in Lithuania it is 29 September. In France it is 16 July – chosen because it was on that day in 1942 that the deportation of stateless Jews from Paris began. Official French national ceremonies on this day took place only from 1993 onwards, with the presidential enacting of a 'National Day of Commemoration of the Racist and anti-Semitic Persecutions Committed under the *de facto* Authority called "Government of the French State" (1940–1944)'. This day began to replace in significance the 'National Day of Memory of the Deportation' which had been held at the end of April from 1954 onwards. In many ways this earlier day commemorated something entirely different. Not only did it not specify the Jewishness of the victims, but it was held at a time that celebrated liberation (France was liberated in April 1945) rather than deportation (which began in July 1942) and thus side-stepped the controversial question of French complicity in the Holocaust. Such difficult issues have been addressed – to some extent at least – in the 16 July ceremonies.

What this official shift in France from a focus on the anniversary of liberation (it is worth repeating that 27 January too is an anniversary of liberation) to the anniversary of deportation has meant is that the unofficial remembering which had taken place for years on this day has been essentially 'nationalized'. The comments of survivors on this process are interesting. When asked about the first official remembrance ceremony held on 16 July, one survivor replied:

> Of course it was good. They're finally recognizing what they did. But in my heart of hearts I preferred it before. It was just us. There we all were every year. Nobody clapped, it was dignified. And then above all, there weren't all these barriers to channel the people. Barriers, here, they don't realize what that reminds us of.
>
> (Wiedmer, 1999, p. 52)

For this survivor, there is a mixture of emotions. On the one hand there is relief that the role of the state in the deportations has been acknowledged, but on the other there is a sense of the irony of state-sponsored memory of an event enacted by the state. Such concerns are not restricted to the French case. As suggested by Dan Stone's words on the British Holocaust Memorial Day, quoted below in the penultimate reading in this chapter, they resonate much more widely.

However, before thinking about the first British Holocaust Memorial Day, held on 27 January 2001, I think it is worth contrasting it with another series of memorial days recognized by European nations. For the Netherlands, Denmark and Belgium, various days in early May – rather than 27 January – form the focus for memory. In the Netherlands, 4 May is the day of remembrance for all the victims of the Second World War, with no specific memory of Dutch Jewish victims; this is followed by the celebration of 5 May to mark the country's liberation from occupation. In Denmark, 4 May is celebrated as both the day of liberation from Nazi occupation and a day of remembrance. In Belgium, it is 8 May – Victory in Europe Day – which both commemorates the final victory over Nazism and remembers the persecution of Jews and Gypsies. In all three countries, therefore, remembrance of those killed during the Holocaust is combined with wider recollections of the Second World War dead and the celebration of liberation. The focus on liberation casts each nation in the role of victim – each was subject to Nazi German occupation – and therefore evades questions of native collaboration; questions which are now asked in France on 16 July. Rather than specifically focusing on the deportations of Jews, the Holocaust is thus placed within the much broader historical context of the national experience during the Second World War.

The following reading is an extract from a government website giving details of the programme for the ceremony held in London to mark Britain's first official national Holocaust Memorial Day in 2001.

Holocaust Programme

Screen: **Opening**

Stage: **'O The Chimneys'**
Poem by Nobel prize-winning German Jewish poet Nelly Sachs (1891–1970).
Read by Emma Thompson

Screen: **The Final Solution**

Stage: **Roman Halter, Auschwitz Survivor**
Esther Brunstein, Auschwitz Survivor

Stage: **'In Memoriam Anne Frank'**
Choral work by Howard Goodall. Written to
commemorate the 50th anniversary of Anne Frank's
death at Bergen Belsen concentration camp. Anne
Frank and her family were hidden for 2 years from
the Nazis at the back of an Amsterdam office
building. Her diary, with its lucid depiction of events
in the attic hideaway, has sold more than 20 million
copies in 55 languages, making her an international
symbol of the Jews murdered by the Nazis.

Performed by
The Voices Foundation Children's Choir [Plate 21]
Musical Director – Susan Digby, Founder and
Principal of the Voices Foundation

incorporating
Members of Laudibus
Urban Voices UK, Musical Director – Lawrence
Johnson
ReGenesis (Berkshire Young Musicians Trust)
Musical Directors – Gillian Dibden & Alison Bersier
The Scunthorpe Cooperative Junior Choir
Musical Director – Susan Hollingworth
Finchley Children's Music Group
Musical Director – Nick Wilks

And accompanied by Andrusier Ensemble
1st Violin: Mia Cooper
2nd Violin: Alison Dods
Viola: Ralf Ehlers
Cello: Rebecca Gilliver
Double bass: Graham Michell
Artistic Director: Tamar Andrusier
Piano: Howard Goodall

Screen:	**Richard Dimbleby's Liberation of Belsen**
	RICHARD F DIMBLEBY, CBE Journalist and Broadcaster 1913–1965
	Richard Dimbleby joined the BBC in 1936 and was one of the Corporation's first news reporters. He pioneered the development of reporting and public commentary on both radio and television. He was also the BBC's first war correspondent, the first correspondent to fly with Bomber Command and the first reporter in Belsen. Post war, he was the BBC's 'voice' on all major state occasions and general elections.
Stage:	**Sir Ian McKellen – The Forgotten Holocaust**
Stage:	**'Trio', by Gideon Klein, Second Movement – Lento – variations on a Morovian folk song theme (extract)**
	Amid the rich cultural life of Terezin ghetto in Czechoslovakia, Gideon Klein was one of several composers writing, performing and teaching. Before his deportation to Auschwitz and eventual death, he managed to hide the manuscripts of 6 compositions. The style of these works is close to that of the second Viennese school – including Schoenberg and Berg.
	Performed by Andrusier Ensemble
Stage:	**Bob Geldof – Righteous Among Nations**
Screen:	**The Czech Kindertransports**
Stage:	**Vera Gissing, Czech Kindertransport Survivor**
Stage:	**Sir Antony Sher – Post 1945 'Never Again'**
Screen:	**The Killing Fields, Director: Joland Joffe**
	Excerpt courtesy of: Goldcrest Films International
Stage:	**Var Hong Ashe, Cambodia Survivor**

Screen: **Fergal Keane in Rwanda**

Fergal Keane was appointed Southern Africa correspondent of the BBC in 1990. His coverage of the genocide in Rwanda won many awards. These excerpts are taken from two of his Panorama reports; 'Journey into Darkness' and 'Valentina's Story'.

Stage: **'Ubupfubyi' by Cecile Kayirebwa**

A popular recording artiste in her own country, Cecile has lived in Belgium since 1973. Her latest album 'AMAHORO', including this track, reflects the genocide of 1994. It carries the message 'to save, preserve, and to keep alive her African heritage with music, poetry and dance'.

Translation

An orphan who survived the genocide sings: 'War is ordinary, and so is death. But not the one that took away my father and my mother. The sun, the moon and the stars have faded. Night has squandered Rwanda, only darkness remains. My body's glazed, and so are my heart, my eyes, my ears. Everything stopped moving, everything stopped talking. Am I or have I stopped existing?'

Written and performed by
Lead vocals: Cecile Kayirebwa

With:
Bass guitar: Bert Candries
Rhythm guitar: Didier Likeng
Keyboards: 'Ket Hagaha'
Backing vocals: Pauline Uwimfula
Percussion/backing vocals: Innocent Karengera
Percussion: Francis Fuster
Percussion: 'Bilou'
Musical arrangement: Bert Candries
Accompanied by: Diane Kabahizi and Laura Karengera from Amarebe

Screen:	**Zlata – Ethnic Cleansing**

Zlata Filipovic's diary has been described as that of a contemporary Anne Frank. A thirteen-year-old resident of Sarajevo, her diary described the descent into war. Its publication by French publisher Robert Laffont Fixot made Zlata an international celebrity. This film reflects on the upsurge of communal hatred and its ultimate manifestation in 'ethnic cleansing'.

Stage:	**Kemel Pervanic, Bosnian Survivor**
Stage:	**Chief Rabbi Dr Jonathan Sacks**
Stage:	**'El Male Rachamim' – Jewish Memorial Prayer for the Six Million who perished in the Holocaust (Shoah)**

Music Composed by: Moshe Stern

Performed by: Cantor Moshe Haschel and Ne'imah Singers

Conductor: Marc Temerlies

Translation

O God full of compassion, who dwells on high, grant perfect rest in the shadow of Your Divine presence in exalted places among the holy and the pure who shine like the brightness of the skies, to the souls of our six million brothers and sisters holy and pure, who were put to death, executed, slaughtered, burned, buried alive and strangled for sanctifying the Divine Name – by the hands of the German Nazis (may their name and memory be wiped out).

We pray that the souls of our beloved ones rise ever upwards. May the Garden of Eden be their resting place.

May the Lord of Mercy shelter them under the protection of His wings for ever more. May their souls be bound up in the bond of life – the Lord is their inheritance. May they lie in peace in their resting place, and let us say Amen.

Stage:	**Prime Minister Rt. Hon. Tony Blair MP**
Stage:	**Sir Trevor McDonald**

Screen:	**Statements of Commitment**
Stage:	**HRH The Prince of Wales to light a candle on behalf of the Nation**
Stage:	**Lighting of Candle by Ben Helfgott, Chairman, The '45 Aid Society**
Stage:	**Candle-lighting Finale – Holocaust Anthem 'I Believe in the Sun'**

Specially Composed by Howard Goodall to mark Britain's first Holocaust Memorial Day.

Performed by Voices Foundation Children's Choir and Andrusier Ensemble

'I believe in the sun' was an unsigned inscription found on the wall of a cave in Cologne where Jews had been hiding. It is translated from the French by Hilda Schiff and is published in Fount paperbacks/Harper Collins Book of Holocaust Poetry (London 1995).

All Film Commentary by Sir Antony Sher

(Holocaust Memorial Day website)

EXERCISE

After reading this extract, think about what is remembered and what is not remembered here, and to what extent the broader context of the national experience during the Second World War provides the framework for the commemorative ceremony.

DISCUSSION

It is striking that while the Holocaust is clearly the central event being remembered here, it is situated not so much within the context of the Second World War as within the broader context of twentieth-century acts of genocide. And this is not restricted to Europe, but rather is a much wider international category, with the genocides in Cambodia (1975–9) and Rwanda (1994) being remembered alongside ethnic cleansing in Bosnia (1992–5). There is a sense in which the memorial ceremony fluctuates between being a Holocaust Memorial Day and a more general (and universal and 'Americanized'?) 'Genocide Day'. While the official title refers to recollections of the Holocaust, the ceremony itself points to a clear attempt to remember the specific events of 1941–5 within a broader twentieth-century (and not simply European) category: genocide. What is interesting is that the Holocaust is, chronologically, the first 'genocide' featured here – suggesting, I think, that it was the first and most important such event. But there is a (controversial) rival contender for the twentieth-century's first act of genocide: the murder of Armenians during the First World War. However, this episode does not feature in the programme – some would argue that this is because of British sensitivities about offending the Turkish government, which holds that no such mass murder took place. Because this controversial case is not mentioned, the Holocaust retains a position of primacy among the acts of genocide cited which, by implication, suggests that it was also the first.

Of course a country like Britain does not have to face questions of collaboration in the way that France, say, does (although there are questions about British anti-semitism which some commentators feel have not been addressed). Nor does the United Kingdom (apart from the Channel Islands) have the memory of being a victim of Nazi Germany in terms of experiencing occupation – which countries such as Belgium or the Netherlands do have. But it is striking that the context of the Second World War and Britain's role as a combatant in that conflict seem to be somewhat downplayed.

The inauguration of a Holocaust Memorial Day in the United Kingdom engendered a degree of national debate about how and whether such a day should be remembered. In the pages of the journal *Patterns of Prejudice*, two British historians, Dan Stone and David Cesarani, who both write and teach on the Holocaust, offered differing views on the first of these memorial days. Extracts from their reflections are provided in the final two readings in this chapter.

Day of remembrance or day of forgetting?

Herein lies the crux of the matter. The issues of whether or not the memorial day will deflect from a plurality of commemorations, and of who will structure the day, are perhaps satisfactorily resolvable. After all, it is not to be doubted that those within government circles who promoted the idea of a memorial day did so in good faith. But the day nevertheless presents a convenient, if not cynically opportunistic occasion in which the government can shape the country's collective memory with a narrative that will undoubtedly follow the pattern of most mainstream narratives of the Holocaust: catastrophe and redemption. The horror of the

Holocaust will be occluded in a celebration of *our* moral superiority.

In other words, it is less the motives behind the Holocaust memorial day that I am questioning than its possible consequences. A memorial day will, I think, be ignored by the vast majority of the population on the one hand, and provide a convenient smokescreen for politicians' displays of public concern on the other. The problem is that the Holocaust is too important, *too threatening to the very idea of the state*, to be left to politicians and spin-doctors.

(Stone, 2000, p. 57)

Seizing the day

[T]he Holocaust Memorial Day is not being constructed *ex nihilo*. It builds upon years of careful work by a host of national and local organizations. Indeed, without their patient and persuasive efforts it is unlikely that the government would have acted at all. Their prior activity is an example of the plurality of memory, or what [the historian] John Bodnar has called 'vernacular memory'. For decades, when no one else was much interested in it, Holocaust survivors, former refugees, Jewish ex-servicemen and others in Britain kept alive the memory of Nazi persecution and mass murder. The persistence of this memory from below means that the government cannot simply shape memory as it wishes and for its own purposes. Indeed, almost every effort to control or prescribe memory 'from above' in this and other countries has failed.

Of course, the British government has its own agenda in promoting a Holocaust memorial day but it has engaged in an extensive consultation exercise. The name of the event was changed from the original Holocaust Remembrance Day in order to allay anxiety that it might be confused with Remembrance Sunday. The element devoted to education and awareness of genocide and human rights abuses since 1945 was accentuated following criticism that the event appeared to be excessively Holocaust- and Jewish-centred. The 'strap line' ('Remembering genocides – lessons for the future') was introduced to clarify the government's intentions, and greater stress was laid on the educational materials about genocide in general. This is hardly an example of government imposing its own narrative of 'catastrophe and redemption' on an unwilling public.

(Cesarani, 2000, pp. 64–5)

EXERCISE _____

Think about the differences in perspective between Dan Stone and David Cesarani, and why they are cautious or optimistic about the Holocaust Memorial Day.

DISCUSSION _____

It is interesting, I think, that there is a strong difference in opinion between Stone and Cesarani about the ability of the government to institute its own particular memory of this event from above. For Stone, there is a fear that Holocaust Memorial Day will be manipulated by the government for its own purposes. Rather than a day for questioning, it will – he suggests – be an occasion when the government can suggest a certain degree of 'moral superiority' (a sort of 'it didn't happen here' attitude) and tell a simple story of 'catastrophe and redemption'. In contrast, Cesarani questions the ability of any government to force a particular memory of the event from above. He suggests rather that there is a sense of give and take, with a plurality of organizations and individuals negotiating this memory with the government. For Cesarani, in short, memory is not something which is imposed from the top down, but negotiated from the bottom up.

_____

Behind these differing perspectives on how memory operates, there lie, I think, deeper ideological and philosophical positions on questions of structure and agency, and the nature of the state and society. What is significant is that the very issues at the heart of the debate between Stone and Cesarani underlie so many of the examples of Holocaust memory that we have explored in this chapter. There seem to be clear instances of the creation of particular memories from the top down, but those memories have been and are contested and reinterpreted from the bottom up. This suggests the need to think of national memories of the Holocaust – let alone European memory of the Holocaust – as anything but monolithic categories. And that, I believe, raises questions about how we think of the notions of European identity or national identities. Is it possible to talk of singular national memories and identities, and a singular European memory and identity, in the period since 1945? Or should we talk in terms of multiple – and contested – memories and identities? What I've suggested here is that the latter makes more sense. And the implications of this are that memory and identity are not unproblematic and essentially fixed categories, but rather fluid and constantly shifting constructs. They therefore have their own histories, which are deserving of study.

References

Berenbaum, M. (1990) *After Tragedy and Triumph: Essays in Modern Jewish Thought and the American Experience*, New York, Cambridge University Press.

Cesarani, D. (2000) 'Seizing the day: why Britain will benefit from Holocaust Memorial Day', *Patterns of Prejudice*, vol. 34, no. 4, pp. 61–6.

Charlesworth, A. (1994) 'Contesting places of memory: the case of Auschwitz', *Environment and Planning D: Society and Space*, vol. 12, pp. 579–93.

Cole, T. (1999) *Selling the Holocaust: from Auschwitz to Schindler, How History is Bought, Packaged, and Sold*, New York, Routledge.

Cole, T. (2002) 'Review article. Scales of memory, layers of memory: recent works on memories of the Second World War and the Holocaust', *Journal of Contemporary History*, vol. 37, no. 1, pp. 129–38.

Fulbrook, M. (1999) *German National Identity after the Holocaust*, Cambridge, Polity.

Holocaust Memorial Day website: http://holocaustmemorialday.gov.uk/section/2/main/htm

Koshar, R. (2000) *From Monuments to Traces: Artifacts of German Memory, 1870–1990*, Berkeley, CA, University of California Press.

Kushner, T. (1997) 'The memory of Belsen', in J. Reilly, D. Cesarani, T. Kushner and C. Richmond (eds), *Belsen in History and Memory*, London, Frank Cass.

Levine, P. (1996) 'To choose to go to Birkenau: reflections on visiting a death camp, August 1996', *Multiethnica*, vol. 18/19 (November), pp. 6–11.

Linenthal, E. T. (1997) *Preserving Memory: the Struggle to Create America's Holocaust Museum*, New York, Penguin.

Maier, C. S. (1988) *The Unmasterable Past: History, Holocaust, and German National Identity*, Cambridge, MA, Harvard University Press.

Novick, P. (1999) *The Holocaust in American Life*, New York, Houghton Mifflin.

Rosenfeld, A. H. (1997) *Thinking about the Holocaust: after Half a Century*, Bloomington, IN, University of Indiana Press.

Rubenstein, E. (1993) *For You Who Died I Must Live On ... Reflections on the March of the Living: Contemporary Jewish Youth Confront the Holocaust*, Oakville, Ontario, Mosaic Press.

Smolen, K. (1974) *Auschwitz 1940–1945: Guide-book through the Museum*, 5th edn., Oswiecim, Panstwowe Muzeum.

Smolen, K. (1993) *State Museum in Oswiecim: Auschwitz Birkenau Guide-book*, Oswiecim, Panstwowe Muzeum.

Stone, D. (2000) 'Day of remembrance or day of forgetting? Or, why Britain does not need a Holocaust Memorial Day', *Patterns of Prejudice*, vol. 34, no. 4, pp. 53–9.

Stratton, J. (2000) 'Thinking through the Holocaust: a discussion inspired by Hilene Flanzbaum (ed.), *The Americanization of the Holocaust*', *Continuum: Journal of Media and Cultural Studies*, vol. 14, no. 2, pp. 231–45.

Till, K. E. (1999) 'Staging the past: landscape designs, cultural identity and *Erinnerungspolitik* at Berlin's *Neue Wache*', *Ecumene*, vol. 6, no. 3, pp. 251–83.

USHMM (2002) 'Mission statement', website: http://www.ushmm. org/museum/council/mission.htm

Wiedmer, C. (1999) *The Claims of Memory: Representations of the Holocaust in Contemporary Germany and France*, Ithaca, NY, Cornell University Press.

Young, J. E. (1993) *The Texture of Memory: Holocaust Memorials and Meaning*, New Haven, CN, Yale University Press.

Young, J. E. (2000) *At Memory's Edge: After-Images of the Holocaust in Contemporary Art and Architecture*, New Haven, CN, Yale University Press.

8

Dealing with dictatorship:

socialism and the sites of memory in contemporary Hungary

MARK PITTAWAY

Introduction: 'post-socialism' and memory in central and eastern Europe

In central and eastern Europe the Second World War resulted in a major expansion of Soviet influence, as Red Army troops occupied much of the region. With the onset of the Cold War during the late 1940s many of the political regimes across the region became socialist dictatorships. Flawed democracies were replaced by states in which the leading role of Marxist-Leninist parties was enshrined in the constitution. Non-socialist political parties and social organizations were banned. In the name of socialist transformation a social revolution was initiated that replaced small private smallholdings with large, industrially organized collective farms. Small businesses were confiscated and industrial production was concentrated in large, state-run factories. Political opponents of the regimes were jailed. These processes were bitterly contested by social groups that opposed such changes; for them, socialist regimes were always illegitimate. For many members of these social groups the events of 1989–92, which brought state socialist rule to an end across central and eastern Europe, represented the end of a turbulent period that had begun in the 1930s.

With the creation of 'new' democracies during 1989 measures were introduced that were to serve in part to eradicate the memory of socialist regimes. This was most marked in rural communities where movements for the re-privatization of land sought, with varying degrees of success, to eradicate agricultural collectives. Often they wanted a return to earlier, pre-socialist patterns of landownership, recovering the memory of peasant societies and patterns of landownership from the late 1940s (Cartwright, 2001; Creed, 1998; Lampland, 2002; Swain, 1995; Verdery, 1994). Land and land reform did not constitute the only sphere where memory was put to political uses in the central and eastern Europe of the 1990s. Across the region, those who perceived themselves as victims of dictatorial socialist regimes sought redress through either the courts or the political system. New democratic states sought to use both strategies of reconciliation and the judicial system to differentiate themselves from their socialist predecessors and thus establish their own legitimacy (Borneman, 1997).

This chapter is not concerned with issues of either landownership or retribution, but seeks to examine the politics of memory as they have been reflected in both socialist and post-socialist material culture. In his chapter in *Globalization and Europe* the historian of design David Crowley addresses the issue of how far material goods produced under socialism, or its material culture, constituted distinctly socialist, eastern European identities (Chapter 6 in Pittaway, 2003). Certainly regimes across the region remade material and visual cultures, many of which have survived in the radically different political context since 1989. Cultural commentators have noticed the continued saliency of cultural and artistic forms associated with the old regimes across the area. The 'afterlife' of socialist realism has been widely remarked upon (Hoberman, 1998; Beke, 1992). More mundane aspects of everyday material culture have come to represent the memory of a world lost in an environment of social dislocation. Everyday material culture during the 1990s has come to act as the focus of nostalgic memory of the socialist period and thus a set of identities denied by post-socialist politics. In the former German Democratic Republic, according to the historian of design Paul Betts, everyday material artefacts – ordinary things – 'serve as repositories of private histories and sentimental reflections' (Betts, 2000, p. 753).

The first reading should help you think about the relationship between history, memory, nostalgia and material culture. It was written by the Croatian-born Dubravka Ugrešić. It is a sensitive and stimulating exploration of the relationship of central and eastern Europeans to their recent pasts – a piece which raises issues that are central to the material contained in this chapter.

The confiscation of memory

Shto by stalo vse ponjatno

Nado nachat' zhit' obratno.

A. Vvdenskij[1]

---

[1]   These lines by the Russian avant-garde poet Aleksandar Vvedenskij contain the humorous message that one should start living backwards in order for everything to become comprehensible.

1

I knew them because I was friendly with their son when I was a student. We were 'going out' together, as we said then. Stanko and Vera lived in a small two-roomed flat in the centre of Zagreb. Stanko was a retired officer of the Yugoslav People's Army, Vera a housewife. They had come to Zagreb from Bosnia. Their flat was like a little museum of Yugoslav everyday life. On the walls hung pictures of plump beauties lazing on the shores of romantic lakes densely populated by moorhens and swans. On top of the television was a Venetian gondola, on the fridge wooden herons (the most popular Yugo-souvenir sold at that time on the whole by Gypsies, 'from Triglav to Djevdjelija'). A picture of Tito hung on the wall beside family photographs. The gleaming polish of the heavy walnut furniture (the first post-war Yugoslav-made bedroom fittings) was protected by little hand-embroidered 'throws'. Boxes decorated with shells and other seaside mementoes with inscriptions ('A souvenir from Makarska', 'A souvenir from Cres' ...) made a kind of diary of their summer holidays. Those were years when everyone 'went to the sea' – the Adriatic, of course – every summer. On holidays organised by the trades' unions, of course.

On the shelves in peaceful coexistence resided various kinds of books: the ones my friend read (Schopenhauer, Kant, Hegel, Nietzsche, Kierkegaard ...), Stanko's (books about Tito, monographs on Yugoslavia and the National Liberation War ...) and Vera's (cheap paperback 'romances').

The flat was full not only of things but also of people, just like a station waiting-room. Through the flat came the neighbours' noisy children; they would come for a drink of water or a piece of bread spread with Vera's home-made jam. Every day Vera's friends would come, for 'a coffee' and 'a gossip'. Our friends would come as well, some of them would stop to play a game of chess and drink a glass of home-made Bosnian plum brandy with Stanko.

Vera kept preserves for the winter under the massive walnut double bed. There were tidy rows of jars of jam, gherkins, paprika, pickle and sacks of potatoes and onions. Once Vera called me into the bedroom, dragged a plastic box of soil out from under the bed and proudly showed me her freshly sprouted tomato seedlings. Every day Vera baked Bosnian pies and fed her neighbours, friends, the neighbours' children, everyone who called in. And many people called in, drawn by the life (and the beguiling cultural syncretism!) which bubbled cheerfully in the little flat like water in a kettle.

And then the children (Stanko and Vera had a daughter as well as a son) finished their studies and left home. Concerned for their parents, the children found another, larger, more comfortable flat and moved their parents in. When I went to see them, Vera burst into tears accusing the children of taking away her things, her souvenirs, her furniture, they had taken everything, she had only been able to save one thing. And Vera took me into the modern bedroom and dragged out from under the bed a picture of plump beauties lazing on the shores of a romantic lake densely populated by moorhens and swans.

'I keep it under the bed. The children won't let me hang it on the wall ...' she said in the hurt tone of a child.

Vera still baked Bosnian pies, only no one came any more. Stanko invited people every day for a game of chess and a Bosnian brandy, but somehow it wasn't on people's way anywhere, or they didn't feel like playing chess. Yes, the flat was certainly larger and better, but with the change for the better life had definitively changed its taste.

In the name of a brighter future, Stanko and Vera's belongings, the guarantee of their emotional memory, had been 'confiscated'. The two old people found themselves, like fish out of water, deprived of their natural surroundings. People are not fish, so Stanko and Vera did not expire, but they had somehow abruptly aged, or at least that's how it seemed to me when I visited them ...

2

As I travelled, I knew that I would turn up among people who at some stage would start talking enthusiastically about things I would not understand. So it was that I once found myself in the company of some American acquaintances who were talking about children's books, their shared cultural inheritance.

'My favourite book was *Winnie the Pooh* ...' I said, not quite truthfully. It wasn't until much later, when I was already an adult, that Pooh had become my favourite literary character.

My acquaintances looked at me in surprise. No one ever talked about Milne. Although I had been in America many times, I suddenly found myself on quite unfamiliar territory. For a moment I was a complete stranger, a being from another planet. And now, what a nuisance, this stranger would have to be told something that we never usually have to explain. Something like the fact that one and one makes two.

Some time ago I happened to be in the company of some Dutch friends. After a pleasant conversation about this and that, my Dutch friends and I were overjoyed to find that both they and I always watched the annual Eurovision Song Contest. The thought of the silly television spectacle aroused a childish gaiety in these grown-up people. And suddenly the atmosphere became warmer and more relaxed. For a moment we were a family, a European family.

As I travelled, I discovered that my American, Dutch, English friends and I easily talk about all kinds of things – about books and exhibitions, about films and culture, about politics and everyday life – but in the end there is always a bit of space that cannot be shared, a bit of life that cannot be translated, an experience which marked the shared life in a particular country, in a particular culture, in a particular system, at a particular historical moment. This unshareable and untranslatable layer in us is activated by a Pavlovian bell. And we salivate unfailingly, without really knowing why. That unknown space in us is something like a shared 'childhood', the warm territory of communality of a group of people, a space reserved for future nostalgia. Particularly if it should happen that this space is violently taken from us.

3

There is an old joke about the Scots who, when they get together, shout out numbers and laugh at the numbers instead of telling the jokes. Why waste unnecessary words?

I believe that I can cross cultural borders easily, but nevertheless I observe that, while I may communicate with 'Westerners' with greater interest, I definitely communicate with 'Easterners' with greater ease. It somehow turns out that we know each other even when we don't, that we pick up nuances more easily, that we know we are lying even when we seem to be telling the truth. We don't use footnotes in our conversation, they are unnecessary, it's enough to mention 'The Golden Calf' and our mouths already stretch into a smile.

An encounter with an 'Easterner' is often an encounter with our own, already forgotten past. I have met Russians who enthusiastically mentioned the name of Radmila Karaklaijić[2] and

---

[2] A Yugoslav pop star who was more popular in the, now former, Soviet Union than she was in, now former, Yugoslavia.

Djordje Marjanović[3] or proudly displayed their Yugoslav-made shoes bought in the Moscow 'Jadran' shop. I have met Chinese people who when they heard where I was from delightedly pronounced 'Ka-pe-tan Le-shi'[4] and Bulgarians who enquired with incongruous rapture about 'Vegeta'[5].

All these names and things hardly meant anything to me, they belonged to an early socialist Yugoslav past which I hardly knew was 'mine', but the recollection of them provoked the momentary prick of an indistinct emotion whose name or quality I was not able to determine at the time.

'If I haven't seen something for thirty or forty years it will give me that intense "punch" of nostalgia,'[6] says Robert Opie, a passionate collector of objects from everyday life and the founder of the Museum of Advertising and Packaging in Gloucester.

4

Things with a past, particularly a shared one, are not as simple as they might first appear from the perspective of the collector. In this 'post-communist' age it seems that 'Easterners' are most sensitive to two things: communality and the past. Everyone will first maintain that his post-communism is different, implying at the same time his conviction that life in his post-communism is closer to that of the Western democracies than that of the other (post-communist) countries. The 'Easterner' is reluctant to admit his post-communist trauma in public, nor does he have the will to try to articulate it. He has had enough communist traumas (he holds the copyright to them too), but they have worn out, aged, or something, and don't seem to hurt any more. The cursed 'homo duplex', mentally trained to separate his private life from the collective, weary of the constant ideological pressure to live facing

---

[3] Now a completely forgotten Yugoslav 'musical idiot', somewhat like the Czech Karel Gott.

[4] Kapetan Leši, the handsome and brave hero of Yugoslav partisan films, shot in the early nineteen sixties, completely forgotten today. In the meantime, he seems to have 'died' in China as well.

[5] 'Vegeta', seasoning for food, a popular Yugoslav export article, can still be found in Turkish shops in Berlin or Russian shops in New York's Brighton Beach. Together with 'Minas-coffee' (know affectionately as 'minasica'), 'Vegeta' has become a cult object of the Yugoslav diaspora.

[6] [']Unless you do these crazy things ...': An interview with Robert Opie, in *The Culture of Collecting*, ed. John Elsner and Roger Cardinal, Harvard University Press, Cambridge, Mass., 1994, p. 29.

towards the future, exhausted by the excessive amount of 'history' that has happened to him, frightened by memories that keep popping up from somewhere, at this moment the 'Easterner' would most like to sink into the compliant and indifferent present, at least that's how it seems. It is only the younger and more honest of them, like the (former) East German playwright Thomas Oberlender, who will exclaim out loud: 'Why, I have two biographies and one life ...!'

5

Things with a past are not simple. Particularly in a time when we are witnesses and participants in a general trend of turning away from stable, 'hard' history in favour of changeable and 'soft' memory (ethnic, social, group, class, race, gender, personal and alien) and a new cultural phenomenon which, as Andreas Huyssen suggests, bears the ugly name of musealisation. 'Indeed, a museal sensibility seems to be occupying ever larger chunks of everyday culture and experience. If you think of the historicising restoration of old urban centres, whole museum villages and landscapes, the boom of flea markets, retro fashions, and nostalgia waves, the obsessive self-musealisation per video recorder, memoir writing and confessional literature, and if you add to that the electronic totalisation of the world on databanks, then the museum can indeed no longer be described as a single institution with stable and well-drawn boundaries. The museum in this broad amorphous sense has become a key paradigm of contemporary cultural activities.'[7]

6

If we accept the 'museum' as a paradigm of the contemporary sense of temporality, then, at least as far as European-American culture is concerned, the places we occupy in the museum and our attitude to the museum do nevertheless differ.

For instance, although in the American intellectual market the key questions of our time at the end of the century are what is history and what memory, what is personal and what collective memory, and so on, it seems to the European outsider that the American attitude to the 'museum' is different from that of the European, particularly the East European. History, memory, nostalgia are concepts in which contemporary America has recognised a high

---

[7] Andreas Huyssen, *Twilight Memories: Marking Time in a Culture of Amnesia*, Routledge, London/New York, 1995, p. 14.

cultural-therapeutic and, of course, commercial value. The stimulation of the recollection of different ethnic immigrant groups, encouraging the reconstruction of a lost identity (Afro-American, for example), opening immigrant museums (on Ellis Island, for example), establishing chairs at American universities, which, concerned with various cultural identities, are concerned with memory, the publishing industry, newspapers and television which readily commercialise the theme – all of this supports the idea of the new American obsession with 'musealisation'. The American market contains everything, from documentary videocassettes of contemporary history to souvenirs of the recent past. Americans of all ages can purchase instant products to satisfy their 'historical' yearnings. And although in America everything rapidly 'becomes the past', it seems that nothing disappears. Television broadcasts series and films which were watched once by today's grandfathers and are now watched by their grandsons. The old *Star Trek* and *Star Trek, the New Generation,* the old *Superman* and the 'Supermen' of all the subsequent generations, are available simultaneously. In this way, the American lives a kind of eternal present, or at least that's how it seems to the superficial European outsider. The rich market of nostalgia seems to wipe out nostalgia, it appears that real nostalgia for something implies its real loss. But America does not know loss, or at least not in the sense that Europeans do. Thus, through the process of commercialisation, but also through the elasticity of an attitude to recollection which is constantly changing (making – remaking, shaping – reshaping), nostalgia is transformed into its painless surrogate, at the same time as its object.[8]

That, I repeat, is how it appears to the European outsider. Because what our European (or Euro-ego-centric) claims an absolute right to, without the slightest hesitation, is just that, History, and understanding of History.

7

Because for him, the European, History has got involved in his private life, altered his biography, it has caused him to perform 'triple axles', he was born in one country, lived in another and

---

[8] The artistic representation of history often follows the idea of the commercial surrogate. Thus one American artist represents the Holocaust by using miniature children's toys (little SS officers, little camps and camp inmates), then he transfers the posing figurines to photographs, reproducing well-known documentary scenes. The children's toys in the photograph imitate the past horrific reality to perfection, only the most attentive eye will observe that it is a question of a surrogate.

died in a third; it has caused him to change his identity like shirts, it has given him a feline elasticity. Sometimes it seems to him that, like a cat, he has nine lives ...

Recently Europe produced the biggest souvenir in the world, the Berlin wall. The Berlin wall shattered into millions of little souvenir pieces: some turned into senseless objects and ended up in the rubbish-bin, and others into pieces of shrapnel which hit wounds which had long since healed, and opened up new ones. Today Europe rummages through drawers of memories, particularly those which contain the traumatic files of the First World War, the Second World War, fascism and communism. This feverish activity, connected with remembering, may have its origin in the fear of the possibility of forgetting. At this moment Europe is concerned with repeating the process of historical guilt: the old rubbish which European countries, in the process of creating and re-creating their own memory, have shoved under each other's doors, is trying to return to its owners. The processes are often sensitive and painful, particularly in the relationship of (former) West and (former) East Germany. The politics of remembering is connected also with artistic questions of its representation, the media, its consumability, commercialisation and morality. Europe is like the Teufelsberg with its contents bubbling out. (The Teufelsberg is the highest hill in Berlin, whose surface is covered in grass; under the grass lie millions of tons of Berlin ruins piled up after the Second World War.) Old souvenirs which had surfaced – flags, relics, red and yellow stars and black swastikas – are joined by new, still warm grenades, bullets and bombs freshly arrived from Bosnia.

(Ugrešić [1995] 1999, pp. 217–24)

EXERCISE

After you have read this extract, I should like you to consider the following questions:

1 What do you think Ugrešić means by 'the confiscation of memory', in both its post-Yugoslav and, more generally, its central and eastern European context?

2 What role, according to Ugrešić, does the museum occupy within contemporary culture, both east and west?

3 What is/are the key difference(s) that Ugrešić identifies in eastern and western European attitudes to the past, and to nostalgia?

DISCUSSION

1   The notion of the 'confiscation of memory' is explored powerfully by Ugrešić through her description of the Zagreb flat of an elderly couple, Stanko and Vera. Their memory, identity and sense of place are embodied in the way in which they have decorated their home. Having grown up in multinational and socialist Yugoslavia, their choices of furniture and decoration evoke both the common past of the country and the material 'heritage' of its socialist regime. With the removal of that regime and the subsequent collapse of Yugoslavia, the memories and identities embodied in the way the couple have laid out their home have come to be defined as illegitimate. Ugrešić argues that the change of regime in Yugoslavia, and by extension throughout central and eastern Europe, has denied many people their memories and identities. It is this process that has given 'nostalgia' much of its power.

2   Ugrešić implicitly argues that 'history' is central to the constitution of identity within contemporary cultures. She quotes a passage from Andreas Huyssen, a scholar in the field of comparative literature, contending that contemporary culture is becoming 'musealized'; in other words that the museum is 'occupying ever larger chunks of everyday culture and experience'. Consequently,

> the museum can ... no longer be described as a single institution with stable and well-drawn boundaries. The museum in this broad amorphous sense has become a key paradigm of contemporary cultural activities.

3   The fundamental difference in attitude lies in what Ugrešić terms 'post-communist trauma'. Whereas in a western (and certainly a North American) context 'nostalgia' can seem apolitical, in the context of central and eastern Europe the remembering of the past is infused with political meaning. This is because the cultural artefacts that act as triggers of nostalgia carry meanings connected to a past which can sometimes be painful and which to some extent has disappeared; in nearly every case such meanings mark a person as a citizen of a post-socialist state.

This chapter explores the issues of central and eastern European memories of the recent past. It does this by taking post-socialist Hungary as a case study to examine the politics of memory and two expressions of that memory in material culture. Central and eastern Europe are not a homogeneous entity; they were not so even during the Cold War. Hungary had a distinctive national history under socialism. It was initially governed by a Stalinist dictatorship headed by Mátyás Rákosi (1892–1971), but then experienced a popular uprising that led to outright revolution in October 1956. The regime's authority was only restored by Soviet armed intervention. Despite the circumstances of its installation, the next government, headed by János Kádár (1912–89), gained a degree of legitimacy from the Hungarian population over the course of the following two decades as a result of the social and economic policies – known as '*gulyás* communism' – that it pursued. These policies considerably improved living standards for most Hungarians. This combination of a long socialist period characterized by eight years of Stalinism (1948–56), revolution (1956) and then three decades of halting reform (1956–89) have shaped a deeply divided and contested memory of socialism among the Hungarian population. The country has also seen important attempts to create museums or monuments that reflect these divided memories of the recent past.

I shall begin by exploring the 'politics of memory' in post-socialist Hungary in general terms. This discussion is merely designed to set the scene for the main subject of this chapter: a detailed discussion of two of the most prominent 'sites of memory' of the socialist dictatorship. These are Budapest's Statue Park, opened in 1993–4, and the city's House of Terror, opened to the public amid political controversy in 2002.

Coming to terms with the past? The politics of remembering socialism in post-socialist Hungary

With the advent of a democratic republic in 1989 and the election of a government committed to asserting the 'national Christian' elements of Hungary's past in 1990, a line was drawn under the socialist era. Over the next few years the archives of the former regime were partially opened, although confused legal regulations and cuts in public expenditure hampered access to them. Attempts were made by the Ministry of Justice to investigate the worst atrocities of the 1956 revolution with a view to bringing their perpetrators to justice, but this met with limited success at best. Moreover, a so-called agents' law (*ügynök törvény*) was enacted in 1994 to expose all those in public life who had passed information to the state security services prior to 1989 – but this law was unevenly implemented at least prior to the mid 1990s. Even at the peak of the system change, when politics was dominated by a 'national Christian' conservative government and a liberal opposition, no consistent attempt was made to call former leaders to account, either judicially or morally, for their role in the earlier dictatorship.

Yet the very fact of the 'negotiated revolution' and the peaceful transfer of power it engendered broke many of the taboos of the Kádár era of reformist socialism. The new republic was proclaimed on 23 October 1989, a date full of symbolic significance as the thirty-third anniversary of the outbreak of the 1956 revolution. Indeed 23 October was instituted as a national public holiday, implicitly giving it official recognition along with 15 March – the anniversary of the outbreak of the 1848 revolution in the country: the event that had given birth to modern Hungary (Nyssonen, 1999). A multitude of personal memoirs covering both 1956 and the political repression that preceded and immediately followed it then became available to a broader public. Also at this time the Institute for the History of the 1956 Revolution was founded by two groups of historians – an older generation who had participated in the reform communist opposition during the revolution and had been jailed afterwards, and a younger generation who opposed the dictatorship in the 1980s. This institute bridged the divide between academic and public history, mobilizing archivists and librarians across Hungary in the early 1990s to document the events of the revolution in towns and villages up and down the country. It also housed and extended the Budapest Oral History Archive, collecting the life histories of Hungarians from all backgrounds. During the first half of the 1990s almost every Hungarian town acquired a memorial to the local events of 1956 (Boros, 1997). Yet the memory of 1956 was contested and divisive. Intellectuals who had been reform communists in the 1950s, and who tended to be members of the liberal Alliance of Free Democrats or the former communist Socialist party, tended to stress the reform communist roots of the revolution. But conservatives stressed its fundamentally anti-communist nature, as did the organizations that were formed to represent political prisoners and the veterans of the largely working-class armed groups who had fought the Soviet tanks in Budapest.

The memory of 1956 did not reveal the consciousness of a nation united against socialist dictatorship so much as a country deeply divided about both the meaning of the past and Hungary's future direction. Socialists, liberals, conservatives and the radical right battled over the reform communist, democratic, anti-communist or nationalist nature of 1956. Attempts to eradicate the material manifestations of socialism revealed the traces of an ambiguous relationship to obviously politicized socialist forms of public culture. The disappearance of some of these material manifestations met with little opposition – for example, the removal of a red star from the spire of Hungary's neo-Gothic parliament building (which, incidentally, in an example of communist kitsch, had been illuminated during the hours of darkness) was not lamented. Street names across the country which had obvious political associations were changed. In 1989 Pest's major boulevard – the Avenue of the People's Democracy (*Népköztarsaság Útja*) was renamed Andrassy út, after the late-nineteenth-century Austro-Hungarian foreign minister. After the 'negotiated revolution' street names were changed wholesale. Surprisingly, Budapest's inhabitants were not happy about all of these alterations. They included changing the name of Marx Square, opposite the Western railway station, to Western Square; altering Engels Square, site of the city's central bus station, to Elisabeth Square; and changing Liberation Square to Franciscans Square, after the friary that graces one corner. None of these changes was readily accepted. The removal of many statues associated with the socialist regime in Budapest was also greeted with a surprising lack of popular acclaim. Some of these sculptures, however, have remained; the most prominent being the Liberation Monument on Gellért Hill that dominates the city.

The deep-seated ambivalence of a large section of the population towards the anti-communist consensus of new parties established at the fall of the dictatorship was revealed in the 1994 parliamentary elections. The 'national Christian' government was extremely unpopular as a result of the deep recession and consequent economic hardship that followed the 'negotiated revolution'. This unpopularity was reflected not in an increase of support for the liberal opposition parties but in a surge in popularity for the former communist Socialist party, which benefited as a result of nostalgia for the security of the Kádár years and discontent with the new political elite. The Socialists' leader, Gyula Horn, a former party apparatchik who had served as foreign minister in the last communist government, admitted to having served in a paramilitary unit that had operated alongside Soviet troops during the suppression of the 1956 revolution. Though no one was able to establish the truth of what Horn had done as a result of his service in this unit, his political opponents used his service against him. The election campaign effectively became a referendum on Horn's record and, by extension, the record of Hungary's dictatorship. Nevertheless, to the surprise of many commentators and to dismay in liberal and conservative circles, the Socialist party easily won.

The elections revealed an electorate that was deeply divided about the past; a significant section was openly nostalgic for the socialist years and some were at least indifferent to the human rights abuses and atrocities committed under the dictatorship. Though Horn, despite his party's absolute majority, pursued a policy of conciliation, forming a coalition with his liberal opponents, he found himself vilified by the right until his loss of office in 1998. This was despite the fact that while he was in power Horn pursued policies which demonstrated to the country that any return to even the more benign aspects of the dictatorship was all but impossible, given the economic situation.

Nostalgia persisted, however, surviving the disappearance of the illusion that liberal democracy and capitalism could somehow be combined with the full employment-based welfare society of the Kádár years. Positive views of the Kádár era even survived the aggressive anti-communism of the right-wing coalition government of Viktor Orbán (1998–2002), which was in part a manifestation of a reaction among conservatives to the political saliency of nostalgic memory. In June 2002 the Hungarian arm of the Gallup opinion polling organization asked a representative sample of the population to evaluate three periods in the country's recent past on a five-point scale, with a score of five being overwhelmingly positive and that of one being overwhelmingly negative. Forty-nine per cent of the sample (including those who chose not to respond to the pollsters' questions) judged the Kádár era of reform communism as an 'outstanding' or 'good' period in the country's recent history (awarding a total of five or four on the five-point scale). Only thirty-two per cent evaluated the post-1989 period in the same way (Magyar Gallup Intézet website).

Nostalgia also infused cultural memory in a way that was much more ambiguous in terms of its relationship to politics. The popularity of Péter Timár's 1997 film *Csinibaba* (*Glamour Girl*), which stormed the Hungarian box-office, could be seen as a manifestation of this phenomenon. Set in industrial Hungary during the early 1960s, this film revolves around the attempt of a group of young people to found a band in order to attend the Festival of World Youth in Helsinki. It combines an attempt to catch the atmosphere of the early years of Kádár's 'compromise' with a soundtrack drawn from the popular music of the period, just as Hungarian youth culture began to be influenced by the west. The film is both avowedly commercial and seeks to play on nostalgia for the period. Later in the same year Hungarotron, the country's major record company, released a collection of digitally re-mastered recordings of political anthems from the socialist years entitled *Best of Communism*. Boosted, among other things, by coverage in Hungary's tabloid press, it topped the album charts in late 1997.

The naked commercial exploitation of aspects of nostalgic memory for the later years of socialist dictatorship was not the only manifestation of the politics of memory in the second half of the 1990s. Many members of the former liberal opposition, excluded from the anti-socialist bloc by their bitter conflicts with the conservative right and their party's coalition with the Socialist party between 1994 and 1998, developed a subtle engagement with popular memory. At the time of the 'negotiated revolution' they had attempted to shape the memory of socialism through the publication of collections of photographs and documents that dealt with subjects which shed light on the human costs of the excesses of the Stalinist years. Publications such as the photographic collection *Hol zsarnokság van, ott zsarnokság van* (Where there is tyranny, one can find tyranny) (Kardos et al., 1990) attempted to present an image of ideological dictatorship, smashing opposition and reshaping society in its own image. By the middle of the decade many liberal intellectuals began to engage directly with nostalgia. In 1996 the journal *Beszélő*, which prior to 1989 had been the *samizdat* journal of Budapest's dissidents and afterwards became the theoretical journal of Hungary's leading liberal party – the Alliance of Free Democrats – began to run a series called *Beszélőévek* (speaking years). Focusing on a year from the Kádár era in each issue, the journal produced a series of articles, recollections, documents, photographs and even poems, counterposing both the nostalgic and the critical. The success of the series was reflected in the publication of an anthology of the collected articles in 2000 (*Beszélő*, 2000). Another manifestation of this trend was the photographic collection *Befejezetlen Szocializmus*, published in 1997 to such commercial success that it appeared in an English translation in 1999 (Gerő and Pető [1997] 1999). The authors/editors of the collection were both historians with links to the former liberal opposition. Iván Pető, for example, an archivist and economic historian, served as leader of the Alliance of Free Democrats from 1992 until 1998. Their intention was to challenge nostalgia on its own terms, counterposing photographs of everyday life with texts that demonstrated the shortcomings of the system itself. The next reading is an extract from András Gerő and Iván Pető's introduction to the English edition of their book.

Unfinished Socialism

This volume is an attempt to evoke the period extending from the installation of the new regime after the suppression of the 1956 uprising until just before the transformation of 1988–89: what we might call the Kádár era. The beginning and the end seem obvious: on the one hand, the cessation of armed struggle, and on the other, the moment before the certainty that the regime had come to an end. Because our object is the completed but still extant recent past, we have sought not only to portray these three decades, but to confront existing memories.

We know that each individual's recollections of the Kádár era must in large measure be determined by personal impressions and experiences, by events and circumstances that determined individuals' and families' fates. The overwhelming majority of today's adults lived the decisive portion of their lives during this period; and although a twenty-year-old of today has no adult memories of the years before 1988–89, the lives and material environments of parents, grandparents and teachers link him or her to those years. (Approximately half of the Hungarian population is over the age of 40, another quarter is between 20 and 40.)

Those who were committed communists or socialists and believed in the construction of the world they had dreamed about, in the remediability of the system's problems, their possible correction via reforms – that is, those who feel that socialism raised the quality of their lives – have a very different image of this era from others, who, say, went about their daily lives without caring much about the regime, merely observing the rules and ten years later remember the Kádár era only as a time when the world seemed calculable and secure.

Among those whose attitude to everyday life was determined by their stance toward the regime, some believed that the system was good, and that its problems, mistakes, and lapses were the consequences of human frailty, and therefore without significance in the 'scales of history'. Others held, on the contrary, that the system was fundamentally bad, and that its putative accomplishments – for example, improved living standards – did not significantly alter the case. Among the latter some saw, and still see, in the socialist regime nothing but a system forced upon the nation by a foreign power, or as the product of an inherently evil design. Yet others felt that 'Satan cannot be dislodged by Beelzebub': that is, even if socialism intended to eliminate the problems of capitalism, the system which came into being did not turn out to be any better or more humane, while the economy necessarily became wasteful and non-competitive. Furthermore, crimes committed in the name of the promise of a beautiful future are all the more unforgivable.

In compiling this volume we did not intend to accuse or to rehabilitate, or to evoke the atmosphere of our bygone youth. In other words, we have tried to avoid an emotional approach to the period. We have also tried to avoid adopting a so-called sympathetic attitude toward socialism, one that concedes 'there were mistakes, but there were also significant achievements'.

Needless to say, we do have firm views toward the Kádár era – or more precisely, the former socialist system. At the same time, we believe that virtues and vices stem from the same source and that they cannot be separated from or weighed against one another. They were divergent yet interdependent aspects of the previous regime that constituted a single, integrated entity, an entire social, political and economic system.

(Gerő and Pető, 1999, pp. 6–7)

EXERCISE _____

1   How does this extract complement and reinforce what you have read above?

2   How does it add to what you have read?

DISCUSSION _____

1   The question of nostalgia that we have examined is addressed only indirectly in the extract, in relation to those

> who, say, went about their daily lives without caring much about the regime, merely observing the rules and ten years later remember the Kádár era only as a time when the world seemed calculable and secure.

Yet a desire to confront popular nostalgia seems to underscore the whole extract; the authors' intention is 'to confront existing memories' and to show that the 'virtues and vices' of the regime 'stem from the same source and ... cannot be separated from or weighed against one another'. The other point made above that they usefully underline is the way that the memory of the socialist system divides Hungarians; it highlights the degree of disagreement and division between those on the right of the political spectrum, those on the left and the apolitical. Political identities are thus crucial to shaping individual and group memories of socialist dictatorship.

2   The two things, I think, that this extract adds which are crucial to any consideration of memory of the dictatorship are the individual dimensions of memory and the mundane, everyday aspects of life under socialism. 'We know', say the authors,

> that each individual's recollections of the Kádár era must in large measure be determined by personal impressions and experiences, by events and circumstances that determined individuals' and families' fates. The overwhelming majority of

today's adults lived the decisive portion of their lives during this period; and although a twenty-year-old of today has no adult memories of the years before 1988–89, the lives and material environments of parents, grandparents and teachers link him or her to those years. (Approximately half of the Hungarian population is over the age of 40, another quarter is between 20 and 40.)

This statement clearly suggests that a parallel can be drawn between the Croatian experience discussed by Dubravka Ugrešić in the first reading and the situation in Hungary by the late 1990s. Material culture acts as a site of private memory of a world that has almost completely disappeared.

Even this engagement with nostalgia has not been uncontroversial, and groups with other political allegiances have sought to shape alternative public memories of the socialist period. Conservative intellectuals have adopted a much more aggressive attitude towards nostalgia, seeking to replace it with an alternative memory stressing the terroristic nature of the socialist regime. This programme underpinned the policies of Orbán's right-wing coalition government towards historical research into the recent past and the public presentation of that past more generally. These policies have sharply politicized debate about the socialist period.

At the time the Orbán government came to power in 1998 the writing of the history of the socialist period was dominated by two research institutes; the Institute for the History of the 1956 Revolution and the Institute for the History of Politics. The second of these, the successor to the socialist-era Institute for Party History, was closely connected to the opposition Socialist party. The first, the 1956 Institute, had advanced an interpretation of the 1956 revolution that placed its origins in the reform communism of intellectuals and anti-Stalinists within the party. This had made it a target for conservative veterans of 1956 and the political right more generally, who accused it of rehabilitating communists.

In November 1998 the government cut off the 50 million forints of state support to the Institute for the History of Politics and reduced the 1956 Institute's funding from a planned 73 million to 6 million forints for the year 1999 (V. Gy., 1998). The motivation for these cuts was clearly political, with one adviser to the government describing the intention as an attempt to end a situation where public money was being used to subsidize the writing of 'socialist party history' (Tóth Gy. László, 1998). The money saved was used to create a new Institute for the Twentieth Century under the auspices of a private organization, the Foundation for Research into the History and Society of Central and Eastern Europe. This institute's connections to the government were clear in that its director, Mária Schmidt, was a senior adviser to the prime minister and a historian with controversial views on the Holocaust: the subject of her own research. The institute has sought to publish historical writings emphasizing right-wing views of the country's recent past. Meanwhile, in 2000 the Foundation for Research into the History and Society of Central and Eastern Europe began to establish a museum to present its view of the country's recent history. Using a substantial government subsidy, it bought number 60 Andrássy út in central Budapest with the intention of transforming this into a museum of communist and national socialist crimes in Hungary. Named the House of Terror and opened in February 2002, it has caused considerable controversy. However, with the defeat of the right in the April 2002 elections its future is uncertain.

Shaping the politics of memory: Budapest's socialist statues and the park of tyranny

Having discussed the politics of the memory of socialist dictatorship in contemporary Hungary and the various manifestations of the public memory of the era, I want now to turn to a specific case, a site of that memory. One of the most striking and public sites of the memory of socialism is the Budapest Statue Park. Opened to the public in 1993, it sits on the far southwestern edge of Greater Budapest in the suburban district of Budatétény, some 10 kilometres from the centre of the Hungarian capital. Poorly served by public transport – there is only one half-hourly bus service to it from the city centre, run by the National Bus Company – it is geographically isolated. Operated by a private entrepreneur under licence from the local authority, the park provides a home for the major public statues of the socialist period – torn down from their original locations in central Budapest and transferred to the edge of the city. Despite its geographic isolation and the difficulties many visitors have in reaching the park, it has attracted between 25,000 and 30,000 visitors a year since its opening. It has not only attracted attention in Hungary itself, but has gained considerable international notice, becoming almost by default Hungary's national museum of the socialist era, at least prior to 2002. In recognition of its success Hungary's Ministry of National Cultural Heritage has granted funding to transform the Statue Park into what has been called a Memento Park, to include a museum, a visitor centre and a series of new exhibitions of the symbols of both the 1956 revolution and the 1989 'negotiated revolution' (N. K. J., 2001).

The park and its success embody a project to shape the public memory of socialism in Hungary. Its existence as a museum and its extraordinary success exemplify some of the ambiguities and contradictions embedded in the popular memory of socialist dictatorship in the country. In order to explore these themes in more depth I shall concentrate first on how the park came into existence, before shifting my focus to examine how it presents socialism and then considering some of the ambiguities of popular memory that are embodied in some of its exhibits.

The park essentially grew out of the debate of what should be done with the political statues of Hungary's socialist era. The notion of the crowd occupying public space was of central importance to the legitimacy of political movements in the country, from the failure of the 1848 revolution onwards (Freifeld, 2000). Associated with this was the rise of a culture in which the decoration of public space by political sculptures was seen as a claim to legitimacy. In the late nineteenth century such sculptures became as much a means of shaping political identities as a way of simply decorating Hungarian towns (Pótó, 1989, pp. 11–16). The significance of these statues was tied not only to the occupation of public space, but also to the importance of symbols – whether these were national in character or more specific to political movements 'within' the Hungarian nation (Hofer, 2000). Both Soviet occupation in 1945 and the creation of the socialist dictatorship in 1948 were marked by moves to banish statues of figures associated with conservatism from their public places. There was also a concerted attempt to replace them with statues that supported the socialist regime's ideology and its view of history (Pótó, 1989). Public statues in Budapest were to continue to have tremendous importance in the socialist era, to the popular politics of both the regime and the opposition. In 1956 and 1989 the capital's public statues served as both objects of hatred (Beke, 1989) and more significantly as rallying points for demonstrators (Hofer, 2000, pp. 635–6).

With the 'negotiated revolution' of 1989–90, the removal of the political statues of the socialist era became almost inevitable. Sections of the triumphant former opposition developed a series of proposals for exhibiting these sculptures in a context where their connections to socialist dictatorship could be explored. One anti-communist party in the provincial town of Békescsaba suggested exhibiting Hungary's statues of Lenin next to the town as a tourist attraction. Former political prisoners advocated turning one of the most notorious labour camps of the Stalinist years at Recsk in northeastern Hungary into a statue park, while one literary historian argued for creating a Lenin park to serve as a resource for future historians (Boros, 1993).

The national government legislated in 1991 for the removal of the statues of the socialist era from public squares. It made local authorities legally responsible for maintaining these sculptures, but said nothing about what precisely was to be done with them. The key to the future plans for a statue park was the capital, both the site of the largest and most spectacular of the statues and the city with the best financial resources to realize any plans for a park. In December 1991 the Greater Budapest assembly decided to proceed with the removal of all socialist-era political statues. A large number of Budapesters opposed the decision to remove some of the more prominent sculptures, arguing that they had become part of the city landscape and therefore should be spared. The notion of a statue park to house the most prominent and popular of the monuments was investigated and supported by the liberal majority in the capital's assembly, much to the displeasure of the conservative opposition and veterans of the 1956 revolution. The leader of one veterans' association wrote to the local authority

> to demand that the authority immediately abandons the plans for a completely unnecessary and expensive statue park. That they stop any works on the park and that they remove any exhibition of these symbols and statues that lie so far from the interests and feelings of the Hungarian people
>
> (Quoted in Szűcs, 1994, p. 161)

Despite the political division over whether or not the material remnants of socialist dictatorship should be exhibited, work on the Statue Park proceeded. Land was donated by the local authority of Budapest 22nd district on the fringes of the Greater Budapest conurbation. During 1992 an architectural competition was launched to find a design for an environment suitable for displaying the statues. The winner was a young architect, Ákos Eleőd, who designed a space that consciously aimed to criticize the ideology that had given birth to the statues exhibited inside it. Built during 1993 and operated by a private entrepreneur, Ákos Réthly, it opened initially as a temporary exhibit that year and then permanently in 1994.

The Statue Park as a site of memory

The park itself is a direct engagement with certain aspects of the memory of socialism and an attempt to interpret the socialist system and lay it bare. As Ákos Eleőd has explained:

> the design was drafted with the aim of breaking through a mire of objections in order to achieve an accurate and fair presentation of the statues (it's not a jokey park, absolutely not). Through the entire atmosphere of the park a critique of the ideology that gave birth to these statues would be

attempted, though it would also strongly stress certain elements.

(Quoted in Szűcs, 1994, p. 162)

The park was designed to represent certain aspects of and contradictions within the ideology of Hungary's socialist dictatorship, as stressed by the architect. Eleőd took his inspiration from a poem by the respected mid-twentieth-century writer Gyula Illés, *Egy Mondat a Zsarnokságról* (A sentence on tyranny). Illés, who is perhaps most famous outside Hungary for his book *Puszták Népe* (People of the Puszta), depicting the poverty faced by manorial workers in interwar Hungary, wrote the poem in 1950 at the height of the Stalinist show trials in the country. This work, which was not published until the outbreak of revolution in 1956, is a powerful and damning indictment of the force and power of the state during the early years of dictatorship. Following Illés, Eleőd entitled his proposed park 'The Sentence on Tyranny Park', envisaging something more ambitious than the simple display area for the statues that was opened in 1993. His original plans included both a visitor centre and a stage, elements that were instead incorporated into the plans for a Memento Park announced in 2000.

Eleőd's attempt to critique the statues was based initially on taking advantage of their separation from their original context and placing them into a new space that would represent the architect's interpretation of the ideological context in which they were produced. This very act, by its nature, was about reshaping the popular memory of socialist dictatorship and directly confronting notions of nostalgia and attachment to socialist public culture. Its effects could be powerful; as one provincial Hungarian visitor to the park remarked to a journalist from the United States in 1998,

> Under communism, such statues stood in particular places, and you got used to them. But seeing dozens of the things brought together like this makes you realise how ghastly they really were.

(Quoted in MacLeod, 1998)

EXERCISE _____

Before looking at the park in some detail, I should like you to think about the information I have just given you. In justifying his approach to designing the park Eleőd has stated that 'this park is about dictatorship. At the same time, however, it is about democracy, because it can be talked about, described and built' (quoted in N. K. J., 2001). Before we go on to talk about the park as a space and the meanings held within it, I want to ask you what Eleőd's intention was in designing the park in the way that he did.

DISCUSSION

Eleőd plainly believes that by placing the statues in a particular material context they would act as powerful tools for discussing the nature of dictatorship and thus underpinning democracy. His intention is both to draw a line under the socialist era and to some extent to shape public memory of it, by laying bare the problems and contradictions of its ideology. By taking what were everyday objects out of their daily context and placing them within a representation of what Eleőd feels is their ideological context, he presents a challenge to nostalgic ways of remembering the past. You might also have noted from our discussion of the politics of memory in contemporary Hungary that his critique of socialism is based on a particular view of socialism that may not be shared by all of his fellow citizens.

Many people felt that Eleőd's attempt to use socialism's material relics to shape a critique of the socialist system would be unsuccessful. You might, for example, remember from earlier in this chapter the response of the 1956 veteran who opposed the whole concept of a statue park. When the park opened to the public on a permanent basis in 1994, press coverage was dominated by the fear that it would be used as a site of commemoration by members and supporters of the neo-Stalinist Workers' party, who were openly nostalgic for Kádár's socialism. The questions of Eleőd's success or failure are ones that I want to leave open for now, however. Instead I want to explore his interpretation of socialism.

The Statue Park is not large; it contains only forty-one statues. As Figure 8.1 shows, it is organized around one path and three figures of eight. As I describe the features of individual parts of the park, I want you to bear in mind its plan as represented in this aerial photograph.

The first thing that struck me was the gate. It is the most imposing building – in fact the only real building in the park. It draws attention to the isolated location, just off the main road between the southwest Budapest suburbs and the nearby town of Érd. The space in front of the gate is simply a dusty car park. The park is surrounded by suburban housing – when I first saw it I was driven to wonder what the local residents make of the monument to the legacy of socialist dictatorship that has appeared in their midst. On the left-hand side of the gate stands a 4-metre-high statue of Lenin, cast in bronze in 1965 and removed from its original site near Budapest's city park in 1988 before the 'negotiated revolution' of 1989. On the right-hand side is a 1971 granite statue of Marx and Engels, over 4 metres high, which used to stand outside the building of the central committee of the **HSWP** in central Budapest. In the centre of the gate can be seen

The HSWP (Hungarian Socialist Workers' party, or *Magyar Szocialista Munkáspárt*) was formed in November 1956 and disbanded in September 1989. It was Hungary's ruling and only legal political party during the rule of János Kádár (1956–88).

Figure 8.1 Aerial photograph of the Statue Park. Photo: Szoborpark

some of the lines from the Illés poem that inspired Eleőd's original design.

The gate does not lead to an imposing building– it is simply a gate, a way into the park. The visitor walks between two buildings, one used to house the park's gift shop (Plate 26) and the other open in summer as a coffee shop, and out into open space. One path forms the centre of the park, leading from the gate to a solid brick wall at the end. Midway along the central path at the very heart of the park lies a circular area of grass with a flowerbed organized in the shape of the five-pointed red star, the symbol of communism.

This circular area is a reference to an element of public culture under socialism. The roundabout on the Buda side of the river Danube at Budapest's Chain Bridge – now know as Adam Clark Square, after the Scottish engineer who built the bridge – is the symbolic, though not the geographic, centre of Hungary, the point in

Figure 8.2   The gate, with the statues of Lenin, Marx and Engels. Photo: Mark Pittaway

Budapest from where all distances in the country are measured. While today the centre of the roundabout is decorated with an apolitical flowerbed, prior to 1989 it was adorned by an arrangement in the form of the five-pointed red star, thus asserting that communism stood at the heart of the country. By using the reference to the 'centre' of socialist Hungary in the layout of the Statue Park, Eleőd has sought to assert that, in its own way, the grounds are symbolic of the ideological universe that underpinned the Hungarian People's Republic.

The wall at the very end of the Statue Park symbolizes the end of the socialist universe; as I have noted, the one central path that clearly leads anywhere in the park ends abruptly in a brick wall. The implication – that the road of communism effectively leads to nowhere, to a dead end – is fairly obvious. In front of the wall stand the only two statues that flank the central path. These statues are related, although they stood at different ends of Budapest prior to 1989. Both sculptures are of soldiers with the Red Army in 1944 who became martyrs to the communist cause as a result of their conduct during the siege of Budapest. Steinmetz was of Hungarian origin, from a communist family who left the country after the suppression of the Soviet republic in 1919, while Ostapenkó (Plate 27) was

Figure 8.3   The Steinmetz and Ostapenkó statues in front of the wall in the Statue Park. Photo: Mark Pittaway

Ukranian. At the beginning of the siege both were sent, Steinmetz from the southeast and Ostapenkó from the southwest, to negotiate a surrender with the Nazi and Arrow Cross (*Nyilások*, or Hungarian fascists) forces defending Budapest. Both men were killed, though the circumstances of their deaths were never clearly established. Nevertheless, they were treated as martyrs by the socialist regime.

These statues were erected at the borders of the city; the Steinmetz statue used to stand on the southeastern border, and the Ostapenkó statue on the main southwestern road out of the city, which by the 1980s had become the beginning of the motorway to Vienna. Though most nostalgic memories of the Ostapenkó sculpture were connected with the fact that it was the last monument Budapesters saw in their city before leaving it to holiday at Lake Balaton, and the first they saw on their return, it also represented the last thing that people seeking to travel to the west saw of Budapest.

For an open space, I found the Statue Park strangely claustrophobic. Examining the aerial view in Figure 8.1, you will have noticed that the statues are arranged along three figures of eight that cross the central path. These figures of eight have all been labelled 'the endless parades'. One forms 'the endless parade of liberation monuments', the second 'the endless parade of personalities of the workers' movement', the third (rather oddly) 'the unending promenade of workers' movement concepts'. These identify the key themes of the many ideas that the political statues represented. Wandering among the sculptures, I was conscious that there is nowhere, literally, to go. The circular paths between the statues lead back to the one central path and the single exit to the park.

The feeling of being shut in the park is at its strongest at its edges. On the western side, beyond the boundaries of the park one can see private housing, a small local grocery shop and a pub. On the eastern side there is the main road and pylons carrying the capital's electricity supply that march across the suburban landscape surrounding the park. Consider the image in Figure 8.4 of the Béla Kun memorial, on the far eastern fringes of the park exposed to the world outside. Here one is cut off from the landscape beyond the grounds by the fence that surrounds them. The feeling of exposure to the outside world and the simultaneous sense of being excluded from that world are both generated by these aspects of the park's design. This seems, at one level, to mimic the way that socialist Hungary was experienced by many of its people. It was exposed to cultural influences from the world beyond its borders, and indeed beyond the borders of all the Warsaw Pact countries. At the same time Hungarians were prevented from travelling outside a world that had the five-pointed red star at its centre.

EXERCISE

Now that you have read the description of the park above in conjunction with the images provided, I should like you to think about how far Eleőd achieves his intention of placing the statues in their ideological context. Write a few sentences on why you think he achieves or fails to achieve his aims.

DISCUSSION

Your answer will of course depend on whether you agree with Eleőd's interpretation of socialism as presented in the way the Statue Park is designed. For Eleőd, socialism is fundamentally about oppression – this can seen in the way that Illés's 'A sentence on tyranny' became the inspiration for his design. It can also be seen in the way in which the park is conceived almost as an enclosed and artificial space separated from the world around it. It is as if ideology is regarded as something that decorates a socialist prison. The bankruptcy of socialist dictatorship is also suggested in the way that the central path through the Statue Park leads to nothing – to an effective dead-end. In short, Eleőd presents us with a space that links Budapest's statues

Figure 8.4   The Béla Kun memorial photographed against the electricity lines. Photo: Mark Pittaway

to a political system which was fundamentally interested in denying the freedom of its citizens and enclosing them in a prison that could be dominated by the ideology of the regime. This interpretation is certainly contentious; by stressing what some commentators see as the 'totalitarian' practice of socialist rule, it understates the Marxist-Leninist goals of the regime. Yet it does provide a space that prompts discussion on the nature of the dictatorship. In this sense it could be said to fulfil the architect's vision of creating a space that provokes discussion of dictatorship.

Certainly the interpretation of dictatorship presented by Eleőd in the park stresses aspects of the socialist experience that were real to many Hungarians: the denial of certain basic freedoms – for example, of the right to vote, and of freedom of speech, assembly and travel. It also clearly represents an intervention into the politics of memory; by re-presenting some of the material manifestations of socialism in a new context it is, at its heart, about shaping a politics of memory.

EXERCISE

I want you now to retrace your steps a little. Refresh your memory, using whatever notes you may have taken at the time, of the earlier section in this chapter entitled 'Coming to terms with the past? The politics of remembering socialism in post-socialist Hungary'. Then try to set the Statue Park in the context of the politics of remembering socialist dictatorship. This, when expressed in these terms, is certainly a tall order. I should therefore like you to organize your thoughts around the following points.

1   With what trend or direction outlined in the section on the politics of remembering socialism does the Statue Park have most in common?

2   How does it diverge from other attempts to shape memory that belong to the trend with which it is most associated?

3   Which manifestation(s) of memory for socialism does the Statue Park not engage with, or ignore all together?

DISCUSSION

There are of course no single correct responses to these questions. My own attempts to answer them should be treated as guidance only; you should feel more than free to disagree with them.

1   The Statue Park would seem to stand broadly with those publications that attempt to engage directly with nostalgic memories of socialist dictatorship, in the sense that it takes some of the material remnants of that dictatorship and seeks to reinterpret them in the light of an assumed ideological context. It certainly does not endorse nostalgia, though it should be noted that the gift shop sells many of the products which have been emblematic of the nostalgia characterizing popular memory and that the private businessman who operates it, Ákos Réthly, has produced a CD entitled *The Best of Communism*. It furthermore emphatically rejects, by its very existence, positions that argue that the memory of socialism should be eradicated – views associated with many on the right of the political spectrum.

2   Unlike the collections picked out in the previous section, *Befejezetlen Szocializmus* and *Beszélőévek*, the park does not directly engage with nostalgic memories. This is not surprising – it was created at a time before nostalgic consumerism became a cultural phenomenon during the late 1990s. It was conceived in 1991 and 1992, in the shadow of 1989, before nostalgia for the past had begun to interest Budapest intellectuals. Rather, the park reflects a desire to draw a line under socialist dictatorship by confining

that regime within the fences of an open-air museum, while asserting that publicly remembering dictatorship and what lay behind it is essential to the strengthening of Hungary's young democracy. In short, the ambition of the originators of the Statue Park should not be understated. It represents an attempt to shape the memory of socialist dictatorship in a way that reinforces democracy.

3   It appears that the fact the Statue Park fails to engage explicitly with nostalgia for the later years of socialist dictatorship, even when its gift shop is stuffed with artefacts that formed the basis of nostalgic cultural consumerism in Hungary during the late 1990s, is its major omission. This may not be a fair criticism, given that nostalgia was not a major concern for the creators of the park in the early 1990s when memories of 1989 were still relatively fresh.

A site of different memories? The House of Terror and the politics of memory

Some 12 kilometres northeast of the Statue Park on the eastern side of the Danube is the central area of Pest. Just north of the Oktogon, one of the major road junctions along Pest's so-called Great Ring, or *Nagykörút*, can be found number 60 Andrássy út. Like many of the buildings in the street, it was originally built as an apartment block in the late nineteenth century for Pest's burgeoning upper middle classes to satisfy their demand for luxury housing during a period of spectacular industrial and commercial expansion in the city. During the late 1930s part of the block was rented by factions of Hungary's national socialist movement, before it became the headquarters of the country's fascist Arrow Cross party in 1940, which renamed it the 'House of Loyalty'. With the installation of the Arrow Cross leader Ferenc Szalási as Hungary's dictator by the Nazis in October 1944 it became, albeit briefly, a seat of power in the country. Following the siege of Budapest in February 1945 it fell into the hands of the Ministry of the Interior. The building then became the headquarters of the political department of first the Budapest and then the Hungarian national police force, which was given responsibility for rounding up fascists. During the late 1940s, as the communists' grip on power in the country tightened, the force's activities were directed at opponents of the emerging dictatorship. With the creation of the Agency for the Protection of the State (*Államvédelmi Hatóság*, or ÁVH) in 1949, the site became the new organization's headquarters. Thus 60 Andrássy út became associated with the crimes of both national socialism and Stalinism in the country. After the 1956 revolution it

Figure 8.5 60 Andrássy út, Budapest. February 2002.
Photo: Tivadar Domaniczky

played no prominent role in Hungarian public life, until it was revived as a museum in the early twenty-first century.

During the 1990s the building carried symbolic meaning, especially for the victims of Stalinist repression during the late 1940s and early 1950s. Its dark past was common knowledge to most Budapest residents, though its role was only commemorated in a plaque to the victims of 'communist repression' placed on its walls by a liberal political party. But this was to change when the building was bought in 2000 by the Foundation for Research into the History and Society of Central and Eastern Europe for 3 billion forints. Another substantial sum – believed to be 340 million forints per year of construction – was spent on transforming the block into a museum

(*Népszabadság munkatársai*, 2002). The creation of this museum, known as the House of Terror (*A Terror Háza*), was headed by Mária Schmidt, the historian and prime ministerial adviser encountered in an earlier section of this chapter. It was intended to present the official, state-sponsored view of Hungary's recent past, under the government of Viktor Orbán, to the population and especially to the younger generation who knew little of life under socialist dictatorship. The museum was therefore conceived to articulate three arguments about Hungary's socialist regime. First it sought to stress the fundamentally terroristic nature of that regime. Secondly, and more controversially, it asserted a fundamental kinship between state socialism and fascist national socialism. Thirdly, and most controversially, it argued that both systems were 'foreign' impositions on the country. This argument in the Hungarian context implied that supporters of the country's main opposition party, as former communists, had been the agents of a foreign power and at the same time implied a denial of Hungarian responsibility for the Holocaust of the country's Jewish population in 1944. For these reasons alone the House of Terror attracted considerable public criticism from historians of contemporary Hungary, including this author, when it opened in February 2002.

Rather than a museum in the traditional sense, the House of Terror was designed, according to Schmidt, to 'give the visitor the sensation of what terror felt like' (La Bruyere, 2002). The building was redesigned by the architect Attila F. Kovács; its interior was completely remade to be (as we shall see below) at one and the same time a museum, an experience and a memorial to the victims of dictatorship. Certain aspects of the building's transformation attracted controversies of their own. Figure 8.5 shows the additions to the exterior of the late-nineteenth-century apartment block. These additions attracted controversy in part because they were erected without planning permission from the appropriate authority. Furthermore, in May 2002 they provoked a debate in the national press between architects over their aesthetic merit.

It was, however, the blatantly political uses to which the House of Terror was put by Hungary's right-wing parties in the run-up to the April 2002 parliamentary elections that attracted the most attention and controversy. Its opening on 24 February 2002 was used as an election rally by supporters of the conservative coalition then in office and by the extreme right-wing Hungarian Justice and Life party. Supporters of the far right explicitly used the demonstration to link the then opposition Socialist party to the 'terror' depicted inside the museum. Supporters of the governing conservative coalition were less vocal, but their message was fundamentally similar. Opening the museum, Prime Minister Orbán argued that it was necessary to teach the young about the fear that had existed in the country's recent past (Rab, 2002). Not only was the House of Terror to figure prominently in the right's campaign for the 2002 elections but its opening set the tone for much of this campaign, in which the right mobilized its vote by bringing its supporters on to the streets of the capital with aggressive right-wing anti-communist rhetoric. It was a campaign, however, which did not prove successful – Orbán's government was defeated by a coalition of the Socialist party and the Alliance of Free Democrats.

Exploring the House of Terror

The House of Terror purports to be much more than a museum, however experiential much of its content may be. It is also designed as a memorial. A visitor might approach it by walking southwest towards the centre of Pest down the right-hand side of Andrássy út. The wide boulevard would be to their left and late-nineteenth-century apartment blocks to their right. All of a sudden our visitor would come to the so-called bladed, black walls of the House of Terror and would turn right immediately through the doors.

The entrance hall architecturally resembles those in any of the late-nineteenth-century apartment blocks along the street outside, except that at its end stand two memorials. One, in black, depicts the

Figure 8.6 The 'Gulag' room and the 'changing clothes' exhibit, House of Terror, Budapest. Photo: Tivadar Domaniczky

Figure 8.7   The courtyard, House of Terror, Budapest. Photo: Tivadar Domaniczky

four-pointed cross that was the symbol of the fascist Arrow Cross movement in the 1940s. This memorial contains a dedication to the victims of the 'Arrow Cross terror'. To its right is a red memorial with a representation of the five-pointed star that symbolizes Soviet socialism; its inscription commemorates the victims of 'communist terror'. Taken together, the two memorials enlist the memories of victims in the service of advancing the argument that lies at the core of the museum's conception; namely that the Arrow Cross dictatorship of 1944–5 can be directly equated with the state socialist dictatorship of 1948–89.

In front of the two memorials our visitor would turn left to enter a lounge. They would then be faced with a choice: to go to a coffee shop to their left, or to turn to their right towards the courtyard.

The central courtyard is an architectural feature common to most of Pest's nineteenth-century apartment houses. At the centre of the block the doors of individual family apartments open out on to the balconies above the courtyard. Larger, more expensive apartments within the block would have had windows that looked out on to the street; the smallest of the units often only looked on to the courtyard. This seems to have been the way in which 60 Andrássy út was originally designed. In his transformation of the former apartment block into a museum, Attila F. Kovács has made considerable use of this architectural feature. In the centre of the courtyard is a Soviet tank, its gun turret pointed directly at the lounge. One of the walls of the courtyard, stretching to the full height of the buildings, contains the portraits of 3,600 people. These photographs, acquired by the museum from the Historical Authority (*Történeti Hivatal*) – the body that administers the archives of the country's socialist-era internal security forces – depict the victims of dictatorship. The emphasis of this memorial is on the victims of socialist dictatorship rather than those of national socialist occupation. Furthermore, the Soviet tank serves as the symbol of the foreign power that is held responsible for Hungary's postwar past.

The exhibition is designed to present an argument about the nature of the socialist dictatorship, rather than its national socialist counterpart. Indeed national socialism is only introduced as a way of sustaining a parallel with its Soviet successor. The exhibition spans three floors (the second and first floors and the cellar), beginning on the second floor. Of thirty exhibition rooms only three are devoted to the period of Arrow Cross rule. Even here, what the exhibition leaves out is as notable as what is included. Because the period covered by the museum only begins in October 1944 there is virtually no mention of the Holocaust; the deportation of Jews to Auschwitz by Hungary's German occupiers with the collaboration of the Hungarian gendarmerie in June–July 1944 is not touched on. In fact the Holocaust is not explored at all.

The purpose of including the Arrow Cross period in the exhibition is only made clear two rooms later. One chamber concentrates on what it terms the process of 'changing clothes', meaning the way in which many members of the fascist Arrow Cross simply exchanged their political clothes and joined the Communist party after 1945. While this process did undoubtedly occur, the exhibit places special weight on it. According to the museum management's own description of the room, 'after 1945 ... the Hungarian Communist Party had a minimal number of members, for this reason the party had to recruit the former Arrow Crossists at that time' (House of Terror website). In short, the exhibit attempts to stress the essential continuity between Hungary's dictatorships, thus equating socialist dictatorship with the earlier national socialist regime.

The rest of the exhibition on the second floor is about asserting that Hungarian socialism was fundamentally a Soviet import. From a chamber that examines the Soviet gulag, the visitor is propelled through rooms that represent the early period of socialist rule, portraying various aspects of the Stalinism of the 1950s. Through a display devoted to the subject of 'Soviet advisers', great weight is placed on the role played directly by Soviet citizens in the creation of the socialist system. The first floor of the exhibition continues this theme with a stress on the terroristic nature of the Stalinist system during the early 1950s; note that the later more reformist period of

Figure 8.8 The torture chamber, the House of Terror exhibition, Budapest. Photo: Tivadar Domaniczky

Compulsory deliveries were the system by which the Hungarian state directly requisitioned a proportion of the harvest of every agricultural producer in the country. The system was introduced as an emergency measure after Hungary's entry into the Second World War in 1941, but gained notoriety during the dictatorship of Mátyás Rákosi (1948–56) when it was used to starve farmers into entering collective farms. It was abolished during the 1956 revolution and, in the interests of political stabilization, not reintroduced after the suppression of the revolution.

the dictatorship is not discussed or considered at all. The role of the internal security services is strongly emphasized, as are some aspects of everyday terror such as the system of **compulsory deliveries** that was designed to starve Hungarian peasants into the collective farms. Representations of everyday life are contained in one small room in one corner of the first floor. The end of the exhibition takes the visitor to the cellar through a reconstruction of the prisons of the internal security services in the early 1950s, to rooms that deal with the 1956 revolution, its repression and the wave of emigration that followed it.

EXERCISE

Think carefully about my description of the House of Terror and my brief overview of its permanent exhibition. What are the differences between it and the Budapest Statue Park? How do you account for these differences?

DISCUSSION

There is of course no single correct way of approaching either of these questions. For me the Budapest Statue Park represents a subtle attempt to engage with nostalgic memories of socialism in Hungary by using its space to reinterpret the material remnants of the period. The House of Terror's creators, however, do not seem to be remotely interested in engaging with nostalgia for the past; rather they have eradicated and replaced that nostalgia with a memory of their own. This reaches back to recollections of the Stalinist 1950s rather than the reformist 1960s and 1970s. The presentation is of socialism as fundamentally based on terror and thoroughly dictatorial. There is no room within the museum for those who believe that socialist dictatorship had any positive benefit whatsoever.

While the Statue Park allows some space for discussion of its interpretation and the artefacts it contains, the House of Terror presents a very specific version of the recent past, a memory that can only be accepted at face value or rejected. In this way it may be said to be providing a site of memory for those on the political right who are already convinced anti-communists. It does, however, offer the possibility of providing a collective memory of socialism for a newer, younger generation growing up in Hungary who have no strong personal memories of the socialist period.

Perhaps you might account for the differences between the two sites in terms of the directly political role of the House of Terror and the more indirect role of the Statue Park. The House of Terror has been used and could be said to have been designed as a political instrument in order to help those of a certain political persuasion to shape public memory in a particular direction.

You might, however, account for the differences between the two sites in terms of a basic dichotomy between what is being remembered. Socialism in both its reformist and its Stalinist variants is being recalled in the context of the Statue Park; furthermore, its focus is on an engagement with memories of everyday life during the dictatorship. But in the House of Terror it is the violence and political repression that dictatorship brings in its train that are being remembered.

Conclusion

This discussion, I hope, reveals that something of what Ugrešić terms 'post-communist trauma' is very much present in the Hungarian case. The memory of the recent past divides Hungarian society, and indeed bolsters and reinforces political disagreement in a society already fundamentally split between right and left. This raises basic questions about the nature of political identities and the possibilities of writing a history that would enable the divisions about the past in Hungarian society to be overcome. Opinion polls and election results suggest that an apolitical nostalgia for the later years of socialism remains strong among about half of the country's adult population, but this has yet to find its own 'site of memory'. Both the places discussed in this chapter are anti-communist, even though the aggressive anti-communism of Hungary's right-wing parties is a world away from the motives that informed the Statue Park. One wonders whether open discussion of the past would allow divisions to heal, or would merely deepen old wounds.

Given the role of the museum in contemporary culture, the museological representation of Hungary's recent past can only reflect the seriously divided memory of that past. The example of the House of Terror, used as part of the 2002 campaign for parliamentary elections, shows in dramatic fashion the links between memory, the museum and political identities in the Hungarian present. It also demonstrates how memory can be manipulated and shaped by political elites to actively mould political identities among the population.

Although this chapter has focused on Hungary, it is important to bear in mind that issues about the memory of the recent socialist past are current throughout central and eastern Europe. Election results across the former Soviet bloc show that the successor parties to communism are significant political forces, in part because they represent to some extent the political manifestation of nostalgic memory. Budapest's museums and Statue Park are not the only attempts in the area to 'musealize' the socialist system. There are other examples, such as the Museum of Everyday Life in Eisenhüttenstadt in the former East Germany, and counterparts in the Czech Republic. Berlin's *Haus am Checkpoint Charlie* is another attempt to 'musealize' an aspect of central and eastern Europe's defunct socialist regime, namely the Berlin Wall. Right across the region the manipulation of the memory of the recent past has been striking, as demonstrated by revelations about the 'secret police' pasts of certain politicians in the Czech Republic, Hungary and Poland – and, more tragically, by anti-communist nationalists in former Yugoslavia.

References

Beke, László (1989) 'A budapesti Sztálin-szobor ledöntése', *Belvedere*, no. 3, pp. 3–6.

Beke, László (1992) 'The strange afterlife of socialist realism', in Péter György and Hedvig Turai (eds), *Art and Society in the Age of Stalin*, Budapest, Corvina.

Beszélő (2000) *Beszélőévek 1957–1968. A Kádár-korszak története 1. Rész*, Budapest, Stencil Kulturális Alapítvány.

Betts, P. (2000) 'The twilight of the idols: East German memory and material culture', *Journal of Modern History*, vol. 72, no. 3, pp. 731–65.

Borneman, J. (1997) *Settling Accounts: Violence, Justice and Accountability in Postsocialist Europe*, Princeton, NJ, Princeton University Press.

Boros, Géza (1993) 'A Lenin-kertektől a Tanú térig', *Kritika*, no. 8, pp. 11–3.

Boros, Géza (1997) *Emlékművek '56-nak*, Budapest, 1956-os Intézet.

Cartwright, A. L. (2001) *The Return of the Peasant: Land Reform in Post-communist Romania*, Aldershot, Ashgate.

Creed, G. W. (1998) *Domesticating Revolution: from Socialist Reform to Ambivalent Transition in a Bulgarian Village*, University Park, PA, Pennsylvania State University Press.

Freifeld, Alice (2000) *Nationalism and the Crowd in Liberal Hungary, 1848–1914*, Washington, DC, Woodrow Wilson Center Press.

Gerő, András and Pető, Iván (1999) *Unfinished Socialism: Pictures from the Kádár Era*, transl. James Patterson, Budapest, Central European University Press.

Hoberman, J. (1998) *The Red Atlantis: Communist Culture in the Absence of Communism*, Philadelphia, PN, Temple University Press.

Hofer, Tamás (2000) 'Harc a rendszerváltásért, 1989 március 15-e Budapesten', in András Bozóki (ed.), *A Rendszerváltás Forgatókönyve. Kerekasztal-Tárgyalások – Alkotmányos Forradalom. Tanulmányok*, Budapest, Új Mandátum Könyvkiadó.

House of Terror website: http://www2.terrorhaza.hu/hu/muzeum/bemutatkozas

Kardos, Sándor et al. (1990) *'Hol zsarnokság van, ott zsarnokság van'*, Budapest, Hét Torony Kiadó.

La Bruyere, Florence (2002) 'La droite hongroise ouvre la "Maison de la Terreur"', *Libération*, 23 February.

Lampland, M. (2002) 'The advantages of being collectivized: co-operative farm managers in the postsocialist economy', in C. M. Hann (ed.), *Postsocialism: Ideals, Ideologies and Practices in Eurasia*, London/New York, Routledge.

MacLeod, Alexander (1998) 'Budapest finds profit in "ghastly" public art', *Christian Science Monitor*, 8 May.

Magyar Gallup Intézet website: http://www.gallup.hu/Gallup/release/ppref020621.htm

Népszabadság munkatársai (2002) 'Vizsgálatok a Népstadiontól a Terror Házáig', *Népszabadság*, 28 June.

N. K. J. (2001) 'A múltba kalauzol a Tanú tér', *Népszabadság*, 19 April.

Nyssonen, Heino (1999) *The Presence of the Past in Politics: 1956 after 1956 in Hungary*, Jytäskylä, SoPhi Academic Press.

Pittaway, M. (ed.) (2003) *Globalization and Europe*, Milton Keynes, Open University.

Pótó, János (1989) *Emlékművek, Politika, Közgondolkodás*, Budapest, MTA Történetudományi Intézet.

Rab, László (2002) 'Sok ezren a Terror Háza megnyitásan', *Népszabadság*, 25 February.

Swain, N. (1995) 'Decollectivizing agriculture in the Visegrad countries of central Europe', *Labour Focus on Eastern Europe*, no. 51, pp. 65–85.

Szűcs, György (1994) 'A "zsarnokság" szoborparkja', *Budapesti Negyed*, vol. 1, no. 3, pp. 151–65.

Tóth Gy. László (1998) Interview: 'Szocialista párttörténet – közpénzen', *Napi Magyarország*, 9 December.

Ugrešić, Dubravka [1995] (1999) *The Culture of Lies: Antipolitical Essays*, transl. Celia Hawkesworth, London, Phoenix House.

V. Gy. (1998) 'Megszűnhet két kutatóintézet', *Népszabadság*, 27 November.

Verdery, K. (1994) 'The elasticity of land: problems of prosperity restitution in Transylvania', *Slavic Review*, vol. 53, no. 4, pp. 1071–109.

9

Identity and managing the memory of war.

Yugoslavia: a case study

CELIA HAWKESWORTH

Introduction: early history and its interpretation

General context

> Who should fail to come to Kosovo Field –
> May nothing more ever grow from his hand:
> May no more white wheat stand tall in his fields,
> And no grapes ripen on vines on his slopes!
>
> ('The Prince's Curse')

Traditional songs were a vital means of transmitting culture through the largely illiterate populations of pre-modern southeast Europe. They cover a wide range of theme and mode, broadly divisible into lyric songs (usually sung by women) and epic or 'heroic' narrative songs (chanted for the most part by men, accompanying themselves on the *gusle*, a simple, single-stringed lute).

At the time of writing, there is still a country called Yugoslavia, but it consists of only two of the previous six constituent republics of post-Second World War Yugoslavia (Serbia and Montenegro). The other four were Slovenia, Croatia, Bosnia-Herzegovina and Macedonia.

These are the words with which the fourteenth-century Prince Lazar of Serbia is said, in a **traditional folk song**, to have summoned his fellow Christians to defend Serbia from the advancing Ottoman army on the famous battlefield of *Kosovo polje* (the field of the blackbirds) on *Vidovdan* (St Vitus's Day), 28 June 1389. For a farming culture such as that of the Serbs at the time, such a curse would have been chilling indeed. The curse is part of a song in the rich south Slav oral tradition.

Over the centuries, to very many citizens in innumerable countries, the call to arms has had irresistible power. It is rarely expressed, as here, in terms of a curse. Far more frequently it is a personal appeal to the individual's noblest impulses, for example in the familiar First World War poster 'Your Country Needs YOU'. Concepts such as courage, pride, dignity, self-sacrifice, duty and honour are all bound up in the call to arms. And memories of battles are used to engender such emotions in peacetime too. In this chapter, I want to consider the management of this kind of memory of conflict as a vital element in the construction of national identity, using the example of the constituent peoples of the country known between 1928 and 1991 as **'Yugoslavia'**.

Why should these memories be particularly prominent in state and identity building in this region? The answer to that question is what we are going to try to investigate here, and I hope that some version of the answer will also be found to be applicable to other peoples and nations, not only in Europe but in many other parts of the world as well.

The first issue to consider is the particular problem of trying to forge an identity that confers the vital emotions of pride and dignity, even among the subject peoples of large empires – a situation that may be perceived as inherently humiliating. It is perhaps hard for us now, in the twenty-first century, to think back beyond the familiar pattern of nation-states to a time when most of Europe was divided among a few powerful ruling houses or empires. But this pattern of dominance and subjection has been a determining factor in the formation of every European identity. In the case of the Yugoslav peoples, by the beginning of the early modern period all were subjects of either the Ottoman or the Habsburg empire. The fact that a significant part of the frontier between these two huge states cut the territory they inhabited in two has been one of the chief factors in determining the self-perception of these peoples, their history and culture. They are essentially peoples from 'borderlands', inherently unstable regions; subject to constant friction, conflict, population movement, incursion, attack and defence in the course of fixing and maintaining these borders. The population of the whole region has witnessed successive waves of refugees and displaced people: the huge migrations caused by the Yugoslav wars of the 1990s were just the latest in what has been a very lengthy process.

For most of their early history we can safely assume that these various peoples thought of themselves not in terms of any 'nation', but in terms of the immediate locality in which they lived: as belonging to a particular village or town, or perhaps to a larger region of speakers of the same language, connected by trade. They cultivated their own way of life and culture, passing this on to future generations through their customs and their traditional songs. The songs in this tradition cover a vast range of subjects. But the ones that have been especially influential are those which preserve the memory of locally significant historical figures and events. In the nineteenth century, when individuals began to think in terms of larger groupings of peoples, of 'nations', inhabiting a defined geographical area and sharing a common language, it was to these songs that they turned in order to foster a sense of what was most particular to their specific group.

Construction of identity under foreign rule

We should now narrow our focus to the early nineteenth century. It was at this time that thinking about questions of national identity and nationhood began to take shape in many parts of Europe. In the Yugoslav lands there were two broad groups of peoples. These were, in the Habsburg lands, Slovenes and Croats (who speak related but distinct languages), and, under Ottoman rule, Bosnians, Serbs, Montenegrins and Macedonians. Macedonians speak a language closely related to Bulgarian, while all the other peoples of the Yugoslav lands speak one language with regional variations, codified in the mid nineteenth century as Serbo-Croat.

Since the disintegration of Yugoslavia into independent states, each has favoured a separate name for its version of the language, so that the official designations are now Bosnian in Bosnia-Herzegovina, Croatian in Croatia and Serbian in the territory still called Yugoslavia. At the time of writing, however, it is not clear whether or not an official Montenegrin language may also emerge. If Montenegro opts for independence from Serbia, this will probably happen.

Just to confuse the picture, Bosnia-Herzegovina, part of the Ottoman empire since the fifteenth century, came under Habsburg rule in 1878 and was formally annexed by Austria-Hungary in 1908. In other words, at different times it was a component part of each of the two dominant imperial structures.

In the Christian Habsburg lands the religion and culture of the ruling power were shared by its subject peoples. This presented one set of problems in the process of fostering a sense of national identity. In order for the Habsburg subject peoples to develop a sense of their specific identity and separateness other components of identity would have had to be emphasized. In the case of Ottoman Europe, where the ruling power was Islamic, questions of distinction from and resistance to the 'other' (a vital component of every sense of identity) were clearer-cut. I therefore propose to concentrate on the lands under Ottoman rule, particularly Serbia. In both cases, however, it is clear that the mythic construction of history by subject peoples inevitably offers them only a passive role, since they can play no active part in the government of their country. Those who seek to mobilize support for a 'national idea' foster the memory (or invention) of a so-called glorious past where action was once possible. Ever since such ideas began to take shape in late eighteenth-century Europe, the traditions, customs and oral culture of a given 'nation' have been seen as having the ultimate aim of recording shared memories and enabling communities to maintain a sense of separateness from others around them.

I shall focus first on the oral traditional literature of the Serbs, its stereotypes and moral imperatives. This is because of the dominance of such literature (and particularly of the Kosovo myth) in the formation of the independent principality of Serbia in the nineteenth century and again in the Yugoslav wars of the 1990s. At both these times political aims gave a new urgency and coherence to the

Figure 9.1 Serbs gathered around a *gusle* player, mid nineteenth century. Photo: L'Épopée Serbe, Paris, Ernest Leroux, Editeur, 1888

disparate elements of the tradition. This led to the evolution of a distinct mythic sense of Serbian history and the historical destiny of the Serbs.

How is it that the story of the battle of Kosovo in 1389, in which the Serbs see themselves as having lost the remnants of their medieval state (in other words, they see this as a catastrophic defeat), became such a potent symbol in Serbian culture? To find part of the answer, let us look at the opening of another traditional song. It is known as 'The downfall of the Serbian empire'.

The Downfall of the Serbian Empire

This poem was recorded from a blind woman of Grgurevtsi in [the region of] Srem by Lukijan Mushitski, the abbot of the neighbouring monastery of Shishatovats, and sent to Vuk Karadzhich [a collector of folk songs] in 1817. It has pronounced religious features typical of such singers who were usually closely associated with local churches and monasteries. Lazar's choice between Turkish vassalage and honourable death in battle is seen here as the dilemma between the earthly and the heavenly

kingdom, which is, in fact, an echo from Serbian medieval
literature. The Holy Communion on the eve of the battle was part
of Byzantine military protocol and probably customary in the
Serbian army. The poem is of considerable interest for the
hagiographical imprint on its epic subject matter.

[Svetozar Koljević]

Flying hawk, grey bird,
out of the holy place, out of Jerusalem,
holding a swallow, holding a bird.
That is no hawk, grey bird,
that is Elijah, holy one;
holding no swallow, no bird,
but writing from the Mother of God
to the Emperor at Kosovo.
He drops that writing on his knee,
is speaking to the Emperor:
'Lazar, glorious Emperor,
which is the empire of your choice?
Is it the empire of heaven?
Is it the empire of the earth?
If it is the empire of the earth,
saddle horses and tighten girth-straps,
and, fighting-men, buckle on swords,
attack the Turks,
and all the Turkish army shall die.
But if the empire of heaven
weave a church on Kosovo,
build its foundation not with marble stones,
build it with pure silk and with crimson cloth,
take the Sacrament, marshal the men,
they shall all die,
and you shall die among them as they die.'
And when the Emperor heard those words,
he considered, he considered and thought,
'Kind God, what shall I do, how shall I do it?
What is the empire of my choice?
Is it the empire of heaven?
Is it the empire of the earth?
And if I shall choose the empire,
and choose the empire of the earth,
the empire of the earth is brief,
heaven is lasting and everlasting.'
And the Emperor chose the empire of heaven
above the empire of the earth.

He wove a church on Kosovo,
built its foundation not of marble stone
but with pure silk and with crimson cloth.
He called for the Patriarch of Serbia,
he called for the twelve great bishops,
he took the Sacrament with his men;
and when the Prince had marshalled his men
the Turkish army struck at Kosovo.
Jug Bogdan the old moves his army
with his nine sons, the nine Jugovichi,
nine grey hawks, grey birds,
every one has nine thousand men,
Jug has twelve thousand men,
beating and slashing at the Turks.
They battled, they slaughtered seven pashas,
they battled with the eighth pasha,
and Jug Bogdan the old man was killed,
and the nine Jugovichi were killed,
nine grey hawks, grey birds.
And all of their men were killed.
The three Merljavchevichi move their men,
the Ban Ugljesha, Gojko the Duke,
Vukashin the King,
every one has thirty thousand men,
beating and slashing at the Turks,
they battled, they slaughtered eight pashas,
they battled with the ninth pasha,
the two Merljavchevichi were killed,
the Ban Ugljesha, Gojko the Duke,
Vukashin dropped loaded with wounds,
Turkish horses trampled him under,
and all of their men were killed.
The Herzog Stephen moves his men,
his force is strong and great,
sixty thousand, a great army,
beating and slashing at the Turks,
they battled, they slaughtered nine pashas,
they battled with the tenth pasha,
the Herzog Stephen was killed,
and all of his men were killed.
Lazar, Prince of Serbia, moved his men,
Lazar had Serbs without number,
seven and seventy thousand men,
hunting the Turks across Kosovo,
moving too swiftly to be seen by them.

And how could there be battle with the Turks.
God be the death of Vuk Brankovich,
traitor to his kinsman on Kosovo:
the Turks dragged down Lazar,
Lazar, Prince of Serbia, was killed,
and all of his men were killed,
seven and seventy thousand men:
with holiness and honour
good in the sight of God.

(*Marko the Prince*, 1984, pp. 17–19)

EXERCISE _____

1   What is the significance of the opening lines?

2   What does the symbol of the 'church [of] pure silk' suggest to you?

3   How does the central message of this song contribute to fostering a sense of dignity which can motivate further deeds of valour and self-sacrifice?

DISCUSSION _____

1   The opening lines link the person of the Serbian Prince Lazar directly with God, giving him an aura of saintliness. This invests his words with particular gravity.

2   The 'church [of] pure silk' may be seen as standing for the practical expediency of having to hold the sacrament of Holy Communion on the battlefield in a tent – here this is a tent decked out in regal splendour. But it may also be seen as the evocation of an abstract dedication of the individual to God: a flimsy silk tent is fragile, yet as an image carried in the heart it is unassailable.

3   Dignity is conferred by the self-denial and sacrifice inherent in the conscious choice of 'the empire of heaven', with its associations of eternal values, over the inferior goal of mere survival in the material world.

We have now seen two of the crucial components of the whole 'Kosovo myth'. It should be clear that the ringing curse of the first combined with the superior moral force of the second offers an extraordinarily potent self-image. However, it is also clear that this self-image is offered above all to men. They are the ones who are the active participants in the myth, the heroes. They are also of course the main victims of heroic action, and for them the conscious choice between heroic death or cowardice and betrayal is stark. The woman's role in this tradition is different but equally limited. It is illustrated by two other songs included as an Appendix to this chapter. The first, 'The Kosovo Girl', describes a young woman searching for her fiancé among the heaps of blood-drenched bodies on a battlefield, giving succour where she can to the dying soldiers. The second, 'The Mother of the Jugovichi', tells of the role of the mother – which is to lament the inevitable death of her husband and their nine fine sons, and then herself to die of grief. Please read the lyrics of these songs and think about the profound contrast they suggest between the kinds of demand made on men and women, respectively, in this tradition. This contrast continues to have considerable resonance even today.

The extent to which these stereotypes have entered into the consciousness of successive generations of Serbs is astonishing. In times of war, men have been regularly called upon to perform deeds of great courage in the name of the 'Kosovo idea': there are many stories, particularly from the First World War, of soldiers testifying that they were inspired to daring action by the image of one of the traditional heroes, Marko the Prince, appearing before them and leading them forward. Stereotypical roles for women are no less enduring. For example,

> In a ceremony in Priština on Vidovdan, 28 June 1993 (the date of the 1389 defeat of the Serbs at Kosovo and a national holiday), dignitaries of the Serbian Orthodox Church honoured Serbian mothers of more than four children with medals called after the Mother of the Jugovići ... (*Politika*, 29 June 1993, p. 10)

(Bracewell, 1996, p. 30)

In times of conflict, it is a woman's duty to produce Serbian sons to carry on the fight, to take on the sacred obligation to 'avenge Kosovo'.

An example of how the traditional culture was exploited in a nineteenth-century text with the specific aim of fostering national consciousness is provided by a work published in 1847 by the poet Petar Petrović Njegoš, ruler of the small territory of Montenegro. Today Montenegro is a mountainous region to the southwest of Serbia, with a clear sense of its own identity. This is partly because it was once a separate province of the Roman empire and then an independent medieval state, but mostly because its largely mountainous terrain prevented it from ever being fully occupied by

Figure 9.2 Statue of the hero of oral traditional epic song, Marko the Prince, made by the Croatian sculptor Ivan Meštrović (1930s). Photo: © Ivan Meštrović. With kind permission of the National Museum of Belgrade

the Ottomans. Nevertheless, for most of their history the Montenegrins have also considered themselves Serbs – in the same way as, say, Yorkshire people are also English. In the nineteenth century, as Ottoman power was declining, the Serbs embarked on a process of liberation from Ottoman rule. This took the form of two uprisings, in 1804 and 1813. By 1847, when Njegoš published his long poem *The Mountain Wreath,* much of central Serbia was in effect an independent principality.

The poem is set in the eighteenth century and deals with the problem of Montenegrin converts to Islam who are perceived as undermining the integrity and potentially the survival of Montenegro. It is a useful text for us in the context of national identity and the management of memory, for two main reasons. First, it illustrates key facets of the Montenegrin way of life, traditions and values, contrasting them always with those of 'others' – the **Turks** on the one hand, and the Venetians on the other. The Turks are presented as cruel and self-indulgent and the Venetians as corrupt. The Montengrins, by contrast, are courageous, resilient,

It is important in this context to bear in mind that the term 'Turk' was widely used in the Yugoslav lands to designate any Muslim.

compassionate, ever ready to sacrifice their own lives for a higher cause. In other words, the poem sets out to convince the reader that the Montenegrin way of life is intrinsically worth preserving. This is one crucial aspect of a sense of national identity: each nation is in its own eyes superior to others, particularly those which are its immediate neighbours.

Secondly, in this poem the management of memory is achieved through the words of a chorus (similar to those in classical Greek plays), reminding the Montenegrins of their history and their historical obligation to preserve the values of Kosovo and the heroes who died to defend them.

The second reading is an extract from this poem, at the point where the Chorus is reprimanding the Montenegrins for not honouring the memory of the battle of Kosovo and for allowing the Serbian nation to be weakened by dissension and by conversion to Islam.

In many contexts, Montenegrins are considered a branch of the whole Serbian nation, so the term 'Serbs' in the first line here includes the Montenegrins.

Miloš Obilić was the hero who slew the Turkish sultan at the battle of Kosovo in 1389.

The Mountain Wreath

Our God hath pour'd His wrath upon the **Serbs**!
A seven-headed monster He sent forth
To plague and extirpate the Serbian Name,
Be they betrayers or be they betray'd.
On falling ruins of a realm heroic
Did **Miloš** shine with firm and constant justice;
Crownèd be too, with an undying glory,
Those pòbratims [brothers in blood] who steadfast were to Miloš;
Not less the lovely Jugovitch bouquet!

So passed the Serbian Cap and Name away:
Warrior lions gave place to ploughmen,
While selfish poltroons took Mohammed's creed, –
Their Serbian milk shall ever bring them plague!

All those who 'scaped from death by Moslem sword,
All those who still held true to Christian faith,
Who with abhorrence thought of bonds and chains,
All such as these took flight to mountain grey,
To wane and perish and pour out their blood;
'Mid mountains, trust and heritage to guard,
Our sacred Freedom and our glorious Name.

Thereto our leaders Providence hath called,
Our Serbian Youth as radiant as the stars,
The children of these mountains wild,
In bloody combats falling day by day,
For sake of Honour, Faith, and Freedom dear;

A *gouslar* (*gusle*) was a player of the single-stringed lute used to accompany the chanting of epic songs.

Yet all our tears are wiped away
When skilful **gouslar** comes with rousing lay.
Oh, let our losses all be light,
If the hard mountains of our land
Become the grave of Moslem might!
Lo! what the cause, that long time now,
Our homeland hills have silent grown,
No longer echoing to heroic shout?
Our idling armour is consum'd by rust,
And without chieftains is our country left,
Our hillsides reek with tramp of Moslem feet. –
In the same fold behold both wolves and sheep!
United now the Turk with Montenegrin,
The hodja [Muslim priest] calls upon Cetinje's plain;
The artful Turk hath run the lion to cage;
The Montenegrin Name is underground,
The Cross **with fingers three** is no more found!

(Nyegosh, 1930, pp. 85–8)

The Orthodox sign of the cross is made across the body with three fingers.

Figure 9.3 Illustration for the satirical story by the Serbian writer, Radoje Domanović, 'Marko the Prince once again among us'. The story describes the disastrous consequences of Marko's visit to Serbia at the beginning of the twentieth century after he had grown tired of hearing his countrymen's pleas for his return. Etching: by kind permission of Radoje Domanović, *Satire*, Zagreb, 1966

EXERCISE _____

Consider the different elements of the Chorus's reprimand to the Montenegrins.

DISCUSSION _____

What we see here is the power of the appeal to an individual's sense of duty towards his or her nation. We should remember that this appeal is irrational: it has no need of facts. It depends on a mythic interpretation of the nation's history. As such, it can be exploited by politicians to excite popular passions, particularly in times of crisis or war. Therefore it is also dangerous. During the war in Bosnia, Serbian soldiers were given copies of *The Mountain Wreath* to help stiffen their resolve to perform deeds of valour in the name of the memory of Kosovo. They were encouraged by this poem to think in terms of late twentieth-century Bosnian Muslims as synonymous with the despised and hated Turks.

_____

The heritage of the First World War in the Yugoslav lands

I have already mentioned the stories told about Serbian soldiers in the First World War, who claimed that they were led into battle by Marko the Prince, one of the great traditional heroes of the Kosovo songs. There is little doubt that the model of self-sacrificing courage which the songs fostered helped the Serbs to fight the superior Habsburg forces and even to claim a temporary victory over them in 1914. Men who survived the subsequent retreat of the Serbian army through Albania to the coast told of the troops sitting round camp fires at the end of the day's battle or march, listening to a singer playing the traditional one-stringed instrument known as the *gusle* and chanting tales of epic heroism to motivate the men to face the demands of the following day.

The First World War led to the creation of the first Yugoslav state. That conflict brought about the definitive collapse of both the Habsburg and the Ottoman empires. The Serbs could legitimately claim a significant role in this process: it was the Bosnian Serb terrorist group *Mlada Bosna* (Young Bosnia), responsible for the assassination of the Austrian crown prince, Archduke Franz Ferdinand, in Sarajevo on 28 June 1914 (the anniversary of the battle of Kosovo), that provided the final spark for the outbreak of hostilities. Serbia's role in the war was widely seen in Europe as heroic: it was regarded as a valiant little country taking on the might of the great Habsburg empire and resisting for several months against the odds of a superior force and the devastating effects of typhus

Figure 9.4 The retreat of the Serbian army in the First World War over Mount Čakor in Montenegro towards Albania and the sea. Photo: *Trnovit Put Srbije 1914–18*, Beogradski Izdavačko-Grafički Zavod, Belgrade, 1974

which claimed the lives of more than 70,000 people. During the war many young British women were moved by the news to volunteer to serve in Serbia as nurses, several themselves succumbing to the disease.

Despite the enormous cost of the war to Serbia – 1,500,000 people lost in battle, to typhus and through the retreat in winter through the mountains of Albania – the country emerged victorious, in the sense that it was on the winning side, together with its British and French allies. In the course of the war, talks were held among the Allied powers to discuss the future of Europe after the great imperial structure of the Austro-Hungarian (Habsburg) empire had been eliminated. New countries were envisaged, including Czechoslovakia and Yugoslavia, to be known initially as 'The Kingdom of the Serbs, Croats and Slovenes'.

It is necessary at this point to consider briefly the position of the other two components of this new kingdom: the Slovenes and the Croats.

The Slovenes had constituted a small but distinct group in the Habsburg lands, identified by their language, adjoining the territories inhabited by Croats. After a century of independence in the early Middle Ages, the Slovene lands were incorporated into the Frankish state and from then until 1918 the Slovenes lived in the various state formations that succeeded that state in central Europe. The language and cultural traditions of the Slovenes were preserved all this time by the largely peasant population. Slovene Protestant reformers wrote the first books in the Slovene language in the mid sixteenth century;

the first translation of the Bible into Slovene was made in 1584. The Enlightenment gave a new stimulus to Slovene national self-awareness, and by the end of the eighteenth century there was a network of schools using Slovene as the language of instruction. The European Romantic movement fostered the national self-awareness of marginal cultures, and during the nineteenth century the Slovenes joined in political activities with other minority Slav groups within the Habsburg monarchy.

The Croats, who share a common language with the Serbs and the inhabitants of Bosnia-Herzegovina, have had a complex history. Having developed a relatively extensive and prosperous medieval state, in 1102 they were obliged to enter into an alliance with the Kingdom of Hungary, under the 'Joint Crown of St Stephen'. This was inevitably an unequal partnership: until the Ottoman forces' invasion of the Hungarian lands in 1526, and after their retreat in the late seventeenth century, the Hungarian part of the joint kingdom was clearly the stronger element. The Ottomans were driven out of Hungary by the Habsburgs, who then incorporated this territory into their empire while allowing the Hungarians a certain degree of autonomy in dealing with their own internal affairs.

As Habsburg power began to wane in the early nineteenth century, particularly under pressure from Napoleon, so the Hungarians began to foster ambitions of greater independence. In this jostling for power, the marginal groups began to feel exposed – notably the Slovaks (a large minority in Hungary) and the Croats. By the beginning of the nineteenth century the lands inhabited by Croats were divided into three separate administrations. First, a broad swath of land from the coast and north of the Sava river, which then formed the northern border of the Ottoman lands, was known as the Military Frontier and administered by the government in Vienna. Secondly, what had been Venetian Dalmatia and later formed part of Napoleon's 'Illyrian provinces' was also administered directly from Vienna, but separately from the Military Frontier. Finally a small section of central Croatia, around Zagreb, continued to form part of the Hungarian crown lands, but with a certain degree of autonomy in internal affairs and its own assembly (parliament), answerable to the Joint Hungarian–Croatian Assembly.

During the first half of the nineteenth century, as a response to Hungarian efforts towards greater independence from Austria, a small group of Croatian intellectuals formed the so-called Illyrian Movement and sought the unification of all the lands inhabited by Croats. Since the Croats were divided not only administratively but also by three distinct dialects, the first step in this process involved establishing a standard language. After much discussion, the dialect selected was the most widespread one, which was also shared by the Croats' neighbours in the territories of Bosnia, Serbia and Montenegro. Under a joint agreement signed in Vienna in 1850, this language came to be known as 'Serbo-Croat'. In the second half of the nineteenth century many Croats were convinced that their best prospect for greater autonomy lay in some kind of union with their south Slav neighbours, particularly with their fellow Serbo-Croat speakers.

The brief account given here is necessary in order to show that the three components of the new kingdom of Serbs, Croats and Slovenes formed after the First World War became 'partners' under very different conditions. In the simplest terms, the Slovenes and Croats had been citizens of the Habsburg empire which had lost the war. Many of their young men had been obliged to fight in the Habsburg army. The Serbs, on the other hand, had fought against the Habsburgs and emerged from the war on the winning side. In fact there had also been a large community of Serbs in southern Hungary, to which country they had emigrated from Ottoman-administered Serbia. The young men of this community were also conscripted into the Habsburg army, which placed them on the opposite side to their fellow countrymen. We have seen that it was possible for the Serbs in the nineteenth century to make a story of national pride and self-sacrifice out of their defeat at Kosovo by the Ottoman forces. A similar process of mythic interpretation of national history enabled them to see themselves as the liberators of their Slovene and Croat neighbours, since they (the Serbs) were involved in the destruction of the Habsburg empire. They had after all fought for and attained the status of an independent kingdom in the course of the nineteenth century. In addition, they had fought in two Balkan wars (in 1912 and 1913) and again emerged on the winning side. It was thus natural that many Serbs at this time would have seen themselves as the freedom-loving centre of the new state and, inevitably, to some degree, as inherently superior to their new fellow citizens.

At the same time, it is equally understandable that the Croats and Slovenes at this point would have had their own interpretation of their national history in relation to that of the Serbs. Theirs was a story which offered them a degree of self-satisfaction and pride, even if it had not been forged through the memory of military prowess and courage in war. Notably, they had a shared residual memory of the split between the eastern and western churches, between Byzantium and Rome, which was later overlain by the division between Christian western Europe and the Ottoman Muslim Balkans. In the Croatian national myth, the concepts of 'Byzantium' and 'Balkan' are synonymous with notions such as 'primitive, backward, barbaric' by comparison with the civilized west. For Croats who subscribed to this myth, the Balkans began at the eastern borders of their land. And within such a view, it was only natural that their disadvantaged cohorts to the east and south should look to Zagreb as the true European centre of the new state.

EXERCISE

Consider the following questions.

1   Which components of the Serbian national myth were likely to give Serbs a sense of superiority in the new kingdom of Serbs, Croats and Slovenes?

2   How was it possible for Croats and Slovenes in turn to see themselves as inherently superior?

3   What do you imagine would have been the consequences for the new state of these two different types of self-perception?

The Yugoslav lands, 1918–90

Legacy of the First World War

The first years of the new kingdom of the Serbs, Croats and Slovenes were characterized by two contradictory pressures: one tending towards unification and the other tending towards decentralization. The complexities of trying to forge a unified state out of the disparate administrative systems the new country inherited would have been taxing for the most united and experienced government, let alone for one riven from the outset by division. And even if the will to make a success of the new state had existed at a political level, it would have taken a long time to instil a real sense of belonging to it in the ordinary population. As one writer has put it,

> It may be that the sense of Yugoslav unity had some meaning to the middle-class professional politicians, lawyers, writers, artists and teachers who promoted the idea of a South Slav state, but it had not penetrated deeply into the consciousness of the mass of the peasantry, who constituted over 80 per cent of the population. To them government was a remote and alien force which descended upon them from time to time, usually with unpleasant consequences. Tax collectors came to take away some of their hard-earned money; recruiting officers came to conscript their sons to fight in distant wars; or policemen came to harass them for breaches of laws which

they had no part in making. Their loyalties were first of all to their own kinsfolk, who belonged to the extended family which was the basis of the social organisation throughout the Balkans ... Religion, local customs and traditions were part of the heritage which provided bonds of cultural identity far stronger than the abstract concept of a nation.

(Singleton, 1985, pp. 132–3)

These circumstances meant that individual politicians disaffected with the common project of a unified state could always rely on the support of their local populations. It is useful to bear this in mind when considering the ultimate fragmentation of the country: even fifty years of communist rule could have only a superficial effect on this underlying situation.

Meanwhile, political structures had to be put in place. The first constitution was approved by the assembly, or parliament, on the Serbian national day, 28 June 1921, and is therefore known as the *Vidovdan* (St Vitus's Day) constitution. You are beginning to be familiar with the symbolic significance of this date! In this case it meant an obvious strengthening of the position of the Serbs, as the constitution was based on the 1903 Serbian constitution, adapted to the needs of the larger state. For the non-Serb population this must have seemed like the brazen embodiment of 'Greater Serbia', particularly given the associations of the date when the constitution was adopted.

Nevertheless, for the first ten years of the country's life there was a genuine attempt to operate a parliamentary democracy based on west European models. But the strains were too great, and by June 1928 political life had reached breaking point: deputies in the assembly with no experience of reasoned deliberations or controlled arguments exchanged insults and abuse, and eventually, during a debate on government corruption, a Montenegrin deputy produced a revolver and shot several members of the opposition, including the popular leader of the Croatian Peasants' party, Stjepan Radić. Three politicians were killed on the spot, and Radić died of his wounds six weeks later. The following January, King Aleksandar Karadjordjević abolished the *Vidovdan* constitution and imposed a royal dictatorship, renaming his country Yugoslavia. This action led directly to the foundation of a group known as the **Ustasha** Croat Revolutionary Movement under the leadership of Ante Pavelić.

Ustasha means 'insurgent'. (*Ustashe* is the plural form of the word.)

The group was dedicated to the creation of an independent Croatia. In 1934 the Ustashe assassinated King Aleksandar in Marseilles while he was on a state visit to France. The heir to the throne, Peter, was only 10 years old, so his cousin Prince Paul, an Oxford graduate, became regent. He set about trying to reconcile the Croats to the idea of Yugoslavia, and indeed made some headway in this during the brief spell before the outbreak of the Second World War. By the late 1930s, however, Prince Paul found himself forced by economic necessity to enter into ever closer relations with Germany.

The Second World War

The processing of memories of the Second World War in Yugoslavia offers a particularly vivid instance of the way in which wars can be harnessed to promote particular political projects. The story of this conflict in the Yugoslav lands has two distinct aspects: on the one hand it may be told as a tale of exceptional self-sacrifice and courage; on the other it brought appalling brutality and suffering, inflicted not only by the occupying German and Italian forces but also by one group of Yugoslavs against another. The far from glorious fact about the Second World War in Yugoslavia is that of the 1.7 million people who died as a result of it, 1 million were killed by their fellow citizens rather than by their external enemies.

Why did this happen?

Chetnik means member of a group or band, a *četa*.

We have seen that the nationalist tensions developing in Croatia between the two world wars had resulted in the emergence of the Ustashe movement. In Serbia groups loyal to the king and the Serbian Orthodox church also formed, calling themselves '**Chetniks**'. Both these groups, at different times in the war and for different reasons, were involved in resisting the third and ultimately successful grouping, that of the communist partisans. We should look at each of these three groups in turn in order to understand how this situation came about.

The Second World War reached Yugoslavia when, in March 1941, Hitler demanded that his troops be granted free passage through the country in order to attack Greece. When the Yugoslav government capitulated to this demand, there were large-scale demonstrations in favour of resistance in many of the country's main cities. A coup was carried out in Belgrade and young King Peter was declared of age. Prince Paul, who was in Greece at the time, fled into exile, settling eventually in London – where Peter followed him a month later, when Belgrade fell to Hitler's advancing troops. Units of the Royal Yugoslav Army then took to the hills and forests, under the command of Colonel Draža Mihailović, and formed armed insurgent bands known as Chetniks. The whole country was occupied by Axis forces: the Germans established themselves throughout the central and eastern areas, with a quisling government installed in Belgrade, while the Italians occupied the south and west. Slovenia and Croatia, including Bosnia-Herzegovina, were annexed to Germany as puppet states. With terrible irony, Croatian aspirations to statehood were

The NDH represented the realization of the 'thousand-year dream of Croatian statehood', as formulated by President Franjo Tudjman (1922–2000), first president of Croatia, when its independence from the rest of Yugoslavia was declared in 1990.

realized with the declaration of the fascist 'Independent State of Croatia' (*Nezavisna Država Hrvatske*, or **NDH**).

We have seen something of the way that grievances and resentment had been able to grow among certain groups in Croatia in the period between the two world wars. Many of these disaffected people now felt that the new independent state was the solution to their aspirations. The prevailing fascist ideology, which promoted the idea of exterminating 'lesser breeds' of people – notably Jews and Gypsies – also encouraged extremists to seek vengeance for these accumulated grievances by persecuting the Serbs living in Croatian territory, including Bosnia-Herzegovina where there was a substantial Serbian population. In their turn, the armed Chetniks were bound to respond in kind, in order to protect their fellow Serbs.

To both of these groups, the communist partisans represented a serious threat. For those Croats who saw their future in an independent state of Croatia, the fact that the partisans comprised a pan-Yugoslav movement was anathema. And of course the partisans' communist ideology was very far removed from the fascist beliefs of such people. Meanwhile the Chetniks, with their allegiance to the monarchy and traditional Orthodox faith, also found these godless communists utterly unacceptable. Extremists in both these groups therefore seized every opportunity to attack the partisans and remove them from the scene.

Figure 9.5 Partisan army crossing a river. National Library of Serbia

The partisans, however, were the most effective force fighting against the German and Italian occupiers. Their guerrilla tactics pinned down large numbers of German troops for a considerable length of time. They were rewarded with Allied support: weapons, supplies and personnel were airlifted or parachuted into the territory which they began steadily to reclaim.

EXERCISE

Consider the following questions.

1   What were the main Croatian grievances against the Serbs?

2   What were the main Serbian grievances against the Croats?

3   Why were the partisans unpopular with both groups?

The partisan movement as the foundation myth of the second Yugoslavia

When the communist partisans, with the support of the Soviet Red Army, took over the government in 1945, following the final defeat of the Axis powers, they immediately set about consolidating their position. This was done in two main ways. The first involved the removal of potential opponents, either through open trials in which individuals were accused of collaboration with the enemy, condemned and executed, or through less visible methods, with the same outcome. Fearing such reprisals, large numbers of people fled – Ustashe and Chetnik supporters and also representatives of the now despised middle class, the 'bourgeoisie'. Many of these people settled abroad in like-minded groups, particularly in the United States, Canada, Australia and South America. There they kept alive their own versions of reality, passing on their memories of suffering and strife to their descendants.

Having successfully eliminated much of the opposition to its rule and silenced the rest, the second way for the new communist government to consolidate its power was through positive action. Thus it set about harnessing cultural activities – painting, monuments, film, literature – to a specific memory of the war. In this story, the partisans were heroes of infinite courage, sacrificing their lives in deeds of incredible valour. Much of the portrayal of the partisans, particularly in the immediate postwar years, had the crude black-and-white quality of the approved Soviet 'socialist realist' style or the most primitive kind of 'spaghetti westerns'. Other manifestations were subtler, and had the compelling power of all myths which aim to ennoble the memory of conflict by investing it with solemn dignity. The best painters and sculptors were enlisted to honour the memory of the dead and inspire the population to a new pride in their nation.

In this way the partisan movement was gradually moulded to become the foundation myth, legitimating the power of the new communist Yugoslavia. The bourgeois past was declared forgotten and with it all the years of conflict between its constituent peoples. The new principle governing all aspects of public life was 'brotherhood and unity'. Roads were built (often by international volunteer brigades), railways restored, new institutions founded, festivals held – all in the name of this principle.

One of the cruder aspects of communist practice in Soviet-dominated eastern Europe in the twentieth century was the tendency for party loyalists to believe that they could alter reality through language: a statement was 'true' simply if it was made with the authority of the prevailing dogma. As a result, public life was dominated by a kind of Orwellian 'New-speak'. But even if the authorities were perhaps hypnotized by their own words, it was always possible for the ordinary citizen to perceive the discrepancy between accounts of the 'socialist paradise' and day-to-day reality – and yet to be powerless to affect official versions of the 'truth'.

Discrepancies were particularly blatant between the official Yugoslav version of the story of the Second World War and individual memories of its reality. The new government sought to play down the extent of the conflict between the different nations which were now, overnight, to accept the new ideology of unity. On the surface, this may have appeared to succeed. New generations, nourished through their school textbooks, and through film, television and fictional tales of the partisans and their victorious struggle, in large part accepted what they were told. And the Yugoslav project was successful in many ways. Moreover, the break with Stalin in 1956 obliged the government to forge an independent path through the invention of the grouping, which Yugoslavia headed, of 'non-aligned' countries outside the Cold War power blocs of the United States and the Soviet Union. The regime also devised a system of 'workers' self-management' which had some attractive features for many ordinary people and was certainly complex enough to keep the majority of the population occupied in trying to work it out in practice in the reality of their individual workplaces.

But naturally the older people who had lived through the Second World War could not forget what had happened. A great many of them had personal stories of tragedy and suffering which no amount of ideological wishful thinking could erase.

EXERCISE

What do you think were the potential areas of friction in the second Yugoslavia that might have caused problems in future times of conflict?

The Yugoslav wars of the 1990s

Disintegration of the Socialist Federal Republic of Yugoslavia

The previous two sections were intended to explain some of the inherent tensions in the complex state of Yugoslavia. These should not be seen as causes of the wars of the 1990s, but rather as potential areas of friction which might have been exacerbated at any time of conflict.

There are many interpretations of the reasons for the collapse of Yugoslavia. Among them are undoubtedly economic decline after years of living beyond the country's means. Yugoslavia's apparent economic success in the immediate postwar years owed a great deal to extensive foreign loans, and by the 1970s the extent of the country's debt was having crippling effects. Indeed the economies of the whole of eastern Europe were in deep trouble.

Politically, too, problems were steadily building up, The necessary process of decentralization, which gave increasing powers to the republics, was bound to result in rivalry. This might not have been a major issue in a more prosperous country. But the gap between the richest republic of Slovenia, whose priorities were good roads and other means of commercial communication with the rest of Europe, and the poorest regions of Macedonia or the autonomous region of Kosovo in Serbia was unbridgeable and inevitably destabilizing.

Josip Broz, or Marshal Tito (1892–1980), leader of the partisans, formed the country's first government and ruled as president of the Socialist Federal Republic of Yugoslavia, 1945–80.

Much has been made of **President Tito**'s ability to hold the country together by insisting on the slogan of 'brotherhood and unity' and ignoring national tensions. However, Tito was himself responsible for establishing a system of parliamentary representation based on the republics, which meant that allegiance to individual republics was built into the fabric of political life. This was the result of a deliberate attempt to go some way towards satisfying the aspirations of the republics for a measure of control over their own affairs. Combined with the restrictions of a one-party system, this made for an inherently fragile central structure.

When Tito died in 1980 there was an obvious power vacuum, exacerbated by the general decline of the whole communist project throughout eastern Europe. The only mechanism available to aspiring politicians was the appeal to national feeling among the populations of the individual republics. The elaborate system of the collective presidency (with one president for each of the republics and the position of head of state rotating between them), set up to deal with the unanswerable question of the succession to Tito, was hardly viable as a long-term solution. And when the communist system throughout the Soviet bloc collapsed following the dismantling of the Berlin Wall in 1989, the most obvious way for the power vacuum in Yugoslavia to be filled was by appeal to the nationalist emotions of the republican populations. Among the politically uneducated broad mass of the people, alternative, more sophisticated kinds of solution, based on collaboration in a genuine market economy (which many committed Yugoslavs favoured), simply did not have a chance.

Slobodan Milošević (b. 1941), was president of Serbia, and then of Yugoslavia (1986–2000). At the time of writing he was held by the International War Crimes Tribunal at The Hague, charged with genocide and crimes against humanity.

As a shrewd politician, **Slobodan Milošević** had foreseen this situation and began to use it to his advantage from as early as 1987. On 28 June 1989 he held a rally to mark the 600th anniversary of the battle of Kosovo on the very field where the contest had been fought. The compelling appeal of this symbolic act for vast numbers of ordinary Serbs may easily be imagined. By the time Milošević embarked seriously on his bid for power following this event, he could be certain of very substantial support among Serbian voters.

Similarly, in Croatia the collapse of communism opened the way for an appeal to the Croatian people in the name of their long frustrated aspirations to autonomy. Franjo Tudjman made his bid for power on the basis of the same kind of crude nationalist emotions that Milošević had reached out to, touching a similar nerve of wounded national pride. Indeed it appears that the two men had agreed a plan to divide between them the central part of Yugoslavia, the republic of Bosnia-Herzegovina: this seems to have been the substance of their meeting in Tito's former hunting lodge at Karadjordjevo in the spring of 1991 (their discussions there have been widely reported; see, for example, Bennett, 1995, pp. 146–7).

In order to explain the rationale behind this agreement, we need to consider the geography of ethnic distribution throughout Yugoslavia. The map reproduced as Figure 9.6 shows that there were large concentrations of Orthodox Serbs who had lived for hundreds of years in parts of Croatia and Bosnia. The division of Yugoslavia proposed by Milošević would have gone a long way towards achieving the long-standing nationalist ambition of having 'all Serbs in one state'. Under this plan Tudjman would have taken the southern half

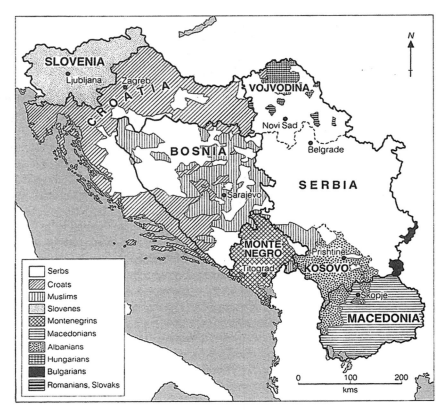

Figure 9.6 National and ethnic distribution in Yugoslavia before the outbreak of war, 1992. Source: Thompson, 1992, p. 97

of Bosnia and all of Herzegovina. Interestingly, at this stage of the negotiations he seems to have been prepared to concede some Croatian land to Serbia for the purposes of preserving peace.

Meanwhile, the whole of the joint presidency met repeatedly in an attempt to devise an equitable future for the Yugoslav republics that would satisfy all parties. Slovenia and Croatia favoured a loose confederation, but in the end what may be interpreted as obstructionism on the part of Milošević drove these two republics to declare unilateral independence. This was allowed for in principle in the constitution, and in a different political climate might have had quite different consequences. As it was, Milošević and the Yugoslav People's Army, which he controlled, were ready for armed conflict to impose their will on their former partners in the federation.

Figure 9.7 Cartoon by the Belgrade cartoonist Corax, showing Serbian President Slobodan Milošević and Croatian President Franjo Tudjman strangling Alija Izetbegović, president of Bosnia Herzegovina. Cartoon: Corax

At this point, it should be emphasized that any attempt to write an account of the Yugoslav wars of the 1990s offers a vivid illustration of the problems involved in writing historical narrative and highlights questions of choice of perspective, of starting point, of cause and effect – of every aspect of the construction of a narrative, in other words. A simple glance at the titles of some of the large numbers of books written on the subject is enough to give an idea of the range of possible interpretations: *A Witness to Genocide* (Gutman, 1993) and *Genocide in Bosnia* (Cigar, 1995), for example, may be contrasted with titles such as *Yugoslavian Inferno: Ethnoreligious Warfare in the Balkans* (Mojzes, 1994) and *Civil War in Bosnia* (O'Ballance, 1995). The main division is between those writers who speak of the conflict as 'civil war', implying equal responsibility for the wars and atrocities among all parties, and those who talk of 'Serbian aggression' and genocide against Muslims.

It is not my intention here to attempt to write yet another account of the wars, which would necessarily entail adopting a point of view. Rather, I want to look at some of the ways in which memories of conflict and cultural assumptions based on those memories have been mobilized.

Memory as an instrument of division: manipulation of the media

As early as the late 1960s, dissatisfaction with the centralist policies of Belgrade began to be manifested in cultural life. This was particularly evident in Croatia, where attempts to introduce new political ideas were accompanied by a new emphasis on a distinct Croatian culture. This initiative, known as the 'Croatian spring', was decisively crushed by Tito in 1971. A recent study (Wachtel, 1998) describes this period of Yugoslav history as one in which the 'brotherhood' of the familiar slogan 'brotherhood and unity' was emphasized, at the expense of the 'unity' which had dominated cultural life for the first twenty years of the existence of the second Yugoslavia. Wachtel argues that cultural trends were in fact of primary importance in the steady disintegration of the country. This may be an overstatement, but it is at least clear that political and cultural tendencies were moving in the same direction: towards greater autonomy for the republics. By the late 1980s the state-owned media in both Serbia and Croatia had joined wholeheartedly in the process of widening and deepening the gulf between the country's constituent peoples – ultimately, preparing the population for war.

The next reading is an extract from the introduction to an edited collection that offers a painstaking analysis of Serbian and Croatian television and the two daily papers with the widest circulation, *Politika* (in Serbia) and *Vjesnik* (in Croatia). The data were gathered between 1992 and 1994, and the book was published in 2000.

UNDERSTANDING AND JUDGING

There is ample material used in the analyses of fourteen authors working under the same research project whose papers are collected in this book. The analyses encompass the production of Serbian and Croatian TV, as well as newspapers with the largest circulation (*Vjesnik* and *Politika*). It is established that on both sides there are the same frameworks of propaganda, repeating: 'we' are the victims, 'they' are the culprits; there is no way to save 'ourselves' other than by annihilating and vanquishing 'them'; it is 'us' who have been sanctified, while the 'others' have been satanised. Each of the parties in the conflict aims to homogenise 'itself' from the inside, and to crush and destroy 'others'. Not only is the other 'ethos' signified as the 'enemy', but also the much wider surrounding ('Europe the bitch'), the abominable 'new world order', as well as ghostly 'mondialism'.

Propaganda, as these works of research have also shown, relies primarily on emotions, and not on reason. It yields to the destructive passions of individuals and the masses, inflames and justifies them. Implanting the feeling of victimisation into people contrives to justify revenge. From 'the silence of hatred', it is easy to proceed to 'the speech of hatred'. A collectivist and antagonistic ideology (a 'class' one) is easily substituted by another (a 'national' one). All the knowledge, wisdom and art are contained in the past of an ethos, in myths and legends. The only thing to do is just to remember them and revive them. The institutions of communication and the procedures of the modern age are declared tight clothes that should be ripped off. We must 'return to nature', to the community of 'earth and blood'. The aim is to expand the territory and 'clean it' of 'impure blood', even by destruction never seen before, and even at the cost of terrible casualties. Until the moment the otherwise vague goal, the 'final solution of the national question' is reached, let there be 'permanent fighting'.

The rejection and destruction of institutions and procedures reduces politics to rule, and rule increasingly to sheer force. Power encourages some, while it intimidates others. This is precisely one of the important roles of the media which are transformed into a device for war propaganda – to stop communication and stimulate confrontations. Everything that happens resembles the cruel clashes of wild tribes. Where does such a power of propaganda come from?

Any serious analysis, including the one discussed here, takes us to a link with ideology.

PROPAGANDA AND IDEOLOGY

Terrifying messages of war propaganda and the views of the cruelty accompanying them are enough to produce a media shock. The shock is intensified by the fact that a great number of media operate as if being under the control of an 'invisible hand'. This brings us to the very edge of the beguiling trap: to come to believe that there is an organised plot behind everything (thus, conspiracies are the favourite subject and one of the postulates of the propaganda we would like to comprehend). Of course, there are particular centres of power that bring up a certain form of co-ordination (say, some apparatus of the old regime – first of all, the political police – which have remained almost intact for decades). However, there is a factor that strongly and broadly directs propaganda. This is ideology as a peculiar form of social consciousness.

The emergence of and zest for war propaganda have been most extensively studied on the 'Serbian side of the war'[1], so we may rely on the results of this research in the course of further investigation of the ideology–propaganda relationship.

During the long and permeating crisis of society and the common state, especially after Tito's death, some expected a turn towards democracy, similar to the one in the countries of 'real socialism', while others, the stronger ones, put forward 'the national question' as a priority. All the 'inflammable' ideas about the Serbs being victims of the common state were spread around. The slogan 'the remains of the slaughtered people' clearly called for retaliation or revenge. Confrontations with other nations occurred one after the other, from the Albanians in Kosovo, the Slovenians, and to Croats and Muslims in Bosnia and Herzegovina. The wave of Serbian ethno-nationalism spread over streets and city squares, with the 'antibureaucratic revolution' and the 'happening of the people'. A new leader acquired increasing power on that wave – Slobodan Milošević, the head of the leading party in the old regime (League of Communists) and in the new order (SPS [Socialist party of Serbia]). The new ideology was supported and promoted by the most significant national institutions. The Serbian Orthodox Church, among other things, organised the carrying of the relics of 'Saint Duke Lazar' (as in the Old Testament stories) just moments before the war, from Srem, over Bosnia and Herzegovina, to Kosovo, through the places that would soon be caught up in the fire of the war. The turning away from the New Testament God of love to the cruel Old Testament deity was accompanied by threatening spiritual vibrations. The zest of the new ideology rested, among other things, on secular institutions – on the University and the Serbian Academy of Arts and Sciences. Their authority had been used for years to promote ethno-nationalism. The ruling party – both the League of Communists and the SPS – did not abandon communism, but it used nationalism profusely to enforce its power and gain wider support. Many rising political parties that stayed within the dominant ideological matrix helped the ruling party. The regime had the army as its most important lever. The media, from the old and respectable *Politika*, through the increasingly powerful electronic media, to many of the emerging media, all have their place within that gravitation.

(Skopljanac-Brunner et al., 2000, pp. 10–12)

---

[1] The text collection *Serbian Side of the War: Trauma and Catharsis in the Historical Memory,* Republika, Belgrade, 1996.

EXERCISE _____

What do you think constituted the particular power of the media in Yugoslavia in the build-up to the war?

DISCUSSION _____

The most important instrument at the disposal of the media is language, and the specific 'language of hatred' or 'hate-speak' which vilifies the 'other' as distinguished from the innocent 'we'. The media are exploited by ruling power groups, effectively making communication seem impossible and increasing the likelihood of confrontation.

The media 'of the other side', which includes internal opposition, are vulnerable to interpretation as the instrument of a 'controlling hand', thereby feeding ideas of a conspiracy against 'us'.

The media in the hands of the ruling groups are able to spread the prevailing ideology – in this case, first communist and then ethno-nationalist. In other words, already practised in the propagation of one ideology, it is easy for the media to adapt to the promotion of a new or different one. In this instance, the ideology of ethno-nationalism has the powerful backing of the Serbian Orthodox church as a potent symbol of Serbian identity, and also of newer institutions such as the Serbian Academy of Arts and Sciences. The media may thus be seen as having been instrumental in the process of transferring public allegiance from the symbols of the old (communist) ideology to the new (ethno-nationalist) ideology.

_____

One of the topics that had been taboo during Tito's rule – the extent of internecine strife during the Second World War – was now reopened for discussion. Newspapers and television in Serbia began to raise the spectre of the number of Serbs killed in camps run by the Croatian Ustashe, especially the camp at Jasenovac. The Croatian media, meanwhile, tended to play down the numbers involved, suggesting that they had been exaggerated by the Serbs.

Franjo Tudjman, the future first president of independent Croatia, was a historian who prided himself on his revisionist scholarship. He calculated that no more than 70,000 people of all nationalities had been killed at the Jasenovac camp. This was a fraction of the million or more that Serbian historians were claiming at the time. As one British historian has put it:

> during the many years [Tudjman] brooded in political disgrace, he clung to his new beliefs with the zeal of a convert. In his own mind he came to personify Croatia and

Croat suffering, while the question of war dead evolved into a crusade. Anyone who disagreed with his findings or even anything which appeared to contradict them became to Tudjman part of a conspiracy to make Croatia appear 'odious in the eyes of the world'. As the years went by and Tudjman became increasingly bitter, his views became more extreme, distanced from his original research and tinged with anti-Semitism. In time, Tudjman effectively became an apologist for the NDH, and the concept of an independent Croatian state, if not for the Ustašas, while his estimates of the Jasenovac dead edged conveniently downwards.

(Bennett, 1995, p. 129)

With the victory of Tudjman's party, the HDZ (Croatian Democratic Union), in the elections of 1990, there was a new, blatant emphasis on numerous Croatian cultural symbols, notably the distinctive red and white chequerboard flag. And as soon as the republic declared its independence in 1991, a new currency, the *kuna*, was introduced. Tudjman claimed simply to be restoring the flag and currency of the glorious medieval kingdom of Croatia. Unfortunately, however, both had already become fatefully associated with the fascist 'Independent State of Croatia' during the Second World War and as such were deeply provocative for the Serbs living on Croatian territory.

However much the politicians may have claimed that such symbols were a simple expression of the cultural aspirations of their respective peoples, the effect of their use was to spread fear throughout the population. In many different ways, memories of the terror of the Second World War were deliberately and cynically revived. One simple mechanism was the widespread use of the labels 'Ustasha' and 'Chetnik'. It takes very little to transform fear into hatred and provoke people into taking pre-emptive action in the belief that it is self-defence. The role of the state-run media in this process was crucial.

As Mark Thompson expresses it in his book *Forging War: the Media in Serbia, Croatia and Bosnia,*

The new media language avoided moribund socialist terminology in favour of a language of demagogy and headlong irrationality, of rhetorical questions and exclamations, of destiny and mission: a 'celestial people' confronting its fate; a language of menacing ultimatums, of infinite self-pity, of immense accusations backed by no evidence or investigation; of conspiracy-mongering, paranoia and brazen incitement to violence. It was, in fact, a language of war before war was even conceivable in Yugoslavia.

(Thompson, 1994, p. 53)

Figure 9.8 Cartoon by the Belgrade cartoonist Corax, showing Milošević's wife Mira Marković bringing him coffee in bed and carrying placards promoting his election as president of Yugoslavia. At this stage (1997) the couple was said by many to be living in a fantasy world. Cartoon: Corax

The hysteria of the state-run media was such that within a very short time all attempts to publicize the truth were rendered ineffective. Those who had been hypnotized by government propaganda could see this only as slander against the heroic Serbian (or Croatian) nation which was engaged in a desperate struggle for survival.

The mobilization of culture in conflict

As we have seen, the fundamental nature of the Yugoslav wars is a matter for debate. For some people, they represent the expression of 'ancient ethnic hatreds': forces barely kept under control for centuries which then erupted into inevitable conflict. For others they are wars of religion, with Croatian Catholics pitted against Serbian Orthodox believers and Muslims engaged in a fanatical war with all Christians. For still others, including the writer of this chapter, they are essentially about the crude desire for territory and power.

The expression 'ethnic cleansing' rapidly came to characterize the whole conflict. However we interpret the concept, it is important to try to establish what this notion of 'ethnicity' entails. In the case of the Yugoslav peoples, we should be clear that the majority of the population consists of Slavs, who settled in the Balkan peninsula in the course of the sixth and seventh centuries CE. Later there were influxes of other peoples across the whole territory, with slight regional variations (there were more Italian and Germanic settlers in the northern areas, for example, and a greater concentration of other peoples, including Slovaks, Romanians, Hungarians, Turks, Greeks and Jews, in other parts). In other words, the vast majority of people living in the Yugoslav lands are indistinguishable from one another in terms of their origins. This includes the Yugoslav Muslims, who are in the main the same Slav people who converted to Islam at various stages of the Ottoman occupation. The greatest concentration of these people was in Bosnia-Herzegovina and the neighbouring region of the Sandžak, bordering on Montenegro.

In the Yugoslav context, then, 'ethnicity' denotes religious and cultural allegiance. As we have seen, the initial separation of the territory according to the spheres of influence of the Catholic church of Rome on the one hand and the Orthodox church of Byzantium or Constantinople on the other was then reinforced by the country's division into areas of Habsburg or Ottoman rule. In the case of the Serbs and Croats, the equation of Orthodoxy with Serbian nationality and Catholicism with Croatian nationality was straightforward. The fundamental drive 'legitimating' Serbian territorial ambitions, or the desire to form a 'Greater Serbia', was based on the existence of large groups of Orthodox Serbs outside Serbia itself, as we have seen in the ethnographic map (Figure 9.6). This drive was expressed in the old nineteenth-century formula promoted by Milošević of 'all Serbs in one state'. Similarly, large areas of Bosnia, and particularly Herzegovina, were inhabited by Catholic Croats, giving rise to aspirations for the inclusion of these territories in Croatia, which formed the basis for Tudjman's proposed division of the republic between himself and Milošević.

The situation of the inhabitants of Bosnia-Herzegovina themselves is far more complex. There are Serbs and Croats, particularly among urban dwellers, who see themselves primarily as Bosnian. But there are many more who think of themselves as either Serbs or Croats living in Bosnia, for whom the concept of 'Bosnian' as a nationality has no meaning. For them, the break-up of Yugoslavia was hard to accept because an independent Bosnia-Herzegovina left them effectively cut off from people who shared their faith and, by extension, their nationality. The remaining inhabitants of Bosnia-Herzegovina, who comprised the majority in the area at the outbreak of the war, are Bosnian Muslims, regarding whom it was decreed in 1971 (bizarrely, but understandably in the circumstances) that their allegiance to Islam marked them as a distinct 'nationality'. For these people, there is no alternative to Bosnia: their co-religionists inhabit other countries (Iran, the Arab world and so on) and have been subject to quite different cultural influences.

The last element in this confusing picture is the fact that, at the outbreak of hostilities, the majority of Bosnian Muslims were not necessarily believers, having shared a largely secular culture with their Yugoslav compatriots at least since the Second World War. For them,

Muslim allegiance was primarily a question of tradition and customs. But what clearly distinguished them in the eyes of the Serbs and Croats (both within and outside the territory of Bosnia-Herzegovina) was precisely their Islamic culture. And it does not take much imagination to see that for Christians, in the hysterical circumstances of war, Islam could easily be equated with 'the Turks' – with all the attendant hostility that this term could engender.

The outbreak of conflict was a trigger for the public expression of the frenzy nurtured by the media in the preparation for war. All sides set about distancing themselves from the culture of their neighbours, who had been starkly identified as 'others', as enemies bent on the annihilation of those who did not belong to their respective group. Culture, with all its accumulated 'ethnic' memories, was mobilized in the service of war in a variety of ways.

Destruction of cultural monuments

The most obvious expression of this frenzy was the destruction of cultural monuments. Orthodox churches were destroyed by Catholics and Muslims; Catholic churches by Muslims and the Orthodox; mosques and other Islamic monuments by Christians of both denominations. Three of the most enduring symbols of this vicious destruction are the sixteenth-century mosque, known as **Ferhadija**, in Banja Luka, the **ancient arched bridge** built by the Turks in Mostar and the former National and University Library, the Vijećnica, in Sarajevo, built by the Austrians.

Efforts to lay the foundation stone of a new mosque on the former site of the Ferhadija provoked furious demonstrations by Bosnian Serbs in the spring of 2001.

Both the bridge and the library are in the process of reconstruction at the time of writing (summer 2002).

Figure 9.9 A view of an improvised bridge at the Old Bridge site in Mostar, 23 September 1997. The Old Bridge, made during the Turkish empire over 400 years ago, was destroyed during the Muslim–Croat war in 1994. Photo: Associated Press/Zina H. Efendic

341

Figure 9.10 This famous poster was photographed in the destroyed National and University Library, where concerts were held before the war. The cellist, Vedran Smajlović, is a legendary figure in Sarajevo. He defied all odds by staging open-air concerts in Sarajevo at the height of the conflict. Photo: 'Untitled' by Enis Selimovic, Sarajevo, 1993

Language as a tool of division

One of the primary and enduring ways of creating a sense of difference from the inimical 'other' is through language. Ever since nationalistically inclined Croats had begun to try to resist what they saw as oppressive Serbian centralism and its dominance over all aspects of Yugoslav national life, they had insisted on the differences between their own (Croatian) variant of the shared Serbo-Croat or Croato-Serbian language. With independence, the Croatian government and its sympathizers began systematically to revive obsolete Croatian words and invent new ones, in order to distance themselves as rapidly as possible from their Serbian neighbours and be seen as a legitimate nation-state with its own distinct national language.

Music as propaganda

A particularly important role in generating and fuelling fear and hatred was played by music. We have seen something of the role of the media in this process. Popular music evolved as an especially potent form of hate-speech. There was a long-standing tradition in Yugoslavia of adapting the rhythms and melodies of folk songs to contemporary themes. In the build-up to the outbreak of war, a new form of these newly composed folk songs developed, known as 'turbo-folk'. It became enormously popular in Serbia and a major factor in fostering hatred among the broad mass of the population, but variations on the style flourished in Croatia and Bosnia-Herzegovina as well. As a recent article expresses it: 'Music was used not only as the cultural weapon of choice by all warring parties in Bosnia but also as a fuel for the war machine' (Laušević, 2000 p. 290) The author describes the way in which all the parties to the conflict blasted music at the enemy. The music itself had been 'ethnically cleansed', or given new meaning, in order to symbolize a particular group (whether Serb, Croat or Muslim) and thus send a clear message.

As one review of a cassette of turbo-folk music puts it,

> Get rid of your collection of classical music, stand against the potential disdain of your friends, prove your fearlessness and buy the cassette 'Stop pashas and ustashas'. If this cassette were not there, I am sure (and convinced from my own experience and that of my fellow fighters) that the results of our fighting would be maybe even 30 percent worse, and again I am convinced by experience that nothing would change with all the speeches of our academics, string quartets, Serbian parties and movements and all our 'culture'. These simple melodies, despised by the cynicism of godless intellectuals without soul, are winning this war.

> (Quoted in Laušević, 2000, p. 299)

343

EXERCISE _____

What do you think is the basis of the appeal of this style of music?

DISCUSSION _____

As with the media, discussed above, this kind of music appeals primarily to the emotions. Because it is based on traditional folk songs, the suggestion is that it somehow expresses the 'spirit of the common people' (or nation) whose legendary courage has been celebrated in song throughout the ages. Hence it is possible for Laušević, the reviewer quoted above, to see this kind of music as expressing military prowess and to appeal to the pride of its young listeners and encourage them to go willingly into battle. In other words, this appeal is a modern version of the earlier call to arms in the name of avenging Kosovo, and plays the same role as that of the traditional folk songs in the nineteenth-century uprisings against Ottoman rule and subsequent wars in the twentieth century.

Rape as an instrument of cultural destruction

It may be hard at first sight to see rape as another form of cultural destruction, but there is little doubt that it was used systematically as a weapon of war in the Yugoslav lands. Rape has always been considered an inevitable part of warfare, and even sanctioned as such in various forms: as encouragement for the attackers, reward for the victors or compensation for the vanquished and soldiers returning home from battle. So endemic did it seem in the context of war that it was not internationally recognized as a war crime until the year 2000. During the Yugoslav wars it was used so widely and blatantly to further the policy of ethnic cleansing that it eventually came to international public attention (see Stiglmayer, 1994). There were several aspects to this policy. It was pursued as a device to engender fear and hence drive the unwanted (for the most part Muslim and Croatian women) from their homes; for the satisfaction of the soldiers and to increase their sense of limitless power; as a preliminary to the murder of women, after their menfolk had been removed; as a way of forcing (again mostly Muslim and Croatian) women to give birth to little members of the soldiers' own nationality. Whatever form the rape took, the women concerned became depersonalized, instrumentalized or, as one writer has put it, 'used as post-boxes to send messages to those other men, _the enemy_' (Dubravka Ugrešić [1995] 1999, p. 122).

The manipulation of new memories

The destruction of cultural monuments in former Yugoslavia has been followed with astonishing speed by the establishment of new cultural markers to lay claim to territory acquired in war. The town of Banja Luka in western Bosnia, where the exquisite sixteenth-century Ferhadija mosque was razed to the ground and immediately replaced by a functional twentieth-century car park, has been cleansed of all buildings that could act as a reminder of its past as an Ottoman town close to the westernmost frontier of the empire. Such a denial of history has been a repeated phenomenon in the Balkans, giving successive generations a frequent sense of having to start again from scratch. Other blatant instances of new cultural markers are the enormous, garish white cross that claims for the Catholic church the ancient settlement of Počitelj between Mostar in Herzegovina and the Adriatic coast. This old village winds up a steep hillside; it used to be graced by a fine mosque with a slender minaret and an old Turkish *amam*, or public bath, with distinctive domed roofs. In Mostar itself, where fanatics among the Catholic population on the west bank of the Neretva river are finding it hard to accept the survival of the town as a multicultural community, the foundations of an enormous cathedral have already been laid.

School textbooks of course offer abundant opportunities for the rewriting of national histories. In Bosnia-Herzegovina the problem is glaring: in the Serb-dominated *Republika Srpska* textbooks are imported from Serbia, while in the Croat-dominated areas of the Croat–Muslim federation which makes up the remaining territory they are imported from Croatia.

Until all parties to the wars can sit down together and work out a balanced, shared interpretation of their recent past, the divisions will become steadily entrenched. But there are already encouraging signs that the kind of manipulation of history seen in the Yugoslav lands in the last decade of the twentieth century will become increasingly difficult. In the successor states that were the main parties in the wars non-governmental organizations have taken on the task of monitoring the ways in which textbooks are used to perpetuate the lies that characterized their public life in the years of fanatic nationalist rule. With Tudjman dead and Milošević at last incarcerated in The Hague, the prospects for a reclamation of the truth are looking at least a little brighter.

In Belgrade, in 1999, a huge monument was commissioned by Milošević's wife, Mira Marković. It was to mark the heroic moral victory of the Serbian people over the combined might of all the Nato countries in their bombing campaign of 1999 to end the Serbian persecution of the Albanian population of Kosovo. The tall

Figure 9.11 The monument in Belgrade commissioned by Milošević's wife, Mira Marković, to mark the moral victory of the Serbian people over Nato forces, 1999. Photo: Celia Hawkesworth

white pyramid was topped by a gas-fired 'perpetual' flame. When Milošević was dramatically removed from power in the course of one memorable day in October 2000, the flame went out. It is to be hoped that the monument itself will not be obliterated, along with so much of the complex past of the Yugoslav peoples, but will be allowed to stand as a memorial to the ultimate vanity of all attempts to distort history, to manipulate collective memory for political ends.

Conclusion

This chapter has attempted to explore one instance of the manipulation of the memory of conflict and its role in the formation of national identity. It has included a considerable amount of historical information, as this seemed essential to explain the role of memory in a recent conflict that has often baffled commentators by its complexity and appalling violence.

My insistence on the theme of the Kosovo idea in shaping my narrative may seem to fall into the same trap of the mythic interpretation of history that I have been trying to analyse. But I believe it has been necessary, as it has been woven into the history of the Yugoslav lands at many different levels. One has only to bear in mind that the final impetus towards independence in Slovenia was fuelled in part by popular indignation at repressive Serbian policies in Kosovo in 1989 (see Bennett, 1995, p. 107). In the judgement of many, it was the Nato response to a new wave of repression in Kosovo in 1999 that led eventually to the fall of Slobodan Milošević in October 2000. There is a highly satisfactory symmetry in the fact that it was on the anniversary of the battle of Kosovo (28 June 2001) that Milošević was extradited to face the United Nations International Criminal Tribunal in The Hague on charges of crimes against humanity.

There is no doubt that the traditional songs about Kosovo have added an enormous amount that is positive to Serbian culture. What has proved finally to be misguided is the instrumentalization of the tradition, its deliberate use and consequent distortion for political ends. We should bear in mind, however, that every nation has its own mythic interpretation of its history and every nation manages the memory of conflict in ways that suit those who hold power. This case study offers a particularly vivid instance of a process of which we should all be aware in the context of the states in which we ourselves live.

Appendix

The Kosovo Girl

Like 'The Downfall of the Serbian Empire' this poem was recorded from a blind woman of Grgurevtsi in Srem by Lukijan Mushitski, the abbot of the monastery of Shishatovats, and sent to Vuk Karadzhich in 1817. The poem does not deal with a historical subject, but it contains some elements of great historical accuracy. Such are the gifts which the heroine receives before the battle from her betrothed and his two blood-brothers: 'a tunic embroidered in circles', a gilded ring and a scarf embroidered with gold: not only do these gifts reflect actual customs, but the monograms on the tunic and the gold-embroidered scarf are historically accurate. Even the circular patterns on the tunic are correct; and the most beautiful Serbian rings at the end of the fourteenth century were made not of gold but of silver gilt. This astounding accuracy may be the result of memorisation of particular formulas or of whole runs of lines in particular poems, though a tunic embroidered with circles may have come from a fresco painting.

[Svetozar Koljević]

The Kosovo girl wakes early,
wakes early on a Sunday,
on a Sunday before the bright sun:
she rolls up her white sleeves,
she rolls them back to the white elbows,
she carries white bread on her shoulder,
and in her hands she has jugs of gold,
she has one jug of cold water,
she has one jug of red wine.
She makes her way to Kosovo meadow,
a young girl, to walk the battlefield,
the battlefield of the honoured Prince.
She turns the heroes over in their blood,
and every hero she finds alive
she washes the hero in cold water,
she gives the sacrament of red wine,
she gives him the white bread to eat.
And fortune fell on the hero,
on Pavle Orlovich, the young man
who carried the Prince's battle-standard:
and she discovered him alive,
and his right hand had been cut off,

and his left leg cut off at the knee,
and his supple ribs were in fragments,
his liver showing pale;
she took him from the floods of his blood,
she washed him in the coldness of water,
and she gave the sacrament of red wine,
she gives him the white bread to eat.
And the hero's heart began to dance,
and Pavle Orlovich is speaking:
'Kosovo girl, my darling sister,
what troubles you so terribly,
that you turn over heroes in their blood?
Young girl walking the battlefield,
who are you looking for?
Is it your brother, is it your cousin?
Or is it your old father, God forgive him?'
The Kosovo girl is speaking:
'My darling brother, soldier I do not know,
I am not looking for my family,
it is not my brother, it is not my cousin,
it is not my old father, God forgive him.
But you could know, soldier I do not know,
when Lazar the Lord with his army
took the sacrament together,
at the wonderful church of the Almighty,
with thirty monks for three weeks of days
the Serbian army took the sacrament,
and three dukes at the end, lords of war;
and the first is Milosh the Duke,
and the second is Ivan Kosanchich,
and the third one is Milan Toplitsa.
I was standing there in the gates
when Milosh the Duke walked out,
an honourable hero in this world,
trailing a long sword on the cobbled road,
with a silk handkerchief around his neck,
and capped in silk and feathers set in silver,
and long tunic embroidered in circles.
Then turning where I was and seeing me,
he took his tunic off and gave me it:
"Here, young girl, my tunic with circles,
and you shall remember me by this,
by my tunic and by my name.
Look, my dear, I am on my way to die,
in the battle-camp of the glorious Prince,

and, O my dear, pray to God
I may come home to you safe from my regiment,
and good luck shall come on you also:
and I will take you for my Milan's wife,
for Milan my brother in God,
who named me by God his brother,
by the most high God and by Saint John,
and I will hold the crown at your wedding."
Ivan Kosanchich came after him,
an honourable hero in this world,
trailing a long sword on the cobbled road,
and capped in silk and feathers set in silver,
and a tunic embroidered in circles,
and a handkerchief of silk around his neck,
and a gilded ring on his hand,
he turned where I was and he saw me,
he gave the ring from his own hand:
"Here young girl, my gilded ring,
and you shall remember me by this,
by my ring and by my name.
Look, my dear, I am on my way to die,
in the battle-camp of the glorious Prince,
and, O my dear, pray to God
I may come home to you safe from my regiment,
and good luck shall come on you also:
and I will take you for my Milan's wife,
for Milan my brother in God,
who named me by God his brother,
by the most high God and by Saint John,
and I will lead you in at your wedding."
Milan Toplitsa came after him,
an honourable hero in this world,
trailing a long sword on the cobbled road,
and capped in silk and feathers set in silver,
and a tunic embroidered in circles,
and a handkerchief of silk round his neck,
over his hand a scarf embroidered gold.
He turned where I was and he saw me,
he drew the scarf of gold from his own hand,
he took it from his hand, he gave me it:
"Here, young girl, my gold-embroidered scarf,
and you shall remember me by this,
by my scarf and by my name.
Look, my dear, I am on my way to die,
in the battle-camp of the glorious Prince,

and, O my dear, pray to God
I may come home to you safe from my regiment,
and good luck shall come on you, my dear,
and I will take you for my faithful love."
And the three dukes, the lords of war, went;
now I look for them on the battlefield.'
And Pavle Orlovich is speaking:
'Kosovo girl, my darling sister,
look, my dear, at the battle-lances,
where they are so tall and so dense:
that is where the blood of the heroes bled,
stirrup-iron deep to a high horse,
stirrup-iron deep and girth deep,
and deep as the silk belts on fighting-men.
And that is where those three died.
Go home now to your whitewashed house,
with an unbloody hem, unbloody sleeve.'
And when the young girl heard his words
she dropped tears down on her white face,
she went away to her whitewashed house,
and her white throat lamented:
'Unhappy! Evil luck has come on me.
Unhappy, if I were to grasp a green pine,
even the green pine would wither.'

(*Marko the Prince*, 1984, pp. 21–4)

The Mother of the Jugovichi

Recorded from an unknown singer in Croatia, this song translates the disaster of Kosovo into the drama of a mother's mind. The mother is able to sustain the loss of her husband and her nine sons until the moment when two ravens, birds of bad omen, bring her the hand of her youngest son. Then she breaks the simple formal pattern of survival in a waste-land of sorrow: her heart breaks and so she attains the fate which has been the privilege only of heroes in action.

[Svetozar Koljević]

Kind God, a great wonder!
When the army assembled on Kosovo,
and the nine Jugovichi served in it,
and the tenth one, Jug Bogdan the old,
the mother of the Jugovichi prayed

for God to give her a hawk's eyes
and give her a swan's white wings,
to fly away above flat Kosovo,
to see the nine, the Jugovichi,
and the tenth one, Jug Bogdan the old.
She got her prayer from God,
and God gave her a hawk's eyes
and gave her a swan's white wings.
She flies away to flat Kosovo,
she comes on nine Jugovichi dead,
and on the tenth, on Jug Bogdan the old,
and the nine war-lances over them,
with nine hawks on the nine lances,
nine good horses by the nine lances,
nine wild lions beside the horses.
And the nine good horses whinny,
the nine wild lions roar,
the nine hawks scream.
Then that mother was strong-hearted,
she let fall no tears from her heart,
she took the nine good horses,
she took the nine wild lions,
she took the nine hawks,
and home she went to the whitewashed house.
The wives of her children see her coming,
they walk out to her, she comes close,
the nine widows are lamenting,
the nine orphan children are weeping,
the nine good horses are whinnying,
the nine wild lions are roaring,
and the nine hawks are screaming.
Then that mother was strong-hearted,
she let fall no tears from her heart.
And at midnight in the night
Damjan's grey horse whinnied.
The mother said to Damjan's bride:
'Daughter, Damjan's bride,
why is his grey horse whinnying?
is he hungry for white wheat?
thirsty for the Zvechan water?'
Damjan's bride is speaking:
'Mother, Damjan's mother,
he is not hungry for white wheat,
not thirsty for the Zvechan water;
Danjan taught his horse

to eat his small feed before midnight
and travel the roads after midnight.
The grey horse is pining for his rider,
because he did not carry him home.'
Even then that mother was strong-hearted,
she let fall no tears from her heart.
And in the morning, daybreak of morning,
two black ravens flying,
with bloody wings to the shoulder-bone,
with beaks dripping white foam,
they are carrying a hero's hand
with a gold ring on his hand,
they throw the hand down on his mother's lap.
The mother of the Jugovichi holds it,
she turns it around and over,
she cries out to Damjan's bride:
'My daughter, Damjan's bride,
do you know this hand?'
Damjan's bride speaks:
'Mother, Damjan's mother,
this is our Damjan's hand.
I know the ring, mother.
I brought him the ring at my wedding.'
The mother takes Damjan's hand,
she turns it around and over,
she is whispering to the hand:
'My hand, O green apple,
where did you grow from, where were you ripped off?
You grew on my lap,
you were ripped off on flat Kosovo.'
The mother of the Jugovichi swelled,
she swelled, she broke into pieces,
for her nine Jugovichi,
and for the tenth, for Jug Bogdan the old.

(*Marko the Prince*, 1984, pp. 24–6)

References

Bennett, Christopher (1995) *Yugoslavia's Bloody Collapse: Causes, Course and Consequences*, London, Hurst.

Bracewell, Wendy (1996) 'Women, motherhood, and contemporary Serbian nationalism', *Women's Studies International Forum*, vol. 19, nos 1/2, pp. 25–33.

Cigar, Norman (1995) *Genocide in Bosnia*, College Station, TX, A & M University Press.

Gutman, Roy (1993) *A Witness to Genocide*, Shaftesbury/Rockport, MA, Element.

Laušević, Mirjana (2000) 'Some aspects of music and politics in Bosnia', in Joel Halpern and David Kideckel (eds), *Neighbors at War: Anthropological Perspectives on Yugoslav Ethnicity, Culture and History*, Pittsburgh, PA, University of Pennsylvania Press.

Marko the Prince: Serbo-Croat Heroic Songs (1984) transl. Anne Pennington and Peter Levi, London, Duckworth.

Mojzes, Paul (1994) *Yugoslavian Inferno: Ethnoreligious Warfare in the Balkans*, New York, Continuum.

Nyegosh, Petar Petrovich (1930) *The Mountain Wreath*, transl. James W. Wiles, intro. Vladeta Popović, London, Allen & Unwin.

O'Ballance, Edgar (1995) *Civil War in Bosnia, 1992–94*, Basingstoke, Macmillan.

Singleton, Fred (1985) *A Short History of the Yugoslav Peoples*, Cambridge, Cambridge University Press.

Skopljanac-Brunner, Nena et al. (eds) (2000) *Media and War*, Zagreb, Centre for Transition and Civil Society Research.

Stiglmayer, Alexandra (ed.) (1994) *Mass Rape: the War against Women in Bosnia-Herzegovina*, Lincoln, NE/London, University of Nebraska Press.

Thompson, Mark (1992) *A Paper House: the Ending of Yugoslavia*, London, Hutchinson Radius.

Thompson, Mark (1994) *Forging War: the Media in Serbia, Croatia and Bosnia-Herzegovina*, London, Article 19.

Ugrešić, Dubravka [1995] (1999) *The Culture of Lies: Antipolitical Essays*, transl. Celia Hawkesworth, London, Phoenix House.

Wachtel, Andrew Baruch (1998) *Making a Nation, Breaking a Nation: Literature and Cultural Politics in Yugoslavia*, Stanford, CA, Stanford University Press.

Acknowledgements

Grateful acknowledgement is made to the following sources for permission to reproduce material in this book:

Chapter 1

Lawson, D. (1990) 'Saying the unsayable about the Germans', *The Spectator*, 14 July 1990. *The Spectator* (1828) Ltd.

Tixhon, A. (1995) 'Thèse annexe', 'Le Souvenir des massacres du 23 Août 1914'. Université catholique de Louvain.

Chapter 2

Lersch, H. (1918) 'Der Kriegsinvalide'. *Deutschland. Gesänge von Volk und Vaterland*. Eugen Diederichs Verlag.

Bridgewater, P. (1985) 'Battlefield' and 'The war invalid', *The German Poets of the First World War*. Croom Helm Ltd.

Chapter 3

Celan, P. (1952 and 1955) 'Todesfuge', *Mohn und Gedachtnis* and *Von Schwelle zu Schwelle*, copyright © Deutsche Verlags-Anstalt GmbH, Stuttgart, 1952 and 1955. In transl. 'Death fugue', copyright © Michael Hamburger, 1972, 1980, 1998, 1995. Reproduced by permission of Anvil Press Poetry Ltd.

Schlink, B., *The Reader*, translation copyright © 1997 by Carol Brown Janeway. Used by permission of Pantheon Books, a division of Random House, Inc.

Chapter 4

Tippett, M. (2003) *A Child of Our Time*. Schott and Co. Ltd.

Buketoff, I. (1970–2) 'Parts 1–V: Transliterations and English translation', *Babi Yar*. RCA Records, Nashville. RCA Red Seal and Victor Group.

Chapter 5

Combs, R. (1982) 'Boot, Das (The Boat)', *Monthly Film Bulletin*, vol. 49, no. 580, May. British Film Institute. By permission of the British Film Institute/Sight and Sound.

Chapter 7

'Erinnerungspolitik at Berlin's Neue Wache', *Ecumene*, vol. 6, no. 3, July. Arnold Publishers. By kind permission of Hodder & Stoughton Educational.

Chapter 8

Ugrešić, D. (1998) 'The confiscation of memory', in transl. Hawkesworth, C., *The Culture of Lies*. Phoenix/Weidenfeld & Nicolson.

Gerő, A. and Pető, I. (1999) 'Introduction', *Unfinished Socialism: Pictures from the Kádár Era*. Central European University Press.

Chapter 9

Nena Skopljanac-Brunner, et al. (eds) (2000) 'Understanding and judging', *Media and War*. Centre for Transition and Civil Society Research.

Pennington, A. and Levi, P. (transl.) (1984) 'Kosovo and the aftermath', *Marko the Prince: Serbo-Croat Heroic Songs*, Duckworth. By permission of Gerald Duckworth & Co. Ltd.

Every effort has been made to contact copyright holders. If any has been inadvertently overlooked the publishers will be pleased to make the necessary arrangements at the first opportunity.

Index

A

Abstract Expressionism 223
Abstraction 200
actuality films 163, 164, 166
Adorno, Theodor 72–4, 75
Albert, RN 179
Aleksandar, king of Yugoslavia 325
Alexander Nevsky 170
All Quiet on the Western Front (film)
  44–5, 46, 47, 163, 168–70, 171, 184
All Quiet on the Western Front (novel)
  44, 55, 163, 168, 214
Anderson, Benedict 80, 81
Anderson, Lindsay 173–4
Annaud, Jean-Jacques 193
anti-capitalist demonstrations, and
  remembrance of war 58
Anzio 161
archetypes, and Tippett's *A Child of
  Our Time* 106
Armistice Day 57–8, 61, 62, 63
Arp, Jean (or Hans), *Dadaland* 210,
  211–12
art music *see* music
artists *see* painting
the arts 4, 197–228
  assemblage 228
  Britart 198
  changes during the twentieth
    century 197–9
  and the Cold War 4, 221, 222
  and the cultural revolution 223–7
  and the First World War 4, 197,
    200–20, 221
  and Modernism 199–200, 201–3,
    204–5, 221, 224
    and music 104, 117, 159, 199,
      208
  and postmodernism 4, 223, 224,
    225–7, 228
  and the Second World War 221–3
  see also literature; music; painting;
    poetry
Arts in the West since 1945 (Marwick)
  197, 222
Ashes and Diamonds 191, 192
assemblage 228
Au revoir les enfants 190
Auschwitz concentration camp 56, 95,
  231
  attempts to 'Catholicize' 236–7,
    241
  and Bergen-Belsen 232
  and Holocaust memories 4, 232–42
    Catholic 236–7, 239
      March of the Living 237–9, 242
      memorial museum guidebook
        233–6, 244–5
      and the Polish communist state
        233–6, 241
  Memorial 30
  moral justification for the arts after
    73, 74, 79, 80
  musical activities at 103
  Paul Levine's reflections on visiting
    240–1, 243
  and western European memory
    232
Austin, Guy 190
Austria, memory and legacy of the
  Second World War in 23
Auteil, Daniel 191
author, death of the 226–7
autobiographies, Jünger's *Storm of Steel*
  48, 49–50, 51–2

B

Bach, J. S. 135
  St Matthew Passion 114–15, 118, 134
Balkan wars (1912 and 1913) 323
Ball, Hugo, *Cabinet Voltaire* 209–10,
  211, 212
Banja Luka, Bosnia, destruction of the
  Ferhadija mosque 341, 345
Barbusse, Henri 204, 212–14, 220
  Hell 212, 214
  Le Feu (Under Fire) 44, 208, 212–14,
    215
Barker, Pat 163
  First World War trilogy 42
Barthes, Roland 225
*Battle of the Ancre and the Advance of the
  Tanks* 164
Battle of Britain 161
Battle of the Bulge 161
The Battle of the River Plate 179, 182,
  185
Battle of the Somme 163, 164–7, 168
'Battlefield' *see* Stramm, August
Battleship Potemkin 168
Beckmann, Max 201
  Night 204
Beethoven, Ludwig van
  Ninth Symphony 154, 157
  Wellingtons Sieg 114
Belgium
  and the European Coal and Steel
    Community (ECSC) 34
  and Holocaust Memorial Day 258
  memory and legacy of the Second
    World War in Dinant 23–9
Bennett, Christopher 337–8
Berenbaum, Michael 230
Berg, Alban 157, 204
Berlin
  memorials 63, 231
    Die Neue Wache 39–41, 59, 62,
      250–4
    plans for a Holocaust memorial
      254–6
Berlin Wall 41, 66, 224, 277, 307
Berri, Claude 190

Bethge, Hans 155
Betts, Paul 270
Beuys, Josef 228
Bildungsroman (novel of education), and Schlink's *The Reader* 88–9, 99–100
Binyon, Laurence 204
Bismarck 170
Bismarck, Otto von 89
Bitburg Affair 251, 254
A Bitter Truth see Cork, Richard
'Blighters' (Sassoon) 43–4
blood sacrifice, and First World War remembrance ceremonies 58
Bloom, Harold 117
Böll, Heinrich 79, 88
Borchert, Wolfgang, *The Man Outside* 79
Bordwell, David 191
Bosnia-Herzegovina 311, 322, 326, 327
    Bosnian Muslims 320, 340–1
    and the disintegration of Yugoslavia 331–2
    manipulation of new memories in 345
    and music as propaganda in the Yugoslav wars 343–4
Boulez, Pierre 222
Bouquet, Carole 191
Bowen, Meirion 116
Bracewell, Wendy 316
Brahms, Johannes 154
Brandt, Willy 18, 22
Braque, Georges 203, 212
Brecht, Bertolt, *Švejk in the Second World War* 54
Bresson, Jean-Jacques de 22
Breton, André 204
Briand, Aristide 32
The Bridge on the River Kwai 178, 179, 180
A Bridge Too Far 161
Britain
    Britart 198
    British identity and popular memories of war 10–14, 19
    and Churchill's 'United States of Europe' idea 34
    euroscepticism in British politics 7–10
    and the First World War
        Armistice Day 57–8, 61, 63
        Christian and classical imagery in war cemeteries 60
        local war memorials 60–1

Owen's poems and remembrance 123
        remembrance ceremonies 58, 59
        war veterans' associations 58
    and Holocaust Memorial Day 70, 257, 258–66
    pacifist sentiments between the wars in 167
    post-Impressionism 198
    and Schlink's *The Reader* 84
    and the Second World War 10–14, 19, 33
Britain at Bay 173
Britain Can Take It! 173
Britart 198
British cinema
    films in the interwar years 170
    First World War films 164–7, 171
    Second World War films 172–81, 186, 193
        and Britain's postwar decline 181, 194
        and the critics 179–81
        documentaries 173–7
        postwar 178–81
        and the postwar generation 162
        prisoner-of-war films 179
        and propaganda 172–3, 177–8
British Legion 58
Britten, Benjamin
    and Mahler 155
    Peter Grimes 121
    and Tippett's *A Child of Our Time* 114, 120–1
    War Requiem 3, 121–39, 159, 222
        'Anthem for Doomed Youth' 134
        Britten's recording (1962) 122, 137
        and celebrated requiem settings of the past 134–6
        and the consecration of the new Coventry cathedral 121–2
        and Derek Jarman's film *War Requiem* (1988) 137–9
        First World War poetry in 104, 123, 133, 222
        harmony in 136
        première 122, 137
        reconciliation message in 137
        religious imagery in 122–3, 133
        and the Second World War 157
        and Shostakovich 153, 157, 158
        texts 123–33

    and Tippett's *A Child of Our Time* 122, 133, 134, 135–6, 137
        'Tuba mirum' 135
Britten, Vera 43
Brontë, Charlotte, *Jane Eyre* 88
Browning, Christopher, *Ordinary Men* 17
Bryant, Sir Arthur 11
Bubis, Ignatz 252
Budapest
    Holocaust memorials 4, 231, 242–9
        around the Jewish ghetto 242–5, 247–8
        at the main synagogue 246–7
        in the central Jewish cemetery 245–6, 247
    House of Terror 4, 279, 287, 298–306
        courtyard 302, 303
        entrance hall 301–3
        history of the building 298–300
        and Hungary's right-wing political parties 300–1
        torture chamber 304
    Liberation Monument on Gellért Hill 281
    removal of statues from the city centre 281, 288–9
    Statue Park 4, 279, 287–98, 305–6, 307
        aerial view 292, 294–5
        Béla Kun memorial 295, 296
        circular area 292–3
        gate 291–2, 293
        plans for Memento Park 287, 290
        Steinmetz and Ostapenkó statues 293–4
    street names changed in 281
Budapest Oral History Archive 280
Burleigh, Michael, *The Third Reich* 70

C

Cabinet Voltaire (Ball) 209–10, 211, 212
Callot, Jacques 201
Camden Town School 198
Canaris 181
Carve Her Name with Pride 179, 180
The Case of Sergeant Grischa (Zweig) 44, 55
Catholic church
    and Auschwitz 236–7, 239

and Croat nationality 339, 340
destruction of churches in the
  Yugoslav wars 341
Celan, Paul 95
  'Todesfuge' 74–8
central Europe, post-socialism and
  memory in 269–79, 306–7
Cesarani, David, on Holocaust
  Memorial Day 264–6
Chapman, James 173, 174
Charlesworth, Andrew 236
The Charnel House (Picasso) 222
Chetniks 326, 327, 328, 338
A Child of Our Time see Tippett,
  Michael
Chirac, Jacques 22
Christian imagery
  in war memorials 59–60, 61, 62
  pietà at Berlin's (*Die Neue Wache*)
    41, 251
Christmas Under Fire 173
Churchill, Winston 11, 13
  'United States of Europe' idea
    33–4
Cicero 91
cinema 3, 161–94
  actuality films 163, 164, 166
  distortions of historical 'truth'
    about war 163–4
  First World War films 44–5, 46, 47,
    163, 164–71, 194
    anti-war 167–70, 171, 194
    Derek Jarman's *War Requiem*
      (1988) 137–9
    and propaganda 166–7
    and the Second World War
      170–1
  in Hungary 282
  Le Chagrin et la Pitié (documentary
    film) 22
  and myths about war 162–3, 187–8
  narrative feature films 163, 164
  Schindler's List 230, 248
  Second World War films 172–93
    British 162, 172–81, 186, 193,
      194
    French 162, 187–92, 193, 194
    German 162–3, 181–6, 194
    Hollywood films of Britain at
      war 177
    and the Hollywood western 161
    Polish 191–3, 194
    Soviet films 162, 167–8
  and war as allegory 194

and war as a national experience
  193
and war as a personal narrative
  193–4
citizenship laws, Germany 83
class
  and First World War films 171
  in Yugoslavia 324–5, 328
classical literature, and Schlink's *The
  Reader* 92–3
Cold War 1, 66
  and the arts in Europe 4, 221, 222
  and Britten's *War Requiem* 104, 137
  and East Germany 18
  ending of the 224
  films 179
    Derek Jarman's *War Requiem*
      (1988) 139
  and Holocaust memory 231
    at Auschwitz 241
    in Germany 249–50
  and popular memory 41, 42
  and Shostakovich's Symphony no.
    13, 'Babi Yar' 153
  and socialist dictatorships in
    central and eastern Europe 269
  and spy thrillers 66
  tourist attractions 66
The Colditz Story 179
collective amnesia 1
  and the Second World War 16, 61,
    65
collective unconscious, and Tippett's
  A Child of Our Time 106
Combs, Richard, review of *Das Boot*
  184–6
communism
  anti-communist films and British
    cinema 179
  communist partisans in Yugoslavia
    326, 327–9
  and eastern European cinema
    191–3
  and the French Resistance 20
  and Holocaust memory of
    Auschwitz 233–6, 241
  in Hungary 4
  and political identities 31
  and the Popular Front government
    in France 21
  and Yugoslavia 5
  see also Marxism
concentration camps
  Bergen-Belsen 232
  musical activities in 103

see also Auschwitz concentration
  camp
Convoy 173
Cooke, Mervyn 134
Cork, Richard 200, 205, 209, 212
  *A Bitter Truth: Avant-Garde Art and
    the Great War* 201
Coudenhove-Kalergi, Richard
  Europe Must Unite 32–3
  Pan-Europe 32
Coventry cathedral, and Britten's *War
  Requiem* 121–2, 222
Coward, Noel 172–3
Croatia 311
  and the 'Croatian spring' 334
  and the disintegration of
    Yugoslavia 331, 332
  and the Second World War 326–7,
    337–8
  Ustasha Croat Revolutionary
    Movement 325, 326, 337, 338
  and the Yugoslav wars
    and culture in conflict 339, 340
    media manipulation 334–9
    music as propaganda 343
Croats 321, 322–4
  and the Illyrian movement 322–3
  and the Serbo-Croat language 323,
    343
Cross of Iron (film) 185, 193
Crowley, David, in *Globalization and
  Europe* 270
The Cruel Sea 178
Csinibaba (Glamour Girl) 282
Cubism 198, 199–200, 203, 212, 217
cultural artefacts, and the
  understanding of war 65–6
cultural revolution, and the arts in
  Europe 223–7
culture, conception of 2
Czech Republic 307

D

Dad's Army 162
Dada manifesto (Tzara) 210–11, 212
Dada movement 201, 203, 204,
  209–12, 224
Dadaland (Arp) 210, 211–12
The Dam Busters 178
Danger Within 179
Das Boot (The Boat) 164, 182–6
David Copperfield (Dickens) 88
Davies, Norman 35

De Gaulle, General Charles 20, 21, 22, 177, 187
democracy, and industrialization 14, 15
Deneuve, Catherine 190
Denmark, and Holocaust Memorial Day 258
Depardieu, Gérard 190
Der Grosse König 170
Derouet, Christian 215, 220
Derrida, Jacques 225
The Devil's General 182
diaries, and Holocaust memories 82
Dickens, Charles, *David Copperfield* 88
dictatorship
    and Budapest's House of Terror 301–6
    and Budapest's Statue Park 289–98
    in central and eastern Europe 269
Dimbleby, Richard 260
Dinant (Belgium), memory and legacy of the Second World War 23–9
discourse and the discursive, and postmodernism 225–6
Dix, Otto 52–3
    Krieg 44
Documentary News Letter (DNL) 174–8
Doktor Faustus (Mann) 79
Domanović, Radoje, 'Marko the Prince once again among us' 319
Donahue, William Collins, 'Illusions of subtlety' 84, 98
Douglas, James, review of *Battle of the Somme* 164–7, 168
Douglas, Keith 74
Drake of England 170
Dubuffet, Jean 223
Dunkirk 179, 180

E

East Germany *see* GDR (German Democratic Republic)
eastern Europe
    cinema of resistance in 191–3
    and euroscepticism in British politics 9
    memory and legacy of the Second World War 30
    music 224
    post-socialism and memory in 269–79, 306–7
    see also Hungary; Poland

ECSC (European Coal and Steel Community) 34, 182
Eisenman, Peter 256
Eleőd, Ákos 289–91, 292, 293
Eley, Geoff 13
Elgar, Edward, *The Spirit of England* 204
Eliot, T. S.
    The Waste Land 118
    and Tippett's *A Child of Our Time* 113
Enemy at the Gates 193, 194
England
    'bourgeois revolution' in, and Germany 15
    see also Britain
English language, and the idea of a united Europe 33
Enright, D. J. 84
Epstein, Jacob 122
ethnic cleansing
    and Holocaust Memorial Day 262, 263
    in the Yugoslav lands 339, 340, 344
ethnicity
    and citizenship laws in Germany 83
    in the Yugoslav lands 339–40
European Atomic Energy Community (Euratom) 34
European Coal and Steel Community (ECSC) 34, 182
European Commission, history of Europe project 35–6
European Economic Community (EEC)
    Britain's entry into the (1973) 12
    and Dinant (Belgium) 26
    and European identity 34–5
European identity 31–6
    and Holocaust memory 266
    post-socialist, eastern Europe identities, and material culture 270–8
European monetary policy, and Germany 7–8, 36
European Union
    and Germany 101
    and national identities 36–7
euroscepticism in British politics 7–10
Expressionism 200, 204, 223

F

false memory syndrome 69

Faulks, Sebastian, *Birdsong* 42
Fautrier, Jean 223
Fauves 198, 199
FDR (Federal Republic of Germany)
    and Auschwitz 234
    Dinant (Belgium) and the German flag 26–8
    and the European Coal and Steel Community (ECSC) 34
    and the German *Soderweg* 14–15
    and the *Historikerstreit* debate 16–18, 79–80, 251
    and Holocaust memories 249, 250
    and the *Holocaust* television series 79
    and memories of the Second World War 16–18, 55–6
    and *Ostpolitik* 18
    and the politics of memory 277
    and *Stunde Null* (zero hour) 78–9
    writers in, and responsibility for the Nazi past 72
    see also German cinema
feminism, and the First World War 43
Fentress, James 13, 29
Ferguson, Niall, *The Pity of War* 42
Ferhadija mosque, destruction of the 341
FFI (French interior forces) 20
Fiennes, Joseph 193
Filipovic, Zlata 262
films *see* cinema
Fire Over England 170
Fires Were Started 173–4
The First of the Few 172
First World War 42–55
    and the arts in Europe 4, 197, 200–20, 221
    and Britain
        Armistice Day 57–8, 61, 63
        Christian and classical imagery in war cemeteries 60
        local war memorials 60–1
        Owen's poems and remembrance 123
        remembrance ceremonies 58, 59
        war veterans' associations 58
    culture of memorial 56–61
        Armistice Day 57–8
        Britain 57–8, 59
        France 56, 59–60
        Germany 59–60
        war memorials 57
        war veterans' associations 58, 59

films 44–5, 46, 47, 163, 164–71, 194
  anti-war 167–70, 171, 194
  Derek Jarman's *War Requiem*
    (1988) 137–9
  and propaganda 166–7
  and the Second World War
    170–1
and gender 42–3
and Germany
  and Berlin's (*Die Neue Wache*)
    39, 250
  films 167
  remembrance 59–60
images of corruption and
  incompetence 42, 43
and the memorialization of the
  Second World War 123
memory and legacy of 7–38
  Belgium (Dinant) 23–9
  Britain 11, 57–8, 61, 63
  France 20, 56, 58–9, 60
  Germany 15–16, 59–60
paintings 44, 45, 52–3, 203–4
poetry 43–4, 46–9
  in Britten's *War Requiem* 104,
    123, 133, 222
  in Tippett's *A Child of Our Time*
    123
and the Soviet Union 62–3
and the term 'no man's land' 45–6
and trench warfare 42, 50
in the Yugoslav lands 320–6
  and the 'Kosovo idea' 316
Fischer-Dieskau, Dietrich 137
Flaubert, Gustave, *L'Éducation
  sentimentale (Sentimental Education)* 88
football, British/English identity and
  popular memories of war 12
*Forging War: the Media in Serbia, Croatia
  and Bosnia* (Thompson) 338
Foucault, Michel 225
Fox, Edward 161
Fragments: Memories of a Childhood
  (Wilkomirski) 100
France
  the arts in
    Nouveau Réalisme 224
    post-Impressionism 198
  'bourgeois revolution' in, and
    Germany 15
  and Churchill's 'United States of
    Europe' idea 34
  cinema 162, 187–92, 193, 194
  and the European Coal and Steel
    Community (ECSC) 34

and the First World War 20
  counter-demonstrations on
    Armistice Day 58
  films 167
  Remembrance ceremonies 58–9
  war memorials 56, 60
historical memories 81
and the Holocaust 22
and Holocaust Memorial Day
  257–8
pacifist sentiments between the
  wars 167
Popular Front government 21
and the Second World War
  and the idea of a Franco-British
    union 33
  massacre of Oradour-sur-Glane
    27
  memory and legacy 20–2
  relations with Britain 177
  remembrance 61
  Resistance 20, 21, 22, 187–92
  Vichy regime 20, 21, 22
  student riots (1968) 21–2
Franco-Prussian war (1870–1) 14, 24
Frank, Anne 82, 248, 259
Franz Ferdinand, archduke of Austria
  320
Fréchuret, Maurice 223
French cinema, Second World War
  films 162, 187–92, 193, 194
French Revolutionary wars 11, 212
Freud, Sigmund 204
'front' or war generations 66
Fulbrook, Mary 70, 249
Furhammar, Leif 164
Fussell, Paul 45, 55, 114, 123
Futurism 200

G

Gance, Abel, *J'Accuse* 44, 45
GDR (German Democratic Republic)
  14
  and Berlin's (*Die Neue Wache*) 39,
    40–1
  and German reunification 18–19
  and Holocaust memory 249–50
  and the *Holocaust* television series
    79
  literature 72, 79
  Museum of Everyday Life 307
  and *Ostpolitik* 18
  and the politics of memory 277

post-socialist identities and
  material culture 270
Gellhorn, Martha 82–3
gender
  and the First World War 42–3
  and the Kosovo myth 315–16
A Generation/Pokolenie 191–2
genocide 1, 30
  and Holocaust Memorial Day
    263–4, 265
German cinema
  in the interwar years 170
  and the Second World War 162–3,
    181–6, 194
German language, and Nazism 74, 75
*The German Retreat and the Battle of
  Arras* 164
Germany
  Blue Rider movement in the arts
    200
  British historians on 11–12
  and Churchill's 'United States of
    Europe' idea 34
  citizenship laws 83
  and England's football fans 12
  and euroscepticism in British
    politics 7–10
  first and second generation of
    postwar Germans 72, 94, 98–100
  and the First World War
    and Berlin's (*Die Neue Wache*)
      39, 250
    films 167
    memory and legacy 15–16,
      59–60
    remembrance 59–60
  and Holocaust memories 249–56
  Langemarck Day 60
  national identity 19, 89
    and the European Union 36–7
    and the Holocaust 70
  relations with Dinant (Belgium)
    23–9
  reunification 72
    and Berlin's (*Die Neue Wache*)
      39, 251
    and Britain 8
    and the GDR 18–19
    and Holocaust memory 80, 250
    and plans for a Holocaust
      memorial in Berlin 255
    and right-wing extremism 82–3
  and the Second World War
    memory and legacy 14–19, 39,
      41, 55–6, 59

remembrance 62–3
Sonderweg (special path) 14–16, 19
unification under Prussia (1871)
14, 15
Weimar Republic 14, 24, 59
see also Berlin; FDR (Federal
Republic of Germany); GDR
(German Democratic Republic);
Nazi Germany
Gerő, András and Pető, Iván,
Unfinished Socialism 283–6
Gies, Miep 248
Giscard d'Estaing, Valéry 187
Glamour Girl (Csinibaba) 282
Gloag, Kenneth 116
Globalization and Europe 270
Goethe, Johann Wolfgang von 74, 91
Wilhelm Meister 89
Goldhagen, Daniel J., *Hitler's Willing
Executioners* 17
Good Soldier Švejk (Hašek) 53–4
Goodall, Howard
Holocaust anthem 'I believe in the
sun' 263
'In Memoriam Anne Frank' 259
Górecki, Henryk 224
Grass, Günter 79, 80
The Tin Drum 72
Great Soviet Encyclopaedia 62
The Great War (film) 171
Gregory, Adrian 57, 61
Grese, Irma 232
Grierson, John 173
Grosjean, Bruno 100
Gross, Jan, *Neighbours* 30
Grynspan, Herschel 105, 106, 115, 119
Gubaydulina, Sofuga 224
Guernica (Picasso) 221
Gypsies (Sinti and Roma), and
Holocaust memory 253, 255, 258

H

Haas, Pavel 103
Habermas, Jürgen 17
Habsburg empire, and the Yugoslav
lands 310, 311, 320, 321, 322–3, 340
Hamburg Institute for Social Research
18
Handel, George Frederick 134, 135,
154
Messiah 115–17, 118
harmony, in Britten's *War Requiem* 136
Harper, Heather 137

Hašek, Jaroslav, *The Good Soldier Švejk*
53–4
Haydn, Joseph 154
Hayward, Susan 187
Heath, Edward 12
Heine, Heinrich 74
Hell (Barbusse) 212, 214
Hemingway, Ernest 91
Henry V (film) 172
Heym, Stefan 79
High Treason 179
Hindemith, Paul 204, 205–9
letters from the front written by
206–9
Testimony in Pictures 205–6
historians
British
on Germany 11–12
on memories of the Second
World War 13
on Croatia 337–8
on the Holocaust 70
and Holocaust memories in
Germany 249, 250
and national identities 35–6
on Second World War Germany
17–18, 55–6
Historikerstreit (historians' controversy)
16–18, 79–80, 251
history and memory, in America and
eastern Europe 275–6
Hitler, Adolf
bomb plot against (1944) 51–2
British historians on 11, 12
and euroscepticism in British
politics 8, 10
and the Weimar Republic 14
and Yugoslavia 326
see also Nazi Germany
Hockney, David 228
Holocaust 4, 230–66
and the arts 221
and collective memory 69–70
and First World War remembrance
59–60
and France 22, 257–8
and Hungary 300
Budapest's House of Terror 303
memoirs 82
memories 69–70, 82
American 231
and Auschwitz 4, 232–42
Budapest memorials 4, 231,
242–9
Germany 249–56

Holocaust Memorial Day
256–66
and postwar German literature
72–80
and Schlink's *The Reader* 72,
94–100
top-down and bottom-up
approaches to 231–2, 249–50
United States Holocaust Memorial
Museum (USHMM) 230, 231,
237
see also Auschwitz concentration
camp; concentration camps
Holocaust (American television series)
16, 79
Homer, *Odyssey* 91–2
Horn, Gyula 281–2
Horváth, Ödön von 105–6, 115
humour, in First World War novels
53–4
Hungary 279–307
Államvédelmi Hatóság (ÁVH)
(Agency for the Protection of the
State) 298
Alliance of Free Democrats 283,
301
compulsory deliveries and
collective farms 305
Foundation for Research into the
History and Society of Central
and Eastern Europe 287, 299
and the Holocaust 300
Horn government (1994–98)
281–2
Hungarian Socialist Workers' party
(HSWP) 291
Institute for the History of Politics
286
Institute for the Twentieth Century
286–7
Kádár era 4, 279, 280, 283–6, 291
Nyilas (Arrow Cross) government
245, 248
and Budapest's House of Terror
298, 302, 303, 304
and Budapest's Statue Park 294
Orbán government (1998–2002)
286–7, 300–1
parliamentary elections (1994) 281
parliamentary elections (2002),
and Budapest's House of Terror
300–1
politics of memory in post-socialist
279–87
revolution (1848) 280, 288

revolution (1956) 279, 286, 287, 305
see also Budapest
Huyssen, Andreas 275

I

Ice Cold in Alex 182
identity
European 31–6, 266
and 'front' or war generations 66
and memory 69
post-socialist, eastern Europe identities, and material culture 270–8
in Tippett's *A Child of Our Time* 118–20
see also national identity; political identity
ideology, and media manipulation in Serbia and Croatia 335–6, 337
Illés, Gyula, 'A sentence on tyranny' 290, 292, 295
'imagined communities' of nationality 80
In Which We Serve 172–3, 186
Inability to Mourn (Mitscherlich and Mitscherlich) 94
industrialization, and democratization 14, 15
Informal Art 223
Ireland, Easter Rising (1916) 105
Iron Curtain 35
Isaksson, Folke 164
Islam
in the Yugoslav lands
Bosnian Muslims 320, 340–1
destruction of mosques in the Yugoslav wars 341, 345
and the Ottoman empire 311, 317–18, 340
Israel, and Holocaust memories, March of the Living at Auschwitz 238, 239
Italy
and the European Coal and Steel Community (ECSC) 34
First World War films 171
memory and legacy of the Second World War in 23
and Second World War remembrance 62
and the Ventotene manifesto (1941) 33

war veterans' associations 59
Izetbegović, Alija 333

J

J'Accuse (film) 44, 45
The Jackboot Mutiny 181–2
Jane Eyre (Brontë) 88
Janeway, Carol Brown 83
Jarman, Derek, *War Requiem* film (1988) 137–9
Jaspers, Karl, *The Question of Guilt* 79–80
Jedwabne, Poland, massacre of Jews in (1941) 30
Jews
and anti-semitism in Vichy France 21, 22
and the Babi Yar massacre 140, 150–3
and Holocaust memory 4
American Jewish community 230
at Auschwitz 234, 235, 236, 237–9, 240–1, 242
Berlin's *Die Neue Wache* memorial 251–2, 253, 254
and Christian images in memorials 41, 251
Holocaust Memorial Day 257, 258
plans for a Holocaust memorial in Berlin 254–6
and Holocaust memory, Budapest memorials 242–9
massacre of in Jedwabne, Poland (1941) 30
John Paul II, Pope 237
Journey's End 167
Joyce, James 199, 212
Jung, Carl, Jungian symbolism in Tippett's *A Child of Our Time* 106, 119, 120
Jünger, Ernst 47
Storm of Steel 48, 49–50, 51–2, 54–5

K

Kádár, János 4, 279, 280, 281, 291
Kameradschaft 167
Kanal (Polish film) 191, 192, 193
Karlsruhe exhibition (1997) 17, 18
Kayirebwa, Cecile, 'Ubupfubyi' 261

Keane, Fergal 261
Kellogg-Briand Pact (1928) 167
Kelly, Andrew 170
Kemp, Ian 123
Khachaturian, Aram 155
Khrushchev, Nikita 153
Kiefer, Anselm 74
King and Country 171
Klein, Gideon, 'Trio' 260
Klopstock, Friedrich 154
Knight, Arthur 181
Kohl, Helmut 8, 9, 10, 250, 252
and Germany's Nazi past 16–17
Kolbe, Maximilian 236–7
Kolbow, Walter 28
Kollwitz, Käthe
Die Eltern memorial 59, 60
pietà at Berlin's *Die Neue Wache* 39, 40, 41, 251
Koshar, Rudy 250
Kosovo 330, 345, 346, 347
Kosovo, battle of (1389) 312, 318, 347
Kosovo myth 311, 315–16, 347
Kovács, Attila F. 300, 303
Kramer, Josef 232
Krása, Hans 103
Kushner, Tony 232

L

La Grande Illusion 171
Labour party (Britain), and the National Union of Ex-Servicemen (NUX) 58
Lacombe, Lucien 188–90, 191, 192
Lada, Josef 53
Laemmle, Carl Jr 168
land and land reform, in central and eastern Europe 269
Langemarck, battle of (1914) 60
language
English language and the idea of a united Europe 33
and postmodernism 225
in the Yugoslav lands 311, 321–2, 322–3
as a tool of division 343
Language of Silence see Schlant, Ernestine
The Last Metro (film) 190
Laušević, Mirjana 343, 344
Laval, Pierre 167
Law, Jude 193

Lawson, Dominic, interview with Nicholas Ridley 7–10
Lazar, prince of Serbia 309, 315
Le Chagrin et la Pitié (documentary film) 22
Le Croix de bois/The Wooden Cross (film) 167
Le Dernier Métro/The Last Metro 190
Le Feu (Under Fire) *see* Barbusse, Henri
League of Nations 32, 33
Léger, Fernand 204, 212–20
    The Card Game 212, 213, 214, 218
    letters to Louis Poughon 215–20
    statement about the First World War 214–15
Lenin, V. I., music for funeral of 63
Leroux, Georges, *L'Enfer* 44
Lersch, Heinrich, 'The war-invalid' 48–9, 51, 55
Leši, Kapetan 274
Levine, Paul 240–1, 243
Lieven, Dominic 64–5
literature 69–101
    collective memory and the novel 80–3
    and the death of the author 226–7
    First World War novels 42, 43, 44, 53–4
        Barbusse's *Le Feu (Under Fire)* 44, 208, 212–14, 215
    French *nouveau nouveau roman* 228
    memory, nation and the novel 80–3
    and Modernism 199
    post-war German 79
        literature of the ruins (*Trümmerliteratur*) 78
        recalling the Holocaust 72–80
    see also poetry; Schlink, Bernhard, *The Reader*
The Longest Day 161
Lowe, John 133
Lucie Aubrac 190–1
Ludendorff, General Erich 164
Lüdtke, Alf, on national mourning day in Göttingen 61–2
Luther, Martin 89
Lutyens, Sir Edwin, and the Cenotaph in Whitehall 60
Lutz, Carl, memorial to in Budapest 242–3, 247–8
Luxembourg, and the European Coal and Steel Community (ECSC) 34

M

McDowell, J. B. 163
Macedonia 330
MacLeod, Alexander 290
Mahler, Gustav 103, 154–5, 157
    Second Symphony 154
    The Song of the Earth 154–5
Malins, Geoffrey 163
Malle, Louis 188–90, 191
Mallory, Leslie 179
Mann, Thomas 74, 88, 91
    Doktor Faustus 79
Marinetti, Filippo 199
Marko the Prince 316, 317, 319, 320
Marković, Mira 339, 345–6
Marwick, Arthur
    Arts in the West since 1945 197, 222
    on history and identity 13
Marxism
    and the death of the author 227
    and the French *nouveau nouveau roman* 228
material culture, and post-socialist, eastern Europe identities 270–8, 286
Mayer, Arno J. 15
media, and the Yugoslav foundation myth 329
memorials *see* war memorials
memory
    confiscation of in the eastern European context 270–8
    loss 69
    national and individual, and the Holocaust 231, 241
    in Schlink's *The Reader* 89–94
    see also First World War; Holocaust; Second World War
The Men Against (film) 171
Men without Shadows (Sartre) 73
Merridale, Catherine 63–4
Messiaen, Olivier, *Quartet for the End of Time* 103
Messiah (Handel) 115–17, 118
Mihailović, Colonel Draža 326
Milestone, Lewis 168
Millions Like Us 172
Milošević, Slobodan 331, 332, 333, 339, 340, 345, 346, 347
Mitchell, Donald 135
Mitscherlich, Alexander and Margaret, *The Inability to Mourn* 94
Mitterand, François 16, 22

Modernism 199–200
    and the cultural revolution 224
    and the First World War 201–3, 204–5
        poetry 46–7
    and music 104, 117, 159, 199, 208
    and the Second World War 221
Moncarz, Jillian 238
Monnet, Jean 33, 34
Montenegro
    language 311
    and *The Mountain Wreath* (poem) 316–20
Morning Departure 186
Moscow Institute of World Economics 35
Mosse, George 59
Mostar
    destruction of the Old Bridge 341
    new cultural markers in 345
Mountain Wreath (Njegoš) 316–20
Mountbatten, Lord Louis 173
mourning, and the arts in the First World War 202, 203
Mozart, Wolfgang Amadeus 154
Mrs Miniver 177
Müller, Wilhelm 113
Mundy, Toby 84
museums, contemporary culture and 'musealisation' 275, 278, 307
music 3, 103–59, 222
    celebrations of military victory 114
    and the First World War 204
        Paul Hindemith 204, 205–9
    for Holocaust Memorial Day 259, 260, 261, 263
    in Hungary 282
    and Modernism 104, 117, 159, 199, 208
    postmodern 224
    as propaganda in the Yugoslav wars 343–4
    in Russia
        and Lenin's funeral 63
        and Second World War remembrance 64
    Serbian traditional songs 309, 310, 312–15, 316, 344, 348–53
    see also Britten, Benjamin; Shostakovich, Dmitri; Tippett, Michael
Mussorgsky, Modest Petrovich 157, 158

N

Napoleonic wars, and Britain 11
narrative feature films 163, 164
Nash, Paul, *We Are Making a New World* 44
nation-states
  and national identities 36
  Nicholas Ridley's perception of 10
  and war 31
national identity
  British/English identity and popular memories of war 10–14
  German 19, 89
    and the European Union 36–7
    and the Holocaust 70
  historians and the construction of 35–6
  and Holocaust memory 266
  and Shostakovich 157, 158
  and Tippett's *A Child of Our Time* 119–20, 157
  and war 2, 31
  in the Yugoslav lands 309
    construction of under foreign rule 311–20
    and culture in conflict 339–41
National Union of Ex-Servicemen (NUX) 58, 59
nations, memory and the novel 80–3
NATO 35, 182, 345, 347
Naumann, Michael 256
Nazi Germany
  and *All Quiet on the Western Front* 168
  and Brecht's *Švejk in the Second World War* 54
  and concentration camps 232, 234
  and denazification after the war 78
  and eastern Europe 30
  and France 20–2
  and German cinema 181–6
  and the German language 74, 75
  and German memory and legacy of the Second World War 15–16
  and German national identity 19, 70
  historians on 17–18
  and the *Historikerstreit* debate 16–18
  Kristallnacht progrom 79, 105
  and Picasso 221–2
  and Yugoslavia 326–7, 328
  see also Hitler, Adolf; Holocaust; Schlink, Bernhard
Neighbours (Gross) 30

Nelson, B. F. 34
Netherlands
  and the European Coal and Steel Community (ECSC) 34
  and Holocaust Memorial Day 258
newspapers, on Armistice Day in Britain 57–8
Nicoll, Sir William 32
Niemöller, Martin 75
Night (Beckmann) 204
Nine Men 173
Niven, David 172
Njegoš, Petar Petrović, *The Mountain Wreath* 316–20
Nolte, Ernst 80
nostalgia
  and the politics of memory 278
    in post-socialist Hungary 282–6, 290, 297, 305, 306
novels *see* literature
Novick, Peter 230, 253
  The Holocaust and Collective Memory 70
Nuremberg trials 16, 82, 95
  and denazification 78

O

Oberlender, Thomas 275
Obilić, Miloš 318
Objective: Burma! 163
October 168
Odette 178
Odyssey (Homer) 91–2
Oh! What a Lovely War 171
Olivier, Laurence 172
Olphus, Marcel, *Le Chagrin et la Pitié* 22
The One that Got Away 182
Opie, Robert 274
Orbán, Viktor 286–7, 300–1
Ordinary Men (Browning) 17
Orthodox church
  destruction of churches in the Yugoslav wars 341
  Serbian 336, 337, 340
Ottoman empire, and the Yugoslav lands 310, 311, 316–17, 322, 323, 340
Owen, Wilfred 43, 50, 55, 74, 163
  'Dulce et Decorum est' 47
  poetry by
    in Britten's *War Requiem* 123, 133, 134, 135, 137, 222

    and Derek Jarman's film *War Requiem* 138
    in Tippett's *A Child of Our Time* 123
  'Strange Meeting' 137
  The Seed 123
Owings, Alison, *Frauen: German Women Recall the Third Reich* 71

P

Pabst, G. W., *Westfront 1918* 44
painting
  Cubism 198, 199–200, 203, 212, 217
  and earlier wars 201
  First World War artists 44, 45, 203–4
    exhibition at London's Barbican (1994) 52–3
    Léger's *The Card Game* 212, 213, 214, 218
  Informal Art 223
  Modernist movements in 198, 199–200
  Surrealism 204, 223
Papon, Maurice 22
Pärt, Arvo 224
Paths of Glory 171
Pattern Childhood (Wolf) 79
Paul, Prince, regent of Yugoslavia 325–6
Pavelić, Ante 325
Pears, Peter 120, 137
peasantry, in the Yugoslav lands 324–5
Peckinpah, Sam 193
Penn, William 32
Pétain, Marshal Philippe 20
Peter Grimes (Britten) 121
Peter, king of Yugoslavia 325, 326
Petersen, Wolfgang 182, 185
Pető, Iván *see* Gerő, András and Pető, Iván
photographic collections, in post-socialist Hungary 283–6
Picasso, Pablo 199, 203, 212, 221–2
  The Charnel House 222
  Guernica 221
Pick, Daniel 52–3
Piper, John 122
Pistoletto, Michelangelo 228
Pitt, William, the Younger 11
The Pity of War (Ferguson) 42
Plath, Sylvia 75

'Daddy' 232
poetry
'Babi Yar' (Yevtushenko) 141–50,
153, 155, 156, 157–8
Celan's poetry and the Holocaust
74–8
'Daddy' (Plath) 232
First World War 43–4, 46–9
in Britten's *War Requiem* 104,
123, 133, 222
in Tippett's *A Child of Our Time*
123
for Holocaust Memorial Day 258
and Modernism 199
The Mountain Wreath (Njegoš)
316–20
'A sentence on tyranny' (Illés) 290,
292, 295
Pöhl, Klaus-Otto 7
Poland
cinema of resistance in 187, 191–3,
194
memories and legacy of the
Second World War 30
Warsaw uprising (1944) 192
see also Auschwitz concentration
camp
political crisis (mid twentieth
century), musical responses to 104
political identity
in post-socialist Hungary 285, 306
and war 2, 31
Pop Art 224, 228
post-Impressionism 198, 199
postmodernism 4, 223, 224, 225–7,
228
post-socialist, eastern European
identities, and material culture
270–8, 286
Poughon, Louis, Léger's letters to
215–20
prisoner-of-war films 179
Prokofiev, Sergei 155
propaganda
and British Second World War
films 172–3, 177–8
and First World War films 166–7
and the Yugoslav wars
media manipulation in Serbia
and Croatia 334–7
music as 343–4
Prost, Antoine 58
Pynchon, Thomas, *Gravity's Rainbow*
123

Q

Quartet for the End of Time (Messiaen)
103
Question of Guilt (Jaspers) 79–80

R

Radić, Stjepan 325
Rákosi, Mátyás 279, 305
rape, as an instrument of cultural
destruction in the Yugoslav wars 344
Ravel, Maurice 205
Reach for the Sky 178, 179
The Reader see Schlink, Bernhard
Reagan, Ronald 16
Reeves, Nicholas 167
Regeneration 163
religious imagery
in Britten's *War Requiem* 122–3, 133
in war memorials 59–60, 61, 62
pietà at Berlin's (*Die Neue Wache*)
41, 251
see also Catholic church
Rellstab, Ludwig 113
Remarque, Erich Maria, *All Quiet on
the Western Front* 44, 55, 163, 168,
214
Renoir, Jean 170–1
La Grande Illusion 45
Resistance in France 20, 21, 22
and French cinema 187–92
Réthly, Ákos 289, 297
Ridley, Nicholas 7–10, 11, 12
Rivers, Dr William 163
Robbe-Grillet, Alain 228
Robert, Jean-Louis 43
Robertson, Alec 122
Roma, and Holocaust memory 253,
255, 258
Romantic movement
and German national identity 89
and Schlink's *The Reader* 92
and the Yugoslav lands 322
Rosa, Salvator 201
Rosé, Alma 103
Rosenfeld, Alvin 248
Rosh, Leah 254
Rossi, Ernesto 33
Rousso, Henry, and the Vichy
syndrome 21–2
Rürup, Reinhard 255
Russia

First World War remembrance
62–3
Russian identity, and Shostakovich
157, 158
and Second World War
remembrance 63–5
see also Soviet Union (USSR)

S

The Safecracker 180
St Matthew Passion (Bach) 114–15, 118,
134
Salmon, Trevor 32
Salsberg, Leigh 238
San Demetrio, London 173
Sartre, Jean-Paul, *Men without Shadows*
73
Sassoon, Siegfried 52, 55, 163
'Blighters' 43–4
Saving Private Ryan 186
Schiller, Friedrich, 'Ode to Joy' 154
Schindler's List 230, 248
Schinkel, Karl Friedrich 39
Schlant, Ernestine, *The Language of
Silence* 84, 94, 97–8
Schlink, Bernhard
background 75, 83
and crime fiction (*Kriminalromane*)
83, 88
Selb's Deception 83
The Reader 3, 70–101
as a *Bildungsroman* (novel of
education) 88–9, 99–100
English translation 87–8
guilt and atonement in 84, 93–4
and the legacy of the Holocaust
94–100
and literature as a discourse for
recalling the Holocaust 72–80
memory in 89–94
opening chapter 85–8
publication 83
reception in the USA and the
UK 84
reviews 83–4
and the 'second generation' in
Germany 72
worldwide sales 70–2
Schmidt, Mária 287, 300
Schnittke, Alfred 224
Schoenberg, Arnold 117, 118, 157,
205
Schubert, Franz 113

Schulze, Hagen 19
Schuman, Robert 34
Sebald, W. G., *Austerlitz* 100
Second World War
    abiding images of 55, 56
    and the arts in Europe 221–3
    and Britain 10–14, 19
        euroscepticism in British
            politics 9, 10
        plans for a Franco-British union
            33
    and British historians 12
    in central and eastern Europe 269
    cinema
        British 162, 172–81, 186, 193,
            194
        and Derek Jarman's *War
            Requiem* (1988) 139
        French 162, 187–92, 193, 194
        German 162–3, 181–6, 194
        Hollywood films of Britain at
            war 177
        and the Hollywood western 161
        Polish 191–3, 194
    different theatres of conflict 56
    in Dinant (Belgium) 25–6
    and European identity 32–3
    and ideas of a European
        federation 32–4
    memory and legacy of 10–23, 55–6
        Austria 23
        Britain 10–14, 19
        eastern Europe 30
        France 20–2
        Germany 14–19, 39, 41, 55–6,
            59
        Italy 23
        Switzerland 23
    and music 103–59, 222
        Britten 121, 157, 222
        Shostakovich 139, 157, 222
        Tippett's *A Child of Our Time*
            104, 105–21, 157
    plays, Brecht's *Švejk in the Second
        World War* 54
    remembrance 61
    and the Soviet Union 63–5, 162
    and Yugoslavia 326–8, 329, 337–8
Secret People 179
Sentimental Education (Flaubert) 88
Serbia
    Chetniks 326, 327, 328, 338
    and the disintegration of
        Yugoslavia 331–2
    and the First World War 320–1

and the Kosovo myth 311, 315–16,
    347
manipulation of new memories in
    345–6
oral traditional literature 311–16
and the Second World War 326,
    327
traditional songs 309, 310, 344, 347
    'The downfall of the Serbian
        empire' 312–15
    'The Kosovo girl' 316, 348–51
    'The mother of the Jugovichi'
        316, 352–3
and the Yugoslav state 325
and the Yugoslav wars
    and culture in conflict 339, 340
    media manipulation in 334–9
see also Montenegro
Serbian Academy of Arts and Sciences
    33, 336
Serbian Orthodox church 336, 337
Serbo-Croat language 323, 343
Ships with Wings 173
Shostakovich, Dmitri
    and Britten's *War Requiem* 153, 157,
        158
    Lady Macbeth of Mtsensk 153
    memoirs 156
    and national identity 157, 158
    and the Soviet Union 139–41, 153,
        155–6, 157–8
    Symphony no. 5 153
    Symphony no. 7 'The Leningrad'
        139, 222
    Symphony no. 11 'The Year 1905'
        139
    Symphony no. 12 '1917' 139–40
    Symphony no. 13 'Babi Yar' 3, 104,
        139–58, 159
        and the Cold War 153
        and the European tradition of
            art music 154–5
        text of Yevtushenko's poems
            141–50, 155
        and Tippett's *A Child of Our
            Time* 114, 153, 157, 158
The Silent Enemy 179, 180
The Silent Village 177
Singleton, Fred 324–5
Sink the Bismarck! 178
Sites of Memory, Sites of Mourning see
    Winter, Jay
Skopljanac-Brunner, Nena, *Media and
    War* 334–6
Slovenes 321–2, 323

Slovenia 330, 347
Smajlović, Vedran 342
social class see class
socialist dictatorships
    and Budapest's House of Terror
        301–6
    and Budapest's Statue Park 289–98
    in central and eastern Europe 269
Song of the Earth (Mahler) 154–5
Sorlin, Pierre 161, 167, 170, 182
South Africa, Truth and
    Reconciliation Commission (TRC)
    81–2
Soviet Union (USSR)
    and the arts in Europe 221
    and the Babi Yar massacre 140,
        150–3
        memorial to 152, 153
    and British war films 177, 179
    and Britten's *War Requiem* 137
    and Budapest Holocaust
        memorials 244, 245, 246
    and Churchill's 'United States of
        Europe' idea 34
    collapse (1989) 224
    and the EEC 35
    films 162, 167–8
    and the First World War 62–3
    and the French Resistance 20
    and the Great Patriotic War
        films about 162
        remembrance 63–5
    and international identity 31
    and Poland 30
    and Shostakovitch 139–41, 153,
        155–6, 157–8
    and Yugoslavia 328, 329
    see also Russia
Spanish Civil War 203, 221
Spielberg, Steven 186
Spinelli, Altiero 33
spy thrillers 66
Staël, Nicolas de 223
Stalin, Joseph 153, 329
Steiner, George 47, 74, 78, 84
Stendhal (Marie Henri Beyle) 91
Stockholm International Forum on
    the Holocaust 256–7
Stölzl, Christoph 83–4
Stone, Dan, on Holocaust Memorial
    Day 258, 264–6
Storm of Steel see Jünger, Ernst
Stramm, August, 'Battlefield' 48, 51,
    55
Stravinsky, Igor 118, 203–4

Stresemann, Gustav 32
structuralism 224, 225
Stubb, A. C-G. 34
Suez crisis (1956) 181
Surrealism 204, 223
Sutherland, Graham 122
Švejk in the Second World War (Brecht) 54
Switzerland, and the Second World War 23
Szalási, Ferenc 298

T

Target for Tonight 173–4, 177
Taylor, A. J. P.
  The Course of German History 11–12
  The Origins of the Second World War 12
Taylor, Philip 162
Tchaikovsky, P., *1812 Overture* 114
television
  Le Chagrin et la Pitié (documentary film) 22
  and nostalgia in America 276
  and Second World War films 162
  war films on 163
Tell England 167
Terezin transit camp, Bohemia 103
Testimony in Pictures (Hindemith) 205–6
Thatcher, Margaret 7, 8–9, 10, 13
Thompson, Kristin 191
Thompson, Mark, *Forging War: the Media in Serbia, Croatia and Bosnia* 338
Till, K. E. 252
Timár, Péter 282
Tin Drum (Grass) 72
Tippett, Michael
  A Child of Our Time 3, 104, 105–21, 159
    and Bach's *St Matthew Passion* 114–15, 118
    Britten and the première of 120–1
    and Britten's *War Requiem* 122, 133, 134, 135–6, 137
    and Handel's *Messiah* 115–17, 118
    identity in 118–20, 157
    Jungian symbolism in 106, 119, 120

narratives 105–6, 113, 115, 119
  Negro spiritual arrangements in 106, 113, 115, 116, 122
  and Owen's poetry 123
  religious imagery in 106, 116–17
  scapegoat image in 106
  and Shostakovich 114, 153, 157, 158
  text of 106–14
  Tippett's own recording (1992) 137
Tito, Marshal (Josip Bronz) 5, 330–1, 334, 336, 337
Tolstoy, Count Leo, *War and Peace* 165, 166
totalitarianism, and Nazi and Stalinist regimes 18, 56
Touvier, Paul 22
trauma, and memory loss 69
Treitschke, Heinrich von 14
Truffaut, François 190
Truth and Reconciliation Commission, South Africa 81–2
Tudjman, Franjo 327, 331–2, 333, 337–8, 345
Twain, Mark 88
Tzara, Tristan, Dada manifesto 210–11, 212

U

U-571 163
Uccello, Paolo 201
Ugrešić, Dubravka 270–8, 286, 306
Ullmann, Viktor 103
Under Fire see Barbusse, Henri
United Kingdom *see* Britain
United States of America
  and Churchill's 'United States of Europe' idea 34
  Declaration of Independence (1776) 231
  and the EEC 35
  history and memory in 275–6
  Holocaust memories 4, 70, 230–1, 253
  and Schlink's *The Reader* 84
  and the Second World War 176
  and the Suez crisis (1956) 181
Utgaard, Peter 23

V

VE day, fortieth anniversary commemoration at Bitburg cemetery (May 1985) 16–17
Ventotene manifesto (1941) 33
Verdi, Guiseppe 154
  Missa di Requiem 135
Verdun 58
  Léger's letters to Louis Poughon from 216–20
  Trench of Bayonets 60
Verdun, visions d'histoire 167
Viermetz, Inge 95
Vietnam war 171
Virilio, Paul 161
Vishnevskaya, Galina 137
Vvedenskij, Aleksandar 270

W

Wachtel, Andrew Baruch 334
Wagner, Richard 154
Wajda, Andrzej 191, 192
Waldheim, Kurt 23
Wallenberg, Raoul 231, 247, 248
war memorials
  Auschwitz 30
  Babi Yar 152, 153
  Belgium (*Furore teutonico* in Dinant) 25, 26
  Berlin (*Die Neue Wache*) 39–41, 59, 62, 250–4
  Britain 60–1
  Christian and classical imagery in 41, 59–60, 61, 62
  France 56, 60
War and Peace (Tolstoy) 165, 166
War Requiem see Britten, Benjamin
Washington, George 231
The Way Ahead 172
We Are Making a New World (Nash) 44
We Dive at Dawn 173, 186
Weiss, Jiri, on British documentary films 174–8
Weiss, Rabbi Avraham 237
Weizsäcker, Richard von 254
West Germany *see* FDR (Federal Republic of Germany)
westerns, and Second World War films 161
Westfront 1918 (film) 44, 167

Where Eagles Dare 164
The White Cliffs of Dover 177
Whitebait, William 180–1
Whittall, Arnold 136
Wickham, Chris 13, 29
Wiedmer, C. 254, 255, 257
Wiener, Martin J. 15
Wiesel, Elsie 82
Wilkomirski, Binjamin, *Fragments: Memories of a Childhood* 100
Winfrey, Oprah 84
Winter, Jay 46, 200, 205, 209, 212, 221
   Sites of Memory, Sites of Mourning 201–3
Wolf, Christa, *Pattern Childhood* 79
women
   and Berlin's *Die Neue Wache* memorial 251, 252–3
   in concentration camps 95
   and the First World War 42–3
   German women's memories of the Third Reich 71
   and the Great Patriotic War in the Soviet Union 64
   and the Kosovo myth 316
   and memorials 251
   and rape in the Yugoslav wars 344
The Wooden Cross (film) 167
The Wooden Horse (film) 178

Y

Yevtushenko, Yevgeny 104
   'Babi Yar' (poems) 141–50, 153, 155, 156, 157–8
Young, James 241–2, 245, 256
young people
   and the cultural revolution 224
   and Holocaust memories, March of the Living at Auschwitz 237–9, 242
Yugoslav identity, and material culture 270–8
Yugoslav lands 5, 81, 82, 309–47
   communist partisans 326, 327–9
   Croats 321, 322–4, 343
   early history 309–20
   ethnic distribution throughout Yugoslavia 331–2
   and the First World War 316, 320–6
   and the Habsburg empire 310, 311, 320, 321, 322–3, 340
   languages in the independent states 311
   Macedonia 330
   Montenegro 216–20, 311
   and the Ottoman empire 310, 311, 316–17, 322, 323, 340

   and the Second World War 326–8, 337–8
   Slovenes 321–2, 323
   Slovenia 330, 347
   see also Bosnia-Herzegovina; Croatia; Serbia
Yugoslav wars (1990s) 310, 330–46
   and culture in conflict 339–40
   and the destruction of cultural monuments 341–2
   and the disintegration of Yugoslavia 330–3
   ethnicity and ethnic cleansing 339–40, 344
   and language as a tool of division 343
   and the manipulation of new memories 345–6
   memory and manipulation of the media 334–9
   and music as propaganda 343–4
   and rape as an instrument of cultural destruction 344
   writers on the 333

Z

Zhdanov, Andrei 155, 156
Zweig, Arnold, *The Case of Sergeant Grischa* 44, 55